EDUCATION

For Rosslynn,

In these pages, find the inclination of the mind, want of words.

All the best,

Marcelo

EDUCATION

A GLOBAL COMPACT FOR
A TIME OF CRISIS

EDITED BY
MARCELO SUÁREZ-OROZCO
AND CAROLA SUÁREZ-OROZCO

Columbia University Press
New York

Columbia University Press
Publishers Since 1893
New York   Chichester, West Sussex
cup.columbia.edu

Library of Congress Cataloging-in-Publication Data
Names: Suárez-Orozco, Marcelo M., 1956– editor. | Suárez-Orozco, Carola,
1957– editor.
Title: Education : a global compact for a time of crisis / edited by Marcelo Suárez-
Orozco and Carola Suárez-Orozco.
Other titles: Education (Columbia University Press)
Description: New York : Columbia University Press, 2021. | Includes bibliographical
references and index.
Identifiers: LCCN 2021027102 (print) | LCCN 2021027103 (ebook) |
ISBN 9780231204354 (trade paperback) | ISBN 9780231204347 (hardback) |
ISBN 9780231555494 (ebook)
Subjects: LCSH: Education and globalization. | Education—Moral and ethical
aspects. | Children with social disabilities—Education.
Classification: LCC LC191 .E279 2021 (print) | LCC LC191 (ebook) |
DDC 370.9—dc23
LC record available at https://lccn.loc.gov/2021027102
LC ebook record available at https://lccn.loc.gov/2021027103

Printed in the United States of America
Cover image: © Robin Hammond/IDRC/Panos Pictures
Cover design: Lisa Hamm

WE DEDICATE THIS BOOK TO A TRUE FRIEND,
BISHOP CHANCELLOR MARCELO SÁNCHEZ
SORONDO.

"THERE IS NOTHING ON THIS EARTH MORE TO
BE PRIZED THAN TRUE FRIENDSHIP."
ST. THOMAS AQUINAS

CONTENTS

FOREWORD

EDUCATION: THE GLOBAL COMPACT

Address of the Holy Father on the Global Compact on Education

The Apostolic Palace, February 7, 2020

THE HOLY FATHER POPE FRANCIS

I am pleased that in this volume you reflect on the theme of education, since today there is a need to join forces in order to achieve a broad educational covenant aimed at forming mature persons capable of mending—mending the fabric of human relationships and creating a more fraternal world (cf. *Address to the Diplomatic Corps*, January 9, 2020).

An integrated and quality education, and the standards set for graduation, continue to represent a global challenge. Despite the objectives formulated by the United Nations Organization and other bodies (cf. Goal 4), and the important efforts made by some countries, equality of education has not yet been achieved in our world. Poverty, discrimination, climate change, the globalization of indifference, and the exploitation of human beings all prevent the flourishing of millions of children. Indeed, for many, these are an almost insurmountable wall preventing the attainment of the goals of sustainable and guaranteed development proposed by the world's peoples.

Basic education today is a normative ideal throughout the world. The empirical data in this book show that much progress has been made in giving boys and girls access to schooling. Today, the enrollment of young people in primary education is almost universal, and it is clear that the gender gap has been narrowed. This is a praiseworthy achievement. Nonetheless, each generation needs to consider how best to hand on its knowledge and its values to the next, since it is through education that men and women attain their maximum potential and become conscious, free, and responsible. Concern for education is concern for future generations and for the future of humanity. It is a concern profoundly rooted in hope, and it calls for generosity and courage.

Education is not merely about transmitting concepts; that would be a legacy of the learning that has to be overcome; that is, it is not only the transmission of concepts. Education is an enterprise that demands cooperation on the part of all involved—the family, the school, and social, cultural and religious institutions. In this sense, in some countries it is said that the educational compact is broken because this social participation in education is lacking. In order to educate, one has to be able to combine the language of the head with the language of the heart and the language of the hands. In this way, the student can think what he or she feels and does, can feel what he or she thinks and does, and can do what he or she feels and thinks. A total integration. By encouraging this training of the head, the heart, and the hands, intellectual and socio-emotional education, the transmission of individual and societal values and virtues, the teaching of a committed citizenship concerned with justice, and by imparting the abilities and knowledge that can prepare young people for the world of work and society, families, schools, and institutions become essential vehicles for the empowerment of future generations.

Today, what I have called the "educational compact" between families, schools, nations, and the world, culture and cultures, is in crisis and indeed in a state of breakdown. That breakdown is serious, and it can only be fixed through a renewed universal effort of generosity and cooperation. This breakdown in the educational compact means that society, the family, and the different institutions called to educate have all delegated the decisive task of education to others. In this way, the various basic institutions and the states themselves have evaded their responsibilities and faltered in this educational compact.

Today, we are called in some way to renew and consolidate the dedication of all—individuals and institutions—in favor of education, in order to forge a new educational compact, because only thus will education be able to change. To achieve this, there has to be an integration of disciplines, culture, sports, science, relaxation, and recreation; for this reason, bridges have to be built to "jump over" (if you allow me that word) the forms of enclosure that trap us in our little world, and to launch into the global open seas in respect for all traditions. Future generations must have a clear understanding of their own tradition and culture—this is nonnegotiable—in relation to other traditions, in such a way that they can develop their own self-understanding by encountering and appropriating cultural diversity and change. This will enable the promotion of a culture of dialogue, a culture of encounter and mutual understanding, in a spirit of serenity and tolerance. An education that enables young people to identify and foster true human values from an intercultural and interreligious perspective.

The family needs to be given its proper place in the new educational compact, since its responsibility already begins in the maternal womb and at birth. Yet mothers, fathers, grandparents, and the family as a whole, in their primary educational role, need to be helped to understand, in the new global context, the importance of this early stage of life and be prepared to act accordingly. One of the fundamental ways to improve the quality of education on the scholastic level is to achieve greater participation of families and local communities in educational projects. This is essential to an integral, focused, and universal education.

I wish to pay homage to teachers—who are always underpaid—so that, faced with the challenge of education, they will persevere with courage and tenacity. They are "artisans" who shape the coming generations. With their knowledge, patience, and dedication, they communicate a way of living and acting that embodies a richness that is not material but spiritual and creates the men and woman of tomorrow. This is a great responsibility. Consequently, in the new educational compact, the function of teachers, as educators, must be acknowledged and supported by every possible means. If our objective is to offer each individual and every community the level of knowledge needed to enjoy their proper autonomy and to be capable of cooperating with others, it is important to ensure that educators are trained in accordance with the highest qualitative standards at every academic level. In order to support and promote this process, it is necessary that they be given access to suitable national, international, and private resources, in such a way that throughout the world they can carry out their tasks in an effective way.

In this volume on *Education: A Global Compact for a Time of Crisis*, academic leaders from some of the most respected universities of the world have identified new springboards for making education more humane and equitable, more satisfactory, and more relevant to the disparate needs of the economies and societies of the twenty-first century. Here they examine, among other things, the new science of the mind, the brain and education, and the promise of technology in order to reach children who presently lack opportunities for learning as well as the important issue of the education of young refugees and immigrants worldwide. They consider the effects of growing inequality and climate change on education and reflect on the tools needed to reverse their effects and to lay the foundations for a more humane, healthy, equitable, and prosperous society.

I speak of three languages: the mind, the heart, and the hands. When we speak of roots and values, we can speak of truth, goodness, and creativity. Yet, I do not want to finish these words without mentioning beauty. We cannot educate without leading a person to beauty, without leading the heart to beauty. Forcing my remarks a little, I would say that an education is not successful if you do not know how to create poets. The path of beauty is a challenge that must be addressed.

I encourage you in the important and exciting task that is yours: to cooperate in the education of future generations. What you seek to accomplish has to do, not with the future, but with the present, here and now. Go forward, and may God bless you. I pray for you, and I ask you to pray for me.

ACKNOWLEDGMENTS

MARCELO SUÁREZ-OROZCO AND CAROLA SUÁREZ-OROZCO

We are in an age of mounting planetary crises. The human family and, indeed, all living systems are facing new risks. Hydra-like and seemingly everywhere, unchecked climate change, extreme poverty, forced migrations, war, and terror are rearing their ugly heads. In yet another planetary malaise, the COVID-19 pandemic hit with geologic force. COVID-19 suddenly opened a curtain for the world to witness untold suffering and the obscene inequalities that continue to deform economies and societies the world over. The pandemic left in its wake death and untold destruction and ushered in a culture of helplessness and despair.

In the face of despair, we must will hope into being. In 2020, we heard Pope Francis's radical "summons to solidarity," calling on all persons of good will and of every faith and nationality to join together in the hope to reimagine and reengineer schools.

"Education bears within itself a seed of hope: the hope of peace and justice; the hope of beauty and goodness; the hope of social harmony," Pope Francis said in his summons. "We must move forward, all of us together, each as we are, but always looking ahead to the building of a civilization of harmony and unity." Education, Francis added, is essential for building a different world. It must serve the flourishing of children and the cause of solidarity, fraternity, and the ethic of care. In education, we must ensure that human needs are met and our shared home, our planet, is nurtured and restored.

This volume is based on Pope Francis's call for an Global Compact on Education. At the request of Monsignor Angelo Vincenzo Zani, Professor Stefano

Zamagni and Marcelo Suárez-Orozco convened leading scholars, policy makers, and public intellectuals from around the world at the Casina Pio IV in the Vatican Gardens in February of 2020. We invited scholars and practitioners from a range of disciplines—from anthropology to the brain sciences, from the health sciences to demography, psychology, child development, sociology, economics, the learning sciences, and education. Each participant agreed to present new research on the most significant challenges facing education today and the levers of change needed to make education more humane, smarter, and more relevant moving forward. Taken together, the contributors' basic research embodies original work in Africa, the Americas, Asia, Europe, and the Middle East. The papers were developed and discussed at length at the Vatican Gardens workshop. We all headed back home, each of us tasked with revising and refining our contribution.

Within a month, COVID-19 reared its ugly head. The pandemic made our endeavors, already urgent, even more significant by deepening preexisting inequities and derailing schooling for millions of children. In its face, we redoubled our sense of purpose in responding to Francis's summons. The chapters in the book address many of the defining challenges facing global education now and moving forward.

The contributions are all original and purposely developed for this volume. We are grateful to many individuals and organizations for their endeavors in seeing the project through from its inception to the book you are now holding in your hands.

We are grateful to the Dean's Priorities Fund of the School of Education and Information Studies at the University of California, Los Angeles, for the generous financial support, especially critical during the earliest phases of this work. At UCLA, we wish to thank Ms. Leah Wilmore for her exacting work in organizing the myriad details—big and small—needed to organize a major international workshop across multiple time zones and in many languages. The dedicated staff of the Pontifical Academy of Social Sciences at the historic Casina Pio IV in Vatican City welcomed us with exquisite tact, professionalism, and generosity.

We are grateful to Professor Jeffrey Sachs for his dedication to the project and for the generous support in his capacity as cochair of the Sustainable Development Solutions Network in the United States.

We thank Ms. Cherish Collins, a master's student at the University of Massachusetts, Boston, with a keen eye and love of reading, who did wonders helping us review all chapters suggesting a word here, a rephrase there, tracking down references and footnotes, and making the individual chapters and the book as a whole a better work.

Monsignor Marcelo Sánchez Sorondo, Bishop Chancellor of the Pontifical Academy of Sciences and the Pontifical Academy of Social Sciences, supported this project from its inception and wisely guided us through its many iterations. We dedicate this book to Monsignor Marcelo—a true friend of the sciences, a true friend of learning, and a true personal friend for the long run.

EDUCATION

INTRODUCTION

The Global Compact on Education

MARCELO SUÁREZ-OROZCO

The fundamental mission of education is to cultivate healthy, flourishing, and engaged children. In the Platonic tradition, education endeavors to nurture logic and science (truth), ethics and justice (goodness), and aesthetics (the creation and appreciation of beauty). In the face of growing inequities, creating a more inclusive, just, and sustainable world is education's urgent challenge. In the words of Pope Francis, a "summons to solidarity" with the next generation, with each other, and with our ever-more fragile planet is the ethical imperative of our times. This volume engages education as a path for a more humane, sustainable, and equitable future.[1]

In the Kantian sense, our full potential unfolds from and with education—"Man can only become man by education."[2] *Homo sapiens*. Sapiens—the knowing, the wise member of the genus *Homo*—is born of knowledge. "When a human being is not educated, his or her telos is thwarted, as when a plant not does not flourish to the point of blossoming. The intellectual dimension of humans entails that even a healthy and strong person without education is somehow dwarfed with regard to his or her humanity. Of course, there is also in the overwhelming majority of children a subjective desire to be educated" (chapter 9).

Basic primary education in schools has become a normative ideal the world over. In the last five decades, schooling has emerged globally as the most important societal institution for the education of the next generation. There is a lot of good news: "Enrollment of children in primary education is at present nearly universal. The gender gap has narrowed, and in some regions girls tend to perform better in school than boys and progress in a more timely manner."[3] Progress in the participation of children in schools is a laudable achievement, yet the work ahead is significant: "Enrollment does not translate directly into education, and education does not translate directly into good education, which is often the real catalyst for engaged citizenship, emotional awareness and human sensitivity, and a tolerance of the other, along with enhanced potential for working collaboratively, productively, and innovatively" (chapter 2). Education is freedom, and it is "far and away the single most empowering investment for individuals. It is for that reason that the world has long regarded education as a basic human need and as a basic human right. Yet we have not yet achieved universal education" (chapter 1). Indeed, millions remain out of school, and illiteracy remains rampant: 781 million people over the age of fifteen remain illiterate—and women make up well over half of those who are illiterate.[4]

While much remains to be done, education is widely viewed as the main pathway for sustainable development and a driver of wellness (chapter 2). "Seen as part of the global commons, knowledge, learning, and education represent *humanity's greatest renewable resource* for responding to challenges and inventing alternatives" (chapter 20). Ample evidence suggests that education— almost any form that nurtures and supports basic literacy—generates powerful virtuous cycles.[5] As UNICEF researchers have concluded: "An education is perhaps a child's strongest barrier against poverty, especially for girls. Educated girls are likely to marry later and have healthier children. They are more productive at home and better paid in the workplace, better able to protect themselves against HIV/AIDS and more able to participate in decision-making at all levels. Additionally, this . . . furthers [the sustainable development goals of] universal primary education and gender equality."[6]

Woefully, however, the COVID-19 pandemic halted and reversed progress in the schooling and education of children the world over. For millions of children, the pandemic represents a long-lasting "catastrophic education emergency," robbing them of the daily attending-school ritual with all that entails: learning opportunities, socializing with other children, seeking supports from teachers, physical education, accessing health care and nutrition, and the various other scaffolds needed for developmentally appropriate socio-emotional, cognitive, and metacognitive growth. The pandemic stunned education systems with geologic force: by early 2020, approximately 1.5 billion students were no longer attending in-person school, as school closings became mandatory in some 160 countries (chapter 20). And as millions of children would eventually continue their learning remotely, UNICEF data suggest that "for at least 463 million children whose schools closed due to COVID-19, there was no such thing as 'remote learning' "[7] (chapter 20). Millions lacking access to electricity, technology, and internet access could not engage in online learning.

Indeed, during the COVID-19 pandemic, it is estimated that over 830 million students did "not have access to a computer at home." As Bridgit Barron notes, "Although unequal access to information technologies had been documented well before the COVID-19 pandemic, dramatic school closures have brought a significant digital divide into sharp relief and exposed the ongoing cost of inequities, as teachers across the world scrambled to continue the education of millions of children. Radio, television, and the internet were deployed in an attempt to connect schools and homes. Learners in rural areas, citizens from less affluent countries, families who have less wealth, and female students were the least likely to have access to any of these forms of remote learning" (chapter 18).

In many low-and-lower-middle-income countries, school closures put children on the streets. "Families are desperate for money. Children are an easy source of cheap labor."[8] Because of the pandemic, "An additional 100 million children could fall below the minimum proficiency level in reading. . . . Lost learning is being counted in months and taking a rising toll on the mental health of students. Progress made towards narrowing gender gaps in education over past decades could be reversed, with girls at increased risk of exposure of early marriage and drop out" (chapter 20).

By the first quarter of 2021, more than 160 million children "around the world have missed school for nearly a year due to COVID-19 restrictions." Fourteen countries "worldwide have remained largely closed since March 2020 to February 2021." Two-thirds of those countries are in Latin America and the Caribbean.[9] Bloom and Ferranna summarize COVID-19's impact on education, "School closures and difficulties in implementing effective remote learning generally reduce the pleasure of learning, hinder children's socialization opportunities, degrade the emotional and mental health of students, and increase the risk of domestic violence and abuse. In addition, school closures disrupt immunization and other health services that are often provided at school and prevent many children from accessing the only nutritious meal of their day. School closures also exert considerable pressures on parents, who have to balance childcare, home schooling, and work duties" (chapter 2).

The COVID–19 pandemic laid bare for the world the deepening inequalities of opportunities to learn that flow from country-of-origin, race, ethnicity, and immigration background. COVID-19 sent another 100 million human beings into deep poverty—brutally intensifying extreme poverty and reversing years of progress.[10]

Indeed, poverty is the other pandemic exacting a heavy toll on children and youth across the world. The consequences on children are chilling. "Different poverty indicators are associated with lower cognitive and academic performance during several stages of development. Psychological and neural evidence generated in recent years suggests the need to review the interpretations of these associations in the sense of deficit, and to consider the occurrence of adaptive processes instead" (chapter 3). Poverty, war and terror, structural racism, unchecked climate change, the "globalization of indifference," an extreme form of which is modern child slavery, thwart the opportunities for healthy development and wilt the flourishing of millions of children.[11] Indeed, they represent the most significant undertow toward meeting the UN Millennium Development Goal of reaching universal basic education.[12]

As Pope Francis and ample research suggest, it is by nurturing socio-emotional learning—including "patient listening,[13] constructive dialogue and better mutual understanding,"[14] the values and virtues of engaged citizenship, and by imparting the new skills to prepare youth for the ever-evolving world of work—that schools become meaningful vehicles for collective empowerment and positive social action. "In order to educate, one has to be able to combine the language of the head with the language of the heart and the language of the hands. In this way, the student can think what he or she feels and does, can feel what he or she thinks and does, and can do what he or she feels and thinks" (foreword). Education must endeavor to inculcate in children and youth humane sensibilities, empathy and perspective-taking, communication and collaboration skills, and higher-order cognitive skills for critical thinking, as well as the metacognitive abilities to become lifelong learners and civic agents. Today, paraphrasing the words of Damon and Colby (chapter 10) fostering a sense of purpose in young people must be a key educational mission. A humanistic ethic of care (chapter 20)—and not simply a reductive utilitarian logic of market efficiencies—must animate the work of education in troubled times.

Twenty-first-century economies and societies are predicated on increasing complexity and diversity—the twin corollaries of an ever more globally interconnected, miniaturized, and fragile world. This book minds the gap between what education *is* and what it *needs to be* to build a more humane, equitable, and sustainable future for all.

THE CRISES IN EDUCATION

WHAT ARE SOME OF THE MOST IMPORTANT CHALLENGES TO EDUCATION TODAY?

First, *quality education*—from early childhood (chapters 14 and 15) onward remains an elusive mirage for millions of children. It is a scandal that prior to the COVID-19 pandemic, over 260 million children and youth were not enrolled in primary and secondary schools. That is the equivalent of the population of Indonesia, the world's fourth most populous country. For those who are enrolled, the little education provided—especially in the form of literacy (chapter 17), will be vital but perhaps not enough to thrive to their full potential.[15] Too many children in low- and lower-middle-income countries are falling further behind their peers in the wealthy nations. We examine the role of literacy—especially "deep reading" (chapter 16) and the opportunities and limitations of new technologies (chapter 18) to reach children who otherwise have few opportunities for formal learning.

The second challenge facing education is unfolding at *the vital link between the wealthy countries in the northern hemisphere and the metaphorical Global South.* Schools are struggling to properly educate and ease the transition and integration of large and growing numbers of immigrant and refugee youth (chapters 4 and 5) arriving in Europe, North America, Asia, Australia, and elsewhere; many immigrant and refugee youngsters are marginalized as racially, ethnically, religiously, and linguistically marked minority groups. The disparagement of immigrant and refugee youth is ubiquitous. Their social belonging is thwarted (chapter 6). More broadly, the invasion of incivility and intolerance in schools is creating new challenges to teachers and administrators the world over (chapter 11). The virus of anti-Blackness continues to spread unabated and with no vaccine on the horizon.

The third challenge education faces is *how to* educate students to address *our ever more fragile planet* (chapters 12 and 13). Unsustainable development is a global threat. The admirable Sustainable Development Goal (SDG4.7) to provide "education for sustainable development and sustainable lifestyles" remains lamentably elusive for the majority of students.[16]

At a time when education must *communicate values, virtues, and purpose,* we find ourselves reticent and unsure of how to proceed. Yet when it comes to values and purpose (chapter 10), children and youth are clamoring for an integral education outlined by Pope Francis (foreword). We are proceeding with too much caution at a time the education needs "a bold humanistic vision, based on human rights, social justice, dignity, cultural and social diversity, and intellectual solidarity. This vision reaffirms a set of universal ethical principles and the need to strengthen moral values in education and society. It starts with people of all ages and the analysis of development contexts. It is inclusive and equitable, and informed by interdisciplinary research across the sciences, arts and humanities. Finally, it is participatory and international in scope" (chapter 20).

The world is facing multiple crises—pandemics, environmental and climate change catastrophes, racism and xenophobia, growing inequality, and extreme poverty. Stefania Giannini (chapter 20) argues, we have "an education crisis that mirrors a wider global crisis, one that is social, moral, and environmental." Tired-old claims, silver bullets, and magical thinking will no longer do. Nor will averting our gaze to growing inequities in education. Schools, the world over, must endeavor to educate the whole child for the whole world. "Through a humanistic and holistic vision of education and development, which cannot simply be framed in terms of economic growth, learners need the knowledge and the values to live meaningful and purposeful lives in harmony with others and the planet" (chapter 20). Schools need to be laboratories reclaiming the shared ethical principles of reciprocity, solidarity, equity, inclusion, and fighting all forms of discrimination.

In this volume, we examine new levers to make education in public schools more humane, equitable, and caring; more engaging and fulfilling; and more relevant to the disparate needs of economies, societies, and the students they serve around the world. Above all, education needs to be at the forefront of creating a sustainable world. Ours is a plea for a new global compact. Success will require significant national and global donor investments (chapter 1; afterword). It will also require stakeholder cooperation and coordination across multiple sectors (chapter 19). Just as literacy and technologies are key resources, cooperation and coordination are foundational interpersonal and interorganizational resources for improvement and implementation.

PLAN OF THE BOOK

PART I: ADDRESSING OUR MOST VULNERABLE

In part I, we examine the education of our most vulnerable populations. The values and virtues flowing from quality education have been named and memorialized in multiple covenants and declarations by some of the world's most august bodies. The worthy ideals embodied in Article 26 of the Universal Declaration of Human Rights (1948), the right to universal, free, and compulsory education come to mind: Education shall be "directed to the full development of the human personality and to the strengthening of respect for human rights and fundamental freedoms. It shall promote understanding, tolerance and friendship among all nations, racial or religious groups, and shall further the activities of the United Nations for the maintenance of peace."[17]

Yet, as Jeffrey Sachs points out in chapter 1, the world has failed for over seven decades "to realize that right, and other rights in the Universal Declaration. There has been progress, but we should be more interested in the shortfall than the achievement, as children are losing their future prospects at our hands. The failures point us to the urgent work we have yet to do." Sachs's review of the global data on educational disparities and their corollaries with health, wellness, wages, and the transition to the world of work points to a powerful truth: inequities in opportunities to learn and in educational outcomes generate bifurcated pathways. Today qua education, the rich are getting richer, and the poor are getting poorer. In low-income countries, Sachs argues, the elephant in the classroom is the disparity in financial resources. On the global level, Sachs advocates "the need to transfer resources from the richest to the poorest countries to ensure that all children have the chance for education at least through upper-secondary level." Sachs's proposal echoes Pope Francis's "summons to solidarity" and frames the summons in pithy, clear, and entirely feasible terms. Such undertaking must be prioritized by wealthy donor countries and philanthropic bodies the world over (see also afterword).

Investments in quality education are at once ethical (chapter 9) *and* smart policy. In chapter 2, Bloom and Ferranna examine education, population health, and demographics. Their contribution focuses on the economic rationale for devoting resources to education, the best policy levers to enhance progress in education, and the role of education in the context of an aging world population. The returns to investments in education are measurable, profound, and multidirectional: "Education investments can promote health and longevity; reduce fertility and population growth rates; improve living standards; and, ultimately, enhance well-being at multiple levels, ranging from individuals to countries. The causal links are bidirectional: health investments and fertility reductions contribute to increasing the returns to education, and, as a result, induce more investment in education. This complexity implies that educational development is probably best approached multisectorally, through an integrated blend of health, population, and education policies" (chapter 2).[18]

At the same time, poverty is education's implacable foe. In chapter 3, Sebastian Lipina "(a) examines the evidence on the associations between poverty and cognition at different levels of organization, with a focus on those aspects related to the acquisition of learning; (b) the mediation and moderation factors identified in such associations; (c) the impact of different interventions aimed at optimizing the cognitive development of children living in a context of poverty; and (d) the scientific implications of this evidence, according to contemporary perspectives of developmental psychology and cognitive neuroscience." He identifies the dominant poverty indicators linked with lower cognitive and academic outcomes in various stages of development and proposes a roadmap for rethinking basic and translational research interventions in education qua poverty.

As international migration has grown significantly since the turn of the millennium, the education of immigrants and refugees is now a global concern. According to the most recent United Nations data, the number of international migrants worldwide reached 281 million in 2020, "up from 220 million in 2010."[19] The largest international corridors of human migration are in Asia, Europe, and the Americas. Internal migration is also on the rise: "The estimated number of internal migrants (migrants inside of their country of origin) is over 760 million."[20] In the first quarter of the twenty-first century, the world is witnessing the largest number of forcefully displaced human beings in history. While precise numbers are both elusive and changing,[21] United Nations data suggest that almost eighty million people are escaping home into the unknown.[22] The majority of those seeking shelter (approximately 51 million) are internally displaced persons (IDPs), not formal refugees across international borders. In addition, approximately nine in ten international asylum seekers remain in a neighboring country—Asians stay in Asia, Africans in Africa, Americans in the Americas. Millions of people linger in perpetual limbo in confinement zones far away from the wealthy cities of Asia, Europe, North America, and Australia. In the words of Filippo Grandi, UN high commissioner for refugees, "We are witnessing a changed reality in that forced displacement nowadays is not only vastly more widespread but is simply no longer a short-term and temporary phenomenon."[23] From Turkey to Colombia, from Papua New Guinea to Libya, Niger, and Rwanda, from Mexico to Guatemala, a vast empire of suffering is keeping millions of human beings forever in displacement. Indeed, millions are internally displaced, millions are awaiting asylum, and millions more are living in the shadow of the law as irregular or unauthorized immigrants.

As the chapters by Yoshikawa and colleagues, Shuayb and colleagues, and C. Suárez-Orozco suggest, the face of human migration in the twenty-first century is youthful. One in eight international migrants is a child. Worldwide, by 2020, there were over thirty-six million migrant children and well over twenty million children had been forcibly displaced. Additionally, by then there were approximately seventeen million child refugees and approximately one million asylum-seeking children. A staggering one in every two hundred children is a refugee, almost twice the number of a decade ago. Chapters 4, 5, and 6 address various defining features of education for children and youth on the move. For too many, it is a reality of grave peril during all phases of the journey—prior to emigration, in transit, and upon settlement.

In chapter 4, Yoshikawa and colleagues write, "Refugee children are at great risk of exclusion from education. . . . Exclusion from these opportunities represents a serious challenge to Sustainable Development Goal 4, which states that all children should have access to quality preprimary, primary, and secondary education by 2030. In countries affected by conflict, one in three children ages five to seventeen are not in school. These 104 million children represent more than one third of the children globally who are not in school.[24] Refugee children access primary education at substantially lower rates than children globally: whereas 91 percent of all children globally have access to primary education, only 63 percent of refugees do. The difference at the secondary and tertiary levels is even more stark: only 24 percent of refugees have access compared to 84 percent of all children. And at the tertiary level, 3 percent of refugees have access compared to 37 percent of young people globally. Marginalization among refugees is often compounded by other discriminatory factors; for example, refugee girls' rates of access to secondary schooling are 70 percent that of boys (chapter 4). The authors build a strong and detailed case for the structural and relational vehicles needed to foment "inclusion with attention to multiple aspects of learning and development. Ensuring these pathways to lifelong learning and opportunity for displaced, refugee and other marginalized populations should be a central aim of the global compact on education" (chapter 4)

Syria's humanitarian catastrophe has sent the largest number of refugees and asylum-seekers in the world in search of shelter. The Syrian exodus has generated a great deal of attention, especially in Europe—above all in Germany, where approximately eight hundred thousand Syrians have settled since

2010. Yet, the majority of Syrian refugees remain in the Middle East. Turkey is host to the largest number of refugees in the world. In chapter 5, Maha Shuayb, Maurice Crul, and Frans Lelie of the Free University of Amsterdam present new data on the education of refugee children from Syria in Turkey and Lebanon. Their research paints an alarming picture. Most Syrian refugee children endure a harrowing journey.[25] They face long periods of interrupted schooling and, upon settlement, the need to work to help the family make ends meet. Once they are able to enroll in schools, they receive reduced hours of instruction in crowded classrooms with overburdened teachers often unable to engage them in second language instruction. Furthermore, "the fragility of the [family's] legal status, the [lower] socio-economic position of the family and the unsecure and overcrowded living conditions of refugee families result in a range of socio-emotional problems that negatively impact their schooling outcomes" (chapter 5).[26]

The authors develop an empirically derived conceptual model identifying and naming intervening variables and negative loops at play in the education experiences and outcomes for refugee children. Policy makers responsible for responding to the humanitarian crisis of children in flight would do well to go beyond fixing temporary measures when serving children in increasingly protracted periods of life in flight. The work by Shuayb and colleagues offers an excellent place to develop more humane and sustainable approaches to the education of refugee children.

Large-scale migration and demographic change are challenging and generate disequilibrium under the best of circumstances. As millions of immigrants and refugees manage to settle in new societies, they encounter not only new opportunities but also racism, xenophobia, and intolerance. In the age of COVID-19, suspicion came to define feelings toward large swaths of immigrants. In the United States, when the then-president Donald J. Trump framed the COVID-19 pandemic as "the Chinese virus" and "the Wuhan virus" and predictably used the emergency as another excuse to build his totemic wall and shut down the U. S. border to immigrants, he threw kerosene into an already combustible situation. Hate crimes against phenotypically Asian American persons in the United States predictably skyrocketed. Research by the California State University Center for the Study of Hate & Extremism found that "Anti-Asian Hate Crimes Surged 149%, while overall hate crime dropped 7% in 2020."[27]

Immigration is a frontier pushing against cosmopolitan tolerance and the pursuit of our inherent humanitarian obligations to the welfare of others. In chapter 6, Carola Suárez-Orozco writes, "Across the globe, we are witnessing increasingly virulent xenophobic sentiments and repressive immigration policies." How are these broad national and international dynamics playing out in schools tasked with educating immigrant children? Carola Suárez-Orozco writes, "Emerging research now strongly suggests that this xenophobic social hostility has cascaded into schools, contributing to toxic learning environments for both educators and students." In her chapter, she examines the role of social belonging (and its antonyms, exclusion and symbolic violence) in American schools serving immigrant-origin children. She explores ways in which schools must play a role in countering "cascading xenophobia" and its devastating effects on the immigrant child's socio-emotional development and learning.

PART II: ETHICAL AND CIVIC CONSIDERATIONS

In part II, the chapters turn to education as moral, ethical, and civic endeavors. Since Plato and his student Aristotle, philosophers have pondered on education and its purposes for the eudemonic flourishing of human beings. In the modern era, as the idea of educating all children in formal school settings took shape, philosophers entered the conversation. According to Kant's moral philosophy, we become a person only in and with education. Indeed, education is constitutive of our humanity (chapter 9). Over a century ago, Émile Durkheim began lecturing would-be teachers on moral values and collective consciousness, articulating what would become his enduring conceptual contribution to the social sciences: the moral nature of the relationships between the individual and society.

John Dewey remains philosophy's most influential voice in education. Dewey's rich conceptual work evolved as the idea of universal, free, compulsory, nondenominational public education was becoming firmly rooted first in the United States and then elsewhere (see chapter 11). In Dewey's early writings, education mediates between the individual and society and is constitutive of the practice of democratic citizenship. In a passage echoing Durkheim's sentiments, Dewey wrote, "I believe that the school is primarily a social institution. Education being a social process, the school is simply that form of community life in which all those agencies are concentrated that will be most effective in bringing the child to share in the inherited resources of the race, and to use his own powers for social ends. I believe that education, therefore, is a process of living and not a preparation for future living."[28] The rise of fascism, Nazism, and the diffusion of authoritarian, antidemocratic ethos, redoubled Dewey's focus on education and democracy. The social process in school, Dewey argued, must engage children as active, hands-on, and involved citizen-learners laying in place the pathway for renewal of the democratic ethos and eidos of each generation (see also Rogers, this volume).[29] Perhaps more than any other philosopher Dewey set a tone during the formative years of education as a democratic practice and as a field of inquiry (chapter 11).[30]

While Jerome Brunner and his students at Harvard, such as Howard Gardner, Patricia Greenfield, and other leading psychologists, became increasingly influential in education and educational psychology, with the ascendancy of neoliberal economics, education inched away from its foundations in ethics, morals, civics, and psychology.[31] Indeed, over the course of the last generation, education scholarship became increasingly a province of economic empirical research and conceptual modeling with economic development a sharp focus of concern.[32] But as Stefania Giannini argues, "Development cannot be simply framed in terms of economic growth—human flourishing and the accessibility of lives of meaning and dignity must be primary concerns" (chapter 20).

In chapter 7, in his reflection, the eminent economics theoretician Stefano Zamagni rejects the reductive neoliberal logic qua education in favor of reclaiming an integral view of educating the whole child for the whole world. Zamagni writes, "There is nothing more essential to the sustainable development agenda than access to education for all young people all over the world." He laments that "during the second modernity, we have moved away from the idea that education is about character building, focusing instead on the acquisition of knowledge and skills needed for a career or to meet market requests." Returning to the platonic ideal, he writes, "We need a holistic vision of education, focusing on integral human dimensions, seeking the true, the good, the beautiful. For such an education profile, the utilitarian ethics is clearly inadequate to cope with the aporias of the libertarian-individualistic outlook. The Aristotelian virtue ethics perspective is well-placed to propose an ethics of personhood allowing human flourishing" (chapter 7).

In chapter 8, Harvard educational psychologist Howard Gardner turns his attention to the timeless concern of educating the three virtues. The mission of schools, Pope Francis has noted, is nourishing *Verum, Pulchrum, Bonum,* that is, to develop the tools and sensibilities to pursue *verum* (logic and science), *pulchrum* (aesthetics), and *bonum* (justice). Gardner delves into this fundamental trinity in light of Hegelian dialectics. He asks: Are the virtues inseparable? Is that which is true always beautiful and good and vice versa? He defines, specifically for education, the formal features of each "truth," "beauty," and "goodness." Gardner places the teaching of the virtues in the arc he sees as encompassing the two "*L*'s" in schooling:[33] the span between when teaching must first focus on the basic literacies to the moment education becomes the bridge to the labor market and the professions. He writes,

> Like almost every educator—indeed, like almost every reflective adult—I believe that education must include literacies, on the one hand, and preparation for the world of work, of labor, on the other. But in a reasonably effective educational system, the basic literacies should be covered in the first years of schooling; and explicit preparation for the world of work should take place in late adolescence. Accordingly, that means we have a considerable period—anywhere from five to ten years—to pursue other educational goals. And this is where I favor a valorization and inculcation of the three virtues. . . . As I thought about this trio of virtues, I first reached the conclusion that the pursuit of truth should be the primary focus of education—to repeat, in the interval between literacy and labor. And indeed, in earlier work, I maintained that the best way—indeed perhaps the *only* way—in which to ascertain what's true is to learn and master the methods used by the different disciplines" (chapter 8).

In chapter 9, Vittorio Hosle makes a plea for the recoupling of education and ethics. His reflections cover the ethical claims for the right to an education and the disparate claim for reengaging with ethics in education. He examines, seriatim: Who has a right to be educated? Who has a duty to educate? What should be taught in the curriculum? What are the challenges and opportunities in the teaching of ethics? Hosle argues that intrinsic to the moral evolution of our species "is the recognition that we share a common responsibility to educate all human beings, not only in order to help them maintain themselves as part of the global society but also to comprehend the complex nature of our world and to attain a greater depth by grasping moral values irreducible to self-interest as well as their ultimate source" (chapter 9).

The sense of purpose is a uniquely human achievement closely connected to the flourishing of potential and the directed and well-lived life. Purpose, when aligned with moral character, generates a cascade of virtuous cycles—health and wellness, motivation, resilience, and other constructive outcomes have been empirically linked to the sense of purpose. In chapter 10, William Damon and Anne Colby examine the problem of purpose in education—its development in youth and throughout the life course and what schools the world over are doing to foster the sense of purpose in today's students. They define purpose as "an active commitment to accomplish aims that are both meaningful to the self and of consequence to the world beyond the self." They argue:

> Purpose has long been identified in philosophy and theology as an essential component of a well-directed life. In recent years, support for this longstanding theoretical intuition has come from studies in psychological science and medicine that have documented important life benefits associated with purpose. Such benefits include: energy and motivation; resilience under pressure; a positive personal identity; emotional stability; academic and vocational achievement; faith and trust in the affirmative value of life; and a sense of direction that can withstand episodic periods of uncertainty and confusion.[34] . . . [and] contribute to energy and health throughout the lifespan.[35] (Chapter 10)

In chapter 11, John Rogers returns to the idea of education, civics (and civility), and the practice of democratic citizenship. Massachusetts was an early incubator for the idea of public education in the service of democracy. Rogers writes:

> Horace Mann became a leading voice trumpeting the importance of public education for democracy. He argued that . . . civic education—"instruction respecting the nature and functions of the government"— must be provided in "common schools" open to all.[36] Such schools not only would present civic knowledge, but afford opportunities for social interaction and shared deliberation through which all "parties can become intelligible to each other."[37]

But even as Mann envisioned public schools as sites for preparing citizens to participate in political life, he worried that a fractious partisanship might undermine the democratic project of common schooling. "If the tempest of political strife were to be let loose upon our Common Schools, they would be overwhelmed with sudden ruin. Let it be once understood, that the schoolroom is a legitimate theatre for party politics, and with what violence will hostile partisans struggle to gain possession of the stage, and to play their parts upon it!"[38]

The years the Trump administration governed the United States (2017–2020) saw the "tempest of political strife" often taking the form of intolerance, xenophobia, racism, and fearmongering. It was government by incivility, and incivility invaded nearly all aspects of American life. Rogers presents new data on what happens when public schools "face not only unruly and contentious politics from the broader community but also the bitter seeds of intolerance" (chapter 11). Rogers develops case studies of three different high school principals in the United States struggling to create different strategies for nurturing their pupils' civic ideals in a climate of growing political intolerance and incivility. The lesson Rogers imparts is that the work of education for civility, like the work of democracy itself, is never complete; it must be created and recreated anew each generation in each classroom and in each school.

PART III: EDUCATING FOR A SUSTAINABLE FUTURE

The world is facing multiple threats—unchecked climate change, environmental cataclysms, and forced migrations. As Stefania Giannini argues, "We have an education crisis that mirrors a wider global crisis, one that is social, moral, and environmental" (chapter 20). The chapters in part III by Ramanathan and colleagues and Iyengar and colleagues focus on education and the environment. Schools across the world face the challenge of teaching and learning an ethic of care for a planet facing growing environmental threats.

Schools must be at the forefront of preparing the next generation to engage in problematic times and in catastrophic contexts. In chapter 12, we turn to education and the growing global challenge of unchecked climate change and its effects—known and yet to be discovered—on nature, health, economy, and society. Ramanathan and colleagues note that "the impacts of climate disruption are intensifying across the globe. . . . The COVID-19 pandemic was a canary-in-the-coalmine, illustrating our profound global interdependence and exposing the disproportionate vulnerabilities of poor and marginalized people everywhere. This crisis has also exposed the susceptibility of reliable science information to political manipulation, the fragility of public commitment to collective goods, and the role that education must play in cultivating informed publics across the world committed to tackling climate change as a global public priority" (chapter 12). The chapter presents an overview of a host of climate change educational programs and tools designed to engage all kinds of learners in different contexts. Each program is mindful of age differences and various social considerations in making climate change teaching and learning developmentally appropriate and culturally consonant. The quest for a sustainable planet and sustainable humanity must include climate literacy for all, including pre-K–12 children and youth, college students, and adults all the way to senior citizens. This is a tall order, but there are enormous opportunities for good work in this area. Students the world over are clamoring to learn about science, the environment, and climate change.

The empirical data collected by Iyengar and colleagues in a community in Bhopal, India, near the Union Carbide factory site of the Bhopal gas tragedy of 1984, show that participants have a high level of awareness about climate change–related risks, both locally and globally. They find that some of the key "determinants that influence participants' daily behavior that has environmental consequences in the Indian socio-economic context are religion, environmental factors affecting their lifestyles, economic-wellbeing, and community involvement in tackling environmental hazards" (chapter 13). Climate change education for all, carefully conceived and well-executed, has inherent value and, furthermore, leads to measurable desirable outcomes, including individual behavioral and attitudinal change, and resulting in reductions in carbon emissions of similar magnitude to other large-scale mitigation strategies (see chapter 12). The goal of climate literacy is to educate and empower millions of climate champions across the world who will help solve the problems flowing from unchecked climate change and unsustainable development.

PART IV: THE FOUNDATIONS OF EDUCATION

In part III, we gather the scholarly fruits of colleagues working on several foundational themes in education. Over the last two generations, early childhood education programs, modules, and interventions focusing on socio-emotional learning, impulse control, cognitive stimulation, and nutrition and health have flourished the world over (see chapter 3). As is the case in all matters pertaining to education, access is important, but quality is supreme. Quality early childhood education sets children on a path of readiness to learn and to bloom.

In chapter 14, Carla Rinaldi, president of Fondazione Reggio Children, Centro Loris Malaguzzi, notes that despite enduring global poverty and growing inequality, evidence shows increased attendance at early childhood education centers. Schools and cultural and educational agencies are the backbone of this change, but they are not always able to offer quality education. She examines in detail the educational experience known as the Reggio Emilia approach as an instance of a widely admired, high-quality early education program in northern Italy. The Reggio approach has flourished, and Reggio-inspired schools are now found the world over. Its approach is built on many disparate ideas and experiences, including the notion that in early childhood educators must first endeavor to learn to listen and engage with the "hundred languages" with which children apprehend the world. Rinaldi writes, the Reggio Emilia approach is a philosophy "based on the image of child as holder of rights from birth; a child competent to learn and relate to others from birth; provided with an extraordinary learning potential metaphorically described with the expression of "a hundred languages"—that is, the hundreds, thousands of ways of expressing themselves, of thinking, of understanding, of learning, as described by Malaguzzi" (chapter 14).

In chapter 15, Leslee Udwin claims that socio-emotional learning is the "missing dimension" in education's quest to nurture responsible, caring, and respectful global citizens. She examines Think Equal, a prevention program designed as a foundation for a healthy life for three-to-six-year olds. With replicability and scalability in mind, the program addresses the challenge of the minimal rate of formal teacher training in low- to middle-income countries' early childhood education centers. This innovative program was designed to intentionally address ten of the seventeen UN Sustainable Development Goals, including goal 3 (good health and well-being); goal 4 (quality education); goal 5 (gender equality); goal 8 (decent work and economic growth); goal 10 (reduced inequalities); goal 13 (climate action); goal 14 (life below water); goal 15 (life on land); goal 16 (peace and justice); and goal 17 (partnerships for the goals) (chapter 15). It provides a promising, intentional, and innovative model to move forward with work in this domain.

Reading is foundational in education. As the eminent education scholar Jeanne Chall once noted, children first learn to read and then read to learn for the rest of their lives.[39] A uniquely human capability, there is no gene for reading. Reading and writing, what we now call literacy, is an epigenetic achievement of the human brain. As a species, we began reading some 3,500 years ago—first, a few members of the human family could read—usually individuals with specialized roles in economic, ritual, and religious functions. Today, literacy is a normative ideal the world over. Reading changes the brain; reading changes the world. Maryanne Wolf has examined the neurological underpinnings of reading, language, and related phenomena in the general areas of mind, brain, and education. In chapter 16, Wolf focuses on "the reading brain" and the effects of digital cultures on "deep reading." The processes involved in deep reading, decoding, comprehending, and reflecting upon each sentence and paragraph rely on using "many of our most sophisticated, intellectual achievements: background knowledge and analogical thought; inference and deduction; perspective-taking and empathy; critical analysis; and the still mysteriously generative drive within all forms of language which helps us to create insights and wisdom of our own.[40] Each of these special faculties contribute to what I have called the deep reading processes.[41] And, each of them is under one form of threat or another, as we move ever more imperceptibly into digital-based modes of reading. Understanding both the threat and the promise of digital reading for ourselves and for the next generation is the overarching goal of this paper" (chapter 16).

In chapter 17, Tami Katzir gathers the lessons from an ambitious reading research program she developed in Israel among immigrant and native Israeli school children. Reading is a socio-emotional as well as a cognitive endeavor, and she situates her research in a mind, brain, and education framework. She articulates a persuasive claim on listening—a fundamental skill linking cognition and emotion. Qua reading, listening aids in understanding the text, the reader, and the world (see also chapter 14). She describes Israel's Island of Understanding reading program and argues that well-crafted reading interventions increase academic achievement and much more, as reading fosters a sense of community and purpose and offers meaningful tools for dealing with life in and outside of school. She writes, "Well designed evidence-based reading instruction can prepare children in the three important subcategories of defined twenty-first-century skills: literacy, learning, and life skills" (chapter 17).

PART V: THE FUTURES OF EDUCATION

All authentic learning is relational—we learn with "the hands, the heart and the mind," (foreword). We learn with others, with the natural world, and with the social world. In chapter 18, Brigit Barron writes of the decisive turn from individualistic theories of learning "as largely cognitive phenomenon driven chiefly by knowledge acquisition to learning as a highly social process that takes place over time, setting, and through varied social interactions." Barron locates consequential learning "as interest-driven, linked to emotions, aided by a diverse set of learning partners, and distributed across the settings of home, school, and community, including online virtual spaces." The ever more ubiquitous infor-mation, communication, and social media technologies have opened new fron-tiers in opportunities for children to learn. A recent UNICEF report states, "If leveraged in the right way and universally accessible, digital technology can be a game changer for children being left behind—whether because of poverty, race, ethnicity, gender, disability, displacement or geographic isolation—connecting them to a world of opportunity and providing them with the skills they need to succeed in a digital world."[42] Indeed, the new technologies can be tools for what Pope Francis calls a "humane globalization," fostering curiosity, engage-ment, and fraternity, or they can accentuate elitism, exclusion, and inequality. The strengths, limitations, and dangers of the new technologies have been dra-matically amplified by the COVID-19 pandemic and the global turn to remote teaching and learning.[43] Barron examines in detail three intentional design interventions and suggests that having (1) clear learning goals, (2) explicit cur-ricula, (3) mentoring scaffolds for teachers, and (4) purposely structured oppor-tunities to engage parents to best support their children's learning are significant features in program development (chapter 18).

People of good faith the world over share in the ethos and eidos animating Pope Francis's global compact for education. Indeed, broad sectors of society hold deeply aspirational notions of schooling with access and quality for all children and youth to flourish. But that aspiration remains an elusive mirage for millions. Louis Gomez, Manuelito Biag, and David Imig articulate a claim for the need to build better *systems* to effectively educate the world's more disadvan-taged children and youth. In chapter 19, the authors offer a series of lessons from improvement science to guide the work of the global compact moving forward. Pope Francis's Global Compact for Education, they write, "offers us an oppor-tunity to work together to address undereducation worldwide and especially in the metaphoric Global South. Taking up this opportunity is more than a matter of aspiration. It is hard, fundamental work and requires foundational resources." The work, they argue, requires careful coordination and long-term collabora-tions among the research community, policy makers, faith leaders, the philan-thropic sector, and, above all, education practitioners on the frontlines. They find in improvement science the "social glue to help helpers help" (chapter 19). Helpers endeavoring to help need to mind "voice" and "agency" as basic levers for moving the needle in educational equity. "In education, as in other fields, we find extraordinarily promising innovations that in the sense of equity and reach, fail to have an impact on some of the important constituents for which they were designed. One challenge that leads to mismatches like these is that designers, as helpers, fail to engage the voices of, and provide agency to, those constituents." They review two extraordinary innovations in education that sadly failed to reach underserved children and youth—*Sesame Street* and the Khan Academy.[44] Minding carefully the lessons harvested by Gomez and colleagues from improvement science is a way to disrupt an educational world where, qua innovation, the rich get richer, and the poor get poorer.

In total, the chapters in this book align with the preponderance of the scholarly evidence suggesting that while progress in education has been laudable and teachers and parents are in many cases making extraordinary efforts to innovate in engaging students, and new technologies open up important new avenues for teaching and learning, current education systems are inadequate to meet the defining social, moral, and environmental crises of the day. As Stefania Giannini diagnoses it, "Climate change has become the defining issue of our time. Digital technologies are disrupting long-held assumptions. There are growing tensions within and between countries and new governance challenges at all levels. In today's context, established ideas, such as 'development' and 'education' urgently need reframing. Development does not guarantee sustainability, and although education has huge potential for good, it has also contributed to social inequalities, economic rivalries, and the unsustainable use of natural resources" (chapter 20).

Giannini then articulates a plea and develops a blueprint for rethinking global efforts "so that education systems can develop the capacities that humanity needs for sustainable development. It calls for a bold humanistic vision based on human rights, social justice, dignity, cultural and social diversity, and intellectual solidarity. This vision reaffirms a set of universal ethical principles and the need to strengthen moral values in education and society. It starts with people of all ages and the analysis of development contexts. [This proposed blueprint] is inclusive and equitable, and informed by interdisciplinary research across the sciences, arts and humanities. Finally, it is participatory and international in scope." Giannini's vision is a fitting bookend to Pope Francis's foreword.

In short, following Pope Francis's call for a radical new global education compact, the chapters that follow examine new levers to improve access to quality education and scale up innovative teaching and learning solutions moving forward. We identify and elevate education's virtuous circles qua health, development, and wellness (chapter 2). We address inequality and its consequences in the lives of children (chapters 1 and 3). We delve into the education of special populations, including children in flight: immigrants, refugees, and the forcibly displaced (chapters 4, 5, and 6). We examine the undertow xenophobia, racism, and discrimination create as children of color try to navigate the currents of hate and intolerance in schools (chapters 6 and 11). We foreground education's foundations in virtues (chapter 8), ethics (chapter 9), morals (chapter 7), civics (chapter 11), a sense of purpose (chapter 10), and bold, humanistic ideals (chapter 20). We ground the lessons extrapolated from innovative early childhood education programs around the world (chapter 14 and 15). We focus on purposive programs in education for the era of climate change (chapters 12 and 13). We mind the tools from the new science of mind, brain, and education (chapters 3, 16, and 17), and the promise and challenges new technologies afford to reach and engage children who currently have little or no opportunities to learn (chapter 18). And lastly, we provide a framework using the tools of improvement science to help those engaged in education's global compact assess the effectiveness of their practices (chapter 19).

NOTES

1. In this volume, we approach education as formal schooling but also as the entire range of opportunities to learn that include early childhood education settings (Rinaldi, chapter 14, this volume; Udwin, chapter 15, this volume), as well as informal and out-of-school educational opportunities in informal settings.

2. Kant, Immanuel, *Kant on Education*, trans. Annette Churton, with introduction by C. A. Foley Rhys Davids (Boston: D. C. Heath, 1906), 6. See also Luhmann, Niklas, and Dieter Lenzen, *Das erziehungssystem der gesellschaft*, vol. 1 (Frankfurt am Main: Suhrkamp, 2002), 38.

3. "The World's Women 2015." United Nations, 2015, https://unstats.un.org/unsd/gender/chapter3/chapter3.html.

4. United Nations. "World's Women 2015."

5. LeVine, Robert A., Sarah LeVine, Beatrice Schnell-Anzola, Meredith L. Rowe, and Emily Dexter, *Literacy And Mothering: How Women's Schooling Changes the Lives of the World's Children* (Oxford: Oxford University Press, 2011).

6. "The State of the World's Children: Girls, Education and Development," UNICEF, accessed September 21, 2021, https://www.unicef.org/sowc04/sowc04_special_issues.html.

7. "UNICEF Executive Director Henrietta Fore's Remarks at a Press Conference on New Updated Guidance on School-Related Public Health Measures in the Context of COVID-19," UNICEF, September 15, 2020, https://www.unicef.org/press-releases/unicef-executive-director-henrietta-fore-remarks-press-conference-new-updated.

8.   Gettleman, Jeffrey, and Suhasini Raj, "As Covid-19 Closes Schools, the World's Children Go to Work," *New York Times*, September 27, 2020, https://www.nytimes.com/2020/09/27/world/asia/covid-19-india-children-school-education-labor.html.

9.   "COVID-19: Schools for More than 168 Million Children Globally Have Been Completely Closed for Almost a Full Year, Says UNICEF," UNICEF, March 3, 2021, https://uni.cf/3uZG6ZV.

10. World Bank estimates that "global extreme poverty is expected to rise in 2020 for the first time in over 20 years as the disruption of the COVID-19 pandemic compounds the forces of conflict and climate change, which were already slowing poverty reduction progress. . . . The COVID-19 pandemic is estimated to push an additional 88 million to 115 million people into extreme poverty this year, with the total rising to as many as 150 million by 2021, depending on the severity of the economic contraction. "COVID-19 to Add as Many as 150 Million Extreme Poor by 2021," World Bank, October 7, 2020, https://bit.ly/2Q3ouZY.

11. "The State of Food Security and Nutrition in the World: The World Is at a Critical Juncture," Food and Agriculture Organization of The United Nations, accessed September 21, 2021, http://www.fao.org/state-of-food-security-nutrition/en/; Speciale, Alessandro, "Pope Francis Decries 'Globalization of Indifference,' " *Washington Post*, July 8, 2013, https://wapo.st/3twnkrC.

12. "United Nations Millennium Development Goals." United Nations, 2015, https://www.un.org/millenniumgoals/education.shtml.

13. Listening is at the heart of all teaching and learning. The Reggio Emilia Approach in early childhood education, explored in chapter 14, perhaps best captures the richness of listening in education. The term "listening" is to be interpreted according to a plurality of meanings, listed on p. 265–266 in this volume.

14. "The Invite of Pope Francis," Global Compact on Education, September 12, 2019, https://www.educationglobalcompact.org/en/the-invite-of-pope-francis/.

15. Roser, Max, and Esteban Ortiz-Ospina, "Literacy," Our World in Data, August 13, 2016, https://ourworldindata.org/literacy.

16. SDG4.7: "Ensure all learners acquire knowledge and skills needed to promote sustainable development, including among others through, education for sustainable development and sustainable lifestyles, human rights, gender equality, promotion of a culture of peace and non-violence, global citizenship, and appreciation of cultural diversity and of culture's contribution to sustainable development." See "Index to Proceedings of the General Assembly 2013/2014," United Nations, December 2015, https://doi.org/10.18356/84e5e905-en.

17. United Nations General Assembly, Universal Declaration of Human Rights, December 10, 1948, https://bit.ly/3stD9yb.

18. Education is linked to the fortunes of both nations and individuals. Quality education is literally life-enhancing and is connected to health and wellness outcomes. Darwin briefly noted the nexus between education—especially the education of women—and human improvement. He wrote in the margins of the evolution notebooks, "Educate all classes. Improve the women (double influence) and mankind must improve." Double the influence surely relates to the fact that educated mothers improve the life changes of their children, thus commencing self-propelling virtuous cycle. Two centuries later Robert Levine and his colleagues at Harvard studied young mothers and their children's health in four countries and found that girls' schooling was good for children's health. See LeVine, Robert A., *Literacy and Mothering: How Women's Schooling Changes the Lives of the World's Children* (Oxford: Oxford University Press, 2012).

Subsequent empirical studies have confirmed Levine's findings. A large-scale *Lancet* study of educational attainment and its effect on child mortality in 175 countries shows that education saves lives, "Of 8.2 million fewer deaths in children younger than 5 years between 1970 and 2009, we estimated that 4.2 million (51·2%) could be attributed to increased educational attainment in women of reproductive age." See Gakidou, Emmanuela, Krycia Cowling, Rafael Lozano, and Christopher J. L. Murray, "Increased Educational Attainment and Its Effect on Child Mortality in 175 Countries Between 1970 and 2009: A Systematic Analysis," *Lancet* 376, no. 9745 (2010): 959–974. https://doi.org/10.1016/s0140-6736(10)61257-3.

19. United Nations, *World Migration Report*, New York: United Nations, 2020, https://bit.ly/3j0ZECr.

20. "Migration in the World," International Organization for Migration, last updated March 12, 2021, https://bit.ly/2OB5CQh.

21. "Data on Movements of Refugees and Migrants Are Flawed," *Nature* 543, nos. 5–6 (2017): https://go.nature.com/2D1VqLU.

22. "UNHCR—Global Trends: Forced Displacement in 2019," UNHCR, June 18, 2021, https://www.unhcr.org/globaltrends2019/.

23. Grandi, Filippo, quoted in "UNHCR—Global Trends 2019."

24. Unicef, "More than 104 million children and young people - 1 in 3 - are out of school in countries affected by war or natural disasters," September 19, 2018, https://www.unicef.org/turkey/en/press-releases/more-104-million-children-and-young-people-1-3-are-out-school-countries-affected-war

25. See also Stathopoulou, Theoni, "Surveying the Hard-to-Survey: Refuges and Unaccompanied Minors in Greece," in *Humanitarianism and Mass Migration: Confronting the World Crisis*, ed. Marcelo Suárez-Orozco (Oakland: University of California Press, 2019), 165–185: *Confronting the World Crisis* (Oakland: University of California Press, 2019), https://bit.ly/3srGYnA.

26. See chapter 5 for further exploration of the many difficulties that Syrian refugee children face in schooling.

27. "Anti-Asian Hate Crime Reported to Police in America's Largest Cities: 2020," Center for the Study of Hate & Extremism, March 2020, https://www.csusb.edu/sites/default/files/FACT%20SHEET-%20Anti-Asian%20Hate%202020%203.2.21.pdf.

28. Dewey, John, "My Pedagogic Creed," *School Journal* 54, no. 3 (January 1897). In a note sympatico to Durkheim's views on education and society, Dewey writes, "Education is a regulation of the process of coming to share in the social consciousness; and that the adjustment of individual activity on the basis of this social consciousness is the only sure method of social reconstruction."

29. William James, working in the Anglo-Saxon pragmatist tradition, thought deeply about education, teachers, and pupils. He conducted field research on memory and learning and investigated consciousness. Considered the father of American psychology, James's empirical work led him to privilege the child's own incipient capabilities and resources as a point of entry into all authentic teaching and learning, in that sense, aligning his thinking to the Dewey's learning-by-doing approach to education. James famously noted, "We are like islands in the sea, separate on the surface but connected in the deep." Education is surely what deeply connects us all.

30. Dewey's "learning by doing," became rooted as experimental schools strived to become hands-on, project-based, democratic learning communities. Corinne Seeds, building on her mentor's teachings, was instrumental in turning the UCLA Lab School into an iconic,

constructivist, research-based experimental school where children-as-citizens took active roles in the courses of their own learning. In Europe, Loris Malaguzzi (chapter 14) built a series of early childhood education programs in northern Italy inspired in part by Dewey's ideas. The Reggio Emilia preschools, in turn, came to deeply influence the thinking of the eminent American cognitive and educational psychologist, Jerome Brunner, and many of his students.

31. Lagemann, Ellen, *An Elusive Science: The Troubling History of Education Research* (Chicago: University of Chicago Press, 2002), https://bit.ly/3snnDUx.

32. Increasingly, education research turned to efficiencies, returns to investments, and theories of forever growth. Algorithmic metrics delineated pathways from teacher "inputs" to student "outcomes." In a particularly vulgar reductive move, economists constructed complex research experiments, such as paying poor children to do their homework, to calculate precisely how extrinsic motivational variables (cash for homework) lead to different learning outcomes. The first principle that "every dollar invested in education" shall deliver results in the currency of better skills, jobs, and income became an agreed-upon shared cognitive schema globally. Arguably, no other idea has traveled as well, even across fiercely contested cultural and epistemic boundaries. From preschool to college, the new mentalité announced that education was an investment paying in little and big ways.

33. The two *L*'s are literacy and labor.

34. See https://coa.stanford.edu/publications for an extensive list of scientific studies that have established empirical associations between such psychological benefits and purpose in life.

35. See, for example, Atul Gawande: *Being Mortal: Medicine and What Matters in the End* (New York: Henry Holt, 2014).

36. Mann, "Twelfth Annual Report," 84. Mann speaks of universal public education in which people across lines of class attend school together. Yet, he remained largely silent about the racial segregation of public schools. See "Horace Mann and Colored Schools," *Liberator*, December 24, 1847. However, Mann was not oblivious to issues of race and discrimination. He advocated for the abolition of the slave trade while secretary of the board of education in Massachusetts. Later, while a member of the U.S. Congress, he spoke out against slavery more generally. See, for example, Horace Mann's February 23, 1849 speech, "Slavery and the Slave Trade" in Horace Mann, *Slavery: Letters and Speeches* (Boston: B. B. Mussey, 1853).

   Mann, Horace. "Twelfth annual report to the Massachusetts Board of Education," in *The Republic and the School: Horace Mann and the Education of Free Men* (1848, repr. Columbia University Press, 1957).

37. Mann, "Twelfth annual report," 86.

38. Mann, "Twelfth annual report," 86.

39. Chall, Jeanne S. *The Academic Achievement Challenge: What Really Works in the Classroom?* (New York: Guilford, 2002).

40. See Taylor, Charles. *The Language Animal* (Cambridge, MA: Harvard University Press, 2016).

41. Wolf, Maryanne. *Reader, Come Home: The Reading Brain in a Digital World* (New York: Harper, 2018).

42. United Nations International Children's Emergency Fund (UNICEF), *Summary: Children in a Digital World: The State of the World's Children, 2017* (New York: UNICEF, 2017), https://www.unicef.org/media/48601/file.

43. Barron further notes (see chapter 18), "Although concerns about data privacy, access to inappropriate content, and increased potential for exploitation are raised, the report also highlights the significant equity challenge reflected by growing evidence of differential use by

children and youth with more and financial assets, digital skills, access to devices, or the quality and stability of their Internet connections that can help them use the technology in empowered ways. Over a third of youth worldwide do not have Internet access and most of these young people are in developing countries."

44.   See chapter 19, particularly the section titled "Innovations Missing the Mark: *Sesame Street* and Khan Academy," which begins on p. 340 in this volume.

I

ADDRESSING OUR MOST VULNERABLE

1

EDUCATION AND INEQUALITY

JEFFREY D. SACHS

E ducation is far and away the most empowering investment for individuals. For that reason, the world has long regarded education as a basic human need and human right. But we have not yet achieved universal education. The COVID-19 pandemic may prove to be a devastating blow to universal education for this generation of children, yet it could also be a spur to renewed action. The biggest obstacle is financial—the need to transfer resources from the richest to the poorest countries to ensure that all children have the chance for education at least through the upper-secondary level. In the post-COVID-19 environment, this will also require universal access to high-quality broadband, since much of learning in the coming decade will be online, including blended learning that combines online curricula with in-person education.

What is a human right? A human right is something that every individual is afforded on the basis of human dignity. Education has been recognized as a human right for seventy-two years, since the UN's adoption of the Universal Declaration of Human Rights in 1948. It is good to recall that right as expressed in Article 26:

(1) Everyone has the right to education. Education shall be free, at least in the elementary and fundamental stages. Elementary education shall be compulsory. Technical and professional education shall be made generally available and higher education shall be equally accessible to all on the basis of merit.

(2) Education shall be directed to the full development of the human personality and to the strengthening of respect for human rights and fundamental freedoms. It shall promote understanding, tolerance, and friendship among all nations, racial or religious groups, and shall further the activities of the United Nations for the maintenance of peace.

(3) Parents have a prior right to choose the kind of education that shall be given to their children.[1]

The world has failed for seventy-two years to realize that right and other rights in the Universal Declaration. There has been progress, but we should be more interested in the shortfall than the achievement, as children are losing their future prospects at our hands. The failures point us to the urgent work we have yet to do.

In fact, we not only made the commitment to education for all seventy-two years ago, but we have repeated the commitment with each generation, announcing it anew to great fanfare, going forward, and then falling short again. This brings to mind Albert Einstein's definition of insanity (or at least the one often attributed to him): to keep doing the same thing and expecting a different outcome. We keep setting the same lofty goals but, because we lack a certain seriousness in how we approach them, we fall short of our promises.

Consider, for example, the UN International Covenant on Economic, Social, and Cultural Rights (1966), which again recognized the right of education for all.[2] Article 13 of the covenant proclaims that the state parties recognize the right of everyone to education and that education shall be directed to the full development of the human personality. The state parties specify that primary education shall be compulsory and available free to all. Secondary education should be made generally available and accessible to all by every appropriate means and, in particular, by the progressive introduction of free education. These are the same goals as in the 1948 Universal Declaration, reiterated in the succeeding generation.

Then came Article 28 on the Convention of the Rights of the Child (1989).[3] In this convention, state parties recognized the right of the child to education and, in particular, that primary education should be compulsory and available free for all. We again find the same language and commitment, but we still are not getting the results. We are doing the same thing and hoping for a different outcome!

With a few more steps along the way, including the Millennium Development Goals in the year 2000, we arrive at the situation today. Our generation has crafted the Sustainable Development Goals (SDGs) as part of Agenda 2030, adopted by the UN member states in September 2015.[4] These goals are not new, but nevertheless they are urgent. There is no target more essential among the seventeen SDGs than to ensure universal education.

SDG 4 calls for inclusive and equitable quality education as well as the promotion of lifelong learning opportunities for all.[5] SDG 4 calls specifically upon us to ensure that all children—both boys and girls—complete free, equitable, and quality primary *and* secondary education leading to relevant and effective learning outcomes. This is a kind of advance in the SDGs as compared to earlier declarations: now secondary education should be free as well. We are no longer saying that we should *try* to make it free. As of the commitment made in 2015, it should be free.

Each of the global covenants includes education for technical skills and vocational education. There is also an insistence on equal access for men and women to combat gender disparities in access to education. SDG 4 goes further, recognizing that there must be quality early childhood development or universal pre-K. This is also new and vital, based on scientific insights about the importance of cognitive and social development during the early critical years of brain development.

Another novel point is SDG target 4.7, which states that by 2030, all learners should "acquire the knowledge and skills they need to promote sustainable development, including, among others, through education for sustainable development and sustainable lifestyles. Every student must also acquire the knowledge and skills needed to promote human rights, gender equality, promotion of a culture of peace and non-violence, global citizenship and appreciation of cultural diversity and of culture's contribution to sustainable development."[6]

We know what our goals are; indeed, we have known for more than seventy-two years that we must ensure that every child receives a quality and complete education. Now we *must* achieve this goal. The future of our globally interconnected world society depends on it. Children who do not receive a quality education will not have a viable future.

We live now in the knowledge economy, and the need for education will intensify in the years ahead. The essential fact of a knowledge-based economy is that knowledge reaps returns in the marketplace, whereas raw labor suffers diminishing returns in the marketplace. Most people lacking a high school education today can no longer earn a livelihood above poverty. This is a basic point, and it will become increasingly evident in the years ahead. Agriculture and mining will become far more mechanized, eliminating many jobs for less-educated workers. Many low-skilled jobs that used to at least provide a basic livelihood are rapidly being mechanized, filled by increasingly smart robots, or substituted by artificial intelligence.

In the United States, there has been a vast and sustained increase in inequality according to educational attainment. America has essentially become two societies divided by level of education. Figure 1.1 shows the change in real wage levels of U.S. workers by gender and education from 1963 to 2012. Especially for men, we see the earnings gap widening between those with tertiary education and those with only secondary education or less. If a person has a bachelor's degree or higher, life has never been better in material terms. If a person has a high school diploma or lower, life has become increasingly difficult. This widening of income inequality explains almost everything about the basic sociological patterns of the United States—the political divides, economic divides, and loss of trust in society between different social classes. Education has become the dividing point of a decent life.

One of the most striking findings of the recent two decades is that people in the United States with less education are dying now at much higher rates. There is an epidemic of *deaths of despair,* that is, deaths from drugs, alcohol, and suicide. This epidemic is mainly hitting the portion of the population that have attained a high school degree or less. Figure 1.2 shows the rates of drug, alcohol, and suicide mortality for white, non-Hispanic people ages fifty to fifty-four, disaggregated by education level and gender. We see that those with a college education or more, shown on the bottom, have essentially unchanged trends

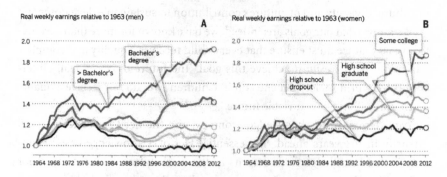

FIGURE 1.1 Changes in real wage levels of full-time U.S. workers by sex and education, 1963–2012.

Source: Roser, Max, and Mohamed Nagdy, "Returns to Education," World in Data, 2013, https://ourworldindata.org/returns-to-education.

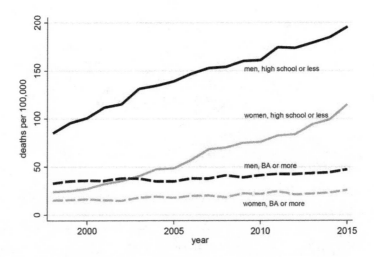

FIGURE 1.2 Drug, alcohol, and suicide mortality, in white non-Hispanic people ages 50–54.

Source: Case, Anne, and Angus Deaton, "Mortality and Morbidity in the 21st Century," *Brookings Papers on Economic Activity*, no. 1 (2017): 397–476. DOI:10.1353/eca.2017.0005.

over the last twenty years. The rising trends are among people with high school degrees or less. It is as if there are two different societies in the United States, divided by level of educational attainment.

We also know that across countries, educational attainment is strongly related to economic progress. The tight correlation of test score quality and economic growth has been shown in repeated studies. In figure 1.3, we see a partial regression line demonstrating this correlation from a 2010 study by E. A. Hanushek and L. Woessmann. The horizontal axis shows the country's test scores according to the Organisation for Economic Co-Operation and Development's (OECD) Programme for International Student Assessment (PISA). The vertical axis shows the country's long-run economic growth rate. The partial regression line controls for initial GDP and years of schooling. We see a strong positive relationship between educational performance, as measured by test scores, and economic growth. The countries at the lower left of the graph (ZAF = South Africa, PER = Peru, and PHL = Philippines) have poor educational outcomes and low economic growth.

There is a strong correlation as well, not surprisingly, between the level of GDP per capita and the performance on standardized international tests (figure 1.4). Children in poorer countries generally go to underresourced

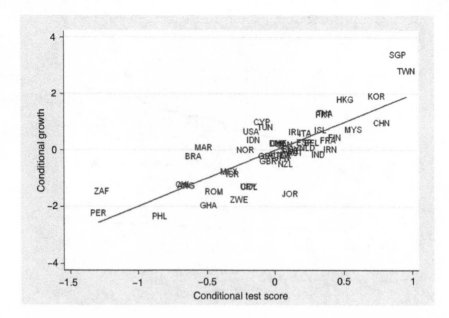

FIGURE 1.3 Association between test scores and long-run economic growth after controlling for baseline GDP and years of schooling.

Source: Hanushek, E. A., and L Woessmann, "Education and Economic Growth," in *International Encyclopedia of Education*, ed. Penelope Peterson, Eva Baker, and Barry McGaw, 245–252 (Oxford: Elsevier, 2010).

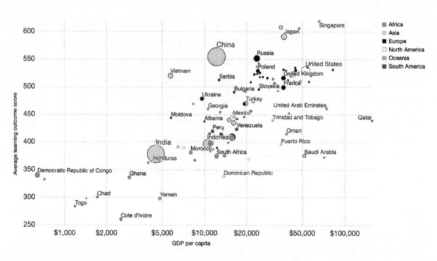

FIGURE 1.4 Average learning outcomes vs. GDP per capita, 2015.

Source: Roser, Max, and Esteban Ortiz-Ospina, "Global Education," Our World in Data, 2016, https://ourworldindata.org/global-education.

schools with fewer teachers, less qualified teachers, fewer supplies, less access to chemistry labs, and so forth. In some of the poorest countries, class sizes are so large, the teachers are so poorly trained, and the materials for schooling are so meager that young children do not achieve even the most basic skills of literacy and numeracy. Often, children in grade five or grade six of low-income countries cannot read basic texts. This is the high cost of poverty on educational quality.

Thus, we continue to fall far short of our global educational attainment goals. Net attendance at the primary level, measured as the proportion of primary-school-age enrollments divided by the total population of primary school–age children, is less than 50 percent in parts of West Africa and Afghanistan (figure 1.5). In many countries, net primary attendance is still less than 70 percent or 80 percent. Total expected years of schooling are between four and eight years across the Sahel of Africa and between eight and twelve years in most of Africa (figure 1.6). This figure is shockingly low.

Each year, UNESCO publishes the *Global Education Monitoring Report*. In 2019, the year before the COVID-19 pandemic began, the report included data showing that only 41 percent of children in low-income countries were completing lower secondary education (figure 1.7). Even more starkly, only 19 percent of children in low-income countries were completing upper secondary education. According to SDG 4, the upper-secondary completion rate is

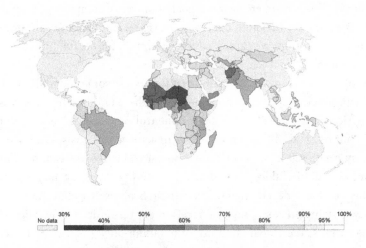

FIGURE 1.5 Net attendance rate of primary school, 2015.

Source: Ortiz-Ospina, Esteban, and Max Roser, "Primary and Secondary Education," Our World in Data, 2013, https://ourworldindata.org/primary-and-secondary-education.

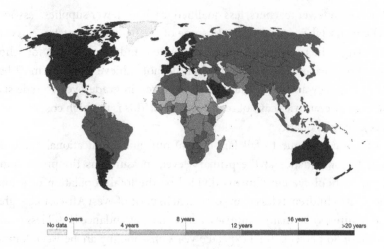

FIGURE 1.6 Expected years of schooling, 2017.

Source: "Expected Years of Schooling," Our World in Data, 2017, https://ourworldindata.org/grapher /expected-years-of-schooling.

supposed to be 100 percent by 2030, but it was just 19 percent in 2019. If the trends up to 2019 were to continue in the post-COVID-19 period, by 2030, just 53 percent of children in low-income countries would complete lower secondary education, and just 26 percent of children would complete upper secondary. This is nowhere near our goal of universal completion. Even before COVID-19, the world community was not yet serious about ensuring universal quality education. We cannot educate and train for the full human being if children aren't even in school.

As of early 2020, it was estimated that there were some 260 million school-aged children out of school. Roughly half of these children live in sub-Saharan Africa (figure 1.8). The number of unenrolled students has been coming down but not with the urgency needed to achieve our goals—and with very little international input to help the poorest countries. Instead, the number of out-of-school children was gradually coming down up to 2019 mainly because of local development. Even though access to education and the ability to complete a secondary education are recognized as universal basic human rights, the global community is taking only small steps to achieve these goals.

Of course, the COVID-19 pandemic made the situation disastrously worse. UNESCO estimates, that as of May 2020, the schooling of more than 1.4 billion

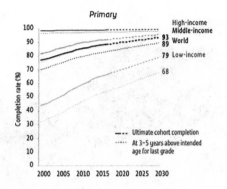

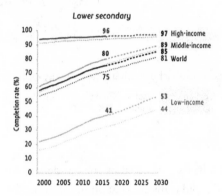

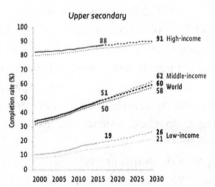

FIGURE 1.7 School completion rate, 2000–2018 and projections to 2030.

Source: UNESCO Institute for Statistics, and Global Education Monitoring Report Team, *Meeting Commitments: Are Countries on Track to Achieve SDG 4?* (Paris: UNESCO, 2019).

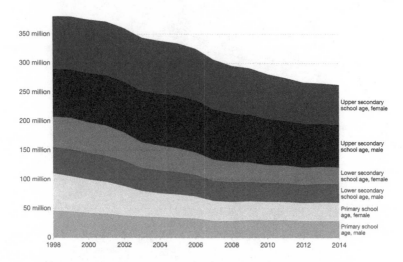

FIGURE 1.8 Number of out-of-school children worldwide, 1970 to 2014.

Source: Roser, Max, and Esteban Ortiz-Ospina, "Global Education," Our World in Data, 2016, https://ourworldindata.org/global-education.

children had been adversely affected by the pandemic, with a combination of school closures and rapid transitions to online learning for those with internet access. As of March 2021, the dislocations were still affecting around 180 million children, and hundreds of millions more dealt with uncertain or unstable schooling due to repeated waves of infection.[7] Now, the hopes for these children depend on three things: (1) vastly improved control of the pandemic, so that schools can reopen and stay open; (2) vastly expanded broadband coverage, so that online learning can reach all learners; and (3) vastly expanded financial resources to equip school systems with teachers, equipment, and safe premises for all children.

Why has global progress towards universal education been so limited, even before the pandemic? Why does such rampant inequality in education persist? The main answer is that developing countries lack the financial resources within families, communities, and government budgets to provide an education for all children through the secondary level. The problem is not the lack of global goals or local desires. The problem is one of poverty combined with insufficient help from rich countries.

There have been several education finance studies to calculate the costs of achieving universal education in low-income settings. Here, I will look at a back-of-the-envelope calculation that comes to basically the same conclusions as the larger studies.

Let us start by examining the cost of educating a student for one year. Each student needs a teacher and a classroom. The classroom must be in a building that has water and electricity. The building should have connectivity.

We start by considering the average salary of a teacher. The average teacher salary in Mali, for example, is about $590 a month, so on the order of $5,000 to 6,000 a year. Of course, on that salary, it may be very hard to get a teacher to stay in a more rural area, but for the sake of this example, let's assume that the teacher's salary is $5,000. If we assume that there are twenty-five children in the class, then per capita, the teacher's salary costs around $200 per student. Now, roughly speaking, teachers' salaries compose about half the expenditure of an education system, taking into account the costs of the school building, electricity, water, internet connectivity, learning materials, and management of the school system. If the teacher's cost is $200 per student, we can estimate roughly the total cost per student at about $400 per year.

This number is an approximation, but it is consistent with the findings of many studies. It is worth noting that in the United States, we spend between $10,000 and $15,000 per student per year. Our estimate of $400 per student per year is surely the lower plausible bound for a meaningful education.

As the next step of the calculation, consider that in a typical low-income country in sub-Saharan Africa, school-aged children (five to nineteen years old) make up around 40 percent of the population. If the cost per student per year is $400, the cost per capita in the country is $400 x 40 percent, or $160 per capita per year.

How does a per capita cost of $160 per year compare to national income? And can a low-income country like Mali afford such an expense? Here is the challenge. For example, in Mali, Niger, Chad, Ethiopia, and Rwanda the per capita GDP is roughly $800.[8] A low-income country typically collects around 20 percent of its GDP in tax revenues. On a per-capita basis, the government collects around $800 x 20 percent, or $160 per capita.

Here's the rub. The education budget for five-to nineteen-year-olds is around $160 per capita, but the total government budget is also around $160 per capita! In other words, for Mali to educate all of its five-to nineteen-year-olds, the government would have to direct its entire budget to education. This, of course, is impossible. The national budget has to fund not only education but also the health system, public administration, the police, water and sanitation, roads, power, electricity, and other infrastructure. It is typically assumed that around 20 percent of the national budget can be devoted to education. That would amount to around $32 per year ($160 x 20 percent), or just one-fifth of what is needed.

So, here is the bottom line. As hard as Mali—or the other low-income countries of sub-Saharan Africa—may try to achieve SDG 4, it simply cannot be done out of national budgets. Children are out of school not because the government doesn't care but because the government doesn't have the financial means. Either the rest of the world helps Mali and countries like it to fund the education system, or we will have hundreds of millions of kids without an education. In the absence of that needed international funding, we will have failed again to secure the right to education of these children. That, of course, is what has been happening for decades.

By looking country by country at the domestic education costs and domestic budget resources, it is possible to estimate the global financing gap for education, meaning the total global funding that low-income and lower-middle-income countries would need to receive to have all children ages five to nineteen in school. According to 2020 UNESCO estimates, taking account of the enormous setbacks due to COVID-19, the global financing gap between 2020 and 2030 is around $148 billion per year, a large part of which will be needed by African countries.[9]

In summary, it is no mystery why students are not completing primary and secondary education. It is their poverty and the lack of adequate budget revenues of their governments. We in the rich world can follow those who blame the developing countries for not trying hard enough (or who charge that they are corrupt, uncaring, or similar slanders), or we can choose to be decent and recognize that we must not leave 260 million children without an education simply because they are too poor.

The correct decision is clear: we must do something about it.

The IMF has worked over the past couple of years to understand the financing gaps not only for education but also for healthcare (SDG 3) and other basic infrastructure, such as safe water and sanitation (SDG 6) and roads (SDG 9). The IMF found that if the poor countries are to meet the key SDGs, there is roughly a $358 billion per year financing gap as of 2030 (figure 1.9). This is based on incremental SDG costs estimated at $528 billion in 2030 and increased domestic taxes that could cover around $170 billion in 2030, leaving a gap of around $358 billion ($528 billion—$170 billion).

That number—$358 billion as of 2030—may seem very big, but it isn't. The first rule of macroeconomics is to always know the right denominator.

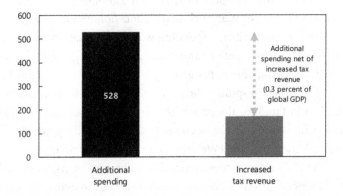

FIGURE 1.9 Low-income developing countries: additional spending and increased tax revenues in 2030 (billions of 2016 US$).

Source: Gaspar, V., M. D. Amaglobeli, M. M. Garcia-Escribano, D. Prady, and M. Soto, "Fiscal Policy and Development: Human, Social, and Physical Investments for the SDGs," International Monetary Fund, January 23, 2019, https://www.imf.org/en/Publications/Staff-Discussion-Notes/Issues/2019/01/18/Fiscal-Policy-and-Development-Human-Social-and-Physical-Investments-for-the-SDGs-46444.

In our case, the correct denominator is the annual output of the world economy, which was around $87 trillion in 2019 and will be around $120 trillion in 2030 (measured at 2019 prices). Suppose we divide $358 billion by a world output of around $120 trillion. In that case, we find that the financing gap for health, education, water and sanitation, and roads of fifty-nine low-income countries with 1.7 billion people comes to just 0.3 of 1 percent of world output. In other words, for far less than 1 percent of world output, we could *secure basic economic rights for all*, including education for all children.

Suppose that just the high-income countries pay to close the $358 billion gap. The high-income countries will constitute perhaps around 45 percent of the total world income in 2030, or around $54 trillion. Thus, the financing gap would come to approximately 0.7 percent of the income of the rich countries.

Here, then, is the point. For just 0.7 of 1 percent of the income of the rich countries, we could ensure universal economic rights. For around 0.1 percent of the income of the rich countries today, around $40 billion per year, we could ensure that all children are in school. The required sums are tiny, but we are not mobilizing them. Currently, development aid from the rich countries for primary and secondary education is about $13 per child. When we divide that by the $400 per child that we need for a year of schooling, we can immediately see that we are not coming close to meeting global needs.

Let's look at just the continent of Africa for a moment. How can we raise the needed $26 billion per year to close the education financing gap? Here are two ways. First, annual military spending worldwide is currently around $1.5 trillion, so less than 2 percent of annual military spending would do the trick. Pope Paul VI called for this in his great 1967 encyclical, Populorum Progressio, calling for diverting some military spending to the fight against poverty to create a World Fund for the poor.[10] The United States alone could close the gap by diverting just two weeks of current military spending, which amounts to around $2 billion per day. (We note that since the original presentation of this paper, the United States spent around $5 trillion on emergency COVID-19 relief for American citizens between March 2020 and March 2021, suggesting how easy it would be financially for the United States and other high-income countries to cover Africa's educational financing gap.)

Alternatively, the world's super-rich billionaires could easily close the financing gap. As of April 2021, *Forbes* magazine estimates that there are 2,755 billionaires, 660 more than in 2020, and with a combined net worth of a staggering $13.1 trillion, up $5 trillion from a year earlier.[11] Just 1 percent of that wealth, or $130 billion per year, could easily pay not only for the worldwide education financing gap but also for the healthcare financing gap. If that's not shocking enough, consider that the world's wealthiest four people (Jeffrey Bezos, Elon Musk, Bernard Arnault, and Bill Gates) have a combined wealth of over $600 billion (as of April 2021). With a 5 percent return on this combined wealth, *these four individuals* could close the entire education financing gap of Africa ($30 billion = $602 billion x 5 percent). We can also note that the world's richest five hundred individuals enjoyed gains in their financial wealth of around $2 trillion between January 2020 and April 2021, even as the pandemic ravaged the world economy.

The money needed to ensure the world's basic economic needs is available in the GDPs of the rich countries, the military budgets of the world, or the bank accounts of the world's super-rich billionaires. The poor suffer from lack of access to schooling and even die from undernutrition and lack of health care—not because this is inevitable or because the costs of solutions are astronomical but because we are not really trying to fulfill our long-standing global commitments.

Pope Francis is the greatest mobilizer for decency in the world, an inspiration and hope for all of us. When Pope Francis calls for a global compact for education, let us use the occasion to mobilize the basic financing so that universal education can be a reality for all rather than merely a lofty ideal. Pope

Francis's leadership, unique in the world, will stir the global conscience. We can get all children in the world into school. Let us get this done.

NOTES

1. United Nations General Assembly, Universal Declaration of Human Rights, December 10, 1948, https://www.un.org/en/about-us/universal-declaration-of-human-rights.

2. UN General Assembly, International Covenant on Economic, Social and Cultural Rights, December 16, 1966, https://www.ohchr.org/en/professionalinterest/pages/cescr.aspx.

3. UN General Assembly, Convention on the Rights of the Child, November 20, 1989, https://www.ohchr.org/en/professionalinterest/pages/crc.aspx.

4. UN General Assembly, Transforming Our World: The 2030 Agenda for Sustainable Development, September 25, 2015, https://sdgs.un.org/2030agenda.

5. United Nations, Ensure Inclusive and Equitable Quality Education and Promote Lifelong Learning Opportunities for All, accessed March 1, 2021, https://sdgs.un.org/goals/goal4.

6. United Nations, SDG 4.7, https://sdgs.un.org/goals/goal4.

7. UNESCO, "Education: From Disruption to Recovery," accessed September 17, 2021, https://en.unesco.org/covid19/educationresponse#schoolclosures.

8. World Bank, "GDP Per Capita (Constant 2010 US$)—Mali," accessed September 17, 2021, https://data.worldbank.org/indicator/NY.GDP.PCAP.KD?locations=ML.

9. United Nations, "Act Now: Reduce the Impact of Covid-19 on the Cost of Achieving SDG 4," https://en.unesco.org/gem-report/COVIDcostSDG4

10. Pope Paul VI, "Populorum Progressio: Encyclical of Pope Paul VI on the Development of Peoples," Vatican, March 26, 1967, https://www.vatican.va/content/paul-vi/en/encyclicals/documents/hf_p-vi_enc_26031967_populorum.html.

11. Forbes, "World's Billionaires List 2021," https://www.forbes.com/billionaires/

2

EDUCATION, HEALTH, AND DEMOGRAPHY

DAVID E. BLOOM AND MADDALENA FERRANNA

This chapter explores the interplay among education, population health, and demographics. Much literature already addresses the role of education in promoting individuals' and nations' economic development and the links among health, demography, and education. In this chapter, we reflect on the most important lessons learned so far and suggest how to further progress on providing quality universal education at the primary and secondary levels and for adults as well. In particular, we focus on three related topics: the economic rationale for devoting resources to education, the most effective policy approaches to education progress, and the role of education in the context of an aging world population.

The economic rationale for devoting more public resources to education is often based on a narrow definition of education benefits: the earnings premiums more-educated individuals enjoy relative to their less-educated counterparts. This chapter argues that economic models and related evidence need to focus on a broader set of public and private education-related benefits, especially the greater longevity of the educated and the intrinsic value that education confers on people and their families. We review some promising lines of inquiry along with indications that such analyses will likely support major increases in education spending.

The second topic concerns the design of policies to enhance education. Education investments can promote health and longevity, reduce fertility and population growth rates, improve living standards, and, ultimately, enhance well-being at multiple levels, ranging from individuals to countries. The causal links are bidirectional: health investments and fertility reductions contribute to increasing the returns to education and, as a result, induce more investment in education. This complexity implies that educational development is probably best approached multisectorally through an integrated blend of health, population, and education policies, especially those that promote child health such as prenatal care, childhood vaccination, and investments in schools' water and sanitation infrastructure.[1]

The last topic concerns the importance of education in the context of a world population with a historically large and growing share of older people. Rates of illiteracy are relatively high among current and near-future cohorts of older people due to past patterns of school enrollment. Investment in the education and human capital of today's youth is a potent pillar in any societal strategy for addressing the workforce shortages that are likely to accompany population aging. Moreover, addressing older adults' educational shortfalls creates value—both by enhancing the productivity of their market contributions but likely more so by enhancing the productivity of their appreciable nonmarket contributions, which often take the form of volunteer work and caregiving for spouses and grandchildren.

The COVID-19 pandemic highlights the broad value of education, the close links between education and population health, and the benefits of investing in older adults—for example, by enhancing their digital knowledge. We conclude the chapter with some reflections on the implications of COVID-19 for the interplay among health, education, and demographics.

THE FULL VALUE OF EDUCATION

Several arguments are traditionally made in support of devoting more public resources to education.[2] Some arguments are moral, ethical, and humanitarian in nature. Some are rooted in international law and the notion of education as a fundamental human right or are related to political commitments and the prominent place of education in the Sustainable Development Goals (see chapter 20). Other arguments are more pragmatic in nature, highlighting, for instance, the contribution of education to societies that are peaceful, cohesive, equitable, and secure. The economic rationale is also pragmatic. Governments should invest in education because it promotes economic well-being, from the micro-levels of individuals and families to the macro-levels of communities and countries.[3]

Economic arguments for education investments have played a fundamental role in educational expansion during the past half-century. Prior to the 1960s, education was widely and severely neglected as a public investment. The watershed moment came when labor economists began to pay substantial attention to education, conceptualizing it as a form of human capital and conducting numerous careful studies comparing its costs and benefits. Gary Becker and T. W. Schultz—both of who received a Nobel Prize in Economics for work they did in the 1950s and 1960s—pioneered this type of cost-benefit analysis.[4] In their work and in the studies that followed, the costs of education encompass tuition fees and the income students forgo by being in school, while the benefits are mainly the higher productivity and income of students after they leave school and enter the workforce.

Another key figure in promoting public investments in education was George Psacharopoulos, a University of Chicago–trained economist working at the World Bank. Psacharopoulos made a career of collecting empirical studies on the return to investment in education for different countries, different demographic groups, and different time frames. He noticed that these studies consistently suggested that education offered a high return on investment by any reasonable financial standard. For example, the latest published review of studies on the rate of return to investments in schooling covered 819 analyses of data from 139 countries that are home to 92 percent of the world's population.[5] These studies indicate that the average rate of return to investment in schooling is 9.7 percent, well above rates of return on standard financial instruments, like long-term U.S. Treasury bonds, which have had yields in the 3–5 percent range for the last decade and a half. Returns to education are even higher for women: an additional year of schooling boosts women's earnings by almost 12 percent.[6]

Psacharopoulos leveraged his compelling observation of high rates of return into a colossal boost in education lending and spending at the World Bank and subsequently in many countries. The fact that the message spoke directly to those with the power of the purse—ministers of finance, ministers of planning, treasury secretaries, and economic advisers to presidents and prime ministers—resulted in that boost. The message was expressed in the financial and economic language these policy makers spoke, and it relied on standard return on investment metrics economists routinely use to guide resource allocation decisions.

However, the estimated returns to schooling that George Psacharopoulos so effectively brought to policy makers' attention are conservative. They are conservative because they only capture as benefits the higher annual earnings that accrue to the individuals who receive the schooling and neglect the broader societal benefits of more education. Those societal benefits include the consumption or intrinsic value that people enjoy from education and the additional production from a population that lives longer and thereby works more years. In addition, broader social benefits include value associated with the tendency of more-educated populations to have lower fertility, enabling the escape from the quicksand of poverty traps; greater security enjoyed by future generations; a more robust base of critical human resources in areas such as engineering, medicine, and business administration; and a population with more progressive social values, a more expansive and forward-looking view of the planet's health, and greater sensitivity to human differences in nationality, gender, race, and sexual orientation.

The difference between the narrow economic benefits Psacharopoulos focuses on and the full societal benefits of a more-educated population are substantial. For example, Elina Pradhan, an economist at the World Bank, points out that educated people tend to live healthier, longer lives, presumably because of better nutrition, better access to health information, and better health-seeking behavior (in addition to the income channel that goes from higher educational attainment to higher wages and, as a result, better access to healthcare services and healthy products). Once the impact of education on adult and child mortality is taken into account, returns to education increase from about 10 percent to as much as 15 percent.[7]

As another example, consider the intrinsic value of education—value that is above and beyond the gains associated with higher productivity and income. The intrinsic value of education is, for example, the value associated with increased access to knowledge and ideas; greater pleasure derived from consumption and leisure; a stronger sense of security and the peace of mind that comes with it; hope for future generations to have a more dignified and better life; and an enhanced sense of empowerment, especially among girls and women. The field of economics is replete with life cycle models that are well suited, at least in principle, to comprehensively and consistently monetizing both the intrinsic and the instrumental value of education. However, to the best of our knowledge, little has been done to develop or apply them in this sphere.

Notice that if all the economic, health, and social benefits of improvements in educational quantity and quality—in other words, all the instrumental and intrinsic benefits at the micro and macro levels—were conceptualized and monetized, rates of return would likely be well above 10 percent. Educational spending is mainly accounted for as a social cost, so it stands to reason that when we make resource allocation decisions, we should compare those social costs with their full societal benefits and not merely the portion of them that takes the form of annual earnings gains. This principle applies to all decisions about the allocation of social resources. However, it is fair to assume that a full societal appraisal of education will only enhance its favorability as an investment in comparison with many other potential uses of public spending, such as militarization, mass incarceration, and building border walls.

Future research could usefully focus on estimating the full value of education. Countries have already invested so much in education on the basis of 10 percent social rates of return. If rigorous evidence indicated that the rate of return was actually 15 percent, 20 percent, or higher, we could make a strong case for increasing global education spending. Note that the same idea applies to other welfare-enhancing investments such as vaccination, whose economic evaluation has traditionally focused on a narrow set of benefits.[8]

HEALTH INVESTMENTS TO PROMOTE EDUCATION

That healthy children have better records of school attendance than their less-healthy counterparts is both intuitive and empirically well established. Moreover, healthy children tend to have better cognitive function, so they get more out of every day that they spend in school. Because education is so heavily cumulative, it is also true that healthy children tend to stay in school for longer and have higher educational attainment. In other words, child and adolescent health strengthen the links between enrollment and attendance, attendance and learning, and attendance this year and enrollment next year.[9]

Several studies have also highlighted the importance of fetal health and early child development in promoting health and economic well-being throughout the presumably lengthened life cycle.[10] Almost forty years ago, the British epidemiologist David Barker hypothesized that factors such as low birth weight and premature birth contributed to hypertension and heart disease later in life.[11] Since then, numerous studies have indicated that early childhood health also affects physical and cognitive development, educational outcomes, and adult productivity.[12]

From a population-level perspective, a key research finding is that child survival improvements tend to promote more than proportionate reductions in fertility.[13] Those reductions occur as couples realize they can have fewer children and still reach their desired number of surviving children. Fertility reductions also occur as desired fertility tends to be reduced with increases in the costs and opportunity costs of childrearing that naturally occur in the course of economic development. Education (especially for females) feeds into this process since children of educated women typically have higher survival rates, and educated women have a higher opportunity cost of time.

Reduced fertility, in turn, allows economic units ranging from households to countries to escape the crushing burden of youth dependency and to raise their living standards through a mechanism known as the demographic dividend, in which education plays a prominent role.[14] And low fertility also enables families to invest more in the health, education, and future productivity of each child.

Fertility reduction is especially important to educational progress. As demographer Gavin Jones once observed, trying to improve educational quantity and quality during periods of rapid population growth is like attempting to run up an escalator that is going down. Anyone who has—in a moment of suspended good judgment—tried or seen this knows that it is difficult to do and somewhat hazardous. Similarly, educational progress is harder to achieve during faster population growth, a constraint that health improvements and further education gains ultimately relax.

The relation among health, education, and well-being is complex, characterized by feedback loops and cumulative causality.[15] More specifically, improvements in general health from gestation on lead to lower fertility, thus reducing population pressure and enhancing opportunities to increase educational quantity and quality, which in turn promotes further health gains, fertility declines, and improved standards of living.[16]

Figures 2.1–2.3 document the strong links among health, education, population, and income. Figure 2.1 plots the adult literacy rate against child mortality in 2000 and 2018 for all countries with available data. Although both indicators have improved over time, a clear negative relationship exists in which countries with higher child mortality also have lower education levels in the general population. Figure 2.2 plots life expectancy at birth against the natural logarithm of gross domestic product (GDP) per capita, showing that countries with higher GDP tend to have superior population health. The positive relation has been stable over time. Finally, figure 2.3 plots the percentage of the population that completed at least lower secondary school against the total fertility rate in 2016 for all countries with available data. The relation is not very tight. Still, countries seem to cluster either around a

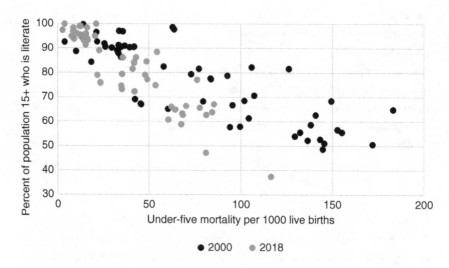

FIGURE 2.1 Child mortality rate (number of deaths under age five per one thousand live births) and adult literacy rate (percentage of people ages fifteen and above who can both read and write) in 2000 and 2018.

Source: World Development Indicators, https://data.worldbank.org. Based on fifty-nine countries and world regions for which both indicators are available both in 2000 and in 2018.

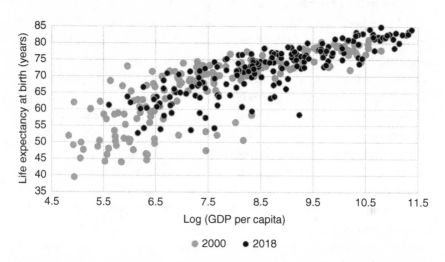

FIGURE 2.2 Natural logarithm of GDP per capita (current US$) and life expectancy at birth (years) in 2000 and 2018.

Source: World Development Indicators, https://data.worldbank.org. Based on 178 countries for which both indicators are available both in 2000 and in 2018.

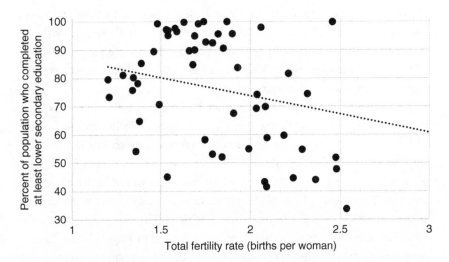

FIGURE 2.3 Total fertility rate (average number of births per woman) and educational attainment of the population ages twenty-five and over (percentage of population twenty-five and over that completed at least lower secondary education) in 2016.

Source: World Development Indicators, https://data.worldbank.org. Based on sixty countries for which there are data on both total fertility rate and educational attainment rates.

low fertility–high educational attainment equilibrium or a high fertility–low educational attainment one.

Although these figures cannot and do not prove a causal relation, they certainly indicate that fully understanding the links among health, population, education, and living standards is fundamental for designing the most effective strategy to catalyze and accelerate educational development. In particular, one key implication is that building and equipping schools, training teachers, and enrolling students are not the only—and may not be the best—ways to promote educational advancement. For starters, enrollment does not translate directly into education, and education does not translate directly into good education, which is often the real catalyst for engaged citizenship, emotional awareness and human sensitivity, and a tolerance of the other, along with the enhanced potential for working collaboratively, productively, and innovatively.

More importantly, the links between education and health imply that an efficient approach to promoting education may be to start by investing in child health. Think here of childhood vaccines against diphtheria, tetanus, pertussis, measles, polio, pneumococcal disease, Haemophilus influenzae type b, and rotavirus. Rigorous and compelling evidence from settings ranging from Ethiopia to India and from the Philippines to Vietnam shows that vaccines promote well-being not just by protecting children from infection by different pathogens but also through the education pathways of school attendance, educational attainment, and engaged learning.[17]

The logic applies equally well to other health interventions, like investing in prenatal care and nutrition and strengthening primary healthcare facilities and their links to other parts of the health system. Investments in safe water and sanitation are also important, especially in schools. For example, the drop off in secondary school enrollment rates among girls might be driven, at least partly, by the absence of functioning toilets and running water in their schools as they mature and begin to menstruate, which often leaves girls exposed to humiliation and harassment that they can best avoid by staying home.[18] Moreover, investments in women's education and health can boost economic development more than similar investments directed to men.[19] Indeed, investing in women increases labor force participation, speeds up the demographic transition, and leads to sustained economic growth.[20]

Given the interplay among health, education, and wealth, we should not limit ourselves to direct approaches to educational development. Rather, we should take advantage of our modern understanding of development processes as complex dynamic systems and recognize the education gains to be realized from focusing on a balanced portfolio of policies that also includes general health and reproductive health. At a minimum, this would require getting ministers of education to work more cooperatively with ministers of health and ministers of finance to understand that their interests are aligned more closely than they otherwise might think.

EDUCATION AND POPULATION AGING

Population aging is the dominant demographic trend of the twenty-first century.[21] Never before have so many people reached ages sixty-five and above (the conventional old-age threshold). We expect to add one billion older individuals in the next three to four decades, atop the more than seven hundred million older people we have today. Although we often think of population aging as a rich country phenomenon, the sharpest growth in absolute and relative numbers of older people will occur in middle-income developing countries

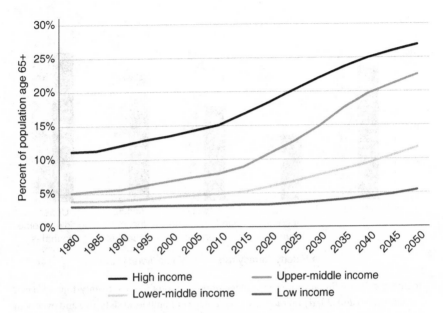

FIGURE 2.4 Percentage of total population ages sixty-five and older from 1980 to 2050 (observed and projected) in different country income groups.

Source: World Population Prospects 2019, United Nations, https://population.un.org/wpp/. The country classification in income levels in based on June 2018 GNI per capita from the World Bank.

(figure 2.4). This aging phenomenon reflects increasing longevity and the progression of large-sized cohorts to the older ages. In this case, lower fertility, which boosts the share of older adults within the population, makes the challenges appear even more daunting.

Population aging is closely connected to our global deficit in education (figure 2.5). Globally, compared with the 8 percent illiteracy rate among adolescents and young adults, illiteracy rates are nearly twice as high among twenty-five- to sixty-four–year-olds (14 percent) and three times as high among those aged over sixty-five (24 percent). The discrepancy is particularly striking in low-income countries and mainly reflects that school enrollment rates in the past were lower than they are today. These gaps will naturally diminish over time, but that will take decades. One issue then is what we can do to accelerate the process of remediation.

Some economists and economic policy makers are willing to write off the remediation of illiteracy among older people on the grounds that older people are relatively unengaged in productive market activities. However, analyses

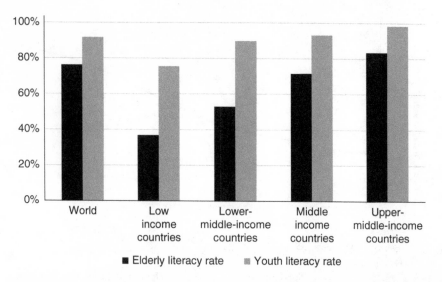

FIGURE 2.5 Youth literacy rate (percentage of population fifteen to twenty-four who can read and write) and elderly literacy rate (percentage of population sixty-five and over who can read and write) in 2018, at the world level and in selected income groups.

Source: UNESCO Institute for Statistics, http://data.uis.unesco.org/.

of time-use studies show that older people create considerable value through productive nonmarket activities like volunteer work and caregiving—both of which also happen to be well-suited to furthering educational advancement of the young and promoting familial and intergenerational connectivity.[22]

Same-language subtitling is a compelling method for accelerating a population's functional literacy. The idea, which originated with Indian academic Brij Kothari, is to subtitle popular movies in the same language as the audio tracks that people know and love.[23] Through this mechanism, illiterate or semiliterate Indians would effectively get a Hindi lesson every time they watched a Bollywood movie. It is a low-tech and low-cost idea but closely attuned to local culture, beneficial for all age groups, and delivering astonishing results thus far.

Population aging is expected to depress economic growth due to labor and capital shortages and to strain government coffers due to the rising cost of pension liabilities and of health and long-term care associated with the expected growth in the incidence and prevalence of chronic diseases. Various responses are available to cushion the economic burden of population aging over different time frames. These include reforming health and pension financing, raising the legal retirement age, and relaxing institutional and attitudinal barriers to international migration.

Wider and deeper investments in the human capital of today's children and adolescents can be a first-order response to the challenge of population aging. Educated and healthy workers are more productive than their less-educated and less-healthy counterparts. As a consequence, an increase in productivity could compensate for the costs associated with a shrinking labor force.[24] In other words, the social value of educational progress will be magnified by its contribution to addressing the ubiquitous challenge of population aging.

Automation is another potential way to alleviate the pressure of population aging and declines in the labor force.[25] However, automation has its own challenges, primarily the displacement of workers, with the consequent rising unemployment among some skill groups—especially among less-educated workers. This is expected to eventually exacerbate existing inequality. Investments in education and skill upgrading by those who are substituted by robots can reduce the negative effects of automation.[26]

EDUCATION, DEMOGRAPHY, AND THE COVID-19 PANDEMIC

Since the first case of COVID-19 was reported in Wuhan, China, in December 2019, COVID-19 has spread explosively around the world, causing more than 5 million deaths as of November 2021 and plunging the global economy into the worst recession since the Great Depression.[27] Nonpharmaceutical interventions to curb the spread of infections (e.g., social distancing policies and sector-specific lockdowns) have contributed to the staggering socioeconomic costs of the pandemic. In particular, school closures and reliance on remote learning (whenever possible) have hindered the educational development of children, thereby harming their future prospects and increasing the learning gaps between rich and poor children due to differential access to effective online learning or alternative schooling methods, for example, private tutoring.[28]

The COVID-19 pandemic strengthens the main arguments of this chapter. First, the pandemic highlights how the full value of education is much greater than the long-term economic benefits in terms of higher labor productivity and wages. School closures and difficulties in implementing effective remote learning generally reduce the pleasure of learning, hinder children's socialization opportunities, degrade the emotional and mental health of students, and increase the risk of domestic violence and abuse.[29] In addition, school closures disrupt immunization and other health services that are often provided at school and prevent many children from accessing the only nutritious meal of their day.[30] School closures also exert considerable pressure on parents, who have to balance childcare, homeschooling, and work duties.

Second, the pandemic clearly shows the interconnection between education and health and that educational development is best addressed by a balanced portfolio of policies. For example, prepandemic school routines can only resume after the COVID-19 threat is over. As a consequence, the full benefits of education can be reaped only if suitable health interventions are implemented. Investments in health (in this case, the health of the general population) are a prerequisite for effective investments in education.

Finally, social distancing and lockdown policies have forced people to rely on remote means of communication to work, talk with friends and family members, or access healthcare (e.g., scheduling a vaccination appointment) and basic services (e.g., ordering food). This requires not only reliable access to social technologies but also the skills and experience necessary to use them in an effective way. Because older adults are most at risk of severe COVID-19 disease outcomes, investments in their digital literacy can keep them safe and connected, enhance their independence, and sustain their contribution to society.

In his celebrated 1995 book entitled *How Many People Can the Earth Support?* Joel Cohen identified three pathways for humanity to escape the consequences of widespread poverty, environmental degradation, and social injustice associated with rapid population growth.[31] First, the "bigger pies" approach, which directs us to use technology and resources to produce more. Second, the "fewer forks" approach, which suggests making reproductive health services available to reduce unwanted fertility and slow population growth. Third, the "better manners" approach, which says to eliminate violence and corruption; improve the operation of markets and government provision of public goods; reduce the unwanted after-effects of consumption; and achieve greater social and political equity between young and old, male and female, and rich and poor.

To Cohen's credit, he also spotted that providing the world's children with the equivalent of a high-quality primary and secondary education, whether through formal schooling or by alternative means, supports all three approaches. In other words, education simultaneously promotes "bigger pies," "fewer forks," and "better manners." With regard to educational progress, the world has accomplished a great deal in recent decades. But the unfinished agenda remains significant.

NOTES

1. Bloom, David E., "Getting Past the Basics: Pursuing Secondary Education," chap. 7 in *Education and Skills 2.0: New Targets and Innovative Approaches*, ed. D. E. Bloom et al. (Geneva: World Economic Forum, 2014).

2. Cohen, Joel E., David E. Bloom, and Martin B. Malin, eds., *Educating All Children: A Global Agenda* (Cambridge, MA: American Academy of Arts and Sciences and MIT Press, 2006).

3. Bloom, David E., Ayla Goksel, Jody Heymann, Yoko Ishikura, Brij Kothari, Patricia A. Milligan, and Chip Paucek, eds., *Education and Skills 2.0: New Targets and Innovative Approaches* (Geneva: World Economic Forum, 2014).

4. Becker, Gary, *Human Capital. A Theoretical and Empirical Analysis with Special Reference to Education*, 3rd ed. (Chicago: University of Chicago Press, 1993); Schultz, Theodore W., *The Economic Value of Education* (New York: Columbia University Press, 1963).

5. Psacharopoulos, George, and Harry Anthony Patrinos, "Returns to Investment in Education: A Decennial Review of the Global Literature," *Education Economics* 26, no. 5 (2018): 445–458, DOI: 10.1080/09645292.2018.1484426.

6. Montenegro, Claudio E., and Harry Anthony Patrinos, "Comparable Estimates of Returns to Schooling Around the World," (World Bank Policy Research Working Paper WPS 7020. Washington, DC, 2014).

7. Pradhan, Elina, Elina M. Suzuki, Sebastián Martinez, Marco Schäferhoff, Dean T. Jamison, "The Effects of Education Quantity and Quality on Child and Adult Mortality: Their Magnitude and Their Value," chap. 30 in *Disease Control Priorities*, 3rd ed., vol. 8, *Child and Adolescent Health and Development* (Washington, DC: World Bank, 2017).

8. Bloom, David E., Logan Brenzel, Daniel Cadarette, and Jessica Sullivan, "Moving Beyond Traditional Valuation of Vaccination: Needs and Opportunities," *Vaccine* 35 (2017): A29–A35, DOI: 10.1016/j.vaccine.2016.12.001

9. Bloom, David E., Alexander Khoury, and Ramnath Subbaraman, "The Promise and Peril of Universal Health Care," *Science* 361, no. 6404 (2018): eaat9644, DOI: 10.1126/science.aat9644; Miguel, Edward, and Michael Kremer, "Worms: Identifying Impacts on Education and Health in the Presence of Treatment Externalities," *Econometrica* 72, no. 1 (January 2004): 159–217, DOI: 10.1111/j/1468-0262.2004.00481.x.

10. García, Jorge Luis, James J. Heckman, Duncan Ermini Leaf, and María José Prados, "Quantifying the Life-Cycle Benefits of an Influential Early Childhood Program," *Journal of Political Economy* 128, no. 7 (July 2020): 2502–2541, DOI: 10.1086/705718; Almond, Douglas, Janet Currie, and Valentina Duque, "Childhood Circumstances and Adult Outcomes," *Journal of Economic Literature* 56, no. 4 (December 2018): 1360–1446, DOI: 10.1257/jel.20171164; Elango, Sneha, Jorge Luis García, James J. Heckman, and Andrés Hojman, "Early Childhood Education," in *Economics of Means-Tested Transfer Programs in the United States II*, ed. R. Moffitt (Chicago: University of Chicago Press, 2016), 235–298.

11. Barker, David J.. *The Fetal and Infant Origins of Adult Disease* (London: BMJ Books, 1992).

12. National Research Council, Institute of Medicine, *From Neurons to Neighborhoods: The Science of Early Childhood Development*, ed. J. P. Shonkoff and D. A. Philipps (Washington, DC: National Academies Press, 2000).

13. Doepke, Matthias, "Child Mortality and Fertility Decline: Does the Barro-Becker Model Fit the Facts?" *Journal of Population Economics* 18 (June 2005): 337–366, DOI: 10.1007 /s00148-004-0208-z; Canning, David, Isabel Gunther, Sebastian Linnemayr, and David E. Bloom, "Fertility Choice, Mortality Expectations, and Interdependent Preferences—An Empirical Analysis," *European Economic Review* 63 (October 2013): 273–289, DOI: 10.1016 /j.euroecorev.2013.07.005.

14. Bloom, David E., David Canning, and J. P. Sevilla, "The Effect of Health on Economic Growth: A Production Function Approach," *World Development* 32 (2004): 1–13, DOI: 10.1016/j.worlddev .2003.07.002; Bloom, David E., David Canning, Günther Fink, Jocelyn E. Finlay, "The Cost of Low Fertility in Europe," *European Journal of Population* 26 (2010): 141–158, DOI: 10.1007 /s10680-009-9182-1; and Bloom, David E., Michael Kuhn, and Klaus Prettner, "Africa's Prospects for Enjoying a Demographic Dividend," *Journal of Demographic Economics* 83(2017): 63–76, DOI: 10.1017/dem.2016.19.

15. Bloom, David E., and David Canning, "Demographic Change and Economic Growth: The Role of Cumulative Causality," chapter 7 in *Population Does Matter: Demography, Growth, and Poverty in the Developing World*, ed. N. Birdsall, A.C. Kelley, and S. Sinding (New York: Oxford University Press, 2001).

16. Bloom, David E., "7 Billion and Counting," *Science* 333, no. 6042 (2011): 562–569, DOI: 10.1126 /science.1209290.

17. Bloom, David E., Victoria Y. Fan, and J. P. Sevilla, "The Broad Socio-Economic Benefits of Vaccination," *Science Translational Medicine* 10, no. 441 (2018): eaaj2345, DOI: 10.1126 /scitranslmed.aaj2345; Nandi, Arindam, Anil B. Deolalikar, David E. Bloom, and Ramanan Laxminarayan, "Haemophilus Influenzae Type B Vaccination and Anthropometric, Cognitive, and Schooling Outcomes Among Indian Children," *Annals of the New York Academy of Sciences* 1449 (2019): 70–82, DOI: 10.1111/nyas.14127; Nandi, Arindam, Anita Shet, Jere R. Behrman, Maureen M. Black, David E. Bloom, and Ramanan Laxminarayan, "Anthropometric, Cognitive, and Schooling Benefits of Measles Vaccination: Longitudinal Cohort Analysis in Ethiopia, India and Vietnam," *Vaccine* 37, no. 31 (July 2019): 4336–4343, DOI: 10.1016 /j.vaccine.2019.06.025; Nandi, Arindam, Santosh Kumar, Anita Shet, David E. Bloom, and Ramanan Laxminarayan, "Childhood Vaccinations and Adult Schooling Attainment: Long-Term Evidence from India's Universal Immunization Programme," *Social Science and Medicine* 250 (April 2020): 112885, DOI: 10.1016/j.socscimed.2020/112885; Oskorouchi, Hamid R., Alfonso Sousa-Poza, and David E. Bloom, "The Long-Term Cognitive and Schooling Effects of Childhood Vaccinations in China" (NBER Working Paper No 27217, Cambridge, MA, 2020), DOI: 10.3386/w27217.

18. Crofts, Tracey, and Julie Fisher, "Menstrual Hygiene in Ugandan Schools: An Investigation of Low-Cost Sanitary Pads," *Journal of Water, Sanitation and Hygiene for Development* 2 (2012): 50–58.

19. Bloom, David E., Michael Kuhn, and Klaus Prettner, "Invest in Women and Prosper," *Finance and Development* 54, no. 3 (2017); Remme, Michelle, Anna Vassall, Gabriela Fernando, and David E. Bloom, "Investing in the Health of Girls and Women: A Best Buy for Sustainable Development," *British Medical Journal* 369 (2020): m1175, DOI: 10.1136/bmj.m1175.

20. Bloom, David E., Michael Kuhn, and Klaus Prettner, "The Contribution of Female Health to Economic Development," *Economic Journal* 130, no. 630 (2020): 1650–1677, DOI: 10.1093/ej /ueaa061.

21. Bloom, David E., "Population 2020," *Finance and Development* 57 (2020): 6–9.

22. Bloom, David E., Alexander Khoury, Eda Algur, and J. P. Sevilla, "Valuing Productive Non-Market Activities of Older Adults in Europe and the US," *De Economist* 168 (2020): 153–181, DOI: 10.1007/s10645-020-09362-1.

23. Kothari, Brij, Joe Takeda, Ashok Joshi, and Avinash Pandey, "Same Language Subtitling: A Butterfly for Literacy?" *International Journal of Lifelong Education* 21 (2002): 55–66, DOI: 10.1080/0261370110099515.

24. Lee, Roland, and Andrew Mason, "Fertility, Human Capital, and Economic Growth Over the Demographic Transition," *European Journal of Population* 26 (2010): 159–182, DOI: 10.1007/s10680-009-9186-x; Prettner, Klaus, David E. Bloom, and Holger Strulik, "Declining Fertility and Economic Well-Being: Do Education and Health Ride to the Rescue?" *Labor Economics* 22 (June 2013): 70–79, DOI: 10.1016/j.labeco.2012.07.001.

25. Abelianky, Ana, and Klaus Prettner, "Automation and Demographic Change" (Hohenheim Discussion Papers in Business, Economics, and Social Sciences 05-2017, Stuttgart, Germany, 2017); Acemoglu, Daron, and Pascual Restrepo, "Demographics and Automation" (NBER Working Paper No. 24421, Cambridge, MA, 2018), DOI: 10.3386/w24421.

26. Prettner, Klaus, and David E. Bloom, *Automation and Its Macroeconomic Consequences: Theory, Evidence, and Social Impact* (London: Academic Press, 2020), DOI: 10.1016/C2018-0-00345-X.

27. Dong, Ensheng, Hongru Du, and Lauren Gardner, "An Interactive Web-Based Dashboard to Track COVID-19 in Real Time," *Lancet Infectious Diseases* 20, no. 5 (May 2020): 533–534, https://coronavirus.jhu.edu/map.html; IMF (International Monetary Fund), *World Economic Outlook: A Long and Difficult Ascent* (Washington, DC: IMF, 2020).

28. Hanushek, Eric A., and Ludger Woessmann, "The Economic Impacts of Learning Losses" (OECD Education Working Papers, no. 225, OECD Publishing, Paris, 2020), DOI: 10.1787/21908d74-en.

29. Singh, Shweta, Deblina Roy, Krittika Sinha, Sheeba Parveen, Ginni Sharma, and Gunjan Joshi, "Impact of COVID-19 and Lockdown on Mental Health of Children and Adolescents: A Narrative Review with Recommendations," *Psychiatry Research* 293 (November 2020): 113429, DOI: 10.1016/j.psychres.2020.113429.

30. Dunn, Caroline G., Erica Kenney, Sheila E. Fleischhacker, and Sara N. Bleich, "Feeding Low-Income Children During the COVID-19 Pandemic," *New England Journal of Medicine* 382 (2020): e40, DOI: 10.1056/NEJMp2005638.

31. Cohen, Joel E. *How Many People Can the Earth Support?* (New York: W. W. Norton, 1995).

3

CHILD POVERTY AND COGNITION

Developmental and Educational Implications

SEBASTIÁN LIPINA

C ontemporary theories of human development are framed in the meta-theoretical postulates derived from the systemic-relational approaches (RDS), which emphasize that the biological, psychological, and social changes occur through multiple and interdependent relationships between individuals and their contexts across the course of life.[1] According to these approaches, every organism is characterized by being active, self-regulated (adaptive), and complex (nonlinear). What would characterize human development would be the coevolution or permanent transformation of the biological and social systems that it involves, which means that the directionality of the trajectories is individually variable. In this sense, the RDS approaches emphasize the study and integration of different levels of organization—from the biological/physiological to the cultural and historical—as a means to understand human development throughout the life cycle.[2]

The contemporary study of the associations between poverty,[3] cognition, and learning fall within the context of RDS metatheories. This implies that its approach considers both individual phenomena that occur at the molecular, neural, cognitive, and behavioral levels and the developmental contexts in which the individual develops her life (i.e., social, cultural, and historical). In this chapter, we present a synthesis of: (a) the evidence on the associations between poverty and cognition at different levels of organization, with a focus on those aspects related to the acquisition of learning; (b) the mediation and moderation factors identified in such associations; (c) the impact of different interventions aimed at optimizing the cognitive development of children living in a context of poverty;

and (d) the scientific implications of this evidence, according to contemporary perspectives of developmental psychology and cognitive neuroscience.

EVIDENCE OF ASSOCIATIONS BETWEEN POVERTY AND COGNITION

COGNITIVE AND BEHAVIORAL LEVELS OF ORGANIZATION

Since the mid-twentieth century, studies conducted in the context of develop- mental psychology, education, and pediatric epidemiology have verified asso- ciations between income, education, parental occupation, and unsatisfied basic needs with: (a) the decrease in developmental quotients of verbal and motor skills in children from three to thirty-six months; (b) the decrease in intellec- tual quotients of language and executive skills in children aged three to eight years; (c) lower performances in cognitive tasks with demands for executive functioning, phonological processing, language, and theory of mind.[4]

In this literature, it has been verified that in some tasks with demands for cognitive control, the association of poverty with cognitive performance is not similar in all domains nor uniform for all ages.[5] This means that there are children living in conditions of adversity due to poverty that may have typi- cal performances for their age in some cognitive domains and that this may vary according to their age and the type of test administered. This is expected because poverty and cognitive development are complex processes that involve multiple interdependent factors and variability across the life cycle.

NEURAL LEVEL OF ORGANIZATION

Regarding the structural aspects of the nervous system, the evidence accumu- lated during the last two decades indicates that: (1) family income and maternal education have been associated with changes in the volume of hippocampus and amygdala—neural structures that participate in the processing of emo- tional information and learning acquisition—between the ages of four and twenty-two; (2) maternal education has been associated with changes in:

(a)   cortical thickness and volume of prefrontal, parietal, and occipital neu- ral networks between the ages of four and eighteen years;

(b)   rate of brain growth and volume of frontal and parietal neural networks in children from one month to four years;

(c)   connectivity between frontal and parietal neural networks between twelve and twenty-four years;

(d)   developmental trajectories of hippocampus in female adolescents aged nine to fifteen years;

and finally (3) parental education and income have been associated with changes in connectivity patterns between different cortical networks and the striatum—a subcortical structure involved in cognitive and motor control processes—between six and seventeen years.[6] In some of these studies, structural changes were also associated with performance in tasks demanding for executive function, language, and learning.[7]

With regard to the functioning of the nervous system, it has been verified that income, parental education, and occupation were associated with changes in: (1) the activation of occipital-temporal networks during tasks with demands for rhyme discrimination and combination of sounds in children from four to eight years; (2) the activation of prefrontal networks during the performance of tasks with demands for associative learning in children aged four to eight years; (3) the activation of prefrontal and parietal networks during working memory and arithmetic processing tasks in children aged eight to twelve years; (4) the increase in activation of amygdala during the performance of tasks with demands for processing threatening faces in adults aged twenty-three to twenty-five with a history of child poverty; (5) the patterns of electrical activity during resting state of infants between six and nine months; (6) the components of electrical activity associated with the attention control to irrelevant information in children from three to eight years; (7) the patterns of electrical activity associated with the processing of speech and environmental sounds; (8) the frontal electrical activity related to error detection and *theta* power—an electric band associated with cognitive control processes—in children aged sixteen to eighteen months and four years old; and (9) the prediction of cognitive performance at fifteen months of age based on electrical activity at resting at one month of life.[8]

This evidence allows us to sustain that child poverty in terms of family income, parental education and occupation, and material deprivation could be associated with a diverse set of structural and functional changes in the nervous system and low performance in tasks with demands for emotional and cognitive self-regulation, language, and learning.[9] This evidence complements that generated by other disciplines during the twentieth century (i.e., human, social, and health sciences), which has also verified that lower levels of cognitive performance in the early stages of development can be associated with lower cognitive performance during adulthood,[10] which in turn could contribute to the effects of intergenerational transmission of poverty.[11]

The associative nature of this evidence does not allow us to infer the causal mechanisms through which such associations are produced, which requires further investigation.[12] The initial interpretation of the evidence has been in the sense of attribution of the poverty deficit.[13] However, there is evidence that contributes to questioning that necessarily, and in all cases, it can be interpreted in such a sense.[14] On the one hand, longitudinal studies that analyze the association between child poverty and adult cognitive performance recommend deepening the analysis of such associations considering the multiplicity of mediating and moderating factors of such association (see next section).[15] On the other hand, there are recent studies indicating that the neural resources involved in the processes of reading and arithmetic can vary according to poverty in a qualitative sense and not only according to what or how many neural networks are activated during their solution. Specifically, there are studies showing that there are children living in poverty that express expected reading and arithmetic performances for their age and that, at the neural level, such performances are associated with the activation of different neural networks compared to what happens to their peers from nonpoor households.[16] In addition, recent evidence also indicates that the neural resources involved in attention control and reading tasks can be modified by interventions in children living in poor households (see "Interventions Aimed at Optimizing Cognitive Development" section below).[17] This evidence should not be considered a priori as of universal value in the sense that in any social context, the same results will be found at the behavioral and/or neural levels of organization,[18] because of the existence of several modulators of such associations.

MEDIATION AND MODERATION FACTORS

As mentioned, the RDS approaches assume the existence of multiple individual and contextual factors that mediate or moderate the associations between poverty and neural and self-regulatory development. Knowing such factors and their dynamics is crucial to identify potential mechanisms that could improve knowledge about child development and contribute to the design, evaluation, and implementation of interventions and policies of educational interest. This is important since self-regulatory performance during childhood can predict academic performance, interpersonal behaviors, mental health, and healthy lifestyles in later stages of the life cycle.[19]

From the perspective of developmental psychology and pediatric epidemiology, mediators and moderators of the relationship between poverty and cognitive development have been identified for decades in different developmental contexts: (a) *Ontosystem*: perinatal exposure to infections, legal and illegal drugs, toxic environmental agents, malnutrition, physical and mental health status of children from birth; and state of children's self-regulatory, social, and language development. (b) *Microsystem*: number of controls of mothers during pregnancy; security of attachment; stressors in care, parenting, and educational contexts; and quality of learning stimulation at home and in childcare centers or schools. (c) *Mesosystem*: mental health and lifestyles of parents, caregivers, and teachers; contextual stressors in homes and schools; learning stimulation; quantity and quality of school resources; and teacher training and teaching styles. (d) *Exosystem*: access to social security systems through health, education, and social development policies; community resources; social mobility; and social, political, and economic crises. (e) *Macrosystem*: cultural norms and expectations, which may eventually induce exclusion phenomena such as discrimination or stigmatization. (f) *Global system*: exposure to natural disasters or consequences of climate change. (g) *Chronosystem*: time and duration of exposure to different types of early adversities.[20]

The available evidence from cognitive and neuroscientific studies accounts for: (1) the moderation of the socioeconomic status in the association between neural structures and functions and self-regulatory performance; (2) the moderation of neural structures and functions in the association between socioeconomic status and self-regulatory performance; (3) the mediation of different risk and protective factors in the association between socioeconomic status and neural structure and function;[21] and (4) the mediation of executive function performance in the association between poverty and academic performance in language and mathematics tasks during primary and secondary school.[22] Some concrete examples of such modulations are:

(a)   the verification of epigenetic changes in the expression of genes that encode the reception of glucocorticoids in preadolescents from poor households exposed to abuse during their childhoods as a mediating factor between stress exposure and self-regulatory performance;

(b)   the volume, thickness, and cortical surface of different neural networks as mediators of the association between income and academic performance in populations from four to twenty-two years;[23] and

(c) the connectivity between hippocampus and amygdala as mediators of the association between admission and symptoms of depression in preschoolers living in poverty,[24] or between maternal education and self-regulatory and academic performance in school-aged children.[25]

In addition to the accumulation of potential risk factors, it is necessary to consider that poverty is a complex phenomenon that can co-occur with other types of adversities, such as orphanhood and consequent institutionalization or exposure to domestic or community violence. In this sense, it is necessary to differentiate experiences due to a lack of material resources from those characterized by the presence of threats to physical integrity. This means that exposure to different types or combinations of early adversities could generate needs for different types of specific interventions, including teaching practices within the classroom.[26]

In summary, the current consensus in developmental science is that the association between poverty and cognitive development is modulated by at least four factors: the accumulation of risks; the co-occurrence of adversities; the individual susceptibility to risks and adversities; and the time of exposure to adversities.[27] Such evidence contributes to the hypothesis that two of the most important pathways in which child poverty would modulate the cognitive and emotional neural and self-regulatory development during the first two decades of life would be the quality of parenting environments and stress regulation.[28] Threats, negative life events, exposure to environmental hazards, family and community violence, family separations, parental job loss or instability, and economic deprivation occur throughout the socioeconomic spectrum but are usually more prevalent conditions of poverty.[29] In turn, the neuroendocrine systems associated with the regulation of stress communicate with the immune and cardiovascular systems, which together regulate the physiological and behavioral responses to stressors, contributing to the processes of adaptation of each individual to their contextual circumstances. In the short term, the activation of these systems functions as a factor of protection against the action of stress, such as, for example, in a typical circumstance of school examination. However, under conditions of continuous exposure— for example, when a child faces material and affective deficiencies for months or years—stress response may be associated with physiological deregulations (i.e., neuroendocrine and metabolic) with the potential to affect health in the long term,[30] or costly strategies that could promote adaptation.[31]

Recently, such approaches began to include the study of the modulation of epigenetic mechanisms during early childhood development in different socioeconomic conditions. At the moment, the results allow us to support the hypothesis that epigenetic changes would be involved, at least partially, in the long-term influences of early experiences.[32] Our understanding of the role of the epigenome in behavioral modifications driven by early life experiences could eventually contribute to our understanding of child poverty and neural development. However, genetic polymorphisms in humans should be analyzed with caution because similar experiences can produce different results in different people, which add another level of complexity to the study of how behavior is modulated by individual differences and experience. In any case, the evidence does not allow us to assume epigenetic causality based on the neuroscientific literature regarding the association between child poverty and adult self-regulatory development.

In summary, the mediation and moderation mechanisms identified in the studies of child poverty and cognitive development involve a diverse set of individual and contextual factors at different levels of organization, which allow us to support hypotheses generated in other disciplines regarding the importance of the quality of early parenting and educational environments. Of greater neuroscientific specificity are the potential mediation and moderation of structural and epigenetic changes. However, neuroscientific research must still increase its efforts to incorporate different sources of variability involved in the processes of neural development in contexts of adversity due to poverty.

INTERVENTIONS AIMED AT OPTIMIZING COGNITIVE DEVELOPMENT

Since the second half of the twentieth century, different types of interventions designed to optimize the cognitive development of children living in poverty have been designed, implemented, and evaluated in different countries. In the field of developmental psychology and cognitive neuroscience, two types of approaches are usually found. On the one hand, interventions have been developed based on the consideration of the multidimensional nature of development during the life cycle. These interventions are usually organized in multiple modules aimed at optimizing different aspects of development and early childhood education, which involve both children and their caregivers. In this context, modules aimed at promoting cognitive development are usually designed based on school-type curricular activities. The rest of the modules are usually aimed at nutritional supplementation, activities to stimulate learning in home and school, and educational workshops for caregivers on child development and sensitive parenting issues.[33] Based on examples of these types of interventions implemented in America, Europe, Asia, and Oceania, it is possible to identify regularities that feed hypotheses on principles or methodological guides for their design. In general terms, the advances observed after the implementation of these types of programs have been associated with the positive impact of a broad set of actions aimed at stimulating learning in children at appropriate times of their development, maintaining or improving the participation of caregivers, coordinating the offer of social and educational actions, applying designs with appropriate controls for the evaluation of impacts and feasibility of the actions, and permanent training of staffs. Depending on the characteristics of the designs and the time of implementation, in general, the impact assessments indicate positive effects on variables such as verbal and executive intelligence quotients and academic performance. In some programs where designs have followed adequate guidelines, long-term effects have been observed in other areas of development (e.g., years of education completed, employment rates, and crime). From the extensive experience of implementation and evaluation of these types of interventions, some conclusions emerge that are relevant to consider for innovation in the area: (a) the positive impact of the interventions depends on their regular application over extended periods, which poses immense challenges to its implementation; (b) not all children who participate benefit equally, due to individual differences in susceptibility and vulnerability to adversity, as well as parenting conditions and intervention activities themselves; and (c) it is not feasible to propose universal formulas of application for different contexts and populations, given the social and cultural conditions of each sample to determine the feasibility and relevance of the interventions.

Another approach, closer to the experimental explorations of the mechanisms of plasticity and cognitive change, consists in the design of unique intervention modules aimed at optimizing processes of cognitive control, emotional regulation, metacognition, reading, and mathematics. The experience of the last three decades in this field of study indicates that: (a) it is possible to positively modify different cognitive aspects of populations of children living in poor households through interventions; (b) that such changes are usually more frequent in the same stimulated domain (i.e., near transfer); and (c) that it is less frequent to verify the effects of generalization of interventions to other domains than those trained (i.e., far transfer).[34]

In both types of intervention approaches (i.e., uni- and multimodular), the changes that are verified in cognition continue to be associative in nature—even in cases where designs with control groups are implemented. This implies that the identification of the underlying causal mechanisms still requires further investigation. Likewise, the literature of the area has also identified the importance of implementing good practices in the design of these interventions that contemplate factors of feasibility, impact evaluation, and dissemination of results in a great diversity of contexts and disciplines,[35] as well as the need to consider the specific needs of children with and without developmental disorders.[36]

In particular, neuroscientific approaches began to be implemented only recently. One of the first studies aimed at optimizing processes of selective attention of preschool-aged children living in poverty through the implementation of two intervention modules in the school.[37] One of the modules consisted of attention training activities for children through manual and group games. The other consisted of meetings with families during which they discussed issues of parenting and stress management and communication at home, following parenting scripts designed by an interdisciplinary team. The results showed not only improvements in children's cognitive performance but also at the electrophysiological level for a selective attention component. The researchers also found that parents had reduced their perception of stress at home. A second study corresponds to a computerized intervention for children six to nine years from different socioeconomic contexts and with reading difficulties. After six weeks of training, the researchers verified an increase in scores on standardized reading tasks and an increase in the thickness of neural networks involved in this type of processing.[38] A third study corresponds to a computerized intervention for preschoolers from poor homes. After ten weeks of training, the researchers found a more mature electrophysiological pattern of activity for an inhibitory control component.[39] The preliminary nature of these studies requires cautiousness regarding the implications of the results. However, its importance lies in supporting the hypothesis that the efficiency of different neural systems can be modified by specific interventions.

IMPLICATIONS OF THE EVIDENCE

The evidence reviewed in this chapter indicates and suggests the following:

(1) Different poverty indicators are associated with lower cognitive and academic performances during several stages of development. Psychological

and neural evidence generated in recent years suggests the need to review the interpretations of these associations in the sense of deficit and to consider the occurrence of adaptive processes instead.[40] In both cases, more research is necessary.

(2) Such associations are modulated by individual and contextual factors (i.e., mediators and moderators), which generate a multiplicity of possible cognitive development trajectories based on the accumulation, co-occurrence, and susceptibility to adversities.

(3) In general, the cognitive and neuroscientific approaches of the associations between poverty and cognitive development focus on the level of individual and family microsystemic organization. In addition, it is important to consider the potential specific modulations of factors related to the structure of the educational system, such as funding, governance, infrastructure, curriculum, pedagogy, assessments, teacher training and professional development, and the quality of formal and informal learning environments. In addition, it is also necessary to incorporate the specific educational problems faced by children with developmental disorders.

(4) The associations between poverty and cognitive performance are plausible of modification through interventions based on different types of approaches and implemented in several development contexts. Regarding the interventions implemented in the context of the cognitive sciences, it is still necessary to generate efforts that allow translating such evidence into specific and concrete actions for the classroom and meeting the specific needs of different populations of children. The areas of nutrition, physical activity, sleep, and stress regulation could be those in which to concentrate research efforts to generate integrations with educational transfer objectives from the cognitive sciences.[41]

(5) There is still a need to generate and sustain interdisciplinary and cross-sector networks aimed at deepening and innovating knowledge on how to inform the findings and promote the involvement of different academic and political actors in the implementation of policies. This is more critical in low- and middle-income countries. This implies taking into account that the design, implementation, and evaluation of policies is a complex process that involves multiple actors and sectors with different interests and tensions.

(6) This type of effort also requires the discussion of the implicit representations about cognitive development and education that each sector and discipline support, which would allow the updating of ethical, cultural, metatheoretical, conceptual, and methodological notions that efforts in child development and educational merit and require today. Innovating in these efforts

implies rethinking and rationalizing the financing of studies whose questions arise from the interdisciplinary and intersectoral efforts. Innovation should also consider expanding the participation of researchers in different stages of policy design (i.e., design, implementation, and evaluation).

(7) Some of the aspects that such efforts of intervention should consider in the near future are:

(a) The identification of high-risk groups of children and families to avoid falling into cycles of exclusion, inappropriate responses by the governments, and subsequent reproduction of cycles of deprivation.

(b) Interventions should address mediating and moderating factors. Among them, it is important to consider starting as early as possible; addressing maternal stress, diet, smoking, and legal and illegal substance abuse since prenatal stage; and generating education plans for microsystemic and mesosystemic social actors on the importance of learning environments and warm and contingent caretaking for fostering self-regulatory skills.

(c) The identification of specific targets and timely interventions in the areas of nutrition, physical exercise, sleep, and stress regulation in several developmental contexts (i.e., home, school, community).

(d) The provision of adequate structural conditions for developmental needs (e.g., housing, sanitation, access to social and health security systems), which ultimately would impact self-regulatory development.

These efforts imply fostering appropriate and efficient debates on the cultural relevance of conceptions, models and designs of development, assessments, interventions, and the avoidance of replication of standardized formulas in foreign cultures. To accomplish this approach in educational settings would require research not only on the outcomes of curricular interventions but also a deeper understanding of the cultural context of schooling. In turn, this would imply a clear understanding of what innovations in training and ongoing support are required for effective outcomes. This could require further understanding of how to highlight the goals of emotional and cognitive self-regulation in the context of educational policy and to impact on both the rhetoric and everyday behavior of educational leaders and communities.

Finally, it is important to devote time in these debates and efforts to discuss the specific implications of the COVID-19 pandemic. Since its beginning in 2020, the pandemic has been exacerbating many of the threats and harmful effects of poverty and inequality, challenging virtually all aspects of social, health, and educational security worldwide.[42] Several reports indicate that it is expected that the most damaged will be the children in the poorest countries, cities, and neighborhoods.[43]

In 2020, during the first wave of the pandemic, 188 countries imposed countrywide school closures, affecting more than 1.5 billion children and youth.[44] Something similar transpired across the world during new waves and variants of the pandemic.[45] The potential losses that this type of impact may accumulate in learning and development are still hard to estimate. While school districts have been engaged in distance learning, reports indicate wide variations in access to quality educational instruction, digital technology, and internet. Before the pandemic, almost one-third of the world's young people were digitally excluded. School closures worsened the learning gap: children from wealthier families continued schooling with digital tools, whereas poorer children fell further behind, especially in low-to-middle-income countries (LMIC).[46] Specifically, the experience of virtual learning during the pandemic has varied widely and raises significant concerns for educational equity. Research during the pandemic shows that students from low socioeconomic backgrounds have less access to electronic devices, internet connectivity, and quality virtual learning programs.[47] Communities are also struggling to identify the resources required to deliver quality educational experiences, either in-person or virtually, and to identify education solutions that serve children in their district equitably. Schools will also need to contemplate alternative instructional strategies to allow improved access to virtual learning environments for students and their families.[48]

Part of the lens of equity that needs considering and understanding are the implications of closures of schools and care centers for families with children with disabilities. In many public schools, students receive special education. In addition, some children and adolescents have complex medical conditions. These populations are heavily reliant on schools for services to help these children learn and develop in a healthy manner. During the pandemic, children with disabilities have struggled to access services remotely. Special education teaching and rehabilitation services, such as physical, occupational, or speech services, normally provided during the school day, have been difficult to provide in a virtual environment. Owing to safety concerns and inadequate staffing, pushing services into homes has not been an option for most children.[49]

Governments, households, and development partners are among the main funders of education. The ability of each group to fund education will be affected by COVID-19 in different ways. Before the pandemic, governments were spending vastly different amounts on education. The actions being taken to slow the spread of COVID-19 would result in a large drop in global output. In LMICs, the pandemic is expected to reduce planned increases in education spending in 2020 and 2021. Actually, there is evidence that some countries have already cut their education budgets to make space for the required spending on health and social protection. Reductions in income and the need for greater health spending will make it difficult for some families to cover education costs. Declining incomes may also lead to shifts in enrollment from private schools to public schools, adding further pressure on public education budgets. And development assistance for education has only recently recovered from the financial crisis of 2008/2009 in many countries. Aid volume is likely to be negatively affected by the drop in economic growth associated with the pandemic in some of the largest donor countries.[50]

For the WHO-UNICEF-*Lancet* commissioners,[51] currently countries' responses have focused on short-term business relief and social protection and not on the long-term recovery needed to create healthier and more equal societies. For the near and far future, the commission proposes that it would be desirable that country leaders: (a) put child health and wellbeing at the center of recovery plans; (b) include experts on children's issues in the relevant task forces and legislative working groups; (c) engage their ministries to work together for children; and (d) ask children and adolescents what changes they would like to see. For the commission, putting children at the center implies a radical change, which means redesigning neighborhoods to give children spaces to play; valuing care work; ensuring families have time and resources to raise children; ensuring sustainable food systems to nourish growth; and stimulating development and learning.

NOTES

1.   Overton, Willis F., and Peter C. Molenaar, "Concepts, Theory, and Method in Developmental Science," *Handbook of Child Psychology and Developmental Science*, 2015, 9–62.

2.   Overton and Molenaar, "Concepts, Theory, and Method"; Bronfenbrenner, Urie, *Ecology of Human Development: Experiments by Nature and Design* (Cambridge, MA: Harvard University Press, 2009); Gottlieb, Gilbert, "Probabilistic Epigenesis," *Developmental Science* 10, no. 1 (2007): 1–11, https://doi.org/10.1111/j.1467-7687.2007.00556.x; Lerner, Richard Martin, *Concepts and Theories of Human Development* (New York: Routledge, Taylor & Francis, 2018).

3.   This chapter considers *poverty* to any experience of adversity due to material and symbolic deficiencies involved in different indicators regardless of the basic criteria for their operational definition (e.g., income, education, and parental occupation).

4. Bradley, Robert H., and Robert F. Corwyn, "Socioeconomic Status and Child Develop-
    ment," *Annual Review of Psychology* 53, no. 1 (2002): 371–399, https://doi.org/10.1146/annurev
    .psych.53.100901.135233; Brooks-Gunn, Jeanne, and Greg J. Duncan, "The Effects of Poverty
    on Children," *Future of Children* 7, no. 2 (1997): 55–71, https://doi.org/10.2307/1602387; Law-
    son, Gwendolyn M., Cayce J. Hook, and Martha J. Farah, "A Meta-Analysis of the Relation-
    ship Between Socioeconomic Status and Executive Function Performance Among Children,"
    Developmental Science 21, no. 2 (2017): https://doi.org/10.1111/desc.12529; Maholmes, Valerie,
    and Rosalind Berkowitz King, *Oxford Handbook of Poverty and Child Development* (New
    York: Oxford University Press, 2012); Peng, Peng, Tengfei Wang, CuiCui Wang, and Xin Lin,
    "A Meta-Analysis on the Relation Between Fluid Intelligence and Reading/Mathematics:
    Effects of Tasks, Age, and Social Economics Status," *Psychological Bulletin* 145, no. 2 (2019):
    189–236, https://doi.org/10.1037/bul0000182; Sania, Ayesha, Christopher R. Sudfeld, Goodarz
    Danaei, Günther Fink, Dana C. McCoy, Zhaozhong Zhu, Mary C. Fawzi, et al., "Early Life
    Risk Factors of Motor, Cognitive and Language Development: A Pooled Analysis of Stud-
    ies from Low/Middle-Income Countries," *BMJ Open* 9, no. 10 (2019), https://doi.org/10.1136
    /bmjopen-2018-026449; Segretin, M. Soledad, M. Julia Hermida, Lucía M. Prats, Carolina S.
    Fracchia, Eliana Ruetti, and Sebastián J. Lipina, "Childhood Poverty and Cognitive Develop-
    ment in Latin America in the 21st Century," *New Directions for Child and Adolescent Devel-
    opment* 2016, no. 152 (2016): 9–29, https://doi.org/10.1002/cad.20162; Yoshikawa, Hirokazu, J.
    Lawrence Aber, and William R. Beardslee, "The Effects of Poverty on the Mental, Emotional,
    and Behavioral Health of Children and Youth: Implications for Prevention," *American Psy-
    chologist* 67, no. 4 (2012): 272–284, https://doi.org/10.1037/a0028015.
5. Farah, Martha J., David M. Shera, Jessica H. Savage, Laura Betancourt, Joan M. Giannetta,
    Nancy L. Brodsky, Elsa K. Malmud, and Hallam Hurt, "Childhood Poverty: Specific Associa-
    tions with Neurocognitive Development," *Brain Research* 1110, no. 1 (2006): 166–174, https://doi
    .org/10.1016/j.brainres.2006.06.072; Lipina, Sebastián, Soledad Segretin, Julia Hermida, Lucía
    Prats, Carolina Fracchia, Jorge López Camelo, and Jorge Colombo, "Linking Childhood Poverty
    and Cognition: Environmental Mediators of Non-Verbal Executive Control in an Argentine
    Sample," *Developmental Science* 16, no. 5 (2013): 697–707, https://doi.org/10.1111/desc.12080.
6. Farah, Martha J., "The Neuroscience of Socioeconomic Status: Correlates, Causes, and Conse-
    quences," *Neuron* 96, no. 1 (2017): 56–71, https://doi.org/10.1016/j.neuron.2017.08.034; Farah,
    Martha J., "Socioeconomic Status and the Brain: Prospects for Neuroscience-Informed Policy,"
    Nature Reviews Neuroscience 19, no. 7 (2018): 428–438, https://doi.org/10.1038/s41583-018-0023-2;
    Johnson, S. B., J. L. Riis, and K. G. Noble, "State of the Art Review: Poverty and the Develop-
    ing Brain," *Pediatrics* 137, no. 4 (2016): https://doi.org/10.1542/peds.2015-3075; Pakulak, Eric,
    Courtney Stevens, and Helen Neville, "Neuro-, Cardio-, and Immunoplasticity: Effects of
    Early Adversity," *Annual Review of Psychology* 69, no. 1 (2018): 131–156, https://doi.org/10.1146
    /annurev-psych-010416-044115; Pavlakis, Alexandra E., Kimberly Noble, Steven G. Pavlakis,
    Noorjahan Ali, and Yitzchak Frank, "Brain Imaging and Electrophysiology Biomarkers: Is
    There a Role in Poverty and Education Outcome Research?" *Pediatric Neurology* 52, no. 4
    (2015): 383–388, https://doi.org/10.1016/j.pediatrneurol.2014.11.005.
7. Hair, Nicole L., Jamie L. Hanson, Barbara L. Wolfe, and Seth D. Pollak, "Association of Child
    Poverty, Brain Development, and Academic Achievement," *JAMA Pediatrics* 169, no. 9 (2015):
    822, https://doi.org/10.1001/jamapediatrics.2015.1475; Mackey, Allyson P., Amy S. Finn, Julia
    A. Leonard, Drew S. Jacoby-Senghor, Martin R. West, Christopher F. Gabrieli, and John D.
    Gabrieli, "Neuroanatomical Correlates of the Income-Achievement Gap," *Psychological Sci-
    ence* 26, no. 6 (2015): 925–933, https://doi.org/10.1177/0956797615572233; Noble, Kimberly
    G., Suzanne M. Houston, Natalie H. Brito, Hauke Bartsch, Eric Kan, Joshua M Kuperman,

Natacha Akshoomoff, et al., "Family Income, Parental Education and Brain Structure in Children and Adolescents," *Nature Neuroscience* 18, no. 5 (2015): 773–778, https://doi.org/10.1038/nn.3983; Ursache, Alexandra, and Kimberly G. Noble, "Neurocognitive Development in Socioeconomic Context: Multiple Mechanisms and Implications for Measuring Socioeconomic Status," *Psychophysiology* 53, no. 1 (2015): 71–82, https://doi.org/10.1111/psyp.12547.

8.   Farah, "Neuroscience of Socioeconomic Status"; Farah, "Socioeconomic Status and the Brain"; Johnson, Riis, and Noble, "State of the Art Review"; Pakulak, Stevens, and Neville, "Neuro-, Cardio-, and Immunoplasticity"; Pavlakis et al., "Brain Imaging and Electrophysiology Biomarkers."

9.   *Self-regulation* is a psychological construct that refers to different cognitive and emotional processes that contribute to adjusting thoughts, emotions, and behaviors depending on the context. Consequently, they contribute to adaptation in the face of the changes that take place in the environments of parenting, education, work, recreation, and spiritual cultivation.

10.   Greenfield, Emily A., and Sara M. Moorman, "Childhood Socioeconomic Status and Later Life Cognition: Evidence From the Wisconsin Longitudinal Study," *Journal of Aging and Health* 31, no. 9 (2018): 1589–1615, https://doi.org/10.1177/0898264318783489.

11.   Magnuson, Katherine A., and Elizabeth Votruba-Drzal, *Enduring Influences of Childhood Poverty* (Madison: University of Wisconsin-Madison, Institute for Research on Poverty, 2008).

12.   Sheridan, Margaret A., Feng Shi, Adam B. Miller, Carmel Salhi, and Katie A. McLaughlin, "Network Structure Reveals Clusters of Associations Between Childhood Adversities and Development Outcomes," *Developmental Science* 23, no. 5 (2020): https://doi.org/10.1111/desc.12934.

13.   *Deficit* refers to the lack or shortage of something deemed necessary, which implies that it is possible to modify by intervention, as in the case of income or other economic variables. In the context of mental health or cognitive development, such involvement is not always clear given that there are varying degrees of modification by intervention and because some cultures still carry the inertia of assuming irreversibility of the impacts of poverty at the level of mental functioning—probably originated in European psychiatry of the nineteenth century—in particular, when considering the level of biological organization that is still usually meant as a fixed process and immutable (Thomson, Mathew, "Disability, Psychiatry, and Eugenics," chapter 6 in *The Oxford Handbook of the History of Eugenics*, ed. Alison Bashford and Philippa Levine [Oxford: Oxford University Press, 2010) 116–133]).

14.   D'Angiulli, Amedeo, Sebastian J. Lipina, and Alice Olesinska, "Explicit and Implicit Issues in the Developmental Cognitive Neuroscience of Social Inequality," *Frontiers in Human Neuroscience* 6 (2012): https://doi.org/10.3389/fnhum.2012.00254.

15.   Greenfield and Moorman, "Childhood Socioeconomic Status and Later Life Cognition."

16.   Demir-Lira, Özlem Ece, Jérôme Prado, and James R. Booth, "Neural Correlates of Math Gains Vary Depending on Parental Socioeconomic Status (SES)," *Frontiers in Psychology* 7 (2016): https://doi.org/10.3389/fpsyg.2016.00892; Gullick, Margaret M., Özlem Ece Demir-Lira, and James R. Booth, "Reading Skill-Fractional Anisotropy Relationships in Visuospatial Tracts Diverge Depending on Socioeconomic Status," *Developmental Science* 19, no. 4 (2016): 673–685, https://doi.org/10.1111/desc.12428.

17.   Neville, H. J., C. Stevens, E. Pakulak, T. A. Bell, J. Fanning, S. Klein, and E. Isbell, "Family-Based Training Program Improves Brain Function, Cognition, and Behavior in Lower Socioeconomic Status Preschoolers," *Proceedings of the National Academy of Sciences* 110, no. 29 (2013): 12138–12143, https://doi.org/10.1073/pnas.1304437110; Pietto, Marcos Luis, Federico Giovannetti, Maria Soledad Segretin, Laouen Mayal Belloli, Matías Lopez-Rosenfeld, Andrea Paula Goldin, Diego Fernández-Slezak, Juan Esteban Kamienkowski, and Sebastian Javier Lipina, "Enhancement of Inhibitory Control in a Sample of Preschoolers from Poor Homes after Cognitive Training in a Kindergarten Setting: Cognitive and ERP Evidence," *Trends*

in Neuroscience and Education 13 (2018): 34–42. https://doi.org/10.1016/j.tine.2018.11.004; Romeo, Rachel R., Joanna A. Christodoulou, Kelly K. Halverson, Jack Murtagh, Abigail B. Cyr, Carly Schimmel, Patricia Chang, Pamela E. Hook, and John D. Gabrieli, "Socioeconomic Status and Reading Disability: Neuroanatomy and Plasticity in Response to Intervention," *Cerebral Cortex* 28, no. 7 (2018): 2297–2312, https://doi.org/10.1093/cercor/bhx131.

18. Farah, "Socioeconomic Status and the Brain."

19. Blair, Clancy, and C. Cybele Raver, "Poverty, Stress, and Brain Development: New Directions for Prevention and Intervention," *Academic Pediatrics* 16, no. 3 (2016): https://doi.org/10.1016/j.acap.2016.01.010; Robson, Davina A., Mark S. Allen, and Steven J. Howard, "Self-Regulation in Childhood as a Predictor of Future Outcomes: A Meta-Analytic Review," *Psychological Bulletin* 146, no. 4 (2020): 324–354, https://doi.org/10.1037/bul0000227.

20. Bradley and Corwyn, "Socioeconomic Status and Child Development"; Yoshikawa, Aber, and Beardslee, "The Effects of Poverty"; Lipina, Sebastián, Pobre cerebro: Lo que la neurociencia nos propone pensar y hacer acerca de los efectos de la pobreza sobre el desarrollo cognitivo y emocional (Buenos Aires: Siglo XXI Editores, 2016).

21. Farah, "The Neuroscience of Socioeconomic Status."

22. Albert, W. Dustin, Jamie L. Hanson, Ann T. Skinner, Kenneth A. Dodge, Laurence Steinberg, Kirby Deater-Deckard, Marc H. Bornstein, and Jennifer E. Lansford, "Individual Differences in Executive Function Partially Explain the Socioeconomic Gradient in Middle-School Academic Achievement," *Developmental Science* 23, no. 5 (2020): https://doi.org/10.1111/desc.12937; Lawson, Gwendolyn M., and Martha J. Farah, "Executive Function as a Mediator Between SES and Academic Achievement Throughout Childhood," *International Journal of Behavioral Development* 41, no. 1 (2017): 94–104, https://doi.org/10.1177/0165025415603489.

23. Noble, Kimberly G., Mayuresh S. Korgaonkar, Stuart M. Grieve, and Adam M. Brickman, "Higher Education Is an Age-Independent Predictor of White Matter Integrity and Cognitive Control in Late Adolescence," *Developmental Science* 16, no. 5 (2013): 653–664, https://doi.org/10.1111/desc.12077; Hair et al., "Association of Child Poverty."

24. Barch, Deanna, David Pagliaccio, Andy Belden, Michael P. Harms, Michael Gaffrey, Chad M. Sylvester, Rebecca Tillman, and Joan Luby, "Effect of Hippocampal and Amygdala Connectivity on the Relationship Between Preschool Poverty and School-Age Depression," *American Journal of Psychiatry* 173, no. 6 (2016): 625–634, https://doi.org/10.1176/appi.ajp.2015.15081014.

25. Noble et al., "Higher Education Is an Age-Independent"; Hair et al., "Association of Child Poverty."

26. Sheridan, Margaret A, and Katie A McLaughlin, "Neurobiological Models of the Impact of Adversity on Education," *Current Opinion in Behavioral Sciences* 10 (2016): 108–113, https://doi.org/10.1016/j.cobeha.2016.05.013.

27. Lipina, Sebastián J., "The Biological Side of Social Determinants: Neural Costs of Childhood Poverty," *Prospects* 46, no. 2 (2016): 265–280, https://doi.org/10.1007/s11125-017-9390-0; Lipina, Sebastián, "Aportes e implicancias de los estudios neurocientíficos sobre la pobreza infantil," *Infancia, adolescencia y juventud: oportunidades claves para el Desarrollo* (2019): 65.

28. Lupien, Sonia J., Bruce S. McEwen, Megan R. Gunnar, and Christine Heim, "Effects of Stress Throughout the Lifespan on the Brain, Behaviour and Cognition," *Nature Reviews Neuroscience* 10, no. 6 (2009): 434–445, https://doi.org/10.1038/nrn2639; Ursache and Noble, "Neurocognitive Development in Socioeconomic Context"; Blair and Raver, "Poverty, Stress, and Brain Development."

29. Bradley and Corwynn, "Socioeconomic Status and Child Development"; Maholmes and King, *Oxford Handbook of Poverty and Child Development*; Yoshikawa, Aber, and Beardslee, "The Effects of Poverty."

30. McEwen, Bruce S., and Peter J. Gianaros, "Central Role of the Brain in Stress and Adaptation: Links to Socioeconomic Status, Health, and Disease," *Annals of the New York Academy of Sciences* 1186, no. 1 (2010): 190–222, https://doi.org/10.1111/j.1749-6632.2009.05331.x.

31. Ellis, Bruce J., and Marco Del Giudice, "Developmental Adaptation to Stress: An Evolutionary Perspective," *Annual Review of Psychology* 70, no. 1 (2019): 111–139, https://doi.org/10.1146/annurev-psych-122216-011732.

32. Gray, Jason D., Joshua F. Kogan, Jordan Marrocco, and Bruce S. McEwen, "Genomic and Epigenomic Mechanisms of Glucocorticoids in the Brain," *Nature Reviews Endocrinology* 13, no. 11 (2017): 661–673, https://doi.org/10.1038/nrendo.2017.97.

33. Barnett, W. S., "Effectiveness of Early Educational Intervention," *Science* 333, no. 6045 (2011): 975–978, https://doi.org/10.1126/science.1204534; Britto, Pia R., Stephen J. Lye, Kerrie Proulx, Aisha K. Yousafzai, Stephen G. Matthews, Tyler Vaivada, Rafael Perez-Escamilla, et al., "Nurturing Care: Promoting Early Childhood Development," *Lancet* 389, no. 10064 (2017): 91–102, https://doi.org/10.1016/s0140-6736(16)31390-3; Burger, Kaspar, "How Does Early Childhood Care and Education Affect Cognitive Development? An International Review of the Effects of Early Interventions for Children from Different Social Backgrounds," *Early Childhood Research Quarterly* 25, no. 2 (2010): 140–165, https://doi.org/10.1016/j.ecresq.2009.11.001; Melhuish, Edward, Jay Belsky, Angela Anning, Mog Ball, Jacqueline Barnes, Helena Romaniuk, Alastair Leyland, and the NESS Research Team, "Variation in Community Intervention Programmes and Consequences for Children and Families: The Example of Sure Start Local Programmes," *Journal of Child Psychology and Psychiatry* 48, no. 6 (2007): 543–551, https://doi.org/10.1111/j.1469-7610.2007.01705.x; Landesman Ramey, S., and C. T. Ramey, "Understanding Efficacy of Early Educational Programs: Critical Design, Practice and Policy Issues," in *Early Childhood Programs for a New Century*, ed. A. J. Reynolds, M.C. Wang, and H. J. Walberg (Washington DC: American Psychological Association, 2003), 35–70.

34. Strobach, Tilo, and Julia Karbach, *Cognitive Training* (Cham, Switzerland: Springer, 2016).

35. Green, C. Shawn, Daphne Bavelier, Arthur F. Kramer, Sophia Vinogradov, Ulrich Ansorge, Karlene K. Ball, Ulrike Bingel et al., "Improving Methodological Standards in Behavioral Interventions for Cognitive Enhancement," *Journal of Cognitive Enhancement* 3, no. 1 (2019): 2–29.

36. Takacs, Zsofia K., and Reka Kassai, "The Efficacy of Different Interventions to Foster Children's Executive Function Skills: A Series of Meta-Analyses," *Psychological Bulletin* 145, no. 7 (2019): 653–697, https://doi.org/10.1037/bul0000195.

37. Neville et al., "Family-Based Training Program Improves Brain Function."

38. Romeo et al., "Socioeconomic Status and Reading Disability."

39. Pietto et al., "Enhancement of Inhibitory Control."

40. Frankenhuis, Willem E., and Daniel Nettle, "The Strengths of People in Poverty," *Current Directions in Psychological Science* 29, no. 1 (2019): 16–21, https://doi.org/10.1177/0963721419881154.

41. Beddington, John, Cary L. Cooper, John Field, Usha Goswami, Felicia A. Huppert, Rachel Jenkins, Hannah S. Jones, Tom B. L. Kirkwood, Barbara J. Sahakian, and Sandy M. Thomas, "The Mental Wealth of Nations," *Nature* 455, no. 7216 (2008): 1057–1060; Ribeiro, Sidarta, Natália Bezerra Mota, Valter da Fernandes, Andrea Camaz Deslandes, Guilherme Brockington, and Mauro Copelli, "Physiology and Assessment as Low-Hanging Fruit for Education Overhaul," *Prospects* 46, no. 2 (2016): 249–264, https://doi.org/10.1007/s11125-017-9393-x.

42. Ghosh, Ritwik, Mahua J. Dubey, Subhankar Chatterjee, and Souvik Dubey, "Impact of COVID-19 on Children: Special Focus on the Psychosocial Aspect," *Minerva Pediatrica* 72, no. 3 (2020): 226–235, https://doi.org/10.23736/s0026-4946.20.05887-9; Tang, Suqin, Mi Xiang, Teris Cheung, and Yu-Tao Xiang, "Mental Health and Its Correlates Among Children and

Adolescents During COVID-19 School Closure: The Importance of Parent-Child Discussion," *Journal of Affective Disorders* 279 (2021): 353–360, https://doi.org/10.1016/j.jad.2020.10.016.

43. Akseer, Nadia, Goutham Kandru, Emily C Keats, and Zulfiqar A Bhutta, "COVID-19 Pandemic and Mitigation Strategies: Implications for Maternal and Child Health and Nutrition," *American Journal of Clinical Nutrition* 112, no. 2 (2020): 251–256, https://doi.org/10.1093/ajcn /nqaa171; Zar, Heather J., Jeanette Dawa, Gilberto Bueno Fischer, and Jose A. Castro-Rodriguez, "Challenges of COVID-19 in Children in Low- and Middle-Income Countries," *Paediatric Respiratory Reviews* 35 (2020): 70–74, https://doi.org/10.1016/j.prrv.2020.06.016.

44. "Policy Brief: The Impact of COVID-19 on Children," United Nations (website), April 15, 2020, https://unsdg.un.org/resources/policy-brief-impact-covid-19-children; Viner, Russell M., Simon J. Russell, Helen Croker, Jessica Packer, Joseph Ward, Claire Stansfield, Oliver Mytton, Chris Bonell, and Robert Booy, "School Closure and Management Practices During Coronavirus Outbreaks Including COVID-19: A Rapid Systematic Review," *Lancet Child & Adolescent Health* 4, no. 5 (2020): 397–404, https://doi.org/10.1016/s2352-4642(20)30095-x.

45. Panovska-Griffiths, Jasmina, Cliff C. Kerr, Robyn M. Stuart, Dina Mistry, Daniel J. Klein, Russell M. Viner, and Chris Bonell, "Determining the Optimal Strategy for Reopening Schools, the Impact of Test and Trace Interventions, and the Risk of Occurrence of a Second COVID-19 Epidemic Wave in the UK: A Modelling Study," *Lancet Child & Adolescent Health* 4, no. 11 (2020): 817–827, https://doi.org/10.1016/s2352-4642(20)30250-9.

46. Armitage, Richard, and Laura B. Nellums, "Considering Inequalities in the School Closure Response to COVID-19," *Lancet Global Health* 8, no. 5 (2020), https://doi.org/10.1016/s2214 -109x(20)30116-9; Lee, Joyce, "Mental Health Effects of School Closures During COVID-19," *Lancet Child & Adolescent Health* 4, no. 6 (2020): 421, https://doi.org/10.1016/s2352-4642(20) 30109-7.

47. Drane, Catherine, Lynette Vernon, and Sarah O'Shea, "The Impact of 'Learning at Home' on the Educational Outcomes of Vulnerable Children in Australia During the COVID-19 Pandemic" (Literature Review Prepared by the National Centre for Student Equity in Higher Education, Curtin University, Australia, 2020).

48. Fairlie, Robert, and Prashant Loyalka, "Schooling and Covid-19: Lessons from Recent Research on EdTech," *npj Science of Learning* 5, no. 1 (2020): https://doi.org/10.1038/s41539 -020-00072-6; Sheikh, Aziz, Asiyah Sheikh, Zakariya Sheikh, and Sangeeta Dhami, "Reopening Schools After the COVID-19 Lockdown," *Journal of Global Health* 10, no. 1 (2020): https:// doi.org/10.7189/jogh.10.010376.

49. CEPAL, NU, "Persons with Disabilities and Coronavirus Disease (COVID-19) in Latin America and the Caribbean: Status and Guidelines." (2020), https://www.cepal.org/en/publications /45492-persons-disabilities-and-coronavirus-disease-covid-19-latin-america-and-caribbean.

50. Al-Samarrai, Samer, Maulshree Gangwar, and Priyal Gala, "The Impact of the COVID-19 Pandemic on Education Financing," World Bank, 2020, https://doi.org/10.1596/33739; Naidoo, Robin, and Brendan Fisher, "Reset Sustainable Development Goals for a Pandemic World," *Nature* 583, no. 7815 (2020): 198–201, https://doi.org/10.1038/d41586-020-01999-x.

51. Clark, Helen, Awa Marie Coll-Seck, Anshu Banerjee, Stefan Peterson, Sarah L. Dalglish, Shanthi Ameratunga, Dina Balabanova et al., "A Future for the World's Children? A WHO–UNICEF–Lancet Commission," *Lancet* 395, no. 10224 (2020): 605–658.

4

EDUCATION FOR REFUGEE AND DISPLACED CHILDREN

HIROKAZU YOSHIKAWA, SARAH DRYDEN-PETERSON,
DANA BURDE, AND J. LAWRENCE ABER

TRENDS IN FORCED MIGRATION

According to the UN *Convention and Protocol Relating to the Status of Refugees*, a refugee is "someone who is unable or unwilling to return to their country of origin owing to a well-founded fear of being persecuted for reasons of race, religion, nationality, membership in a particular social group, or political opinion."[1] Globally, the current number of refugees is at a historic high. The United Nations High Commissioner on Refugees estimated by the end of 2020 that a total of 82.4 million forcibly displaced people existed worldwide, of whom 26.4 million were refugees, 48.0 million were internally displaced, and 4.1 million were asylum seekers. Some of the largest mass displacements across borders of recent years resulted in over nine hundred thousand Rohingya individuals who fled to Bangladesh since 2017 to escape violence in Myanmar; nearly five million Venezuelans who have fled to neighboring countries to escape the collapse of their country's economy and social services; and close to seven million Syrians who have fled their country during the to-date ten-year civil war, with another seven million displaced within Syria. Environmental disasters are also an increasing cause of displacement and refugee status, with climate change both increasing conflict as well as increasing the likelihood of disasters.[2]

Despite the large numbers of newly displaced people, forced migration has been a phenomenon throughout human history, and refugees—living outside the borders of their country—are part of this larger population of forcibly displaced people worldwide. The largest forced migration prior to World War II was the forced kidnapping, migration, and enslavement of 12.5 million Africans.[3] World War II displaced more than forty million across borders, along with millions of people killed in the Holocaust after migrations by force. Wars of partition and independence in the 1940s in India, Pakistan, and Bangladesh resulted in over one million deaths and close to fifteen million people becoming refugees after fleeing across borders.[4]

Three factors define contemporary refugee and displaced persons' experiences with education: geography, the length of exile, and residence in refugee camps versus host communities. First, over 80 percent of refugees flee to a neighboring country.[5] With the largest displacements occurring in Africa and the Middle East, this means that these regions are also hosting the largest numbers of refugees. The geography of conflicts and their historical, colonial, and geopolitical roots also mean that the neighboring countries that host refugees are largely low- and middle-income countries. For refugee children, experiences of conflict and flight are often overlaid by conditions of poverty, inequality, exposure to violence, and marginalization in exile. Second, over 80 percent of refugees remain displaced for over five years and roughly 20 percent for over twenty years.[6] This length of exile means that refugeehood is not temporary but rather a life-course experience for most refugee children, whose development and opportunities for education and learning may take place largely outside their family's home country. Finally, the large majority of both refugees and internally displaced persons worldwide live outside of refugee camps. For example, over 90 percent of Syrian refugees in Turkey and Jordan, and virtually all in Lebanon, live outside formal refugee camps, largely in urban environments.[7]

In the following pages, we first present various types of exclusion to which refugee and displaced children are subjected and then possible ways forward to address these forms of exclusion and ensure access to quality education and learning opportunities for refugee and displaced children.

REFUGEE CHILDREN AND EDUCATION: THE REALITY OF EXCLUSION THROUGH LENSES OF ACCESS, QUALITY, AND EQUITY

Refugee children are at great risk of exclusion from education. For the purposes of this chapter, we define education not only as formal schooling but also access to broader opportunities for learning, such as early care and education or, in middle childhood and adolescence, informal and out-of-school education. Exclusion from these opportunities represents a serious challenge to Sustainable Development Goal 4, which states that all children should have access to quality preprimary, primary, and secondary education by 2030.[8] In countries affected by conflict, one in three children ages five to seventeen are not in school. These 104 million children represent more than one-third of the children globally who are not in school.[9] Refugee children access primary education at substantially lower rates than children globally. Whereas 91 percent of all children globally have access to primary education, only 77 percent of refugees do. The difference at the secondary and tertiary levels is even more stark. Only 31 percent of refugees have access compared to 84 percent of all children. And at the tertiary level, 3 percent of refugees have access compared to 37 percent of young people globally. Marginalization among refugees is often compounded by discrimination based on other factors such as race, class, caste, language, sexuality, religion, and gender. For example, refugee girls' rates of access to secondary schooling are 70 percent that of boys.[10] School closures related to the COVID-19 pandemic have been devastating to refugee children's school participation, which was tenuous to begin with. A recent analysis by the Malala Fund of UNHCR data from ten refugee-hosting countries suggests that half of all refugee girls will not return when their schools reopen.[11]

EXCLUSIONS IN HOME COUNTRIES AND IN FLIGHT

Processes of exclusion of refugees from education are multiple and occur throughout forced migration and displacement experiences. Experiences of conflict, disaster, or persecution in the home country often result in interrupted schooling in the place of residence. In the case of conflict, schools may close due to physical damage or sociopolitical unrest. Sometimes, as in the case of Boko Haram in northern Nigeria and southern Niger and the Lord's Resistance Army in northern Uganda, schools are prime targets of violence or kidnapping.[12] During flight, either within the home country or after arrival in a host country, schooling can be further interrupted for many reasons, including overcrowded classrooms, language barriers, and/or displaced children's lack of school records to meet entry requirements. The added effects of uncertainty, danger, and exploitation en route to schools and within schools can additionally threaten not only learning but also survival.

While in ongoing limbo, multiple threats can disrupt children's access to education and learning opportunities. For example, in Australia and the United States, detention has recently resulted in the prolonged exclusion of children and youth from education.[13] This exclusion contravenes global rights frameworks and agreements. While in detention, which should be for the absolute minimum of time according to the *Convention on the Rights of the Child (General Comment 6)*, "Children have the right to education which ought, ideally, to take place outside the detention premises in order to facilitate the continuance of their education upon release."[14]

EXCLUSIONS IN HOST COUNTRY SETTLEMENT

After initial settlement in a host country, exclusion from education can occur in ways that threaten basic access as well as quality and equity. For example, access to education may be only available to children with certain categories of status, which can exclude nonregistered and/or registered refugees. Malaysia, for example, is not a signatory to the 1951 Refugee Convention and has no legal system for asylum. Without legal status, children in Malaysia who have fled other countries have no official access to school.[15] Even with access to schools, refugees may not experience schooling in an equitable manner. Important dimensions of the quality of education and learning opportunities, such as instruction time; the language of instruction; implemented curricula or absence thereof; training and qualifications of teachers and school staff; access to learning supports for children with learning difficulties or disabilities; out-of-pocket costs associated with schooling; bullying and discrimination within schools; and family and community engagement are all examples of features of education systems that may be experienced differently by refugee-origin students relative to their nonrefugee counterparts.[16]

INEQUITABLE ACCESS TO QUALITY EDUCATION: THE CASE OF THE ROHINGYA IN COX'S BAZAR, BANGLADESH

The Rohingya, an indigenous group with a large population in Rakhine province, Myanmar, fled violence and bombing of villages there in large numbers starting in 2017 (surpassing in numbers the multiple prior waves of forced migration over the last forty years).

The Rohingya exodus from northern Rakhine province to Cox's Bazar district, Bangladesh, represents one of the largest and most concentrated recent migrations of refugees anywhere in the world. Over nine hundred thousand Rohingya migrants now reside in an area divided into thirty-two contiguous refugee camps in Cox's Bazar.

Since the onset of the exodus in early 2017, the Rohingya have experienced exclusion from formal education. Both structural and instructional aspects of education differ when comparing their schooling experiences to those students in the host community. First, the government does not provide schooling access, so all education services are provided by nongovernmental organizations in the form of informal rather than formal education. Second, this limited access is only provided to five- to fourteen-year-olds (with the five-year-old year being a single year of preprimary education). Third, typically, instruction is provided for only a very small number of hours per day (often two)—defined as "informal" learning in the guidance from the government of Bangladesh. Finally, instruction in Bangla (the mainstream language of instruction of Bangladesh) and access to the Bangladesh national curriculum are generally forbidden, with preference given to instruction in the Burmese language. The military takeover of Myanmar in February 2021 also left the option of Rohingya return to that country blocked. This leaves the schooling of hundreds of thousands of children in a limbo state.[17] The refugee relief and repatriation commissioner, in charge of implementing Bangladesh government policy on Rohingya refugees, stated in February 2019: "If they stay for 20 years, you'll need a curriculum, but if it's just a year or two, then it's different. . . . There is no possibility for them to take the Bangladeshi curriculum."[18] Very recently, this policy has been amended, and access to the national curriculum was to be implemented on a small-scale pilot basis.[19] Yet, as of this writing, these plans have been placed on hold during the COVID-19 pandemic. Ultimately, the current experience of the Rohingya in Cox's Bazar violates the pledge of Sustainable Development Goal 4 to "ensure inclusive and equitable quality education and promote lifelong learning opportunities for all," as well as aspects of the Global Compact on Refugees and more recent frameworks such as Refugee Education 2030, described below.[20]

Beyond the future economic and livelihood consequences of limited access to education, exclusion and inequities in access to education and learning may drive increased conflict. Out-of-school youth may have more opportunities to engage in organized conflict, and perceptions of inequities, particularly if

perceived as associated with ethnicity or other marginalized group membership, can increase intergroup conflict.[21] In contrast, access to equitable education may be associated with greater social cohesion and trust in institutions,[22]
as well as lower incidence of civil war.[23]

NEW DEVELOPMENTS AND TENSIONS IN REFUGEE INCLUSION IN NATIONAL SYSTEMS OF EDUCATION

In 2012, the UNHCR made an explicit shift in its education strategy to encourage refugee integration into national, public systems of education rather than
segregated refugee education.[24] This shift responded to challenges of exclusion, in particular as related to the length of exile and the geography of contemporary refugees.[25] In principle, this inclusion in the structures of national
education reflected a conceptualization of education in the host country as a
long-term endeavor for refugees rather than a short-term, emergency activity
considering trends of protracted displacement. This inclusion also recognized
the geography of marginalization in refugee-hosting countries and the need
for support to refugee education to also benefit national students where access
to education and learning does not meet global goals. Further, in principle,
the inclusion of refugees in national education systems opened access to the
central pathway to economic and social mobility in host countries, including
access to the same schools and teachers as well as curriculum and certifica-
tions as host-country citizens. Whereas in 2011, before the codification of this
policy approach, UNHCR had no formal relationships on education with host
country governments, by 2016, agreements for access to national schools and
established means of coordination were in place in twenty of the twenty-five
priority countries in which UNHCR worked.[26]

The approach of including refugees in national systems, not only for
education but also across other sectors, was echoed in the 2014 UNHCR Alternatives to Camps policy and the 2016 New York Declaration. It was expanded
upon in the 2018 Global Compact on Refugees, which affirms that "In line with
national education laws, policies and planning, and in support of host countries, States and relevant stakeholders will contribute resources and expertise
to expand and enhance the quality and inclusiveness of national education systems to facilitate access by refugee and host community children (both boys
and girls), adolescents and youth to primary, secondary and tertiary education."

The Global Compact on Refugees thus builds on the idea that education is a medium- to long-term social service intervention rather than a short-term crisis intervention. Further, the global compact orients the approach of inclusion toward creating conditions that are productive and beneficial both for refugees and for host country nationals.

Despite these shifts in global policy frameworks, refugees' access to national education systems, to learning in these settings, and to economic, service, and civic opportunities vary across countries and contribute to additional forms of exclusion. Exclusion under this new approach continues to follow some of the same patterns described above. Exclusion can occur in all phases of migration. Most fundamentally, if individuals cannot access refugee status, they have no right to any provision of education in host countries. This is the case for stateless individuals or those deemed otherwise unauthorized, as well as for those denied entry and/or asylum.[27] For example, the Trump administration in the United States issued a policy of returning those who formally apply for asylum at the southern border to their home countries.[28] Policies and laws such as this one perpetuate defining geographic conditions of exile, whereby opportunities outside of the country of first asylum in conflict-affected regions are limited.[29]

Lack of physical access to schools because of distance, safety, or significant overcrowding is also a fundamental exclusion refugees face upon arrival in host countries, even when access by law or policy is in place. This form of exclusion is often most severe in the early stages of displacement when informal systems may not yet be in place to accommodate this population and long before formal education systems have been extended to support new refugees. Yet, given the importance of each passing week to the education of a child, the amount of time children and families must wait before any education facilities are available to them often has stark consequences.[30]

Within host countries, multiple models of inclusion exist, primarily of three types. First is national inclusion under conditions of geographic isolation, such as in the cases of refugee camps. For example, in refugee camps in Kenya, Ethiopia, and Uganda, refugee children follow the national curriculum in the national language of instruction with a combination of national and refugee teachers. They sit for national exams, yet they are not in schools and classrooms with national students.[31] Second is national inclusion under conditions of temporal isolation, such as in the case of second shifts. For example, in Lebanon, refugee and national students share the same school buildings, follow the same national curriculum, often with the same national teachers, and sit for national exams, but they are separated in time, with Lebanese nationals attending school in the morning and Syrian refugees in the afternoon.[32] Third is inclusion, where refugees and nationals share the same schools and classrooms at the same time. This type of inclusion is more frequent in urban areas, such as in Cape Town, Quito, and Nairobi, and at secondary levels.[33] In March 2021, Colombia began to utilize this model, allowing temporary protected status, including access to education to all Venezuelans in the country who can show proof of residence in Colombia as of January 2021 (under prior protected status rulings, roughly 40 percent of Venezuelan refugees who had entered Colombia since 2017 acquired legal protected rather than irregular status).[34] The universal right to education regardless of immigration or legal status is granted in Colombia's constitution, and despite serious gaps in implementation, especially in some of the regions close to the Venezuelan border, all Venezuelan children have the right to access primary and secondary basic education in the country.[35]

In situations of inclusion, while there are fewer policy barriers to accessing education, barriers that impede access to learning continue, including those related to new exclusions that accompany inclusion of refugees in national systems, as related to host-country curriculum, pedagogy, language, and relationships. In national education systems, refugee children encounter curricula that can be exclusionary, discriminatory, hard to relate to, and provide limited opportunity for them to engage with their own experiences of conflict and displacement. Such can be the case when they are within education systems that struggle to address national histories of conflict or that seek to inculcate adversarial attitudes toward perceived enemies.[36] Refugee children also encounter pedagogy that is predominantly teacher-centered and standardized, with limited flexibility and adaptation to engage with the needs of diverse learners.[37] Further exclusion can come through language in the context of national education systems. Refugee children cannot learn when they do not understand the language or are not adequately prepared and supported to learn in the languages of instruction and of examination in the national education system in which they are included.[38] Refugee children encounter relationships at school with peers and with teachers that can be discriminatory and exclusionary, including physical and verbal bullying, as early as kindergarten.[39] These relationships can adversely impact their academic and social-emotional learning.[40]

Exclusion under the approach of inclusion in national education systems also can come in the form of misalignment between this inclusion and the kinds of future opportunities available to refugees—in particular, barriers to using education toward future economic, social, and civic opportunities.[41]

First, schooling and certification obtained in the national education system of the host country may not be recognized in the country of origin or in another settlement site, preventing refugees from accessing livelihoods for which they prepared through their education. Moreover, even in the national host country context in which refugees pursue education, obtaining the national educational qualifications often does not open opportunities for further study or employment, given limitations on the right to work.[42]

RECOMMENDATIONS: POSSIBILITIES FOR INTEGRATING ACCESS, LEARNING, AND EQUITY FOR REFUGEES IN EDUCATION AND OTHER SECTORS

In light of the multiple challenges described above, how can successful refugee education be implemented at scale? The "Global Framework for Refugee Education" includes emphases on (1) inclusion in national education systems; (2) learning, qualifications and skills for work and engagement and opportunities to use such learning, qualifications, and skills; and (3) emergency response.[43]

We integrate these three approaches with the provisions of Sustainable Development Goal 4 for universal access to quality education to consider how both access and quality may be encouraged, with attention not only to the structural aspects of education but also to the instructional content and access to the economic, social, and civic opportunities to pursue productive futures.[44] Although the framework spans many areas of systems and education improvement, several additional challenges could and should be addressed in order to reach these goals and address the new exclusions that have surfaced with inclusion. These challenges represent opportunities for innovation in global education that at the same time address the particular barriers experienced by refugee children: (1) building structural inclusion; (2) building relational inclusion to address underlying causes of conflict; (3) integrating support for social-emotional learning and mental health.

BUILDING STRUCTURAL INCLUSION

Structural inclusion, often also called functional integration, involves refugee children's ability to access institutions and services, including but not limited to the formal education sector. Access to institutions and services intersects with dimensions of quality and equity related to certification, alternative and nonformal education, and connections with families.

With heightened awareness of the importance of credentials in order to gain access to education and other systems, some host countries work with international organizations to resolve these barriers. In addition, many organizations involved in supporting refugee access to education offer alternative forms for studying within the host country and with the host curriculum but outside formal schools. These often take the shape of programs similar to community-based education classes in which a community offers a space in a home or center, provides the teacher, and the implementing organization distributes government curricula and provides training for the teacher. In conditions where state services are weak or nonexistent, community-based education can be highly effective, as recent community-randomized trials have shown.[45]

Technological supports and innovations may also aid in bringing nonformal learning to mobile, home, and community settings. For example, a recent small field experiment in Turkey tested a game-based curriculum provided on tablets to Syrian refugee children ages nine to fourteen. The curriculum aimed to strengthen Turkish language and executive function skills, as well as computational and algorithmic thinking. A waitlist-control design was used to assess exposure to the curriculum. The program produced increases in Turkish language, coding skills, executive function (i.e., cognitive flexibility), and reduced perceived hopelessness.[46]

Another approach to structural inclusion is the integration of education with other multisectoral supports for families and communities. For example, parents, other caregivers, and other family members have to support themselves in displacement and conflict. Yet, very few parenting or caregiver interventions have been evaluated for children from displaced and refugee families.[47] The global Nurturing Care Framework recently developed by UN agencies emphasizes integrated approaches to responsive caregiving, health, nutrition, and learning in early childhood programs and policies. It builds on the global evidence base supporting the strengthening of parenting and caregiving in the first years of life.[48] Its application to refugee and conflict-affected contexts may be promising as an approach that is more multicontext and multisectoral than formal refugee education alone.[49] Early childhood development requires integration of these components, and later development benefits from such integration, too.[50] For example, there is promising evidence that strategic combinations of services—supports for a minimum family income, good parenting, and safe schools, for example—can serve as development accelerators and lead to improvements in multiple Sustainable Development Goal targets.[51] Such integrated attention to income support, health, well-being, and learning is particularly needed for vulnerable populations, such as those displaced by conflict and war.[52]

BUILDING RELATIONAL INCLUSION RATHER THAN CONFLICT IN EDUCATION

Relational inclusion is a sociocultural process that involves both an individual-level sense of belonging or connectedness and group-level social cohesion.[53] Considering relational inclusion in addition to structural inclusion of refugees in national education systems must acknowledge that education can act both to mitigate and to promote conflict.[54] Bush and Saltarelli's influential paper noted what others have since observed in many conflict-affected contexts around the world: that education can promote conflict, not just peace.[55] For example, King observed in the case of Rwanda that in each of three historical periods (including most recently post-genocide), the education system was not only inequitable in ways that increased interethnic conflict but also included instructional content that increased stigma, inequalities, and competition for resources.[56]

Social cohesion accompanies education as a central component of the Sustainable Development Goals, which call for inclusive communities. Fostering inclusive communities is a central goal of the Comprehensive Refugee Response Framework (an annex of the UN's 2016 New York Declaration on Refugees and Migrants), which advocates that "diversity enriches every society and contributes to social cohesion," while countering "racism, racial discrimination, xenophobia and related intolerance against refugees and migrants." Important to its relevance to education is that "direct personal contact between host communities and refugees and migrants" is defined as a mechanism to achieve this goal.[57]

To act on these goals, education for refugees must attend to barriers to relational inclusion described above, particularly as connected to curriculum, pedagogy, language, and relationships. Across time and geography, refugee families have looked outside of formal school structures to support learning about community history, culture, identity, and language, for example.[58] These issues must be addressed in schools. Curricular and pedagogical approaches that emphasize cultural preservation rather than cultural displacement and loss are promising in this regard. The preservation of culture in a new country can be threatened when survival, health, and basic food, shelter, and clothing are unavailable. However, the support of learning and education requires attention to culture and language both to make it accessible to refugee children and to enable productive learning. Curriculum and pedagogy that are culturally sustaining enable refugee children to access learning and build a sense of belonging.[59] Yet, they are often absent in the national schools refugees are included within. At the same time, refugee children experience exclusion from the curriculum and pedagogy of education alongside their national peers, who are often among the most marginalized in the national context.[60] Educational spaces are at the forefront of challenges to sharing scarce resources within already stretched institutional settings in host countries, including the possibilities that support for refugee education can deepen already high levels of poverty and limited services for nationals. These dynamics can lead to tensions among individuals and groups if resources are not consolidated for the benefit of all children in areas of refugee settlement.

Language of instruction is a particularly challenging area to address in situations of inclusion.[61] Research shows benefits to young people of instruction in their home languages both for learning and identity development.[62] Parents express concern that their children are instead "submerged" in other languages, with little opportunity to be taught in their home language, learn about cultural traditions, and maintain means of communication with family or future opportunities in countries of origin.[63] At the same time, challenges to multilingual instruction even in stable but low-resourced contexts result in situations where little learning takes place given the lack of curricular materials in relevant languages and the lack of trained teachers for language teaching.[64] While much more research is needed to develop innovative solutions to these challenges, a recent model of early childhood education developed by the NGO BRAC with and for the Rohingya in Cox's Bazar uses a model of cultural and linguistic preservation in which Rohingya arts—visual, musical, dance, and movement—are central features of a preprimary curriculum and are the vehicles for child protection, hygiene, and sanitation messages, as well as preacademic learning.[65]

SOCIAL-EMOTIONAL LEARNING AND MENTAL HEALTH

Some areas of learning are under particular threat for refugee children—especially those related to mental health and social-emotional development.

Prior exposure to conflict and adversity due to displacement are direct risk factors for heightened anxiety, depression, conduct problems, and externalizing and antisocial behaviors.[66] Many children have undergone family separation experiences—sometimes prolonged—or losses of parents, caregivers, siblings, or other family members. For children who have undergone parental or caregiver loss or family separations, clinically and culturally informed programs implemented in family, school, or community contexts have shown some evidence of improving well-being and mental health.[67]

More broadly, recent evidence shows that children in conflict-affected contexts can benefit from the integration of social-emotional learning (SEL) as a core aspect of formal and informal education curricula. Until recently, almost no impact evaluations have considered the impact on holistic learning outcomes of provision of SEL-infused formal or informal education programs for children from refugee and displaced families.[68] The International Rescue Committee's Learning in Healing Classrooms (LHC) approach, which entails quality literacy and numeracy curricula as well as teacher training and coaching in these curricula, has been implemented in many countries around the world. In a nonrefugee but conflict-affected context, the eastern Democratic Republic of Congo, this model of integrating SEL with traditional emphases on reading and math improved students' perceptions of their schools and teachers as safe and supportive and improved some literacy and numeracy skills; but it did not reduce children's experiences of victimization or mental health symptoms.[69]

A subsequent impact evaluation tested the Learning in Healing Classrooms approach in nonformal retention-support programs to help promote Syrian refugee children's learning and retention in Lebanese public primary schools. The program was implemented for children in "second shift" classrooms with largely Lebanese teachers. This approach was evaluated in a longitudinal site-randomized design.[70] Relative to students in public schools without this additional informal literacy and numeracy support integrated with social-emotional learning, students who had access to sixteen weeks of remedial programs based on the Healing Classroom model showed greater growth in basic reading (decoding) and numeracy (number identification) skills, while more difficult language and quantitative reasoning skills were unaffected. In addition, these students' behavioral regulation as assessed by enumerators showed stronger growth in the sites randomized to include the Healing Classrooms remedial tutoring curriculum. The students with access to the Healing Classroom model, moreover, were more likely to perceive their public school teachers to be caring and supportive and to view their public schools as safe, engaging and motivating, and respectful and inclusive. This study represents some of the first evidence in a refugee context that supporting children's social-emotional learning in informal education programs, in conjunction with traditional emphases on improving reading and math skills, may help children from refugee contexts learn and adapt when included in public schools in a host country.

In the context of the COVID-19 pandemic, remote approaches to building holistic learning, including attention to mental health, have been implemented in contexts of displacement and migration. COVID-19 produced unprecedented internal displacement and economic hardship worldwide (e.g., urban-rural migration in the wake of lockdowns).[71] Supporting learning during lockdown has required integrated attention to health, economic hardship, mental health and well-being, as well as opportunities for learning. Such integration is occurring in the implementation of phone-based programming for caregivers and parents for Syrian refugee populations and the Rohingya in Cox's Bazar district, Bangladesh.[72] Telecounseling approaches are being integrated into these models, with quality assessment incorporating attention to psychosocial support in remote learning interventions.

INTEGRATING REFUGEE AND DISPLACED CHILDREN IN THE GLOBAL COMPACT

The Global Compact on Education is distinguished by its attention to the most vulnerable and excluded in society. Unfortunately, exclusion from schooling and other opportunities for learning—whether in home countries, during flight, or in host societies and communities—is the daily experience of far too many children and youth who are among the over seventy million forcibly displaced worldwide. In this chapter, we have reviewed the kinds of exclusion that can threaten learning and development for this population. In addition, we have described pathways to ensuring structural and relational inclusion with attention to multiple aspects of learning and development. Ensuring these pathways to lifelong learning and opportunity for displaced, refugee, and other marginalized populations should be a central aim of the Global Compact on Education.

NOTES

1.   UNHCR, *Convention and Protocol Relating to the Status of Refugees* (Geneva: United Nations, 1951).

2.   UNHCR, "Global trends," accessed October 30, 2021, https://www.unhcr.org/flagship-reports/globaltrends/.

3.   Richardson, David, and David Eltis, *Atlas of the Transatlantic Slave Trade* (New Haven, CT: Yale University Press, 2015).

4.   Dalrymple, William, *A Deadly Triangle: Afghanistan, Pakistan, and India* (Washington, DC: Brookings Institution Press, 2013).

5.   Global Refugee Forum Education Co-Sponsorship Alliance, "Global Framework for Refugee Education," UNCHR, November 2019, https://www.unhcr.org/5dd50ce47.pdf

6.   Global Refugee Forum Education Co-Sponsorship Alliance, "Global Framework for Refugee Education."

7.   Asgary, Ali, ed. *Resettlement Challenges for Displaced Populations and Refugees* (New York: Springer, 2018).

8.   United Nations, *Transforming Our World: The 2030 Agenda for Sustainable Development*, (New York: United Nations, 2015).

9.   "A Future Stolen: Young and Out of School," UNICEF, September 2018, https://data.unicef.org/resources/a-future-stolen/.

10.   Global Refugee Forum Education Co-Sponsorship Alliance, "Global Framework for Refugee Education."

11.   Grandi, Filippo, "Coming Together for Refugee Education," UNHCR, accessed April 1, 2021, https://www.unhcr.org/5f4f9a2b4.

12.   Yakubu, Moses Joseph, "Child Insurgents in West Africa: The Boko Haram Example in Nigeria, Chad and Cameroon," *African Journal of Governance and Development* 5, no. 2 (2016): 34–49.

13.   Waddoups, Anne Bentley, Hirokazu Yoshikawa, and Kendra Strouf, "Developmental Effects of Parent–Child Separation," *Annual Review of Developmental Psychology* 1 (2019): 387–410.

14.   Committee on the Rights of the Child, *United Nations Convention on the Rights of the Child: Comment 6* (Geneva: Committee on the Rights of the Child, 2005), https://www2.ohchr.org/english/bodies/crc/docs/GC6.pdf

15.   Dryden-Peterson, Sarah, Elizabeth Adelman, Michelle J. Bellino, and Vidur Chopra, "The Purposes of Refugee Education: Policy and Practice of Including Refugees in National Education Systems," *Sociology of Education* 92, no. 4 (2019): 346–366.

16.   Mendenhall, Mary, Sarah Dryden-Peterson, Lesley Bartlett, Caroline Ndirangu, Rosemary Imonje, Daniel Gakunga, Loise Gichuhi, Grace Nyagah, Ursulla Okoth, and Mary Tangelder, "Quality Education for Refugees in Kenya: Pedagogy in Urban Nairobi and Kakuma Refugee Camp Settings," *Journal in Education in Emergencies* 1 no. 1 (2015): 92–130; Dryden-Peterson, Sarah, Elizabeth Adelman, Sagra Alvarado, Katelin Anderson, Michelle J. Bellino, Ranya Brooks, Sayeda Unsa Shah Bukhari et al., "Inclusion of Refugees in National Systems," UNESCO, 2018, https://unesdoc.unesco.org/ark:/48223/pf0000026605.

17.   Human Rights Watch, " 'Are We Not Human?' Denial of Education for Rohingya Refugee Children in Bangladesh," December 3, 2019, https://www.hrw.org/report/2019/12/03/are-we-not-human/denial-education-rohingya-refugee-children-bangladesh.

18.   Human Rights Watch, " 'Are We Not Human?' "

19.   Amnesty Interational, "Bangladesh: Rohingya Children Get Access to Education," January 28, 2020, https://www.amnesty.org/en/latest/news/2020/01/bangladesh-rohingya-children-get-access-to-education/.

20.   United Nations, "Transforming Our World: The 2030 Agenda for Sustainable Development" (2015), 18. https://sdgs.un.org/sites/default/files/publications/21252030%20Agenda%20for%20

Sustainable%20Development%20web.pdf; UNHCR, "Global Compact on Refugees" (2018), https://www.unhcr.org/en-us/the-global-compact-on-refugees.html; UNHCR, "Refugee Education 2030" (2019), https://www.unhcr.org/en-us/publications/education/5d651da88d7/education-2030 -strategy-refugee-education.html.

21. Burde, Dana, Amy Kapit, Rachel L. Wahl, Ozen Guven, and Margot Igland Skarpeteig, "Education in Emergencies: A Review of Theory and Research," *Review of Educational Research* 87, no. 3 (2017): 619–658.

22. Burde, D., M. Lisiecki, J. Middleton, O. Okhidoi, and C. Samii, "Phase Two Endline Report: Can Communities Take Charge? The Assessment of Learning Outcomes and Social Effects of Community-Based Education: A Randomized Field Experiment in Afghanistan," Steinhardt School, New York University, 2019, https://www.jointdatacenter.org/literature _review/can-communities-take-charge-the-assessment-of-learning-outcomes-and-social -effects-of-community-based-education-a-randomized-field-experiment-in-afghanistan/.

23. Thyne, Clayton L., "ABC's, 123's, and the Golden Rule: The Pacifying Effect of Education on Civil War, 1980–1999," *International Studies Quarterly* 50, no. 4 (2006): 733–754.

24. UNHCR, *Education Strategy 2012–2016* (Geneva: United Nations High Commissioner for Refugees, 2012).

25. Dryden-Peterson, Sarah, Elizabeth Adelman, Michelle J. Bellino, and Vidur Chopra, "The Purposes of Refugee Education: Policy and Practice of Including Refugees in National Education Systems," *Sociology of Education* 92, no. 4 (2019): 346–366.

26. Dryden-Peterson, Sarah. *Right Where We Belong: How Refugee Teachers and Students Are Changing the Future of Education* (Cambridge, MA: Harvard University Press, in press).

27. Suárez-Orozco, Carola, "A Compassionate Perspective on Immigrant Children and Youth," *Humanitarianism and Mass Migration: Confronting the World Crisis* (2019): 99–129;UNHCR, *Global Action Plan to End Statelessness: 2014–2024* (Geneva: United Nations High Commissioner for Refugees, 2014).

28. Kao, Jason, and Denise Lu, "How Trump's Policies Are Leaving Thousands of Asylum Seekers Waiting in Mexico," *New York Times*, August 18, 2019, https://www.nytimes.com/interactive /2019/08/18/us/mexico-immigration-asylum.html.

29. Rodriguez Vega, Silvia, and Hirokazu Yoshikawa "Border and Asylum Immigration Policies and Adolescent Development in the United States," in *APA Handbook of Adolescent and Young Adult Development*, ed. L. Crockett, G. Carlo, and J. Schulenberg (Washington, DC: American Psychological Association, in press).

30. Brown, Jill, Jenny Miller, and Jane Mitchell, "Interrupted Schooling and the Acquisition of Literacy: Experiences of Sudanese Refugees in Victorian Secondary Schools," *Australian Journal of Language and Literacy* 29, no. 2 (2006): 150–162.

31. Dryden-Peterson et al., "Inclusion of Refugees in National Systems." https://inee.org/system/files /resources/Dryden-Peterson_Inclusion%20of%20Refugees_2018_Eng.pdf;Kemiso,A.,"Integration and Identity Among Refugee Children in Ethiopia: Dilemmas of Eritrean and Somali Students in Selected Primary Schools of Addis Ababa" (Unpublished PhD diss., Addis Ababa University, Center for Comparative Education and Policy Studies, 2016); Monaghan. C., "Asking 'Why' and 'How': A Historical Turn in Refugee Education Research," *Journal of Education in Emergencies* 5 no.1 (2019): 35–61.

32. Crul, Maurice, Frans Lelie, Özge Biner, Nihad Bunar, Elif Keskiner, Ifigenia Kokkali, Jens Schneider, and Maha Shuayb, "How the Different Policies and School Systems Affect the Inclusion of Syrian Refugee Children in Sweden, Germany, Greece, Lebanon and Turkey," *Comparative Migration Studies* 7, no. 1 (2019): 1–20.

33. Mendenhall, Mary, Sarah Dryden-Peterson, Lesley Bartlett, Caroline Ndirangu, Rosemary Imonje, Daniel Gakunga, Loise Gichuhi et al., "Quality Education for Refugees in Kenya:

Pedagogy in Urban Nairobi and Kakuma Refugee Camp Settings," *Journal in Education in Emergencies* 1 no.1 (2015): 92–130.

34.   Selee, Andrew, and Jessica Bolter, "Colombia's Open-Door Policy: An Innovative Approach to Displacement?" *International Migration* (2021): 1–19.

35.   Selee and Bolter, "Colombia's Open-Door Policy."

36.   Fresia, Marion, and Andreas Von Känel. "Beyond Space of Exception? Reflections on the Camp Through the Prism of Refugee Schools," *Journal of Refugee Studies* 29, no. 2 (2016): 250–272; Mendenhall et al., "Quality Education for Refugees in Kenya," 92–130; Bellino, Michelle J., "Youth Aspirations in Kakuma Refugee Camp: Education as a Means for Social, Spatial, and Economic (Im)Mobility," *Globalisation, Societies and Education* 16, no. 4 (2018): 541–556.

37.   Mendenhall et al., "Quality Education for Refugees," 92–130.

38.   Reddick, Celia, and Sarah Dryden-Peterson, "Refugee Education and Medium of Instruction: Tensions in Theory, Policy, and Practice," in *Language Issues in Comparative Education II*, ed. Carol Benson and Kimmo Kosonen, 208–233 (Leiden, Netherlands: Brill Sense, 2021)

39.   El-Haj, Abu, Thea Renda, Garene Kaloustian, Sally Wesley Bonet, and Samira Chatila, "Fifi the Punishing Cat and other Civic Lessons from a Lebanese Public Kindergarten School," *Journal of Education in Emergencies* 4, no.1 (2018): 13–44. Chopra, Vidur, and Sarah Dryden-Peterson, "Borders and Belonging: Syrian Youth's Experiences of Displacement in Lebanon," *Globalisation, Societies and Education* (forthcoming).

40.   Kim, Ha Yeon, Lindsay Brown, Carly Tubbs Dolan, Margaret Sheridan, and John Lawrence Aber, "Post-Migration Risks, Developmental Processes, and Learning Among Syrian Refugee Children in Lebanon," *Journal of Applied Developmental Psychology* 69 (2020): 101–142; Dryden-Peterson, Sarah, Elizabeth Adelman, Michelle J. Bellino, and Vidur Chopra, "The Purposes of Refugee Education: Policy and Practice of Including Refugees in National Education Systems," *Sociology of Education* 92, no. 4 (2019): 346–366.

41.   Brun, Cathrine, and Maha Shuayb, "Exceptional and Futureless Humanitarian Education of Syrian Refugees in Lebanon: Prospects for Shifting the Lens," *Refuge: Canada's Journal on Refugees* 36, no. 2 (2020): 20–30.

42.   Zetter, Roger, and Héloïse Ruaudel, "Refugees' Right to Work and Access to Labor Markets—An Assessment" (World Bank Global Program on Forced Displacement [GPFD] and the Global Knowledge Partnership on Migration and Development [KNOMAD] Thematic Working Group on Forced Migration. KNOMAD Working Paper. Washington, DC: World Bank Group, 2016).

43.   Global Refugee Forum Education Co-Sponsorship Alliance, "Global Framework for Refugee Education."

44.   Dryden-Peterson, Sarah, Elizabeth Adelman, Michelle J. Bellino, and Vidur Chopra, "The Purposes of Refugee Education: Policy and Practice of Including Refugees in National Education Systems," *Sociology of Education* 92, no. 4 (2019): 346–366.

45.   Burde et al., "Phase Two Endline Report."

46.   Sirin, Selcuk, Jan L. Plass, Bruce D. Homer, Sinem Vatanartiran, and Tzuchi Tsai, "Digital Game-Based Education for Syrian Refugee Children: Project Hope," *Vulnerable Children and Youth Studies* 13, no. 1 (2018): 7–18.

47.   Murphy, Katie Maeve, Hirokazu Yoshikawa, and Alice J. Wuermli, "Implementation Research for Early Childhood Development Programming in Humanitarian Contexts," *Annals of the New York Academy of Sciences* 1419, no. 1 (2018): 90–101.

48.   Britto, Pia R., Stephen J. Lye, Kerrie Proulx, Aisha K. Yousafzai, Stephen G. Matthews, Tyler Vaivada, Rafael Perez-Escamilla et al., "Nurturing Care: Promoting Early Childhood Development," *Lancet* 389, no. 10064 (2017): 91–102.

49. Bouchane, Kolleen, Hirokazu Yoshikawa, Katie Maeve Murphy, and Joan Lombardi, "Early Childhood Development and Early Learning for Children in Crisis and Conflict," UNESCO, 2018, https://unesdoc.unesco.org/ark:/48223/pf0000266072.

50. Black, Maureen. M., Jere Behrman, Bernadette Daelmanns, Elizabeth L. Prado, Linda Richter, Mark Tomlinson, Angela Trude et al., "Nurturing Care Promotes Human Capital and Mitigates Adversities from Preconception Through Adolescence, *BMJ Global Health* 6, no. 4 (April 2021): https://gh.bmj.com/content/6/4/e004436.

51. Cluver, Lucie D., F. Mark Orkin, Laurence Campeau, Elona Toska, Douglas Webb, Anna Carlqvist, and Lorraine Sherr, "Improving Lives by Accelerating Progress Towards the UN Sustainable Development Goals for Adolescents Living with HIV: A Prospective Cohort Study," *Lancet Child & Adolescent Health* 3, no. 4 (2019): 245–254.

52. Moving Minds Alliance, "Supporting the Youngest Refugees and Their Families," December, 2019, http://movingmindsalliance.org/files/moving-minds-brief-supporting-the-youngest-refugees -GRF2019-web.pdf.

53. Dryden-Peterson et al., "Inclusion of Refugees in National Systems."

54. Burde, Dana, *Schools for Conflict or for Peace in Afghanistan* (New York: Columbia University Press, 2014).

55. Bush, Kenneth David, and Diana Saltarelli, "The Two Faces of Education in Ethnic Conflict: Towards a Peacebuilding Education for Children," *Innocent Insights*, no. 4 (2000): https://www.unicef-irc.org/publications/269-the-two-faces-of-education-in-ethnic-conflict -towards-a-peacebuilding-education-for.html; Burde, *Schools for Conflict or for Peace in Afghanistan.* ; Bellino, Michelle J., *Youth in Postwar Guatemala: Education and Civic Identity in Transition* (New Brunswick, NJ: Rutgers University Press, 2017); Davies, Lynn, "Can Education Interrupt Fragility? Towards the Resilient and Adaptable State," in *Educating Children in Conflict Zones: Research, Policy, and Practice for Systemic Change (a Tribute to Jackie Kirk)*, ed. Karen Mundy and Sarah Dryden-Peterson, 33–48 (New York: Teachers College Press, 2011); Mulimbi, Bethany, and Sarah Dryden-Peterson, " 'There Is Still Peace. There Are No Wars': Prioritizing Unity Over Diversity in Botswana's Social Studies Policies and Practices and the Implications for Positive Peace," *International Journal of Educational Development* 61 (2018): 142–154; Freedman, Sarah Warshauer, Harvey M. Weinstein, Karen Murphy, and Timothy Longman, "Teaching History After Identity-Based Conflicts: The Rwanda Experience," *Comparative Education Review* 52, no. 4 (2008): 663–690.

56. King, Elisabeth, *From Classrooms to Conflict in Rwanda* (Cambridge: Cambridge University Press, 2013).

57. United Nations. "New York Declaration on Refugees and Migrants" (2016), https://www.un .org/en/development/desa/population/migration/generalassembly/docs/globalcompact /A_RES_71_1.pdf, 3.

58. Magee, Arran, and Tejendra Pherali, "Freirean Critical Consciousness in a Refugee Context: A Case Study of Syrian Refugees in Jordan," *Compare: A Journal of Comparative and International Education* 49, no. 2 (2019): 266–282.

59. Bajaj, Monisha, and Lesley Bartlett, "Critical Transnational Curriculum for Immigrant and Refugee Students," *Curriculum Inquiry* 47, no. 1 (2017): 25–35; Bellino, Michelle J., Bibi-Zuhra Faizi, and Nirali Mehta, "Finding a Way Forward: Conceptualizing Sustainability in Afghanistan's Community-Based Schools," *Journal on Education in Emergencies* 2, no. 1 (2016): 11–41; Dryden-Peterson, Sarah, and Celia Reddick, " 'When I Am a President of Guinea': Resettled Refugees Traversing Education in Search of a Future," *European Education* 49, no. 4 (2017): 253–275.

60. Piper, Benjamin, Sarah Dryden-Peterson, Vidur Chopra, Celia Reddick, and Arbogast Oyanga, "Are Refugee Children Learning? Early Grade Literacy in a Refugee Camp in Kenya,"

Journal on Education in Emergencies 5, no. 2 (2020): 71–107; Bellino, Michelle J., and Sarah Dryden-Peterson, "Inclusion and Exclusion Within a Policy of National Integration: Refugee Education in Kenya's Kakuma Refugee Camp," *British Journal of Sociology of Education* 40, no. 2 (2019): 222–238.

61. Reddick, Celia, and Sarah Dryden-Peterson, "Refugee Education and Medium of Instruction: Tensions in Theory, Policy, and Practice," in *Language Issues in Comparative Education II*, ed. Carol Benson and Kimmo Kosonen, 208–233 (Leiden, Netherlands: Brill Sense, 2021).

62. Barac, Raluca, Ellen Bialystok, Dina C. Castro, and Marta Sanchez, "The Cognitive Development of Young Dual Language Learners: A Critical Review," *Early Childhood Research Quarterly* 29, no. 4 (2014): 699–714.

63. Benson, Carol, "The Role of Language of Instruction in Promoting Quality and Equity in Primary Education," in *Lessons in Educational Equity: Successful Approaches to Intractable Problems Around the World*, ed. Jody Heymann and Adèle Cassola, 199–221 (Oxford: Oxford University Press, 2012); Piper et al., "Are Refugee Children Learning?" 71–107; Reddick and Peterson, "Refugee Education and Medium of Instruction," 208–233.

64. Piper et al., "Are Refugee Children Learning?" 71–107.

65. Mariam, Erum, Syeda Sazia Zaman, Sakila Yesmin, Sadaf Huq, and Sarwat Sarah Sarwar, "BRAC Humanitarian Play Lab: When Playing Becomes Healing," *Early Childhood Matters*, June 18, 2019, https://earlychildhoodmatters.online/2019/brac-humanitarian-play-lab-when -playing-becomes-healing/.

66. Macksoud, Mona S., and J. Lawrence Aber, "The War Experiences and Psychosocial Development of Children in Lebanon," *Child Development* 67, no. 1 (1996): 70–88.

67. Waddoups, Yoshikawa, and Strouf, "Developmental Effects of Parent–Child Separation," 387–410.

68. Aber, J. Lawrence, Carly Tubbs Dolan, Ha Yeon Kim, and Lindsay Brown, "Children's Learning and Development in Conflict- and Crisis-Affected Countries: Building a Science for Action," *Development and Psychopathology* 33, no. 2 (2021): 1–16. DOI:10.1017/S0954579420001789.

69. Aber, J. Lawrence, Carly Tubbs, Catalina Torrente, Peter F. Halpin, Brian Johnston, Leighann Starkey, Anjuli Shivshanker et al., "Promoting Children's Learning and Development in Conflict-Affected Countries: Testing Change Process in the Democratic Republic of the Congo," *Development and Psychopathology* 29, no. 1 (2017): 53–67.

70. Tubbs Dolan, Caroline, Ha Yeon Kim, Lindsay Brown, Kalina Gjicali, Serena Borsani, Samir Houshaimi, and J. Lawrence Aber. "Supporting Syrian Refugee Children in Formal Education Systems: A Cluster Randomized Controlled Trial of Non-Formal Remedial and Mindfulness Programs in Lebanon." *American Educational Research Journal* (in press).

71. Egger, Dennis, Edward Miguel, Shana S. Warren, Ashish Shenoy, Elliott Collins, Dean Karlan, Doug Parkerson et al., "Falling Living Standards During the COVID-19 Crisis: Quantitative Evidence from Nine Developing Countries," *Science Advances* 7, no. 6 (2021): eabe0997; Lee, Jean N., Mahreen Mahmud, Jonathan Morduch, Saravana Ravindran, and Abu S. Shonchoy, "Migration, Externalities, and the Diffusion of COVID-19 in South Asia," *Journal of Public Economics* 193 (2021): 104312.

72. Ahmad, Jahanara, Erum Mariam, Bushra Humaira Sadaf, Sarwat Sarah Sarwar, Shaheen Nafisa Siddique, and Syeda Sazia Zaman, "Mental Health and Learning: BRAC's Response in Bangladesh During COVID-19," *Early Childhood Matters*, November 5, 2020, https://earlychildhoodmatters .online/2020/mental-health-and-learning-bracs-response-in-bangladesh-during-covid-19/.

5

THE CONSEQUENCES OF EDUCATION IN EMERGENCY FOR SYRIAN REFUGEE CHILDREN IN TURKEY AND LEBANON

MAHA SHUAYB, MAURICE CRUL, AND FRANS LELIE

Without a doubt, the Syrian refugee crisis has been one of the most devastating crises of the past decade. Over five million people have been displaced to other countries, with Turkey hosting the largest number (3.6 million) and Lebanon hosting the largest percentage of refugees per capita (one in three inhabitants now being refugees).[1] Both countries had to deal with an unprecedented crisis in a short period of time. Among the numerous challenges the two countries faced was how to provide an education to over 50 percent of the refugee population who are of school age. For Lebanon, this meant that the public school system had to triple its capacity to absorb the five hundred thousand Syrian school-age children, as the number of enrolled children in public schools prior to the Syrian crisis was two hundred thousand.[2] As for Turkey, the educational system had to absorb over one million new students on top of the 13.5 million students already attending school. Other countries in the region affected by the Syrian crisis are Jordan, Iraq, and Egypt that host 660,000; 244,000; and 130,000 refugees, respectively.[3] In comparison, European countries per capita host far fewer Syrian refugees. However, most research so far has been directed to the European case rather than to Syria's neighboring countries.

While research on the education of refugee children proliferated in the last eight years, comparative research has only recently begun to emerge. However, there still is a paucity of comparative research examining policies and practices in countries that adopted different modalities of education for refugee children (see chapter 4).[4] An overview of the education provisions for refugee children in both the Global North and South yields two different modalities. The first is the so-called education in emergency, where education is part of a larger humanitarian response in host countries in the Global South. These countries are struggling economically and offer temporary settlement for refugees, either in camps or aggregations. Education in emergency is heavily dominated by the humanitarian rationale. Whereas the perspective of education should be long-term and forward-looking, the humanitarian outlook is embedded in the present and, hence, short-term. Humanitarian education is also focused on return, resulting in a myriad of debates around the curriculum that should be taught to refugees, the language of instructions, and certification.[5] In contrast to the humanitarian model mainly present in the Global South, a different, long-term approach is present mainly in the Global North where refugees are resettled either permanently or for a period of time specified by the state's asylum procedures. The policies and practices there are not implemented by humanitarian agencies but by the state. Refugees are, to different degrees, integrated into the national education systems. A route to higher education and employment is also built into this system, whereas in the humanitarian model, refugees rarely complete upper secondary education and are often denied the right to work in many professional jobs, making the pay-off of education more uncertain and precarious.

Analyzing these two main approaches to the education of refugee children (humanitarian temporary approaches versus long-term state approaches) can help us unpack the conditions and factors that might affect the enrollment and attainment of refugee children and further understand the impact on education outcomes of emergency and humanitarian relief provisions and the temporary legal status of the refugee families. In this chapter, we compare the educational provisions for refugees in Lebanon and Turkey. Lebanon has clearly adopted a humanitarian model of education, while Turkey, after an initial humanitarian approach, has now shifted to a longer-term and integrative paradigm of education.

Over the past nine years, the educational response and provision to the crisis in Turkey have shifted from segregation to obligatory integration in the regular school system. At the beginning of the Syrian crisis, the Syrian opposition coalition took control over the education of Syrian refugees in Turkey. Temporary education centers (TECs) run by Syrian educators and NGOs were launched. The Syrian national curriculum was adapted (mainly to remove political and religious connotations celebrating the Baath regime). Yet, as the crisis became protracted, the Turkish government took more and more control of the education response, aiming to close down all TECs and integrate children into the Turkish public schools. Currently, over 630,000 Syrian children are enrolled in public education in Turkey.[6] The education response in Turkey is gradually shifting from an emergency approach to one that is more long-term.

In contrast, Lebanon kept to its initial segregationist approach regarding the education of Syrian refugee children. The government took the lead on the response and formed a special department at the Lebanese Ministry of Education and Higher Education (MEHE). The current enrollment rate among Syrian refugee children in compulsory school age is around 60 percent. However, they study in segregated afternoon shifts designed particularly for Syrian refugees. These shifts are on average only four hours per day, about half a normal school day.

Our chapter aims to examine the effect of temporary educational provisions and the vulnerable legal and socio-economic status of refugee families on the schooling experience of Syrian refugee children in Lebanon and Turkey. The data we present comes from Arabic-speaking refugee children enrolled in formal schools in middle school (grades 7 and 8). We will describe their well-being, development, and progress in school. We decided to focus on this school-age due to the very low enrollment rates in Lebanon and Turkey in upper secondary school.

METHODOLOGY

The study follows a mixed-method research design and, as such, has a qualitative component as well as a quantitative one. Mixed-methods is a valuable approach because it offers different perspectives on the policy environment and students' education experiences. To make sure the data are triangulated, data were collected not only from students but also from parents, teachers, school principals, and other policy actors (actors from the MEHE and UN). We administered a survey to students in school. Quantitative data (student survey results) were collected through paper questionnaires which were completed face to face. Following data entry, the results were analyzed using Stata statistical analysis software.

Convenience sampling was used for this study. In Lebanon, this approach was necessary because of a lack of information regarding the target populations (Lebanese and Syrian students). Convenience sampling was also necessary because access to schools was determined by the Lebanese MEHE, which provided us with a list of public schools that included a large number of Syrian students. To reduce sampling bias, we collected data from all five governorates, from urban and rural areas, and from boys and girls. Convenience sampling does not allow us to make generalizations about our target populations. The quantitative results reported here are indicative and offer valuable insights into the policy environment and education experiences of Syrian students in Lebanese public schools. In total, we interviewed 418 students, of which 247 were displaced.

Similarly, convenient sampling was also followed in Turkey. We selected the two cities with the largest concentration of Syrian refugees: Istanbul and Ghazi Aintab. The sample included both public schools and TECs. In Turkey, we interviewed 710 displaced students and 211 nationals across two districts. In total, 921 students participated in the survey. Students were in grade levels 7 and 8, attended either public school or TECs, with a relatively equal number of boys and girls being surveyed.

POLICY FRAMEWORK OF TEMPORARY EMERGENCY EDUCATION AND "GUEST" STATUS IN TURKEY AND LEBANON

Lebanon has the largest concentration of refugees per capita and the fourth largest refugee population in the world.[7] Lebanon has been hosting refugees ever since it gained independence in 1943. At that time, Lebanon received over three hundred thousand Palestinian refugees who exiled Palestine upon the creation of the State of Israel and the subsequent war between Arab states and Israel.

Lebanon is not a signatory of the 1951 Convention Relating to the Status of Refugees nor its 1967 Protocol and thus does not consider itself as an asylum country nor a final destination for refugees. The government of Lebanon generally advocates the repatriation and "safe and dignified return" of Syrian refugees as soon as possible. However, following the Syrian crisis, efforts were made toward providing humanitarian aid and basic support, increasing the employability of refugees, and granting them access to education that is certified in Lebanon and other countries.[8] There is no route to permanent residency/citizenship for Syrian refugees in Lebanon. This means that Syrian refugees become permanent "guests." The legal status has an effect on the mobility of refugees and consequently on access to assistance and aid opportunities. For not having evidence of legal status, persons can be arrested.[9] Although the Lebanese Labor Code stipulates that foreign workers require a work permit within ten days of their entry in return for social security, the right to a minimum wage, and security protection, these rights mainly exist on paper. Currently, legal provisions allow Syrians to work in agriculture, construction, and cleaning only.[10] The policies in place for refugee families in Lebanon create vulnerability at different levels.

A main feature of the response to the Syrian crisis in Lebanon is the strong presence of UN humanitarian agencies that are working closely with the different ministries and governments. In 2012–2013, MEHE introduced the second-shift classes, strictly reserved for non-Lebanese students. This afternoon shift is specifically tailored to nonnational students.[11] Like for Lebanese students, English and French are used as second languages and languages of instruction, notably for math and sciences [12]. However, unlike Lebanon, Syria did not teach in French and English. This poses an extra challenge to the Syrian students. Second shifts rely on international aid. High numbers of contractual teachers (some of who were inexperienced or underqualified) were assigned to classrooms, threatening the quality of education even more.[13] Second-shift schools open when there is a minimum of twenty students in the classroom, which is a condition that renders the continuity of this program questionable, particularly because in higher grade levels, dropout rates are especially high among Syrian refugees.[14] Children over the age of fifteen have to help support the family income. Across the various reports, the references to secondary and higher education are scarce. [15] Unsurprisingly, but nonetheless dramatic, less than 4 percent are enrolled in upper-secondary school.[16] In sum, refugee children are segregated and are taught in shorter afternoon classes, often led by inexperienced and or overburdened teachers. Following the COVID 19 crisis, while the vast majority of children in Lebanon struggled with access to quality education, refugee children, in particular, had very limited access to school. In the academic year 2019–2020, limited provisions for distance learning were made for Syrian children enrolled in public school shifts.[17]

Unlike Lebanon, Turkey is a party to the 1951 Refugee Convention and 1967 Protocol.[18] Turkey has retained an "open-door" policy since the beginning of the Syrian crisis. The Turkish authorities welcomed the first Syrian refugee convoy in 2011 and referred to them as their "Syrian guests" for a long time. The number of registered Syrians in the country reached 3,642,738 by early

2019, which is 4.4 percent of the total population. On October 22, 2014, Turkey adopted the Temporary Protection Regulation, which determines the rights and obligations along with procedures for those who are granted temporary protection in Turkey.[19]

Turkey is also classified as an upper-middle-income country.[20] Turkey's economic and social development since 2000 has been remarkable. Between 2002 and 2015, Turkey urbanized intensely, halved the level of poverty, and greatly extended access to public services.[21] The gross national income per capita was U.S. $27,640 in 2017.[22]

The Turkish education system is under the administration and control of the Ministry of National Education. Education is obligatory from ages six to fourteen and free in public schools. The vast majority of children (98 percent) attend public schools.[23] Before the first Syrian refugees arrived in Turkey, a "regulation for foreign students" was issued in 2010. The government regulation provided some general rights for foreigners in terms of registration, support for schooling, and so on. International protection status holders have access to many rights and are entitled to temporary protection. Children who are considered to be under protection can enroll in the schools closest to their residence. In 2011, Syrians were welcomed as temporary "guests" expected to return home once the situation in Syria was stabilized. Syrians were permitted to operate their own educational facilities. The ministry of education (MoE) also warranted private entrepreneurs to open schools and even allocated some schools to give education to refugee children after local students were finished for the day. Apart from local public schools, Turkey's local government authorities allowed people to rent private places or municipal properties in which to do their schooling. From 2014, Syrians were able to open their own schools, known as TECs. The local municipalities and governors allocated spaces for the refugees' education. The curriculum for Syrian refugee students was first developed by UN agencies and Syrians promoting the education units in the camps and TECs in the early time of their arrival.[24] The Syrian teachers in TECs were given flexibility in finalizing the curriculum and related materials that students were previously taught with in Syria.

A government regulation of 2014 ordered local agencies of the MoE to take administrative control of all TECs and governorships in consultation with the MoE. Turkish principals and teachers were appointed to the schools, and each school was administered by one Syrian and one Turkish director. Syrian teachers were employed as "voluntary workers" but in effect paid by the local MoE. In 2015, a policy shift came. The MoE devised a strategic program whereby the

TECs would be closed gradually in the following three years (2016 onward), and Syrian refugee students would transfer to the local public schools. All the TECs were closed by the end of 2021. Since the beginning of the 2016–2017 education year, the TECs have not taken on any new registrations and have directed the Syrian refugee students to attend the public schools

In addition to TECs, there are Imam-Hatip schools, which are a type of vocational school mainly focusing on religious training for Imams. Many conservative families, including Syrians, prefer to send their children to these institutions because they feel that religious teaching is very important and that registering their children in such schools will allow them to retain their own culture. They are also often chosen because the curriculum is taught in Arabic.

THE EFFECTS OF EMERGENCY RELIEF ON THE SCHOOL CAREERS AND THE SOCIO-ECONOMIC SITUATION OF REFUGEE CHILDREN

The word *emergency* tends to suggest an urgent need for assistance or relief that is temporary in nature. Today's refugee emergencies mean that displaced families come to live in very precarious living conditions for years on end (see chapter 4). Often the place where people are staying (housing) but also the children's schooling arrangements—when in place—are supposed to be temporary. In fact, they are becoming a permanent new normal for too many refugees. The stigma of being labeled a refugee seems to justify these temporary and often inadequate arrangements. People are only entitled to basic support (food, shelter, provisional education for the children) because of the emergency situation that forced them to leave their normal life behind. The label "refugee" has created a new category of people who do not have the same rights as other citizens. In Turkey and in Lebanon, this becomes clear when we look at the legal status of the Syrian refugees. Basically, they are considered "guests" without any formal legal status. There is significant research on the legal consequences of such guest status. Next, we turn our focus to the practical consequences of the guest status in terms of housing, poverty, and access to school.

We will make use of the data from a unique longitudinal student survey collected among students of grade 7 and grade 8 in schools in Lebanon and Turkey, both countries harboring hundreds of thousands of refugee children.

TABLE 5.1 Syrian refugee children in Lebanese afternoon classes (AC) and in Turkish temporary education centers (TEC): missed school years in country of birth (Syria)

	1 year	2 years	3 years or more
Turkey (TEC)	19%	12%	11%
Lebanon (AC)	20%	16%	5%

Source: A longitudinal survey of the education experience of refugees in Lebanon, Turkey, and Australia (wave 1). Spencer Foundation. Spencer Foundation.

TABLE 5.2 Syrian refugee children in Lebanese afternoon classes (AC) and in Turkish temporary education centers (TECs): missed school years in country of residence (Lebanon or Turkey)

	1 year	2 years	3 years or more
Turkey (TEC)	20%	9%	6%
Lebanon (AC)	34%	20%	8%

Source: A longitudinal survey of the education experience of refugees in Lebanon, Turkey, and Australia (wave 1). Spencer Foundation.

The survey is unique in that it also captures the experiences of those children who attend or attended temporary educational services.

Apart from questions about their experiences in the classroom, we asked about their educational pathways from when they were forced to leave regular education in Syria. Table 5.1 shows how many years of schooling children in the Turkish TEC and the Lebanese afternoon classes had already missed in Syria. Table 5.2 shows missed years of schooling in their present country of residence.

As table 5.1 shows, about half of the children missed one or more years of schooling in Syria. Of those who missed a year or more when still in Syria, three quarters gave displacement as one of the reasons for not attending school. About a quarter reported that their own school in Syria was closed due to the war, and about a quarter reported that it was no longer safe to go to school (more answers possible). It is important to realize that even before becoming a refugee outside Syria, many children were already displaced and missed school years in their own country.

Table 5.2 shows that many students arriving safely in Turkey or Lebanon after fleeing Syria have had difficulties entering education again. In Lebanon, about half of the students again lost one or more years of schooling. In Lebanon, students could not attend school because there was not yet or no opportunity to go to school. Ten percent of these children missed the right documents to go to school, and 7 percent were constantly on the move. Lack of financial resources and safety concerns were also mentioned.

If we combine the outcomes for tables 5.1 and 5.2 for the children in Lebanon, only a small minority (27 percent) did not miss any years of school. About a quarter of the children in total missed three years or more. In Turkey, this is true for one in five children. These survey data show that the globally acknowledged right to education for all children of compulsory school age, including refugee children, has been violated both in their country of birth and in the present countries of residence. This, of course, means that these children lost valuable years of education and have fallen behind with their peers in the country of residence. This will mean, among other things, that they often are older than peers attending the same grade. But one can also imagine that both the experience of not being in school for one or more years and switching school systems and curriculum comes at a high socio-emotional cost and has untold effects on their cognitive development. On top of this, a quarter of the children were not with their father during the displacement journey, which was causing additional stress for the children and the family. No less than 6 percent of the children actually experienced the death of their father or mother in Syria due to the war. For another 10 percent of the children, their father is not living with them because he is either still in Syria or living in another country or city.

One of the reasons for the disrupted school careers has been the precarious nature of housing for refugee families and their economic insecurity. At the time of the survey, the majority of the children were living in an apartment after moving out of the refugee camps. However, often they were sharing apartments with other families. In the case of the children in Turkey, for instance, of those living in a three-room apartment, 26 percent have to share this with five people, 29 percent with six people, and 34 percent even with seven or more people. In Lebanon, this is true for 19 percent, 13 percent, and 30 percent, respectively. In Lebanon, half of the students said that almost everybody in their area had been displaced, which means that stress, problems, and poverty are concentrated in their neighborhoods.

In Turkey, the largest group lived already for three years in Turkey, and 35 percent of these children moved houses at least three times. In Lebanon, most of the refugee children lived there for six or seven years. They also had to move a lot: more than half of this group moved three times or more because they could no longer afford their housing, the landlord asked them to leave, or the apartment was too small or in too bad a condition.

Many refugee families suffer from economic hardship. Eighteen percent of the families reported "always" struggling to pay the bills, and 21 percent reported "often" having to struggle. In Lebanon, the main source of income for the families is UN agencies or other NGOs. The families depending on said aid reported that 52 percent "always or often" struggle to pay the bills. In Turkey, for about a quarter of the families, the host government is the main financial provider. In this case, 45 percent "always or often" struggle to pay the bills. These figures only give a rough indication, they are based on the children's observations, but we can be certain that the limited aid given by the UN, NGOs, and government agencies still results in considerable financial problems in the families. In both countries, families have to resort to child labor to make ends meet. In Turkey, of the children in eighth grade, 23 percent were working during the academic year; in Lebanon, 11 percent of the children in seventh grade. Of those in Turkey who worked (beyond the summer), two-thirds reported having missed one or more years of schooling because they had to work.

In combination, these factors (poverty, poor quality and overcrowded housing, neighborhoods with concentrated problems, and missed school years) impact the children's socio-emotional well-being and their ability to concentrate on their schooling.

THE EFFECTS OF HUMANITARIAN EDUCATION ON THE SOCIO-EMOTIONAL WELLBEING OF REFUGEE CHILDREN

The previous section describes the circumstances of the Syrian refugee children flowing from the precarious situation of their families, beginning with their displacement within Syria. Upon their settlement, the condition of the refugee children is, in most cases, much more stable than during their displacement

TABLE 5.3 Syrian refugee children in Lebanese afternoon classes and in Turkish temporary education classes: "I get a lot of headaches, stomach-aches or sickness."

	Not true	Somewhat true	Very true
Turkey (TEC)	17%	35%	48%
Lebanon (AC)	12%	36%	52%

Source: A longitudinal survey of the education experience of refugees in Lebanon, Turkey, and Australia (wave 1). Spencer Foundation.

TABLE 5.4 Syrian refugee children in Lebanese afternoon classes and in Turkish temporary education classes: "When I get very angry, I usually lose my temper."

	Not true	Somewhat true	Very true
Turkey (TEC)	41%	42%	18%
Lebanon (AC)	44%	38%	18%

Source: A longitudinal survey of the education experience of refugees in Lebanon, Turkey, and Australia (wave 1). Spencer Foundation.

journey. But at the same time, we found them and their families endeavoring to cope with overcrowded and poor-quality housing, poverty, and insecurity. In this section, we will focus on how this impacts their socio-emotional and physical well-being in the classroom.

We asked them different questions regarding their physical and socio-emotional well-being. In table 5.3, we see the answers to the question: "I get a lot of headaches, stomach-aches or sickness."

About half of the students suffer from these physical complaints that typically signal a high stress level. Since these pupils are in classes only with other refugee children, we also have to consider the effect of so many pupils having these symptoms in the same class.

Another important indicator for the problematic situation is how students manage their stress levels. We measured this with the following statement: "When I get very angry, I usually lose my temper."

Looking at the outcomes in table 5.4, we should consider what it means for the educational process if such a large proportion of the children self-identify

TABLE 5.5 Syrian refugee children in Lebanese afternoon classes and in Turkish temporary education classes: "I am constantly fidgeting or squirming."

	Not true	Somewhat true	Very true
Turkey (TEC)	44%	37%	20%
Lebanon (AC)	56%	31%	13%

Source: A longitudinal survey of the education experience of refugees in Lebanon, Turkey, and Australia (wave 1). Spencer Foundation.

TABLE 5.6 Syrian refugee children in Lebanese afternoon classes and in Turkish temporary education classes: "I am often unhappy, depressed, or tearful."

	Not true	Somewhat true	Very true
Turkey (TEC)	38%	43%	19%
Lebanon (AC)	31%	44%	25%

Source: A longitudinal survey of the education experience of refugees in Lebanon, Turkey, and Australia (wave 1). Spencer Foundation.

as a person to lose their temper. The potential disruption this creates in class is hard to underestimate.

Other children will cope by directing the stress inward and start showing nervous behavior. We measure this with the statement: "I am constantly fidgeting or squirming" (table 5.5).

We further asked the students to assess their psychological well-being with a rather straightforward statement: "I am often unhappy, depressed, or tearful." The answers in table 5.6 show the magnitude of the psychological distress these refugee children are experiencing.

How does all this affect their schoolwork? We asked to answer the following statement: "I get distracted easily and find it difficult to concentrate" (table 5.7).

The emergency context of education as provided in the afternoon classes in a second shift in Lebanon and in the temporary education centers in Turkey puts a big toll on the children. It also burdens the teachers who not only have to manage over-crowed classes in Lebanon—many after a day of teaching their regular class—but they have to work with traumatized children who are

TABLE 5.7 Syrian refugee children in Lebanese afternoon classes and in Turkish temporary education classes: "I get distracted easily and find it difficult to concentrate."

	Not true	Somewhat true	Very true
Turkey (TEC)	47%	36%	17%
Lebanon (AC)	43%	40%	17%

Source: A longitudinal survey of the education experience of refugees in Lebanon, Turkey, and Australia (wave 1). Spencer Foundation.

TABLE 5.8 Syrian refugee children in Lebanese afternoon classes and in Turkish temporary education classes: "teacher's disciplining is mostly controlling and punitive (shouting, detention, use of harsh language)"

	Strongly agree	Agree	Neutral	Disagree	Strongly disagree
Turkey (TEC)	9%	14%	16%	28%	33%
Lebanon (AC)	13%	17%	23%	23%	24%

Source: A longitudinal survey of the education experience of refugees in Lebanon, Turkey, and Australia (wave 1). Spencer Foundation.

confronting multiple problems. Many of the children experienced teachers as punitive. When we asked the pupils whether their teacher's way of keeping order is mostly controlling and punitive (shouting, detention, and use of harsh language), a third of the children in the Lebanese afternoon classes agreed or strongly agreed with this statement (table 5.8).

At the same time, school is a real refuge for the children. In schools, children find a respite from overcrowded homes, the hardship of poverty, the insecurity and the stress flowing from the ongoing war in Syria, and the very precarious refugee status many families face. Indeed, over 90 percent of the children say they like going to school (table 5.9). These are figures seldom seen in regular schools.

Also, the children's ambitions are very high, especially given the bleak outlook of their situation. In Lebanon, no less than 91 percent said they aspire to go to university, whereas in Turkey, this percentage is 75. These refugee

TABLE 5.9 Syrian refugee children in Lebanese afternoon classes and in Turkish temporary education classes: "I like going to school."

	Strongly agree	agree	Neutral	Disagree	Strongly disagree
Turkey (TEC)	68%	22%	7%	2%	1%
Lebanon (AC)	70%	26%	4%	0%	1%

Source: A longitudinal survey of the education experience of refugees in Lebanon, Turkey, and Australia (wave 1). Spencer Foundation.

TABLE 5.10 Syrian refugee children in Lebanese afternoon classes and in Turkish temporary education classes: "I am often unhappy, depressed or tearful" vs. academic performances

	Academic performance				
Student response	Very good	Good	Fair	Poor	Very poor
Not true	47%	42%	10%	1%	0%
Somewhat true	38%	43%	16%	2%	1%
Certainly true	38%	35%	19%	5%	4%

Source: A longitudinal survey of the education experience of refugees in Lebanon, Turkey, and Australia (wave 1). Spencer Foundation.

children are still highly invested in education, even under the harsh circumstances they face.

The survey contains a self-reported indication of the overall academic performances of the students. We have analyzed the correlations for four different types of socio-emotional indicators and self-reported academic performance. The results in table 5.10 show a strong correlation between academic performance and feeling more *or* less "unhappy, depressed and tearful" (P<0.005).

For the indicator "I get distracted easily and find it difficult to concentrate" (table 5.11), we also find a strong correlation (P<0.001) with the self-reported academic performances.

For the indicator "I get a lot of headaches, stomachaches, or sickness," we also find a correlation, but less strong (P<0.05), with self-reported academic performances as shown in table 5.12.

TABLE 5.11 Syrian refugee children in Lebanese afternoon classes and the Turkish temporary education classes: "I get distracted easily and find it difficult to concentrate" vs. academic performances

Student response	Academic performance				
	Very good	Good	Fair	Poor	Very poor
Not true	54%	35%	10%	0%	1%
Somewhat true	31%	46%	20%	3%	0%
Certainly true	32%	40%	15%	8%	5%

Source: A longitudinal survey of the education experience of refugees in Lebanon, Turkey, and Australia (wave 1). Spencer Foundation.

TABLE 5.12 Syrian refugee children in Lebanese afternoon classes and the Turkish temporary education classes: "I get a lot of headaches, stomachaches, or sickness" vs. academic performances

Student response	Academic performance				
	Very good	Good	Fair	Poor	Very poor
Not true	46%	38%	15%	1%	0%
Somewhat true	36%	44%	14%	3%	3%
Certainly true	39%	40%	15%	6%	0%

Source: A longitudinal survey of the education experience of refugees in Lebanon, Turkey, and Australia (wave 1). Spencer Foundation.

We also find a correlation in table 5.13 between yet another socio-economic indicator, "anger management," and self-reported academic performances ($P<0.05$).

We have to keep in mind that these are self-reported academic performance data, but there seems to be an obvious consistency in terms of the correlation between different socio-emotional indicators and self-reported academic performance, with difficulties in concentration and depression seeming to be powerful indicators. It is important to consider that many of these children at the time of the survey had been on average four years or even longer in the host country. After such a period of time, one would hope that a stable and safe environment would have been established for the children. The findings, however, show that this is not at all the case for a considerable group of children.

TABLE 5.13 Syrian refugee children in Lebanese afternoon classes and the Turkish temporary education classes: "When I get very angry, I usually lose my temper" vs. academic performances

	Academic performance				
Student response	Very good	Good	Fair	Poor	Very poor
Not true	48%	37%	13%	2%	0%
Somewhat true	36%	42%	19%	2%	1%
Certainly true	38%	45%	10%	4%	3%

Source: A longitudinal survey of the education experience of refugees in Lebanon, Turkey, and Australia (wave 1). Spencer Foundation.

A PLEA FOR A HOLISTIC AND SUSTAINABLE APPROACH

We have endeavored to describe how emergency relief and temporary emergency education influences compulsory school–aged refugee children, their living conditions, their access to education, and their chances to be successful in school. In contrast to the globally acknowledged rights of all children to education, equal to children who are citizens, new types of educational arrangements are created based on the idea of temporality. The opportunities of these children to learn will affect their lives moving forward. To address their education as a "temporary emergency" resulted in a total lack of access to education for some, while the more fortunate students received limited hours of education and/or attended education separate from peers who are citizens of the host country. This framework, which we label "Temporary Humanitarian Education," has become the "normal" schooling regime for many refugee children for years on end. The main justification of humanitarian education is that this arrangement is the best at offer, given the emergency situation. Step by step, this type of provision is normalized by governments, NGOs, and donors and is thus becoming accepted as the standard education paradigm for refugee children in many countries. The chapter highlights the negative consequences of this policy.

In the first part of the chapter, we explained how government policies and relief organizations together have built a framework that allows refugee children to be treated differently than children who are nationals. In both Lebanon and Turkey, the government has used the large numbers of refugee children, their supposedly temporary stay, and the potential negative impact on the education of national students to exclude them from regular education. More research is needed to assess the consequences of these so-called temporary regimes. Our research has identified a number of consequences based on the policy documents and survey data: (1) the majority of children have lost one or more years of schooling; (2) a large proportion of children have to work instead of going to school or have to work while going to school; (3) many children do not receive the same number of hours of schooling and the same quality of schooling (as a result of overburdened teachers and disturbances in over-crowded classes) compared to children who are nationals; (4) second language provisions in these temporary emergency relief education arrangements are often absent; (5) temporary educational arrangements and vulnerable legal sta-tus often hinder access to upper secondary education and tertiary education. This is because of financial problems and poor education outcomes, especially related to socio-emotional problems and second language issues; (6) the fragil-ity of the legal status, the socio-economic position of the family, and the unse-cure and overcrowded living conditions of refugee families result in a range of socio-emotional problems that negatively impact their schooling outcomes.

Based on our findings, we constructed the humanitarian education model (see figure 5.1) that describes these consequences. The model shows how var-ious factors combined produce the negative outcomes we find for the school children. We constructed the model to show the complexity of all the processes at work. Policy makers and educators must be aware that at the very core of all these negative loops shown, there is the choice of temporality in the provisions.

One of the major issues we want to put forward is that children experience a combination of different negative factors. Many children, having lost years of schooling, find it difficult to integrate directly into education again after being absent from school for long periods of time. In such a context, mean-ingfully addressing their needs is almost impossible. Their classes, we found, are often overcrowded and understaffed. Classroom teaching is often inter-rupted because students act out in class and have difficulties concentrating. Some pupils are older than their peers; thus, they have struggles to fit into the classroom. Moreover, because they are older, they are more often pressed to do paid work and are more likely to miss classes. Add to that, the overcrowded living conditions that make doing homework difficult, which means that many children come unprepared for their classes. Due to the second-language issues, children are enrolled in separate classes or not getting enough support from their teachers to learn the new language. Moreover, teachers can have problems communicating with parents.

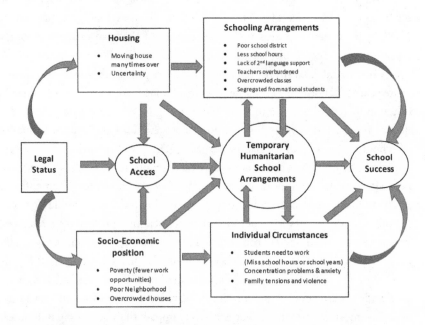

FIGURE 5.1 Humanitarian education model.

Source: Chart created by Maha Shuayb and Mohammad Hammoud.

The fact that these problems cluster and are intertwined is probably the most important characteristic of humanitarian education. The data also point to ways this problematic knot can be unraveled. To address the shortcomings and the challenges of providing education in a humanitarian setting, a long-term vision of education policies and programs is needed. An education that is without a future and is disconnected from other vital rights for refugees risks collapsing into a literacy program.[25] While there is an increasing shift to enroll refugee children into the public educational system of the host state, several conditions need to be met in order to have a smooth and supportive transition. A preparatory program that can support children, many of who might have been out of school for months or years, is needed. Removing all legal barriers preventing the access of refugees to education is needed, including removing document and residency restrictions.[26] Providing language support is key if the language of instructions in schools is different from the native language of the refugees. Adapting the curriculum to tackle acculturation is also critical, especially as many national curricular, such as in the case of Lebanon and Turkey, have strong nationalistic goals that may not allow for diversity.

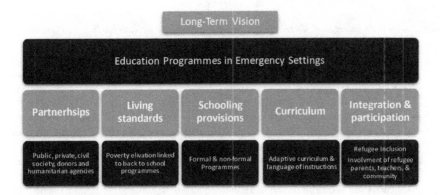

FIGURE 5.2 The protracted reality of Syrian children in Lebanon.

Source: Shuayb M., and M. Hammoud, "The Protracted Reality of Syrian Children in Lebanon: Why Go to School with No Prospects?" Center for Lebanese Studies, 2021, https://lebanesestudies.com/the -protracted-reality-of-syrian-children-in-lebanon-why-go-to-school-with-no-prospects/.

Moreover, participation of the refugee community, including parents and students, is essential for retention and attainment of children. Poverty remains another key challenge that is undermining any back-to-school campaign and retention in education. Thus, any programs aimed at enrolling in and access to education need to be accompanied by poverty alleviation programs. Finally, the large scale of many of the refugee crises necessitates the collaboration and partnerships of various sectors, including the public, private, and civil society. Figure 5.2 summarizes the recommendations presented above.

Only when a holistic approach is taken, which involves different aspects, will it lead to effective improvements for the children. This requires a coordinated effort of school authorities, donors, national policy makers, politicians, and the refugee families themselves. The Turkish government has shown the political courage to leave the path of humanitarian education and move toward integrating the Syrian refugee children in regular education. This has been a major development for refugee children in Turkey. However, the Turkish case also shows that if this is not coupled with additional support measures regarding second-language learning, additional support staff, and improving the socio-economic situation of the families, the educational situation of the children will remain vulnerable. A holistic and sustainable approach will have positive consequences for the learning and the flourishing of refugee children.

NOTES

1. "Syria Emergency," United Nations High Commissioner for Refugees, accessed October 13, 2021, https://www.unhcr.org/uk/syria-emergency.html.

2. "Statistical Report for the Academic School Year 2018–2019, Centre for Educational Research and Development, accessed October 13, 2021, https://www.crdp.org/sites/default/files/2021-03 /Stat_Nashra_Inside_2019_V_13_0.pdf.

3. United Nations High Commissioner for Refugees, "Syria Emergency."

4. For exceptions, see Crul, M., F. Lelie, Ö. Biner, N. Bunar, E. Keskiner, I. Kokkali, J. Schneider, and M. Shuayb, "How the Different Policies and School Systems Affect the Inclusion of Syrian Refugee Children in Sweden, Germany, Greece, Lebanon and Turkey." *Comparative Migration Studies*, 7 (2019): 1–20, https://doi.org/10.1186/s40878-018-0110-6;Crul, M., F. Lelie, E. Keskiner, J. Schneider, and Ö. Biner, "Lost in Transit: Education for Refugee Children in Sweden, Germany and Turkey," in *On Humanitarianism and Mass Migration*, ed. M. Sánchez Sorondo and Marcelo M. Suárez-Orozco, 268–291 (Los Angeles: University of California Press, 2019).

5. Shuayb, M., and C. Brun, "Exceptional and Futureless Humanitarian Education of Syrian Refugees in Lebanon: Prospects for Shifting the Lens," *Refuge: Canada's Journal on Refugees* 36, no. 2 (2020): 20–30.

6. "Turkey: Humanitarian Situation Report #31," UNICEF, January–March, 2019, https://www .unicef.org/turkey/media/7091/file/UNICEF%20Turkey%20Humanitarian%20Situation%20 Report%20-%20Jan-March%202019.pdf.

7. "Vulnerability Assessment of Syrian Refugees in Lebanon," United Nations High Commissioner for Refugees, December 2018. https://www.unhcr.org/lb/wp-content/uploads/sites/16 /2018/12/VASyR-2018.pdf.

8. Janmyr, Maja, "UNHCR and the Syrian Refugee Response: Negotiating Status and Registration in Lebanon," *International Journal of Human Rights* 22, no. 3 (2018): 393–419.

9. Aranki, Dalia, and Olivia Kalis, "Limited Legal Status for Refugees from Syria in Lebanon," *Forced Migration Review* 47 (2014).

10. Khater, Le Bau, "Labour Policy and Practice," *Peace Building in Lebanon* 16, no. 4 (2017).

11. Abla, Z., and M. Al-Masri, "Better Together: The Impact of the Schooling System of Lebanese and Syrian Displaced Pupils on Social Stability," accessed July 31, 2016 file:///C:/Users /2shayr69/Downloads/Lebanon_LebaneseSyrianSchooling_EN_2016. pdf.

12. Refugee, Regional, and Resilience Plan, "3RP Regional Progress Report," 2015; "2014 Syria Regional Response Plan RRP6," United Nations High Commissioner for Refugees, January–December 2014, https://www.unhcr.org/uk/partners/donors/52b170e49/2014-syria-regional -response-plan-rrp6-january-december-2014.html.

13. Janmyr, "UNHCR and the Syrian Refugee Response," 393–419.

14. Carlier, W., *The Widening Educational Gap for Syrian Refugee Children* (Amsterdam: Kids Rights, 2018), https://reliefweb.int/sites/reliefweb.int/files/resources/Background%20Report%202018%20 -%20The%20Widening%20Educational%20Gap%20for%20Syrian%20Refugee%20Children _0.pdf.

15. *Reaching All Children with Education: RACE I*, Ministry of Education and Higher Education (MEHE), 2014; "RACE II Fact Sheet," Ministry of Education and Higher Education (MEHE), September 2019, http://racepmulebanon.com/images/RACE-PMU-Fact-Sheet-September-2019 .pdf; Janmyr, "UNHCR and the Syrian Refugee Response," 393–419.

16. "The Obstacle Course: Barriers to Education for Syrian Refugee Children in Lebanon," Norwegian Refugee Council, June 30, 2020, https://www.nrc.no/resources/reports/the-obstacle-course -barriers-to-education-for-syrian-refugee-children-in-lebanon/.

17.   Abou Moghli, M., and M. Shuayb, "Education Under Covid-19 Lockdown: Reflections from Teachers, Students & Parents," Centre for Lebanese Studies, July 19, 2020, https://lebanesestudies.com/education-under-covid-19-lockdown-reflections-from-teachers-students-parents.

18.   "Refugees and Asylum Seekers in Turkey," UNHCR Turkey, accessed October 11, 2020, https://www.unhcr.org/tr/en/refugees-and-asylum-seekers-in-turkey.

19.   UNHCR Turkey, "Refugees and Asylum Seekers in Turkey."

20.   "Turkey Overview," World Bank, 2020, last updated October 12, 2021, https://www.worldbank.org/en/country/turkey/overview.

21.   "Lebanon Overview," World Bank, 2020, last updated April 12, 2021, https://www.worldbank.org/en/country/lebanon/overview.

22.   World Bank, "Lebanon Overview."

23.   Nimer, M. "Towards an Inclusive Education for Refugees: A comparative longitudinal study, 2018–2020." Education Policy Analysis in Turkey, Centre for Lebanese Studies, 2021.

24.   Culbertson, S., and Louay Constant, "Education of Syrian Refugee Children: Managing the Crisis in Turkey, Lebanon, and Jordan," RAND Corporation, 2015, https://www.rand.org/pubs/research_reports/RR859.html.

25.   Shuayb, Maha, "Lebanon: 'Ahmed Will Not Be Part of the One Percent,'" Daraj, March 18, 2021, https://daraj.com/en/68496/?fbclid=IwAR1U5cFI99c5uRVs3sjuvZzt2RisVl7p7eJx_CkRV83iWb_02PeQcDGrZaA.

26.   Shuayb, "Lebanon: 'Ahmed Will Not Be Part of the One Percent.'"

6

COUNTERING CASCADING XENOPHOBIA

Educational Settings at the Frontline

CAROLA SUÁREZ-OROZCO

Across the globe, we are witnessing increasingly virulent xenophobic sentiments and repressive immigration policies.[1] Emerging research now strongly suggests that this xenophobic social hostility has cascaded into schools, contributing to toxic learning environments for both educators[2] and students.[3] In this chapter, I consider the role of social belonging and its antithesis—social exclusion in the form of xenophobia—for schools, immigrant-origin children, and the future of our societies.[4] Lastly, I consider ways in which schools must play a crucial role in countering cascading xenophobia.

I begin with a brief consideration of the extent to which immigrant-origin children in the United States are aware of xenophobic attitudes. To gain some insight into whether immigrant children and youth register the antipathy directed toward them, we asked four hundred newcomer youth to complete a simple fill-in-the-blank: "Most Americans think that most [people from the respondent's birthplace; i.e., Mexicans] are _____."[5] These data were just a small (but highly illustrative) part of a longitudinal study of the immigrant student adaptation drawn from youth (who were on average twelve years old) arriving from five points of origin in Asia, the Caribbean, and Latin America to the United States.

Sixty-five percent of the children filled in the blank with a negative term. The most frequent word was "bad," though many wrote in more elaborate responses: "Most Americans think that Mexicans are lazy, gangsters, drug addicts that only come to take their jobs away," one fourteen-year-old boy wrote, for example. In addition to choosing words associated with criminality, the children in the study also tended to come up with terms related to contamination (". . . we are garbage," a fourteen-year-old Dominican boy said) and incompetence (". . . we can't do the same things as them in school or at work," said a ten-year-old Mexican girl) as well as invisibility (". . . we do not exist," lamented a ten-year-old Haitian girl).[6]

We also found that the ways in which participants completed the sentence were related to their families' countries of origin. While a little less than half of Chinese youth completed the sentence with negative terms—75 percent of Mexican and 82 percent of Dominicans and Haitians did so. We repeated the task annually for the five years of the study, and these percentages changed little. Young immigrants are clearly aware of negative attitudes about them in the host society.

SOCIAL BELONGING AND EXCLUSION

"The need to belong is a powerful, fundamental, and extremely pervasive" social motivation[7] and human need.[8] Humans are a social species who long to belong across a variety of domains. These include kinship groups, schools, places of work, places of worship, mutual aid societies, voluntary associations, clubs, as well as in political groupings and social movements, and, of course, in the nation-state.[9] Upon entering a new setting, individuals routinely ask themselves, "Do I belong here?"[10] The experience of being socially connected and accepted leads to a sense of social belonging.[11]

The converse of social belonging is the well-theorized concept of social exclusion.[12] For members of stigmatized groups (including, for example, people with disabilities, people of color, immigrants, members of the LGBTQ community, among others), however, a sense of social belonging is routinely compromised and at risk[13] across a variety of domains including the socio-political, spatial, labor market, educational, and relational.[14]

XENOPHOBIC SOCIAL EXCLUSION

Xenophobia is a particular form of social exclusion inflaming and legitimizing toxic rhetoric directed against immigrants and their children.[15] Immigrants (or those perceived as such) become the "quintessential other" in the public imagination delineating who is "us," who is "them," and who may (conditionally) join.[16] Xenophobia serves to normalize stereotypes of danger: criminality, sloth, and filth.[17] Further, it pits newcomers against longstanding residents via perceptions of competition over scarce resources as it delineates "who has the right to be cared for by the state and society."[18] The "terms of permission" of who is deserving and who is not,[19] can be, and are, manipulated according to economic and political winds leading to "civic ostracism."[20]

Historian Erika Lee has painstakingly demonstrated that in the United States—which has long cultivated a foundational myth as a nation of immigrants—there is a long tradition of recurring waves of virulent xenophobia.[21] Drawing on an extensive review of the historical record (e.g., the Chinese Exclusion Act; Japanese family internment camps; Operation Wetback—repatriating over a million individuals of Mexican origin, including U.S. citizens; and the recent Muslim ban). She argues:

> Xenophobia has been neither an aberration nor a contradiction to the United States' history of immigration. Rather, it has existed alongside and constrained America's immigration tradition, determining just who can enter our so-called nation of immigrants and who cannot. Even as Americans have realized that the threats allegedly posed by immigrants were, in hindsight, unjustified, they have allowed xenophobia to become an American routine.[22]

Phenotypic characteristics are frequently conflated with immigration status,[23] and as such, xenophobia can and often is deeply with intertwined racism.[24] While immigrants have long been racialized (e.g., Chinese Exclusion Act; "black" Irish), this pattern of response has been exacerbated in the last half-century as immigrants to the United States are increasingly people of color hailing from Latin America, Asia, the Caribbean, and Africa.[25] As such, immigrant-origin persons of color (including those in the first, second, and beyond generations) are more likely to experience discrimination associated with "perpetual foreigner" status:[26] for the phenotypically marked, becoming a full member of a white-dominant society is often thwarted by perceptions of perpetual outsiderhood.[27]

STRUCTURAL EXCLUSION

For immigrants, xenophobia and the resulting enacted policies contribute to structural exclusion in a variety of ways, beginning with policies on quotas for entry. While worded in the ethic of rights and legal frameworks, immigration policies are ever-shifting, depending upon the political winds of the day and economic priorities. Xenophobia typically "rises and falls along with economic, political, and social crises, war, and rapid demographic changes."[28]

For the unauthorized immigrant population, deportation and the perennial threat to the self as well as to loved ones is the ultimate form of social exclusion.[29] In the condition of actual deportation or its imminent threat, there is no ambiguity whether one is being expulsed from society.[30] For unauthorized individuals and their citizen-children, the continual threat of ejection compromises belongingness in myriad ways.[31] Just how does one establish a sense of belonging to a society that clearly signals in overt actions—"you (and your family) do not belong"?

Social exclusion also actively structures access to resources, including work, housing, healthcare, and education, among others.[32] Unauthorized parents and children are ineligible for government healthcare benefits (with the exception of perinatal and emergency room care). Research has revealed that unauthorized Latinx immigrants in the United States visit doctors less frequently than immigrants who have legal status.[33]

Despite having working parents, children growing up in families in unauthorized homes face high levels of poverty[34] with negative consequences for academic, cognitive, and behavioral development of children and youth.[35] Further, parents' legal status blocks access to necessities of everyday life, like valid social security numbers, driver's licenses, and bank accounts.[36] Citizen children of unauthorized parents are eligible for these benefits, though their parents are often fearful of revealing their own legal status and thus avoid receiving such benefits for their eligible children. Further, the proposed legislation would block the acquisition of permanent residence status if families accessed public resources (including medical services, housing, or food stamps), further contributing to decreased use of services.[37]

Hence, children living in unauthorized families are less likely to be enrolled in programs that help to foster their early learning, such as preschool, with negative longitudinal implications.[38] Compromised access to learning resources in early life places children at a disadvantage for school readiness when compared to children of the authorized.[39] The schools where many unauthorized families typically enroll their children are often characterized by high drop-out rates, inadequate postsecondary educational preparation, and low rates of matriculation into college.[40] For the small percent who make it to college, most begin in community colleges, which often have abysmal graduation rates.[41] Thus, the shadow of perpetual unauthorized status can have educational ramifications that last a lifetime.

SYMBOLIC VIOLENCE AS A FORM OF SOCIAL EXCLUSION

While structural impediments and exclusion have clear implications for social belonging, so do a variety of forms of symbolic violence[42] as well as "recognition gaps."[43] These gaps extend to all those perceived as Other—the immigrant (whether documented and recognized as legal or not) as well as to those associated with potential foreign origins. Messages "marginalizing, silencing, rejecting, isolating, segregating and disenfranchising [are] the machinery of exclusion."[44] Exclusionary messages legitimizing privilege and the status quo are rendered all the more powerful when they are internalized by those who are disparaged.[45] These social messages are transmitted to those who (presumably) do not belong[46] and who are (un)recognized.[47] The resulting identity threats can linger for years to create isolation that negatively impacts well-being, academic self-efficacy, and performance in students.[48]

Notably, while negative rhetoric about immigration has historically been a part of the United States' "ambivalent welcome,"[49] these relentless disparagements have increased significantly in recent years.[50] In the United States, for example, under the Trump administration, those of immigrant-origin have been targeted as potential terrorists and criminals ("rapists," who "bring crime").[51] Anti-immigrant xenophobia now animates efforts to withdraw birthright citizenship to children born of immigrants.[52] The polarizing discourse on immigration has made unauthorized immigrants, in particular, frequent targets of vitriol by politicians and anti-immigrant groups and is persistently played out in mainstream and social media.[53] Further, these narratives reinforce negative stereotypes, legitimizing unabashed acts of covert and overt discrimination.[54] This type of rhetoric is linked to increased acts of violence against the foreign Other, the immigrant,[55] as well as to everyday stigmatizing encounters that "overscrutinize or underestimate" them.[56]

For the objects of xenophobia and symbolic violence, exposure to even experimental simulations of toxic rhetoric elicits a range of negative emotions and is linked to heightened stress responses.[57] For its targets, the coexisting process of xenophobia and racialization are linked ethno-racial trauma—"individual and/or collective psychological distress and fear of danger that results from experiencing or witnessing discrimination, threats of harm, violence and intimidation directed at [one's own] ethno-racial minority group."[58] The effects of symbolic violence, whether directly experienced or vicarious, have significant negative implications for both physical and psychological health.[59]

Notably, ethno-racial trauma adds to the burdens that are concomitant with migration, including *traumatic*,[60] *cumulative*,[61] *acculturative*,[62] and *transgenerational*[63] stresses.

WHY SOCIAL BELONGING, EXCLUSION, AND XENOPHOBIA MATTER FOR EDUCATIONAL SETTINGS

As noted, many of the issues faced by immigrant-origin families and their children are being exacerbated and imposed by the policies fueled by the nativist socio-political landscape. While family separations and deportations intensify, and policy makers continue to debate ever more draconian quotas and immigration reforms, a generation of immigrant children with ambiguous status has come of age in limbo and is still waiting. In the meantime, toxic rhetoric is increasing, and long-settled families live with the chronic threat of deportation[64] with its cascading effect[65] insidiously finding its way into our educational settings.[66]

Ominously, violence, symbolic and otherwise, is on the rise. In the United States, hate crimes occurring in primary and secondary schools as well as post-secondary institutions increased by 25 percent in 2017.[67] A longitudinal study of bullying in Virginia schools before and after the 2016 U.S. presidential election also found that reported bullying incidents were 18 percent higher after the election in schools located in areas where a majority of people voted for Trump compared to schools in non-Trump majority localities.[68] Significantly, the response rate to the survey question asking if students had been teased "because of their race or ethnicity" was 9 percent higher in majority-Trump voting areas. Further, two groundbreaking surveys of principals and school personnel documented widespread and troubling consequences for students' physical and mental health and educational engagement associated with the political climate, immigration enforcement activities, and anti-immigrant sentiment post the 2016 election.[69]

What does this mean for schools?

CASCADING XENOPHOBIA COMPOUNDING TRAUMA FOR IMMIGRANT-ORIGIN STUDENTS

Immigrant-origin students often enter schools having undergone a series of stresses and traumas.[70] Children and their families are frequently exposed to a number of highly stressful events at a variety of junctures; these "compound traumas" are rarely processed or entirely resolved before another trauma is experienced that, in turn, affects "developmental and relational growth."[71]

These are particularly acute for those who have escaped violence in their home countries and/or have undergone arduous journeys as they seek safety in the new homeland.[72] Further, children and youth growing up in mixed-status families live with the chronic fear that beloved family member(s) will suddenly be detained or deported.[73]

Even in less extreme circumstances, immigration is a stressful process, removing youth from predictable contexts and stripping them of significant pre-existing social ties.[74] In the course of migration, many children spend protracted periods of time separated from their parents before joining them in what are often emotionally complicated reunifications.[75] Immigrant children must contend with the particular psychological acculturation challenges of navigating two worlds.[76] They are often asked to take on responsibilities beyond their years, including sibling care, translation duties, and advocacy for their families that, at times, may undermine parental authority.[77] Children of immigrants also face the challenge of forging an identity and sense of belonging in their new homeland while also honoring their parental origins.[78]

When children do not have direct exposure to trauma, caretaker exposures to physical and symbolic violence can lead to transgenerational transmission of trauma.[79] The rapid loss of familial social resources[80] along with chronic exposure to stress has been linked to posttraumatic stress disorder, depression, and somatic complaints and ailments[81] as well as to academic challenges.[82]

Further, the anti-immigrant socio-political context has a clear "trickle-effect" on the academic lives of immigrant-origin students. A survey of 3,600 educators across the United States found that the majority (85 percent) had observed "overt expressions of fear" of immigration enforcement in their (or a loved one's) lives among their immigrant-origin students.

Further, a majority of the educators (79 percent) reported emotional or behavioral problems among their immigrant students that interfered with learning.[83]

In short, the adversity and risks many immigrants encounter before, during, and after immigration can complicate the adaptation process and activate "toxic stress."[84] A growing body of research on trauma has demonstrated both the long-term health implications of exposure to trauma[85] as well as its short-term implications for social-emotional functioning, learning, cognition, motivation, and learning.[86] Simply put, traumatized students cannot learn optimally.

Traumatic exposures negatively affect student learning at school by decreasing their ability to focus attention, regulate emotions and behavior, and -develop positive relationships with adults and peers. Students who have been exposed to trauma often "view the world as a perilous place." Day-to-day events can easily trigger fight, flight, or freeze survival responses that are not under the student's control resulting in students being less able to engage in problem-solving and rational thought.[87] Traumatized students may appear anxious, are prone to being "sensitive" and to perceiving intent of harm when criticized, and often engage in avoidance behaviors (like daydreaming and pencil-sharpening), which are misperceived as willful misbehavior.[88] This leads to more stressful classroom learning environments. Increasingly teachers, principals, school counselors, and other staff report the ripple effects as immigrant-origin students come to schools traumatized and afraid.[89]

CASCADING XENOPHOBIA CREATING HOSTILE LEARNING ENVIRONMENTS

The cascading effects of xenophobia are finding their way into classrooms. In a national survey of over five hundred school principals across the United States, Rogers and his colleagues found a widespread increase in incivility across schools—with "an overwhelming majority of principals report[ing] problems such as contentious classroom environments, hostile exchanges outside of class, and demeaning and hateful remarks over political views." In particular, 60 percent of participating principals reported that they had encountered issues around "derogatory comments about immigrants" (often drawing upon President Trump's 'Build the Wall' rhetoric).[90] A survey of 3,600 educators in the United States, which considered school climate in regard to immigrant-origin students, found particularly high incidents of bullying toward immigrant-origin students in schools with higher percentages of white students.[91]

The problematic school climates that these studies point to should give us pause. Developmental scientists[92] and educators[93] have brought together ample evidence demonstrating that school and class climate have important implications for social-emotional functioning, motivation, and learning. Social scientists are demonstrating what students, parents, principals, and good teachers have always known—a healthy classroom climate is essential for optimal learning. Yet, educational settings find themselves on the frontlines of toxic (un) civil conversations[94] with a concurrent mandate to provide sanctuary learning environments[95] so that their students can thrive with little in the way of a compass on how to proceed.

CASCADING XENOPHOBIA CONTRIBUTING TO THE SOCIAL EMPATHY GAP

A parallel concern for our current and future civil societies is the growing social empathy gap, aptly described as a "severe crisis of disconnection."[96] In this historical period marked by xenophobic rhetoric and partisan divides, educators must find ways to better align their curricula and pedagogical practices with the increasingly diverse students they serve amid a divided twenty-first century.[97]

This xenophobic public climate has serious ramifications for a sense of national unity. At a time of extraordinary demographic shift, our societies need to counter the pressures to divide "them" from "us" by fostering cohesive social relations and strengthening the bonds of solidarity between both new and more established Americans.[98] Schools must work to disrupt the narratives of exclusion and division and nurture practices of inclusion and shared membership in the family of the nation in classrooms and across educational settings.[99] Now more than ever, it is a primary responsibility of schools to bring the ideals of citizenship and democratic principles to life—fostering a sense of citizenship (in the broadest sense) around our responsibilities and obligations to each other and the public good.

WHAT SCHOOLS MUST DO

Educators, already challenged with educational reforms sharply focused on assessments, find themselves ill-equipped to address xenophobia, trauma, and their consequences.[100] At the turn of the twenty-first century, a review of teacher education research demonstrated the invisibility of immigrant students in the field. When this review was repeated a decade and a half later, scholars found "scant attention paid by teacher education scholars" to immigrant students or how to prepare educators to work with them, despite the fact that immigrant students constitute over a quarter of the child population in many postindustrial nations.[101] The educational focus has been on narrow issues of language acquisition. Educators have minimal preparation for how to either address the needs of their diverse newcomer students or manage difficult conversations around cascading xenophobia that trickle into classrooms.

As such, what are fundamental issues that educational settings must address?

A WHOLE-CHILD UNDERSTANDING OF IMMIGRANT-ORIGIN STUDENTS

Increasingly, it is acknowledged that in order to promote short-term learning, long-term success, and development of students, education must expand beyond a narrow focus on academic achievement.[102] At a minimum, a whole-child perspective includes: (1) a focus on supporting and promoting student health and well-being; (2) engaging the family and community in sustaining ways; (3) providing learning environments that are safe, supportive, and caring; and (4) providing a challenging education that prepares students for the future.

In order to take a comprehensive and effective whole-child approach addressing the needs of immigrant-origin students, educators must undertake the following strategies and approaches.

UNDERSTAND IMMIGRANT-ORIGIN CHILDREN WHOM WE SERVE

This work must begin with an understanding of the children educators serve as "We simply cannot teach what we ourselves don't know."[103] At a minimum, educators must become well-versed in the issues facing the diverse children and families they serve. Today, all teachers must be well grounded in an understanding of the realities of the migratory experience and its effects on families and children.[104] To paraphrase Kluckholm and Murray, all humans are at once like all others, like some others, and like no others.[105] Educators should seek to understand what commonalities of the migratory experience are while learning about the communities that they are serving and the individual students they teach.[106]

BE GROUNDED IN A TRAUMA-INFORMED EDUCATIONAL CARE

Given the pervasive nature of trauma in immigrant-origin students' lives, educators must begin by becoming familiar with the types of trauma and chronic stressors these children and families are exposed to. Further, they should be aware of how students' "behavioral and attentional problems may be secondary to trauma," and anticipate and take note of (potential) triggers.[107] Trauma-informed educational practice requires predictable classroom routines and developing deescalation routines for students who may become triggered (e.g., quiet time-out spaces and self-soothing strategies). It is essential to foster warm, safe classroom contexts where relationships are fostered between the teacher and students and among students.[108]

PROVIDE CULTURALLY SUSTAINING PEDAGOGY

Classrooms are spaces where students, at a minimum, should feel recognized and respected. An important foundation to creating learning environments for this to happen is by providing culturally responsive pedagogy (CRP) that builds upon the "cultural knowledge, prior experiences, frames of reference, and performance styles of ethnically diverse students to make learning encounters more relevant to and effective for them."[109] At its most basic levels, CRP incorporates elements of diverse students' historical and cultural legacy by including literature or historical references to often-overlooked individuals or events. At higher levels of CRP, educators provide deep learning opportunities to consider and discuss multiple perspectives of diverse ethnic/cultural groups structured and integrated into the curriculum.[110] The most advanced, rarely achieved level of CRP encourages students to develop solutions to existing social problems using multicultural perspectives.[111]

Through the process of CRP, educators have the opportunity to highlight students' commonalities while acknowledging their individuality. Discussion can foster positive intergroup relations and self-awareness through shared activities, resources, and strategies.[112] At its more sophisticated levels, CRP requires a recognition that experiences do not occur in a social or political vacuum.[113] The discussions that arise as students grapple with these issues (when well-managed) can serve to bridge differences by providing new perspectives and ways of understanding.[114]

IMPLEMENT PERSPECTIVE-TAKING AS A STRATEGY TO BRIDGE THE EMPATHY GAP

A strategy to break the pattern of division, stereotyping, and prejudice is to find ways to minimize the distance across perceived differences.[115] Certainly, the profound social empathy gap faced by so many of our societies today will not likely be easily bridged, as biases are deeply held. A starting point, however, is through the lens of empathy—defined as the capacity to accurately understand the position of others and to "feel this could happen to me."[116] Three variations of empathy have been articulated. The emotional (or sympathetic link) attunement to another's emotional world or pain; this form of empathy is inborn in most children across cultures. A second form of empathy is the cognitive dimension involving the ability to understand another's point of view—in essence, to take on another perspective. Lastly, there is the behavioral dimension, sometimes termed "compassionate empathy," which is linked to mobilization to do something constructive to help.[117]

Alone, neither the emotional nor the cognitive dimensions are effective for bridging the empathy gap.[118] Emotional attunement can lead to sensory overload or burnout, and cognitively recognizing realities while remaining disconnected allows distancing and the decision to remain uninvolved. Both the emotional and cognitive dimensions of empathy must be addressed[119]—one has to imagine another's dilemmas and "explicitly place oneself in the position" of the Other.[120]

Classrooms are spaces where diverse groups of students can regularly come in contact and (optimally) come to know one another—recognizing that perceived differences are indeed less than imagined.[121] Scaffolded curriculum and well-managed classroom dialogues should be places where students are exposed to new perspectives, experiences, and ways of thinking. Classrooms can and should be spaces of sustained conversations where perspectives are exchanged, imagined, and civilly debated. As politicians and social media enact an ethos of discord, divisiveness, and hatred, educators must foster class-rooms that are "sites of possibilities" where an ethic of civility and respect are modeled daily. At a time when it seems everyone is shouting, the classroom must be a place of careful listening.[122]

NURTURE CLASSROOM CULTURES THAT EDUCATE FOR SHARED FATES

As societies, we are in a "crisis of disconnection" with lines of demarcation dividing "them" from "us."[123] Ben-Porath has eloquently suggested schools should strive to prepare the next generation of citizens by cultivating a "shared fate." She defines this shared fate as "a relational, process-oriented, dynamic affiliation" that "accommodate[s] diversity while maintaining a common foundation"[124] Educating for shared fate "connect[s] our very identity to the good of others."[125] It recognizes "that reciprocity is at the heart of citizenship."[126]

The obligation of every school and educator is to foster a democratic ethos where immigrant children come to feel they are full members and contributors to the community with a shared fate. Immigrant youth describe the practices of democratic citizenship as a shared obligation to society, a responsibility to give back, and, above all, kindness when relating to others.[127] The work of education is not to fan the flames of social division but rather to foster a sense of "we."[128] Education must strive to bridge the empathy gap between relative newcomers (and perceived outsiders) and those who self-identify as long-term citizens (or insiders). In short, a central task of education today is to consistently nourish a sense of our "common humanity."[129] More than ever, we must draw upon ample historical lessons that remind us (with hindsight) of shameful xenophobic acts of exclusion and mass complicity.[130] While these may seem like lofty educational goals, they are more necessary now than ever in our increasingly uncivil times.

ASPIRING TO BE SITES OF POSSIBILITIES

These are deeply unsettling times for immigrant-origin students and their families. Multiple forms of social exclusion, ranging from its most extreme form—deportation—to restriction of access to resources, to toxic media messages, to everyday hostile racial and ethnic social encounters, have troubling implications for social belonging. The COVID-19 pandemic has exacted a particularly grueling toll on immigrant communities. Many of our most vulnerable families and children are being conferred heightened stress and profound disadvantage by exclusionary policies and practices.[131] Educational settings have both the opportunity and the obligation to address these challenges directly. By making education for shared fate a guiding principle, schools can become "centers of support and beacons of hope" for their students.[132]

For immigrant-origin children and youth, schools have great potential as "sites of possibilities"[133] and to serve as "sanctuary schools"[134] and safe havens for systematic, intimate, and long-term immersion in the new culture and society. Conversely, by enacting poorly thought through policies and practices noxious to immigrant student needs, schools in too many cases perpetuate disempowerment and reveal a studied indifference to authentically and successfully engage our newest future citizens.[135] We know how to do better and must demonstrate the will and the care to do so.[136] The futures of millions of children and youth *and* our societies are at stake.

NOTES

1. Capps, Randy, Muzaffar Chishti, Julia Gelatt, Jessica Bolter, and Ariel G. Ruiz Soto, "Revving up the Deportation Machinery: Enforcement Under Trump and the Pushback," Migration Policy Institute, May 2018, https://www.migrationpolicy.org/research/revving -deportation-machinery-under-trump-and-pushback; Fomina, Joanna, and Jacek Kucharczyk, "The Specter Haunting Europe: Populism and Protest in Poland," *Journal of Democracy* 27, no. 4 (2016): 58–68; Gündüz, Zuhal Yesilyurt, "The European Union at 50—Xenophobia, Islamophobia and the Rise of the Radical Right," *Journal of Muslim Minority Affairs* 30, no. 1 (2010): 35–47; Poynting, Scott, and Victoria Mason, "The New Integrationism, the State and Islamophobia: Retreat from Multiculturalism in Australia," *International Journal of Law, Crime and Justice* 36, no. 4 (2008): 230–246.

2. Ee, Jongyeon, and Patricia Gándara, "The Impact of Immigration Enforcement on the Nation's Schools," *American Educational Research Journal* 57, no. 2 (2020): 840–871.

3. Rogers, John, Michael Ishimoto, Alexander Kwako, Anthony Berryman, and Claudia Diera, "School and Society in the Age of Trump," UCLA's Institute for Democracy, Education, and Access, March 13, 2019, https://idea.gseis.ucla.edu/publications/school-and-society-in-age-of-trump/.

4. Immigrant-origin students have at least one immigrant parent and may be either of first generation (born abroad) or second (parent[s] born abroad); Suárez-Orozco, Carola, Mona M. Abo-Zena, and Amy K. Marks, eds., *Transitions: The Development of Children of Immigrants* (New York: New York University Press, 2017).

5. Suárez-Orozco, Carola, Marcelo Suárez-Orozco, and Irina Todorova, *Learning a New Land* (Cambridge, MA: Harvard University Press, 2008).

6. Suárez-Orozco, Marcelo, Carola Suárez-Orozco, and Adam Strom, "Backtalk: A Lesson in Civility," *Phi Delta Kappan* 99, no. 4 (2017): 80–81.

7.   Baumeister, Roy F., and Mark R. Leary, "The Need to Belong: Desire for Interpersonal Attachments as a Fundamental Human Motivation," *Psychological Bulletin* 117, no. 3 (1995): 497–529.

8.   Maslow, Abraham Harold, "A Theory of Human Motivation," *Psychological Review* 50, no. 4 (1943): 370–96.

9.   Crisp, Beth R., "Belonging, Connectedness and Social Exclusion," *Journal of Social Inclusion* 1, no. 2 (2010): 123–132.

10. Walton, Gregory M., and Shannon T. Brady, "The Many Questions of Belonging," in *Handbook of Competence and Motivation: Theory and Application*, ed. Andrew J. Elliot, Carol Dweck, and David S. Yeager, 272–293 (New York: Guilford Press, 2017), 272.

11. Walton, Gregory M., and Geoffrey L. Cohen, "A Question of Belonging: Race, Social Fit, and Achievement," *Journal of Personality and Social Psychology* 92, no. 1 (2007): 82–96.

12. Crisp, "Belonging," 123–132; Fangen, Katrine, "Social Exclusion and Inclusion of Young Immigrants: Presentation of an Analytical Framework," *Young* 18, no. 2 (2010): 133–156; Lamont, Michèle, Graziella Moraes Silva, Jessica Welburn, Joshua Guetzkow, Nissim Mizrachi, Hanna Herzog, and Elisa Reis, *Getting Respect: Responding to Stigma and Discrimination in the United States, Brazil, and Israel* (Princeton, NJ: Princeton University Press, 2016).

13. Walton and Cohen, "A Question of Belonging," 82–96.

14. Fangen, "Social Exclusion and Inclusion," 133–156.

15. Xenophobia is defined as the "fear and hatred of strangers or foreigners or of anything strange or foreign" (*Merriam-Webster*, s.v. "xenophobia [*n.*]," accessed September 28, 2021, https://www.merriam-webster.com/dictionary/xenophobia).

16. Fiske, S. T., and T. L. Lee, "Xenophobia and How to Fight It: Immigrants as the Quintessential 'Other,' " in *Decade of Behavior: Social Categories in Everyday Experience*, ed. S. Wiley, G. Philogène, and T. A. Revenson, 151–163 (Washington, DC, American Psychological Association, 2012), 151.

17. Chavez-Dueñas, Nayeli Y., Hector Y. Adames, Jessica G. Perez-Chavez, and Silvia P. Salas, "Healing Ethno-Racial Trauma in Latinx Immigrant Communities: Cultivating Hope, Resistance, and Action," *American Psychologist* 74, no. 1 (2019): 49–62.

18. Wimmer, Andreas, "Explaining Xenophobia and Racism: A Critical Review of Current Research Approaches," *Ethnic and Racial Studies* 20, no. 1 (1997): 17–41, quote at 17.

19. Lee, Erika. *America for Americans: A History of Xenophobia in the United States* (New York: Basic Books, 2019), 11.

20. Sundstrom, Ronald R., and David Haekwon Kim, "Xenophobia and Racism," *Critical Philosophy of Race* 2, no. 1 (2014): 20–45.

21. Lee, *America for Americans*.

22. Lee, *America for Americans*, 8.

23. American Psychological Association, *Crossroads: The Psychology of Immigration in the New Century*" (Washington, DC: APA, 2012), https://www.apa.org/topics/immigration/immigration-report.pdf.

24. Chavez-Dueñas, et al., ""Healing Ethno-Racial Trauma," 49–62; Lee, America for Americans; Sáenz, Rogelio, and Karen Manges Douglas, "A Call for the Racialization of Immigration Studies: On the Transition of Ethnic Immigrants to Racialized Immigrants," *Sociology of Race and Ethnicity* 1, no. 1 (2015): 166–180; Wimmer, "Explaining Xenophobia," 17–41.

25. Saenz and Douglas, "Racialization of Immigration Studies," 166–180.

26. Lee, Stacey J., Nga-Wing Anjela Wong, and Alvin N. Alvarez, "The Model Minority and the Perpetual Foreigner: Stereotypes of Asian Americans," in *Asian American Psychology: Current Perspectives*, ed. N. Tewari, and A. N. Alvarez, 69–84 (New York: Routledge, 2009).

27. Saenz and Douglas, "Racialization of Immigration Studies," 166–180.

28. Lee, *America for Americans*, 4.

29. The unauthorized population in the United States are estimated to be made up of approximately 10.5 million individuals—the lowest level in a decade. Historically, the majority of unauthorized individuals were of Mexican origin and entered at the southern border. These patterns are shifting, however; visa overstayers now surpass southern border crossers, and unauthorized immigrants from Asia and Central American have risen. John Gramlich, "19 Striking Findings From 2019," Pew Research Center, December 13, 2019, https://www.pewresearch.org/fact-tank/2019/12/13/19-striking-findings-from-2019/.

30. Suárez-Orozco, Carola, Guadalupe López Hernández, and Patricia Cabral, "The Rippling Effects of Unauthorized Status: Stress, Family Separations, and Deportation and their Implications for Belonging and Development," in *Racial Minority Immigrants and Trauma in the United States. Minority Immigrants and Trauma in the United States*, ed. Pratyusha Tummala-Narra (Washington, DC: American Psychological Association Press, 2021).

31. Zayas, Luis H. *Forgotten Citizens: Deportation, Children, and the Making of American Exiles and Orphans* (New York: Oxford University Press, 2015); Dreby, Joanna, "The Burden of Deportation on Children in Mexican Immigrant Families," *Journal of Marriage and Family* 74, no. 4 (2012): 829–845; Enriquez, Laura E., "Multigenerational Punishment: Shared Experiences of Undocumented Immigration Status Within Mixed-Status Families," *Journal of Marriage and Family* 77, no. 4 (2015): 939–953; Gonzales, Roberto G., Carola Suárez-Orozco, and Maria Cecilia Dedios-Sanguineti, "No Place to Belong: Contextualizing Concepts of Mental Health Among Undocumented Immigrant Youth in the United States," *American Behavioral Scientist* 57, no. 8 (2013): 1174–1199; Yoshikawa, Hirokazu, Carola Suárez-Orozco, and Roberto G. Gonzales, "Unauthorized Status and Youth Development in the United States: Consensus Statement of the Society for Research on Adolescence," *Journal of Research on Adolescence* 27, no. 1 (2017): 4–19; Yoshikawa, Hiro, "Resisting 'Us versus Them': Immigrants and Our Common Humanity," in *The Crisis of Connection: Roots, Consequences and Solutions*, ed. Niobe Way, Alisha Ali, Carol Gilligan, and Pedro Noguera, 428–443 (New York: New York University Press, 2018).

32. Fagan, Jeffrey, and John MacDonald. "Policing, Crime and Legitimacy in New York and Los Angeles: The Social and Political Contexts of Two Historic Crime Declines," (Columbia Public Law Research Paper 12-315, 2012); Yoshikawa, Suárez-Orozco, and González, "Unauthorized Status," 4–19.

33. Ortega, Alexander N., Hai Fang, Victor H. Perez, John A. Rizzo, Olivia Carter-Pokras, Steven P. Wallace, and Lillian Gelberg, "Health Care Access, Use of Services, and Experiences Among Undocumented Mexicans and Other Latinos," *Archives of Internal Medicine* 167, no. 21 (2007): 2354–2360.

34. Tienda, Marta., and Faith Mitchell, "E pluribus plures or e pluribus unum?" in *Hispanics and the Future of America* (Washington, DC: National Academies Press, 2006).

35. Yoshikawa, Hirokazu, Thomas S. Weisner, and Edward D. Lowe, eds., *Making It Work: Low-Wage Employment, Family Life, And Child Development* (New York: Russell Sage, 2006). See also chapter 3.

36. Yoshikawa, Suárez-Orozco, and González, "Unauthorized Status," 4–19.

37. Bernstein, Hamutal, Dulce Gonzalez, Michael Karpman, and Stephen Zuckerman, "One in Seven Adults in Immigrant Families Reported Avoiding Public Benefit Programs in 2018," Urban Institute, May 22, 2019, https://www.urban.org/research/publication/oneseven-adults-immigrant-families-reported-avoiding-public-benefitprograms-2018.

38. Yoshikawa, Hiro, *Immigrants Raising Citizens: Unauthorized Parents and Their Young Children* (New York: Russell Sage Foundation, 2011).

39. Crosnoe, Robert, "Early Child Care and the School Readiness of Children from Mexican Immigrant Families," *International Migration Review* 41, no. 1 (2007): 152–181.

40. Teranishi, R. T., W. R. Allen, and D. Solórzano, "Opportunities at the Crossroads: School Segregation and Disparate Opportunities for Higher Education in California," *Teachers College Record* 106, no. 11 (2004): 2224–2247.

41. Osei-Twumasi, Olivia, and Guadalupe Hernández-López, "Resilience in the Face of Adversity: Undocumented Students in Community Colleges," in *Immigrant-Origin Students in Community College: Navigating Risk and Reward in Higher Education*, ed. Carola Suárez-Orozco and Olivia Osei-Twumasi, 46–62 (New York: Teachers College Press, 2019).

42. Bourdieu, Pierre, and Jean-Claude Passeron, *Reproduction in Education, Society and Culture*, trans. Richard Nice (London: Sage,1977).

43. Lamont, Michèle, "Addressing Recognition Gaps: Destigmatization and the Reduction of Inequality," *American Sociological Review* 83, no. 3 (2018): 419–444, at 425.

44. Taket, Ann, Beth R. Crisp, Annemarie Nevill, Greer Lamaro, Melissa Graham, and Sarah Barter-Godfrey, eds. *Theorising Social Exclusion* (Abington, UK: Routledge, 2009), 3.

45. Bourdieu and Passeron, *Reproduction in Education, Society and Culture.*

46. Chavez, Leo R., Belinda Campos, Karina Corona, Daina Sanchez, and Catherine Belyeu Ruiz, "Words Hurt: Political Rhetoric, Emotions/Affect, and Psychological Well-Being Among Mexican-Origin Youth," *Social Science & Medicine* 228 (2019): 240–251.

47. Lamont, "Addressing Recognition Gaps," 419–444.

48. Walton, Gregory M., and Geoffrey L. Cohen, "A Brief Social-Belonging Intervention Improves Academic and Health Outcomes of Minority Students," *Science* 331, no. 6023 (2011): 1447–1451; Steele, Claude M., Steven J. Spencer, and Joshua Aronson, "Contending with Group Image: The Psychology of Stereotype and Social Identity Threat," *Advances in Experimental Social Psychology* 34 (2002), 379–440.

49. Simon, Rita James, and Susan H. Alexander, *The Ambivalent Welcome: Print Media, Public Opinion, and Immigration* (Santa Barbara, CA: Praeger, 1993), 1.

50. Chavez, et al., "Words Hurt," 240–251.

51. Washington Post staff, "Full Text: Donald Trump Announces a Presidential Bid," *Washington Post*, June 16, 2015, https://www.washingtonpost.com/news/post-politics/wp/2015/06/16/full-text-donald-trump-announces-a-presidential-bid/?noredirect=on&utm_term=.bee0e57a4f88.

52. Hagan, John, Ron Levi, and Ronit Dinovitzer, "The Symbolic Violence of the Crime-Immigration Nexus: Migrant Mythologies in the Americas," *Criminology & Public Policy* 7 (2008): 95.

53. Chavez, Leo R., Cecila Menjívar, and Daniel Kanstroom, "Illegality Across Generation: Public Discourse and the Children of Undocumented Immigrants," in *Constructing Immigrant "Illegality": Critiques, Experiences, and Responses*, ed. Cecilia Menjívar and Daniel Kanstroom, 84–110 (Cambridge: Cambridge University Press, 2014); Mark Hugo Lopez, Rich Morin, and Paul Taylor, "Illegal Immigration Backlash Worries, Divides Latinos," Pew Research Center, October 28, 2010, http.s://www.pewhispanic.org/2010/10/28/illegal-immigration-backlash-worries-divides-latinos/.

54. Suárez-Orozco, Abo-Zena and Marks, *Transitions*.

55. Steinhardt, Max F., "The Impact of Xenophobic Violence on the Integration of Immigrants" (IZA Discussion Papers, No. 11781, Bonn: Institute of Labor Economics, 2018).

56. Lamont et al., *Getting Respect*, 4.

57. Chavez-Dueñas, et al., ""Healing Ethno-Racial Trauma," 49–62.

58. Chavez-Dueñas, et al., ""Healing Ethno-Racial Trauma," 49.

59. Comas-Díaz, Lillian, Gordon Nagayama Hall, and Helen A. Neville, "Racial Trauma: Theory, Research, and Healing: Introduction to the Special Issue," *American Psychologist* 74, no. 1

(2019): 1–5; Pascoe, Elizabeth A., and Laura Smart Richman, "Perceived Discrimination and Health: A Meta-Analytic Review," *Psychological Bulletin* 135, no. 4 (2009): 531–554.

60. Brabeck, Kalina M., M. Brinton Lykes, and Cristina Hunter, "The Psychosocial Impact of Detention and Deportation on US Migrant Children and Families," *American Journal of Orthopsychiatry* 84, no. 5 (2014): 496–505; Fazel, Mina, Ruth V. Reed, Catherine Panter-Brick, and Alan Stein, "Mental Health of Displaced and Refugee Children Resettled in High-Income Countries: Risk and Protective Factors," *Lancet*, 379, no. 9812 (2012): 266–282; Goodman, Rachael D., Colleen K. Vesely, Bethany Letiecq, and Carol L. Cleaveland, "Trauma and Resilience Among Refugee and Undocumented Immigrant Women," *Journal of Counseling & Development* 95, no. 3 (2017): 309–321; Vizek-Vidović, Vlasta, Gordana Kuterovac-Jagodić, and Lidija Arambašić, "Posttraumatic Symptomatology in Children Exposed to War," *Scandinavian Journal of Psychology* 41, no. 4 (2000): 297–306.

61. Shonkoff, Jack P., Andrew S. Garner, Benjamin S. Siegel, Mary I. Dobbins, Marian F. Earls, Laura McGuinn, John Pascoe et al., "The Lifelong Effects of Early Childhood Adversity and Toxic Stress," *Pediatrics* 129, no. 1 (2012): 232–246.

62. Suárez-Orozco, Suárez-Orozco, and Todorova, *Learning a New Land*.

63. Schwab, Gabriele, *Haunting Legacies: Violent Histories and Transgenerational Trauma* (New York: Columbia University Press, 2010).

64. Menjívar, Cecilia, and Krista M. Perreira, "Undocumented and Unaccompanied: Children of Migration in the European Union and the United States," *Journal of Ethnic and Migration Studies* 45, no. 2 (2019): 197–217; Zayas, *Forgotten Citizens*.

65. Suárez-Orozco, Carola, "Conferring Disadvantage: Behavioral and Developmental Implications for Children Growing Up in the Shadow of Undocumented Immigration Status," *Journal of Developmental & Behavioral Pediatrics* 38, no. 6 (2017): 424–428; Yoshikawa, "Resisting 'Us versus Them.'"

66. Ee and Gándara. "The impact of immigration enforcement." 840–871; Rogers et al., "School and Society." See chapter 11.

67. Keierleber, Mark, "New FBI Data: School-Based Hate Crimes Jumped 25 Percent Last Year—For the Second Year in a Row," 74, November 14, 2018, https://www.the74million.org/new-fbi-data-school-based-hate-crimes-jumped-25-percent-last-year-for-the-second-year-in-a-row/.

68. Huang, Francis L., and Dewey G. Cornell, "School Teasing and Bullying After the Presidential Election," *Educational Researcher* 48, no. 2 (2019): 69–83.

69. Rogers et al., "School and Society";Ee and Gándara, "The Impact of Immigration Enforcement," 840–871.

70. Suárez-Orozco, Carola, and Marcelo Suárez-Orozco, *Children of Immigration* (Cambridge, MA: Harvard University Press, 2001).

71. Cockersell, Peter, "Compound Trauma and Complex Needs," in *Social Exclusion, Compound Trauma and Recovery*, 27–36 (London: Jessica Kingsley, 2018), 27.

72. Suárez-Orozco, López Hernández, and Cabral, "The Rippling Effects"; See chapter 5.

73. Yoshikawa, "Resisting 'Us versus Them.'"

74. Suárez-Orozco, Abo-Zena, and Marks, *Transitions*.

75. Suárez-Orozco, Carola, Hee Jin Bang, and Ha Yeon Kim, "I Felt Like My Heart Was Staying Behind: Psychological Implications of Family Separations & Reunifications for Immigrant Youth," *Journal of Adolescent Research* 26, no. 2 (2011): 222–257.

76. Berry, John W., Jean S. Phinney, David L. Sam, and Paul Vedder, "Immigrant Youth: Acculturation, Identity, and Adaptation," *Applied Psychology* 55, no. 3 (2006): 303–332.

77. Orellana, Marjorie Faulstich, *Translating Childhoods: Immigrant Youth, Language, and Culture* (New Brunswick, NJ: Rutgers University Press, 2009).

78.   Suárez-Orozco, Abo-Zena and Marks, *Transitions*.

79.   Schwab, *Haunting Legacies*.

80.   Hobfoll, Stevan E., "Traumatic Stress: A Theory Based on Rapid Loss of Resources," *Anxiety Research* 4, no. 3 (1991): 187–197.

81.   Fazel, Reed, Panter-Brick, and Stein, "Mental Health," 266–282; Vizek-Vidović, Kuterovac-Jagodić, and Arambašić, "Posttraumatic Symptomatology," 297–306.

82.   American Psychological Association, *Crossroads*; Bean, Frank D., Mark A. Leach, Susan K. Brown, James D. Bachmeier, and John R. Hipp, "The Educational Legacy of Unauthorized Migration: Comparisons Across US-Immigrant Groups in How Parents' Status Affects Their Offspring," *International Migration Review* 45, no. 2 (2011): 348–385; Suárez-Orozco, Abo-Zena and Marks, *Transitions*; Suárez-Orozco, Suárez-Orozco, & Todorova, *Learning a New Land*.

83.   Ee and Gándara, "The Impact of Immigration Enforcement," 840–871.

84.   Shonkoff et al., "The Lifelong Effects," 232–246.

85.   Delva, Jorge, Pilar Horner, Ramiro Martinez, Laura Sanders, William D. Lopez, and John Doering-White, "Mental Health Problems of Children of Undocumented Parents in the United States: A Hidden Crisis," *Journal of Community Positive Practices* 3 (2013): 25–35; Shonkoff et al., "The Lifelong Effects," 232–246.

86.   Nadiv, Sarah, and Nicholson, Julie, *Creating Trauma Informed Learning Environments* (San Francisco: Wested, 2019), https://www.wested.org/resources/trauma-informed-learning-environments/; Van der Kolk, Bessel A., *The Body Keeps the Score: Brain, Mind, and Body in the Healing of Trauma* (New York: Penguin Books, 2015).

87.   Nadiv and Nicholson, *Creating Trauma Informed Learning Environments*.

88.   Van der Kolk, *The Body Keeps the Score*.

89.   Ee and Gándara, "The Impact of Immigration Enforcement," 840–871; Rogers et al., "School and Society"; Sattin-Bajaj, C., and J. J. Kirksey, "Schools as Sanctuaries? Examining the Relationship Between Immigration Enforcement and Absenteeism Rates for Immigrant-Origin Children," in *Absent from School: Understanding and Addressing Student Absenteeism*, ed. Michael A. Gottfried and Ethan L. Hutt, 101–120 (Cambridge, MA: Harvard Education Press, 2019).

90.   Rogers et al., "School and Society," v.

91.   Ee and Gándara, "The Impact of Immigration Enforcement." 840–871.

92.   Immordino-Yang, Mary Helen, Linda Darling-Hammond, and Christina R. Krone, "Nurturing Nature: How Brain Development Is Inherently Social and Emotional, and What This Means for Education," *Educational Psychologist* 54, no. 3 (2019): 185–204.

93.   Cohen, Jonathan, Libby McCabe, Nicholas M. Michelli, and Terry Pickeral, "School Climate: Research, Policy, Practice, and Teacher Education," *Teachers College Record* 111, no. 1 (2009): 180–213.

94.   See chapter 11.

95.   Sattin-Bajaj and Kirksey, "Schools as Sanctuaries?" 101–120.

96.   Yoshikawa, "Resisting 'Us versus Them,' " 428.

97.   Martin, Margary, and Carola Suárez-Orozco, "What It Takes: Promising Practices for Immigrant Origin Adolescent Newcomers," *Theory Into Practice* 57, no. 2 (2018): 82–90; Nieto, Sonia, "Re-Imagining Multicultural Education: New Visions, New Possibilities," *Multicultural Education Review* 9, no. 1 (2017): 1–10; Noguera, P. A., "The Role of Schools in Responding to the Needs of Immigrant and Refugee Children," *Sociology International Journal* 3, no. 5 (2019): 392–399; Yoshikawa, "Resisting 'Us versus Them.' "

98.   Putnam, Robert D., *Our Kids: The American Dream in Crisis* (New York: Simon and Schuster, 2015); Yoshikawa, "Resisting 'Us versus Them.' "

99. Ben-Porath, Sigal, "Citizenship as Shared Fate: Education for Membership in a Diverse Democracy," *Educational Theory* 62, no. 4 (2012): 381–395, at 381.

100. Mittelstadt, Michelle, "Amid Sizeable Increases in Migrant-Background Students, New MPI Europe Report Finds Schools in Europe Are Ill-Equipped to Handle Growing Diversity," Migration Policy Institute, February 8, 2018, https://www.migrationpolicy.org/news/amid-sizeable-increases-migrant-background-students-new-mpi-europe-report-finds-schools-europe.

101. Goodwin, A. Lin, "Who Is in the Classroom Now? Teacher Preparation and the Education of Immigrant Children," *Educational Studies* 53, no. 5 (2017): 433–449, at 439.

102. Lewallen, Theresa C., Holly Hunt, William Potts-Datema, Stephanie Zaza, and Wayne Giles, "The Whole School, Whole Community, Whole Child Model: A New Approach for Improving Educational Attainment and Healthy Development for Students," *Journal of School Health* 85, no. 11 (2015): 729–739; Noddings, Nel, "What Does It Mean to Educate the Whole Child?" *Educational Leadership* 63, no. 1 (2005): 1–11.

103. Goodwin, A. Lin, "Who is in the Classroom Now?" 443.

104. Suárez-Orozco and Suárez-Orozco, *Children of Immigration*; Suárez-Orozco, Abo-Zena, and Marks, *Transitions*; Suárez-Orozco, Carola, Adam Strom, and Rosalinda Larios, "A Culturally Responsive Guide to Fostering the Inclusion of Immigrant Origin Youth," Reimagining Immigration, 2018, https://reimaginingmigration.org/a-culturally-responsive-guide-to-fostering-the-inclusion-of-immigrant-origin-students/.

105. Kluckhohn, Clyde, and Henry A. Murray, *Personality in Nature, Society and Culture* (New York: Knopf, 1948).

106. Banks, James A., Peter Cookson, Geneva Gay, Willis D. Hawley, Jacqueline Jordan Irvine, Sonia Nieto, Janet Ward Schofield, and Walter G. Stephan, "Diversity Within Unity: Essential Principles for Teaching and Learning in a Multicultural Society," *Phi Delta Kappan* 83, no. 3 (2001): 196–203; Hammond, Zaretta, Culturally Responsive Teaching and the Brain: Promoting Authentic Engagement and Rigor Among Culturally and Linguistically Diverse Students (Thousand Oaks, CA: Corwin Press, 2014); Suárez-Orozco, Marks, and Abo-Zena, *Transitions*.

107. Nadiv and Nicholson, *Creating Trauma Informed Learning Environments*, 1.

108. Nadiv and Nicholson, *Creating Trauma Informed Learning Environments*, 1.

109. Gay, Geneva, "Teaching to and Through Cultural Diversity," *Curriculum Inquiry* 43, no. 1 (2013): 48–70 at 49–50.

110. Banks et al., "Diversity Within Unity," 196–203.

111. Karras Jean-Gilles, J., R. Larios, C. Suárez-Orozco, and I. Baaqee, "Systematically Observing Culturally Responsive Pedagogy Across Classrooms: Incorporating Educator Perspectives Through an Iterative Approach" (under review).

112. Banks et al., "Diversity Within Unity," 196–203; Gay, "Teaching to and Through," 48–70; Karras Jean-Gilles, Larios, Suárez-Orozco, and Baaqee, "Systematically Observing Culturally Responsive Pedagogy."

113. Ladson-Billing, G., "Toward a Theory of Culturally Relevant Pedagogy," *American Educational Research Journal* 32, no. 3 (1995): 465–491.

114. Karras Jean-Gilles, Larios, Suárez-Orozco, and Baaqee, "Systematically Observing Culturally Responsive Pedagogy"; Suárez-Orozco, Strom, and Larios, "A Culturally Responsive Guide."

115. Yoshikawa, "Resisting 'Us versus Them.'"

116. Trout, John D., *Why Empathy Matters: The Science and Psychology of Better Judgment* (New York: Penguin, 2010), 21.

117. Goleman, Daniel, Annie McKee, and Adam Waytz, *Empathy* (Cambridge, MA: Harvard Business Press, 2017).

118. Goleman, McKee, and Waytz, *Empathy*; Yoshikawa, "Resisting 'Us versus Them.' "

119. Suárez-Orozco, Suárez-Orozco, and Todorova, *Learning a New Land*.

120. Yoshikawa, "Resisting 'Us versus Them.' "

121. Pettigrew, Thomas F., "Intergroup Contact Theory," *Annual Review of Psychology* 49, no. 1 (1998): 65–85.

122. Suárez-Orozco, Suárez-Orozco, and Strom, "Backtalk: A Lesson in Civility." *Phi Delta Kappan* 99, no. 4 (2017): 80.

123. Yoshikawa, "Resisting 'Us versus Them.' "

124. Ben-Porath, Sigal, "Citizenship as Shared Fate,"381, 383,383.

125. Callan, Eamonn, *Creating Citizens: Political Education and Liberal Democracy* (New York, Clarendon Press, 1997), 76.

126. Ben-Porath, Sigal,"Citizenship as Shared Fate," 383.

127. Suárez-Orozco, Carola, María G. Hernández, and Saskias Casanova, " 'It's Sort of My Calling": The Civic Engagement and Social Responsibility of Latino Immigrant-Origin Young Adults," *Research in Human Development* 12, no. 1–2 (2015): 84–99.

128. Yoshikawa, "Resisting 'Us versus Them.' "

129. Yoshikawa, "Resisting 'Us versus Them.' "

130. Strom, Adam, Veronica Boix-Mansilla, Carolyn Sattin-Bajaj, and Carola Suárez-Orozco, "Teaching Migration and Citizenship Building, " in *The Palgrave Handbook of Citizenship Education*, ed. Andrew Peterson, Garth Stahl, and Hannah Soong (London: Springer, 2020).

131. Suárez-Orozco, Carola, "Conferring Disadvantage," 424–428.

132. Noguera, "The Role of Schools," 394.

133. Fine, Michelle, and Reva Jaffe-Walter, "Swimming: On Oxygen, Resistance, and Possibility for Immigrant Youth Under Siege," *Anthropology & Education Quarterly* 38, no. 1 (2007): 76–96.

134. Sattin-Bajaj and Kirksey, "Schools as Sanctuaries?" 101–120.

135. Allen, Danielle, and Rob Reich, eds. *Education, Justice, and Democracy* (Chicago: University of Chicago Press, 2013).

136. Noddings, Nel, *Caring: A Feminine Approach to Ethics* (Berkeley, CA: University of California Press,1984).

II

ETHICAL AND CIVIC
CONSIDERATIONS

7

EDUCATION AS A MORAL RESPONSIBILITY

STEFANO ZAMAGNI

Education is a human right, which makes it a moral responsibility as well as a societal responsibility. As Pope Francis says, it is a "summons to solidarity" with current and future generations[1]—a concept that the Catholic Church already expressed more than half-century ago in "Gravissimum Educationis."[2] Sustainable Development Goal 4 (SDG4) calls upon the global community to "ensure inclusive and equitable quality education and promote lifelong learning opportunities for all." There is nothing more essential to the sustainable development agenda than access to education for all young people all over the world.

We urgently need to update the educational system, intervening both on its contents and on its organizational setup. Concerning the contents dimension, the new education approach should favor the development of the right skills and attitudes in pupils, including critical thinking, creativity, and imagination. Students in higher education must evolve to become lifelong learners. Unfortunately, during the second modernity, we have moved away from the idea that education is about character-building, focusing instead on the acquisition of knowledge and skills needed for a career or to meet market requests. We need a holistic vision of education focusing on integral human dimensions, seeking the true, the good, and the beautiful. For such an education profile, utilitarian ethics is clearly inadequate to cope with the aporias of the libertarian-individualistic outlook. The Aristotelian virtue ethics perspective is well-placed to propose an ethics of personhood allowing human flourishing.

In recent times, we have witnessed a live-streamed example of some of the negative consequences of a school culture that cultivates privilege. Though, the truth is that every student has the potential to be extraordinary. That is why we need an education that empowers students to be able to change the world—not merely to adapt to it. If we admit that justice as fairness is not just a matter of wealth redistribution since it has to do with inclusion, then we have also to admit that education is the most effective way to enhance the participation through which persons become truly dignified protagonists of their destiny.

As far as the organizational setup is concerned, the time has come to recognize that the Tayloristic model of organization is no longer adequate if we want to meet the challenges of new education.[3] It is not only a matter of moving from vertical to horizontal teaching methods. What is required is an organizational model capable of keeping together three elements: knowledge, skills, and character. Indeed, *wanting* to do the right thing is something different from *knowing* the right thing to do, and that, in turn, is something other than actually *doing* the right thing. It is a specific responsibility of scholars and academic institutions not only to see the world as it is but also to imagine the world as it might be. The point is that knowing—that is, thinking—does not necessarily result in doing—that is, changing behavior. How to put concepts into action? Conation is the answer. The notion of conation appears in the writings of Aristotle in a discussion about how to define concepts such as wishing and desire. "Wishing"—he wrote—"is a conation after the good; desire is a conation after the pleasant."[4] However, in the last couple of centuries, this concept was abandoned in educational practices. Conation, conceived as a desire to learn, connects cognition and emotion to actions. Educators must foster the learner's conation. In this regard, the role of the family is simply fundamental.[5]

Innovation in education is absolutely essential—today more than ever. Digitization and the transition to a knowledge-based economy are changing the learning landscape. Not only are professional profiles changing apace, but students themselves are changing, too. Technology has encouraged us to confuse access to information with knowledge. Because of that, we need a major transformation in learning if we want our students to succeed in our age of precarious work and technological disruption. We should appeal for a more equitable education—a necessary condition for a more just society. A school culture that cultivates privilege is intolerable. It is not only a matter of teaching how to adapt to a changing world but also teaching to change the world. So it is not simply a matter of teaching technologies that have to be updated. What is required is recognition that education is a structural social institution and that its structuring makes huge differences to its intake, process, and outcomes. Unfortunately, education continues to be treated as a homogeneous concept—a taken-for-granted notion that everyone uses in the same way. This has never been the case, historically or comparatively.

The education of its citizens is one of the main areas of government intervention in every country. At the same time, the government is not the only provider of education. Education systems often display a mix of public and privately funded institutions. The share of private involvement varies greatly among countries. Institutional arrangements concerning the funding of private schools also differ among countries. Trying to understand how countries choose the mix of public and private education is not an irrelevant question. More attention should be given to such a question in view of the implications stemming from the adoption of an integrated educational system instead of a regime with segregation between public and private schools. Empirical studies inform us both that public spending on education is negatively related to income inequality and that the quality and extent of public schooling generally increase with the political weight of the poor.[6]

A final remark on the educational role of entrepreneurs: most firms limit internal and external learning of their workforce to subjects that provide knowledge and skills needed to perform specific tasks. Although certainly useful, corporate training is not sufficient. Corporations should move toward corporate education by adding dimensions that deal with soft skills and, above all, thinking skills. Such skills are necessary to navigate a world in flux. The purpose is to stimulate normative reflections and to put daily business activities in perspective of a purpose greater than mere profits maximization.

In this volume, we propose an active contribution toward restructuring the global education system. "Education," Pope Francis stresses, "is meant to be transformative";[7] to educate is always an act of hope. As with the healthcare sector, the education system stands to be profoundly transformed by the COVID-19 pandemic. Despite multiple difficulties, it is not too far-fetched to achieve SDG4, but now it is the appropriate time to do it. A wise American saying proclaims: never waste a crisis! This saying resonates with the famous expression used by St. Ambrose, bishop of Milan (fourth century): "Happy the collapse [of the Roman Civilization] if the reconstruction will make the building more beautiful." The current pandemic crisis affords us a rare opportunity to pause and reflect on where we have been going and where it leads. As with the healthcare sector, the education system stands to be profoundly transformed by the COVID-19 pandemic. The big open question is how to keep students connected to their schools despite physical distancing and remote learning. The goal is to keep students engaged, which is certainly a challenge in a system where barriers have been erected intentionally and specifically to prevent communication between teachers and their students outside the school space. Teachers have to be encouraged to be leaders, designers of innovative learning environments, cocreators, and coaches of their students.

To conclude—those with no hope in the future have only the present. And those who have only the present have no compelling reason to be interested in the future, in innovative endevors. But fortunately, people who continue to entertain hope in the future have not disappeared altogether.

NOTES

1. Francis (Pope), "Laudato si," Vatican website, May 24, 2015, http://www.vatican.va/content /francesco/en/encyclicals/documents/papa-francesco_20150524_enciclica-laudato-si.html.

2. Paul VI (Pope), "Declaration on Christian Education (Gravissimum educationis)," Vatican website, October 28, 1965, http://www.vatican.va/archive/hist_councils/ii_vatican_council /documents/vat-ii_decl_19651028_gravissimum-educationis_en.html.

3. Taylor, Frederick Winslow, *The Principles of Scientific Management* (New York: Harper & Brothers, 1911).

4. Aristotle, *Organon: The Topics*, book IV [350 BCE], translated by W.A. Pickard-Cambridge, Digireads.com, Overland Park, Kansas, USA, 2006.

5. Militello, L. G., F. C. Gentner, S. D. Swindler, and G. I. Beisner, "Conation: Its Historical Roots and Implications for Future Research," *International Symposium on Collaborative Technologies and Systems* (2006), 240–247, https://doi.org/10.1109/cts.2006.31.

6. J.E. Stiglitz, *Economics of the Public Sector*, 4th ed. (New York: Norton, 2015), chap. 16. See also E. Saez, "Public Economics and Inequality: Uncovering Our Social Nature," NBER Working Paper 28387, January 2021.

7. Francis (Pope), "Video Message of His Holiness Pope Francis on the Occasion of the Meeting Organised by the Congregation for Catholic Education: 'Global Compact on Education. Together to Look Beyond,'" Vatican website, October 15, 2020, http://www.vatican.va/content /francesco/en/messages/pont-messages/2020/documents/papa-francesco_20201015_videomessaggio -global-compact.html.

8

ON EDUCATING THE THREE VIRTUES

A Hegelian Approach

HOWARD GARDNER

Though it was likely not apparent to those around me, in one sense, I have always seen myself as embedded in education. As a youth, growing up seventy years ago in Pennsylvania, I daydreamed that over the course of my lifetime, I would teach all grades—from kindergarten through high school. (I did not know about college or university at that time.) I tried to explain things to my peers—probably in a way that was rather bossy. And to make extra money, I occasionally taught piano over a ten-year period.

Despite this inclination to teach, once I attended college, I took a turn toward "pure research" in psychology. I did not begin to teach regularly until I was well into my forties. As it turned out, principally because of the institutional affiliation of our research group "Project Zero," my professorial appointment was in a school of education (with a courtesy appointment in psychology at Harvard and a courtesy appointment in neurology at the Boston University School of Medicine). Over the last thirty years, I have taught a variety of students across a range of subjects, including several topics featured in this volume. As a researcher, I have spanned the educational landscape from preschool through the college years.

Over this period—effectively seventy years—education has undergone massive changes. As several authors in this collection point out, in comparison to past centuries, all over the world, education now begins earlier, lasts longer, and, happily, involves an ever-larger proportion of young people. The conditions of education have also altered. In the time of my grandparents—born toward the end of the nineteenth century—the range of topics, disciplines, media, and institutional settings that we take for granted today would have been unmanageable, indeed unthinkable. Some of the challenges described in this volume—rapid and deleterious climate change, the possibility of nuclear devastation, technologies that silently gather, synthesize, and make use of knowledge about each of us as individuals—would have been (and indeed sometimes were!) the stuff of science fiction. And, not to accentuate the negative, the breakthroughs in science and technology make life much easier and more pleasant for those of us fortunate enough to have been born in the right place at the right time. Alas, as Pope Francis reminds us, progress in science and technology has not been matched by advances in human cooperation, empathy, and service to the wider community.[1] In much of the world, we saw ample evidence of these human failings during the pandemic of 2020–2021.

When a sector of the world—indeed, when the world as a whole—changes so rapidly, it is on occasion appropriate to step back and to consider *what might be the educational constants*, the elements that are worth retaining over time, across space, with respect to the human family and the human condition. And even as one seeks to identify and sustain the constants, it is equally important to consider *how these educational desiderata should be conceptualized, configured, and conveyed in an ever-fast-changing environment.*

When formal education began around the world many centuries ago, it had three primary objectives: (1) to equip young people to handle the important literacies of the era (sometimes termed the "three Rs" of "reading," "[w]riting" and "[a]rithmetic"); (2) to give young people the concepts, attitudes, and moral compasses that helped them to become reasonable, constructive members of their communities; and (3) to prepare youth for the livelihoods that were available, needed, and valued in the ambient culture. The importance and the accents placed on these three educational objectives change over time. For instance, now a non-"R," "coding," is increasingly deemed an essential literacy, and the objectives also change across cultures (explicitly moral lessons are salient in Confucian societies but very much in the background in the secular societies of Northern Europe). But I know of no contemporary culture that altogether dismisses literacies, ignores an introduction to communal and civic life, or ignores preparation for the workplace.

Given this analysis, one might well claim "these goals are more than enough." Or even "we are hardly meeting these goals adequately; what possible need is there for any additional educational goals, means, and 'considerations?' "

That is *not*, however, the message that I have gleaned in reading the words of Pope Francis or in perusing the essays by those who attended the historical meeting in January 2020 at the Pontifical Academy of Social Sciences. And while I was not privileged to attend that meeting, I ask indulgence if I regard this invitation as an opportunity to put forth a vision of education "over the long haul" or even "for the ages."

Before turning to that vision, it's important to point out that education can be construed so broadly that it covers *everything*—every topic from astronomy to zoology and every moment from cradle to grave.

I am not going to be so grand. Instead, I am going to focus on the three virtues that I value the most and reflect on how, in the period going forward, best to conceptualize and nurture them.

INTRODUCING THE THREE VIRTUES

Wyoming Seminary, my secondary school, located in northeastern Pennsylvania, proclaimed its educational goals: Verum, Pulchrum, Bonum—Truth, Beauty, Goodness.[2] Though I had long forgotten this school motto, it clearly made a deep impression on me.

The evidence: like almost every educator—indeed, like almost every reflective adult—I believe that education must include literacies, on the one hand, and preparation for the world of work, of labor, on the other. But in a reasonably effective educational system, the basic literacies should be covered in the first years of schooling; and explicit preparation for the world of work should take place in late adolescence. Accordingly, that means we have a considerable period—anywhere from five to ten years—to pursue other educational goals. And this is where I favor a valorization and inculcation of the three virtues.

But how to think about the virtues? Enter the German philosopher Georg Wilhelm Friedrich Hegel. In a famous conceptual formulation, Hegel sought to describe progress in thinking—which he conceived in dialectical terms. Initially, he claimed, one has a *thesis*—a strong claim of one sort of another. Then, he argued, there is a need for an *antithesis* —a contrasting point of view. And finally, triumphantly (one can hear the trumpets blaring in the background), one progresses to a final *synthesis*. (Of course, the process can be repeated—synthesis A becoming the thesis for a new cycle: and while Karl Marx may have believed that he had arrived a final Hegelian synthesis, among political philosophers, the conversation, the dialectic launched by Marx has continued indefinitely).

So let me now apply Hegel to thinking about the virtues.

THESIS

When I initially thought about the virtues during my early adolescence, I felt that they were akin to one another or even the same thing—yoked together like the proverbial three musketeers. And then, several decades later, when I informally surveyed their formulation in various languages and cultures, I discovered that, in general, *these virtues were considered inseparable.* Perhaps the clearest example is in Confucian societies—where it is assumed that what is true is beautiful and good—and vice versa. You can't have one virtue without the others, and if any virtue is lacking, coherence is not possible.

As evidence from the other side of the globe, one can also cite the memorable couplet by poet John Keats:

> Beauty is truth, truth beauty—that is all.
> Ye know on earth and all ye need to know.

ANTITHESIS

When I, in the early twenty-first century, as a Western-educated scholar, began to reflect on these virtues, it became clear to me—perhaps *too* clear!— that the virtues could *not* be identical and were *not* interchangeable. It's clear, it's *true*, that millions of deaths occurred as a result of the Spanish flu of 1918–1919, but certainly, that is not *good*, nor is it *beautiful*. Many of us consider the paintings of Picasso (like *les demoiselles d'Avignon*) or the music of Benjamin Britten (like his *War Requiem*) to be *beautiful*—but it does not make sense to think of them as being "true," or "good"— at least not in any literal sense. And while the socialist/communist dream of Karl Marx may be good in the eyes of many, it's not yet true, and many do not find it beautiful at all.

Having arrived at this framing, I proceeded to put forth my own definitions of the three virtues. In my 2011 book *Truth, Beauty, and Goodness Reframed* (with the tantalizing subtitle "Educating for the Virtues in the era of Thruthiness and Twitter"),[3] I laid out the following argument.

TRUTH

is the property of propositions, assertions, indeed, sentences. A proposition can be *true or false* and demonstrably so (2+2 is 4 and not 5 or 5,000); *not determinable* at present but perhaps determinable in the future; or *indeterminate* and likely to remain so indefinitely.

Beauty is the property of experiences. An experience is likely to be deemed beautiful if it fulfills three conditions: it initially attracts attention; it is memorable in form as well as content; and one seeks to revisit the experience or one that is quite similar. (Conversely, experiences are NOT beautiful if they are *not* noticeable, do *not* attract attention; if they are forgettable or readily converted into another format; and/or if one is inclined—or even determined—to avoid them in the future.) We think of our contacts with works of art as beautiful or not; but indeed, any of our experiences—from a talk to a walk, from a dialogue to a dream—can be beautiful (or ugly, or erased from memory)

GOOD

is a description of our hopefully benevolent relationship to other individuals—both ones close to us and those who are remote and with whom we have only a transactional relationship. More specifically, our relation to those whom we contact regularly entails what I have termed "neighborly morality"—and the tenets are quite well captured in the Ten Commandments or in the Golden Rule and its variations.

In contrast, and particularly characteristic of our modern, industrial and postindustrial ages, good can also refer to relationships that are primarily transactional and transitory rather than common and long-lasting. I refer to these relations as involving "the ethics of roles." And in particular, I have in mind two roles: the role of a worker, and particularly that of a *professional*. And the role of a member of a community, and particularly that of a *citizen*.

A few more thoughts about the "good": Relationships to others (near or far) can be classified as good to the extent that one considers the impact on others of one's words, thoughts, and actions and tries to perform in ways that are moral and ethical. And one is more likely to achieve an ethical or moral aspiration if one knows the substance of what one is doing (excellence) and if one cares about one's behavior (engagement). Hence, my colleagues and I speak of the "three Es" of the good—as in good work and in good citizenship—excellence, engagement, and ethics.[4]

Clearly, this is a mouthful, indeed a mindful. And there's much more to say—as noted, an entire book! And yet, for my present purposes, I trust that this brief introduction to my perspective on the virtues should suffice.

FULL STOP

In the aforementioned book, I took the position that the three virtues are independent of one another—they need to be conceptualized and realized independently. A statement like "truth is beauty"— however beautiful one may find it— is neither true nor virtuous. That was my *antithesis* to the earlier beliefs in the insolubility of the three virtues.

TOWARD A SYNTHESIS

As I thought about this trio of virtues, I first reached the conclusion that the pursuit of truth should be the primary focus of education—to repeat, in the interval between literacy and labor. And indeed, in earlier work, I maintained that the best way—indeed perhaps the *only* way—in which to ascertain what's true is to learn and master the methods used by the different disciplines. (I also described certain professions and trades where knowledge may not currently be encoded in propositions but has the potential to be so captured and conveyed.) On this account, if we learn about the methods employed by the physicist or the historian, or the moves made by the electrician or the chef, we can figure out what is true in these realms.

I still believe that the heartland of formal education should be focused on the pursuit and the determination of truth. But I have since become convinced of two other things.

THE BEAUTY OF TRUTH SEEKING

Even if one knows how to ascertain truth, that does not suffice. It's necessary, but it's not sufficient.

As any scientist, scholar, researcher, or journalist can tell you, there is a pleasure, a joy—even awe—in pursuing truth, in separating it from myth, mischief, or miscues. Recall the vivid testimony of Sir Isaac Newton: "I do not know what I may appear to the world, but to myself I seem to have been only like a boy playing on the seashore, and diverting myself in now and then finding a smoother pebble or a prettier shell than ordinary, whilst the great ocean of truth lay all undiscovered before me."

Not only "undiscovered," I would add: there can never be a complete, definitive truth. All one can hope for, or aspire to, is to come ever closer to the truth—whether it is about the creation of the cosmos or the causes of the First World War or how the human mind works—or fails to work.

Accordingly, in formal and informal education, we need to share the joys of pursuing truth—as well as the costs of hiding or missing truth and/or spreading false information. Alas, in the era of social media, it is often superficially more pleasurable to spread alluring nonsense: only if one has a prior and firm commitment to the pursuit of truth do we have *any* hope of ignoring the superficial and arriving at the substantive, the claims that have merit and that can withstand scrutiny.

THE CONCEPTION OF THE GOOD

After *Homo sapiens* emerged and began to constitute communities (as small as a family or clan, or ultimately as large as a country or the planet), members of our species began to develop norms of behavior that are acceptable as compared to behavior that is not. Of course, these are not necessarily consistent with one another, nor are they necessarily permanent. Though—having been around for many centuries—neighborly morality has been much more firmly established than has the ethics of roles.

How does this consideration relate to the pursuit and conveyance of truth? In two ways:

First, one needs to believe that the pursuit and the promulgation of truth are important, indeed crucial. Of course, many individuals, including ones with great power and influence, do not value the truth at all. They may either be pathological liars—Hitler famously endorsed "the big lie"—or they may be transactionalists without nuance—"I pursue whatever works for me."

Indeed, that stance, that skepticism, constitutes the great risk inherent in the conception of truth held by some members of the pragmatist school of philosophy (truth is what works— à la William James, on some readings) or of post-modern relativism (there is no such thing as truthfulness (à la Jacques Derrida, on some readings). Under such skeptical formulations, the most that we can hope for is to reach a tentative agreement (à la Richard Rorty).

Second, one must wed the belief in truth to a personal commitment to pursue it, even when it seems easier to go with the crowd, or to sweep doubts under the rug, or even to tell a lie—often protesting it's only a "white" lie. And here is where goodness and truth begin to converge. We need a conception of the good that recognizes and valorizes truth while disdaining perspectives that deny, undermine, or minimize truth value.

THE SYNTHESIS IN BRIEF

So, now I have done it. Having for a decade argued for the independence of the three virtues, I now have come to recognize—to concede, if you will—that they are, in fact, bound together and perhaps quite tightly, perhaps even inextricably.

To state the new synthesis:

1. The pursuit of truth is possible and worthwhile.
2. It's best carried out through a careful understanding and application of the methods used to arrive at propositions of various sorts, in various disciplines, and in various sectors of society.
3. Individuals (and groups and societies) are most likely to pursue truth if . . .

The experience proves pleasurable and worth pursuing and repursuing over the long haul

And

If that course of action fits in with one's overall conception of a good society—one which espouses and pursues neighborly morality and the ethics of roles.

Note that, in reaching this conclusion, I am but echoing the wisdom of Pope Francis: In an address to Italian schoolteachers in 2014, he said, "I speak of three languages: the mind, the heart and the hands. When we speak of roots and values, we can speak of truth, goodness, and creativity. Yet, we cannot educate without leading the heart to beauty."[5]

FROM SYNTHESIS TO ACTION

Having sketched out my key concepts, I propose to return to the challenges of education, with a special focus on the years-long period between literacy and labor. Here are the principal considerations:

1. One has to believe that these three virtues are crucial, that they are worth placing centrally as THE overarching mission of education in the period between literacy and labor.

2. Lessons, assessment, feedback, trophies need to be built around the pursuit of truth, the cultivation of beautiful experiences, and the conceptions of a good society in which these virtues are highlighted.

3. The three virtues need to be conveyed—better, embodied—by teachers, administrators, staff, and older students. For their part, the learners need to have both the motivation to learn and the capacity to draw on their skills and knowledge—one might say, their intelligences— to master new areas of study and practice.

4. Equally important, these virtues need to be built into the DNA, the structure, of educational institutions—whether schools, libraries, museums, or educational media—the institutions need to model and promote the pursuit of truth, the pleasure of finding it out, its importance, indeed its indispensability for the thriving of the broader society.

In this context, it may be helpful for this American observer to mention two of the most powerful educational experiences from the early days of television: the series of Young People's Concerts, choreographed by conductor Leonard Bernstein and the segments of *Sesame Street*, as conveyed by a few live characters and featuring the amazing Muppets. Both of these broadcast series foregrounded powerful indeed (for me) unforgettable, intertwining of the three virtues.

And going beyond formal schooling, this modeling of the virtues should ideally characterize workplaces with which students come in contact— jobs at fast-food restaurants or grocery stores for younger students, internships in workplaces or professional offices for older students. I've come to believe in the power of the atmosphere, the habitus that pervades the first real job that students have. Again, using an example from the United States, it truly matters whether one's first paying job in journalism occurs at National Public Radio or at Fox News.[6]

5. And while the pursuit of truths should overall be a positive experience, we need to be able to pursue truth wherever it leads—that includes understanding the sometimes harsh realities about lethal viruses, climate change, nuclear weapons, forced separation of families, and the many ways in which social media can become vehicles of propaganda.

6. Accordingly, hand in hand with the acknowledgment of difficult truths, we need to be aware of the threats to *truth* (propaganda, lies, facile media),

threats to *beauty* (food that seems pleasurable but is harmful, media messages that are seductive but fallacious), and threats to *goodness* (false gods, xenophobia, misogyny, lies that are big, as well as lies that present themselves as innocuous).

LINGERING QUESTIONS

ARTS AND HUMANITIES

In the proceeding, I have dealt at some length with questions of the truth, as captured in scholarly disciplines, along with their concomitant methods of investigation. But so far, this discussion has largely bypassed an important part of any curriculum—courses and experiences in the arts (music, painting, dance, and the like) and the humanities (history, philosophy, the study of languages, the more qualitative strands of the social sciences, and the like).

As one devoted to the experience of beauty and the search for the good, I fully endorse—indeed, I insist—on a curriculum that features artistic and humanistic, as well as scientific courses of study. To recall a quip uttered by my teacher Nelson Goodman "We don't want an education that is half-brained." Indeed, in view of the synthesis that I have proposed, these lines of study and experience are crucial. That is because unless students are guided to significant experiences in the arts, they will have a restricted (and probably rigid, even unchangeable) sense of beauty—if any at all. And unless they explore the visions of society that have been captured in the arts and humanities, they will have an impoverished sense of what is good and, alas, what does not qualify for that descriptor.

ARTIFICIAL INTELLIGENCE, DEEP LEARNING, AND AUTOMATICALLY INVOKED ALGORITHMS

I have already alluded to the challenges to the virtues posed by social media. Without question, many of us either choose or are seduced into choosing conceptions of the virtues that are presented, implicitly or explicitly, across the spectrum of social media. These clearly challenge a belief, a faith—be it a powerful desire or a lingering hope—that we human beings ourselves *choose* and *can choose deliberately* to follow one course rather than another.

The computer-centric period in which we are living is sometimes seen—and appropriately so—as a test for our species. We need to determine in which individuals, corporate bodies, governmental departments, and/or technologies we will invest a sense of agency or whether, indeed, we will allow or encourage competition among these respective agencies. One can envision a 1984-style rivalry emerging among three different approaches—the United States, a great deal of latitude to corporations, their products, their modes of operation; China, a great deal of centralized control of computational devices and approaches; Western Europe, an attempt to mediate between these polar options.

FORMS OF GOVERNMENT AND GOVERNANCE

For a time, after the fall of the Berlin Wall in 1989, it was assumed that Western-style democratic governance had triumphed—indeed, in Francis Fukuyama's memorable phrase, that we had come to "the end of history."

More than a quarter of a century later, these predictions seem incredibly naïve. If anything, the governance pendulum has swung quite far to the rightwing of the political spectrum, with authoritarian and even totalitarian regimes and systems on the rise and many nations being democratic only in name—or in slogan. Should this trend continue or even accelerate, thoughts or aspirations with respect to the virtues will seem naïve. Governments will control education—indeed, they will BE education. Once again, recall the three chilling, oxymoronic slogans from George Orwell's prophetic allegory *1984*:

War is peace
Freedom is slavery
Ignorance is strength[7]

PROXIMITY AND REMOTENESS IN A GLOBAL CENTURY

In our earlier work on issues of the good, we made a convenient distinction between neighborly morality—how we relate to those who live alongside us— and the ethics of roles—how we relate to those with whom we have a relationship, but it is not a close, or regular, or well-established connection.

But we now live at a time and in a place where we can connect readily to individuals who are thousands of miles away. Moreover, we learn of their needs and their desires, just as they learn about ours, and we discover and affirm our joint membership in the human species—in what has come to be called the Anthropocene era.[8]

We must now take on one of the great challenges of our species: Are we able to think of those whom we may never meet in person in ways akin to how we think of those to whom we are related by our street address or by our genetic heritage? And in raising this question today, we need to think deeply about our relation to the many millions who are now stranded in refugee camps and may never come to know their biological relatives.[9]

THE ROLE OF RESOURCES

I have set forth a very ambitious set of educational goals—one giving as much of a place to the pursuit of the classical liberal arts as to the bread-and-butter issues of literacy and labor. And I have presupposed an educational community that supports these goals and a financial and governance infrastructure that permits—perhaps even encourages—these aspirations.

Without question, it is easier to pursue these goals if one has the resources on which to draw. But at the same time, it is crucial to point out that there are political entities with considerable resources that fail to embrace these virtues.[10] Both over time and at the present moment, there are schools, school systems, and even entire regions that have limited resources and that are nonetheless able to achieve a well-rounded and virtue-filled education. Given a choice between money and mission, I'd put *my* money on mission!

THE ROLE OF RELIGION AND RELIGIONS

When he was generous enough to attend the lectures on which my 2012 book was based, Marcelo Suárez-Orozco pointed out, acutely, "You have left out the eight-hundred-pound gorilla—religion." And, of course, he was right! Wearing the garb of a secular academic, it is not a sphere that I ponder regularly—though as one ages, religious, spiritual, or at least existential concerns tend to loom larger.

To trace out the relationship between the great religions, on the one hand, and the three virtues, on the other, would require a lengthy book—indeed, one much longer than my own essay on the virtues in our time.[11] Just think of the three virtues at the times of the Biblical Moses, or the life of Christ, or the height of the Roman Empire in the early centuries of the Common Era, during the rise of the papacy, or at the time of the challenge from Protestantism or, more recently, the ascendancy of evangelical religion—with its belief in direct knowledge and explicit guidance from The Book. Or think of Karl Marx, who considered religion as the opiate of people, or of critics of Marx, who apply the same characterization to socialism or communism.

Suffice it to say, most individuals require a belief in something larger than themselves—perhaps even larger than their neighborhood, clan, nation, or, for that matter, planet or universe. For many, at present, it is a belief in science,[12] in science tempered by humanism,[13] or in what I have termed "the three sacreds."[14]

Personally, I do not care whether individuals, groups, or societies have a religion, a world view, or consider themselves existential in the Sartrian sense. What's important is that these eschatologies, at a minimum, do not disrupt the aspiration for truth, beauty, and goodness; and that, as a maximum, they work actively toward the achievement of that lofty aspiration. And ideally, if there are more than one of these world views, that they do not cripple one another, at worst, or, more happily, that they work in consort toward the realization of the virtues.

It is not easy to predict the lay of the land in the decades and centuries ahead. We can be sure that, if we survive as a species at all, our successors will encounter surprises of many sorts. While I am politically liberal, I am educationally conservative—we need to preserve and build upon the best ideas and the best methods for educating the next generation and the generations thereafter. Indeed, during the five-to-ten-year period between the achievement of the literacies, on the one hand, and preparation for the labor market, on the other, we need to strive for educational approaches and aspirations that honor, preserve, and extend the three critical virtues. Three cheers for the liberal arts and sciences!

In this perilous time of pandemics and unchecked climate change, I would add that we need a vision of society that is built upon the fundamental importance of truth, beauty, and goodness—one that sees their achievement—or, more accurately, their pursuit—as *the* adventure of a lifetime. Indeed, the goal of lifelong learning should be the pursuit and strengthening of a virtue-filled, flourishing life, one of which Socrates—and his student Plato, and Plato's student Aristotle—would have approved.

A FINAL NOD TO HEGEL

In the preceding pages devoted to the portrait of an education worthy of our species and our planet, I presented a thesis, an antithesis, and what I believe to be a new and appropriate synthesis. But as Hegel would presumably have been the first to agree, *all syntheses are* pro term; and if these words themselves activate a new antithesis and a better and more comprehensive synthesis, I will be pleased.

ACKNOWLEDGMENTS

For helpful comments on an earlier draft, I thank my colleagues Lynn Barendsen, Shelby Clark, Wendy Fischman, Kirsten McHugh, and Danny Mucinskas. Special thanks to Marcelo Suárez-Orozco for his support over the decades and for his sensitive editing. The work described in this essay was generously supported by the Argosy Foundation, the Endeavor Foundation, Yumi and Eiich Kuwana, the Community Foundation of New Jersey, and the Saul Zaentz Charitable Foundation.

NOTES

1. See foreword.
2. Gardner, Howard, *Truth, Beauty, and Goodness Reframed: Educating for the Virtues in the Age of Truthiness and Twitter*, reprint ed. (New York: Basic Books, 2012).
3. Gardner, *Truth, Beauty, and Goodness*.
4. See https://www.thegoodproject.org/; Gardner, Howard, Mihaly Csikszentmihalyi, and William Damon, *Good Work: When Excellence and Ethics Meet* (New York: Basic Books, 2005); Gardner, Howard, ed., *Good Work: Theory and Practice* (Cambridge, MA: Good Work Project, 2010).
5. Address of His Holiness Pope Francis to Participants at the Seminar "Education: the Global Compact," organized by the Pontifical Academy of Social Sciences, Consistory Hall, Friday, 7 February 2020, https://www.vatican.va/content/francesco/en/speeches/2020/february/documents/papa-francesco_20200207_education-globalcompact.html.
6. Gardner, Howard, *A Synthesizing Mind* (Cambridge: MIT Press, 2020).
7. Orwell, George, *The Orwell Reader: Fiction, Essays, and Reportage* (Houghton Mifflin Harcourt, 1984).
8. Jürgen, Renn, *The Evolution of Knowledge: Rethinking Science for the Anthropocene* (Princeton, NJ: Princeton University Press, 2020).
9. See chapter 4.

10. See chapter 9.
11. See chapter 9.
12. Renn, *Evolution of Knowledge*.
13. Pinker, Steven, *Enlightenment Now the Case for Reason, Science, Humanism and Progress* (New York: Penguin, 2019).
14. Gardner, *A Synthesizing Mind*.

9

ETHICS IN EDUCATION AND EDUCATION OF ETHICS

VITTORIO HÖSLE

The idea of the Global Compact on Education is deeply rooted in moral principles; their explicit clarification seems to be an important task that ethics is called to fulfill. But the relation of ethics and education is not limited to the *ethics of education*; the inverse relation, the *education of ethics*, also has to be considered. Even if the two are distinct tasks, it is easy to see that they are not disparate. The ethics of education requires guiding principles that are not limited to the ethicist reflecting on them but hold sway over the course of generations. And this will occur only if these principles are passed on to the younger generation through education. In short, an ethics of education must insist, among many other things, on the necessity of teaching ethics. Thus, it is not complete without reflections on the education of ethics.

In the following chapter, I want to begin by laying out the principles that justify the idea of the Global Compact on Education. I will focus mainly on (1) the formal questions of who has a right to be educated and who has a duty to provide this education. I will also (2) address the material question of what should be taught and will point out some of the gaps that I see in the contemporary curriculum—including, but not limited to, ethics. Finally, I will (3) discuss some of the peculiar challenges, but also opportunities, connected to the teaching of ethics.

THE RIGHT AND DUTY TO EDUCATE

The necessity of the education of humans is rooted in the fact that we are an *altricial* species. Unlike precocious species, the altricial species have young that are not yet able to fend for themselves; their brains still grow considerably after birth, and thus extended parental involvement is indispensable to help them survive. While there are many altricial species, none has such a long juvenile period as ours. This is due not only to physiological phenomena, which render nurture necessary, but also to the fact that our species, by its very nature, relies on culture. While there is an innate biological basis for cultural acquisitions, such as language learning, the concrete cultural products, such as the different languages, are a result of choices that vary from culture to culture. Thus, a language has to be learned in a long process that usually lasts at least six to seven years. But language is not the only achievement of a culture. Discoveries and innovations, based on historical traditions that are often explicitly transmitted together with their content, also have to be appropriated. With the development of science and technology—and modern science and technology, in particular—the amount of knowledge that has to be mastered not only by the scientific elites but also by the general population inevitably increases. At least, this is so if the dominion over nature, and partly also over humanity itself, offered by science and technology is to be maintained. All this deepens and extends the need for education.

Another factor that renders education an anthropological necessity is the radical instinct-reduction that distinguishes us from all other species.[1] Much of animal behavior is directed by instincts. While humans also know internal drive mechanisms, they are in principle able to check them. This can help prevent otherwise dangerous behavior, but it can also lead to the dissolution of salutary mechanisms and the unleashing of drives such as aggression far beyond what we find in other animal species. Such drives become more dangerous when they are accompanied by the scientific-technological knowledge that extends human dominion over nature and fellow human beings. Moral rules, originally grounded in religious traditions, have the function of taming humans, potentially the most destructive of all species, and direct their intellectual capacities so that they become beneficial to other creatures—first to the members of their own communities, later to humankind at large and ideally also to other species.

Because of these traits, humans are in dire need of education—they cannot achieve the full potential of their own nature if they are not educated beyond what nature has bestowed on them by birthright. "Man can only become man by education."[2] When a human being is not educated, his or her telos is thwarted, like when a plant is not allowed to get to the point where it blossoms. The intellectual dimension of humans entails that even a healthy and strong person without education is somehow dwarfed with regard to his or her humanity. Of course, in the overwhelming majority of children, there is also a subjective desire to be educated; but whoever does not believe that desires alone constitute morally relevant goods (for there are silly desires) is more easily swayed by the argument that education is an objective good when it comes to the question of justifying policies of education. A noneducated human is less valuable than an educated one for two different reasons: first, because she or he does not take part in more complex activities of the mind; second, because she or he can benefit her or his fellow human beings less; and this objective value is the reason why the child has a legitimate desire to learn from adults. The value of the unfolding of a mind cannot be denied without performative contradiction in an ethical discussion because it is presupposed by any serious intellectual quest; and if one believes that a basic feature of moral norms is their universality, one cannot deny the value of an education in any human being (even if the level up to which she or he should be educated will vary according to her or his talent). Education has both an intrinsic and an extrinsic value—it is good in itself for the students because it fulfills their deepest reasonable aspiration, and it is useful for them and the rest of society because education increases the level of intelligent cooperation in a society.

The argument starting from the objective value of education instead of the subjective need explains why there is not only a right but also a duty to be educated. In fact, in the system of positive rights, the right to visit a school is quite unique in being at the same time a duty to do so. Most other rights do not carry a corresponding obligation with themselves: one may, but one does not need to marry; one may, but one does not need to engage in certain contracts. A noneducated person is a burden to society, and thus society can impose on each child, more accurately on the family, the duty to be educated. But this does not yet answer the question of who has the duty to pay the considerable costs of education. For most of human history, that duty lay exclusively in the hands of the parents of the child and, in the case of their death or incapacitation, in the hands of the closest relatives, such as grandparents, uncles and aunts, elder siblings, and the like. It was largely left to their discretion what they chose to teach the children entrusted to their care. While limited compulsory schooling has existed elsewhere (for example, in the Aztec empire in the fifteenth century), in Western culture, it was Martin Luther who first vigorously demanded it since every Protestant was supposed to be able to read the Bible. Thus, in a few Protestant German areas in the sixteenth century, compulsory education was introduced, sometimes only for boys, sometimes for boys and girls. Scotland followed suit in the seventeenth century. Prussia introduced mandatory elementary education for all children under Frederick the Great, and in the nineteenth century, it spread to many European countries, to some, however, such as Poland or Finland, only in the twentieth century.[3]

Ernest Gellner has coined the term *exo-training* to refer to an education that does not occur within the family unity or traditional structures, such as guilds, but that is imposed by the state and usually occurs in specific buildings, the schools.[4] What are the reasons for the rise of exo-training? They go hand in hand with those that led in general to the modern welfare state, which has its basis in the national state. With the Industrial Revolution, a specific knowledge became indispensable that most families were not able to pass on. The increased mobility demanded by a rational allocation of labor weakened the bonds of the traditional extended family, and the state had a moral duty to step in to fulfill tasks earlier ascribed to families because it had destroyed the old social order or at least allowed its demise. Furthermore, the competition between states, both economic and military, rendered it imperative for the new nation-states to educate their citizenry. The new ideology of nationalism created a strong incentive to work for the common good of a nation, forge cohesion among the classes by a common education, and lift the poor people from their ignorance, which otherwise would condemn them to lifelong poverty.[5] Not only the family but also the state now acknowledged responsibility for the education of the children.

In many respects, the idea of the global compact extends this process from the national state to the international community. The argument is analogous: in a globalized world, in which the various parts of humanity are more and more dependent on each other and in which universal trade, as well as the uninhibited worldwide spread of information, has widely undermined traditional cultures, there is not only an obligation of the individual state but where for plausible reasons it cannot fulfill its task, of the international community too to step in and help provide for general education.[6] International education was declared one of the various tasks of UNESCO, which was founded in 1946 as a specialized agency of the United Nations. In 2000, together with the

World Bank, the Asian Development Bank, and other institutions, it formed the World Education Forum, committed to achieving education for all by 2015, the second of the eight Millennium Development Goals of the United Nations declared in 2000. Since the goal was not achieved by 2015, it still forms the fourth of the seventeen Sustainable Development Goals (SDGs) set by the General Assembly in 2015. Cooperation of states, NGOs and other institutions of the civil society, particularly religious ones, and individual donors seems to be the best means to help achieve the fourth SDG, which is rooted in recognition of the objective value of an education, without which humans cannot reach their mental telos.

It is true that one major incentive that drove the creation of exo-training in the national states of the nineteenth and twentieth centuries is missing in its extension to the international community: the argument that if one's state does not invest in the education of its citizens, those states that do so will have advantages in economic or military competition. On the contrary, one might argue, supporting the education of foreign citizens may endanger one's own power position and foster potential adversaries. But, first, there is the purely moral argument that leaving any child without education is a grave sin of omission at the moment in which there are amply sufficient resources to fulfill this task—and the money needed for granting every child a decent education is ridiculously low. Not only the subjective utility but also the objective moral value of the education of a child is clearly superior to the enjoyment of luxury goods. Thus, the refusal to help countries and families that have very limited resources to grant their children the education that they yearn for is morally the more objectionable the less the sacrifice one oneself has to make. One could object, though, that such an argument is certainly valid for the individual but cannot bind states that should use their resources for the interests of their own nation. However, also on the level of collective self-interest, nations are well-advised to collaborate to achieve the aforementioned goal (to which they have committed themselves in 2000 and 2015, even if not in a way that is binding according to international law). For, second, in a globalized world, leaving larger strata of a population uneducated, and thus without the chance to get an acceptable job, destabilizes not only the country where they live but, in turn, increases the desire to attempt to migrate into the richer countries. While states have the right to limit access to their territory, their possibilities to do so are limited by technical as well as by humanitarian factors. So, even on purely egoistical grounds, they should have a strong interest in achieving sustainable development in the poorer parts of the world. This will not take place, however, without basic education for every child.

There is certainly no denying that the primary responsibility for the education of children must rest with those who are responsible for their existence, their parents, as well as with the states that legislate, for example, family policies. People should learn to beget only those children that they can raise, and they must be held accountable for their demographic behavior. The principle of subsidiarity rightly demands that institutions at a higher level step in only when those at a lower level, closer to the matter at hand, prove unable to do so. Even when they do, they must ask for substantial cooperation and sacrifices by the lower-level institutions, the state in which the children live as well as the family. Countries must limit their irrational expenses in order to deserve contributions from the international community; the class sizes in such countries will have to be considerably larger than in rich countries. Where there is no way to send all children to school, one might consider limiting access to an equal amount of children for all families in order to create an incentive not to beget more children than can be educated. After all, the costs of child-bearing (opportunity costs included) are an important factor that has contributed to the demographic slowdown in developed countries.[7] They must not disappear.

However, one argument that since Thomas Malthus has been used against welfare policies does not hold water in this case. Malthus (who believes that children have relative rights to food and education but only against their parents) famously argued that the Poor Bill by the younger Pitt, while "framed with benevolent intentions," "possesses in a high degree the great and radical defect of all systems of the kind, that of tending to increase population without increasing the means for its support."[8] Of course, a rights-based account will still claim that one has to help starving people, even if this may lead to an increase in the number of people needing food in the next generation. Yet, a consequentialist account on the basis of average utilitarianism (which maximizes the average utility, not its total sum) could easily object that such generous behavior in the long term would lower the average utility because it would increase the number of starving people. However, at the moment in which the international community, and, as I believe, rightly so, helps eradicate illnesses and famine, even an average utilitarian should recognize that help in installing general education should be added. For it is an empirical fact that a longer and better education of females is one of the factors that lower the natality rate.[9] Since this is a crucial demand of average utilitarians, they too must be in favor of international support of general education, at least for females.

WHAT SHOULD BE TAUGHT?

A crucial part of the curriculum must render pupils able to function in their own societies as well as possibly in the global civil society. Literacy and numeracy are basic requirements; a working knowledge of the global lingua franca (for the moment, this is English, but such things may change) is highly desirable. Pupils must acquire a mental image of central features of reality, such as basic laws of physics, crucial facts about organisms (and far more detailed knowledge about human physiology), as well as a working understanding of the economy and the political system of the country, and some basic knowledge of the geography and history of the world. No doubt, the level of thoroughness of knowledge will vary with the degree of education that a person receives, be it primary, secondary, or tertiary. After the general knowledge, special knowledge corresponding to one's own talent and the desired and needed profession with its specific profile dictated by the division of labor must follow suit.

But despite, or perhaps because of, the enormous increase in the transmission of knowledge at all educational stages, it seems to me that the education system practiced today almost everywhere in the Western world has some considerable shortcomings, which have to be addressed if the education about to be extended to every child shall prove a blessing. First, the knowledge that the student acquires does not simply mirror the world; it facilitates its alteration, particularly in an age dominated by the imperative of technological transformation. The four industrial revolutions have created a world that is much more complex than the preindustrial world; it is not at all guaranteed that the mismatch between the generally spread knowledge and the world was greater in earlier times than it is today. We certainly have an incomparably superior understanding of the workings of nature and partly also of society. But the far-reaching consequences of our alterations of nature that are based on the superior knowledge acquired since the scientific revolution of the seventeenth century often escape the general public's knowledge or are gained long after deleterious processes are set up. The ecological disasters that are threatening us (see chapter 12), as well as the COVID-19 pandemic now raging throughout the world, are clearly due to both our superior scientific-technological knowledge and the incapacity of predicting side effects, natural and social ones, of our actions enabled by that knowledge. Of course, the list of the ecological sins of people in earlier times is long, too. But since they had less knowledge and thus less power than we have, they did not have the capacity of rendering the earth

as a whole uninhabitable. We can, and our system of education is hardly prepared to prevent that. It teaches us an enormous number of superfluous things
but not what is needed for survival.

Second, the sheer increase of knowledge is a mixed blessing even if we
abstract from its deleterious ecological and health consequences. For the
increase of knowledge stored in society at large goes, given human finitude,
inevitably hand in hand with a decrease of the portion of the collective knowledge that can be mastered by a single individual. This in itself would not be
dangerous—after all, one can cooperate with others—if at least there were a
generally shared consensus on the place of one's own knowledge in the whole
of the objective system of knowledge and its relative value. But, on the one
hand, such a consensus, which was traditionally based on a picture of the
whole offered by philosophy, has vanished. There are two main reasons: first,
philosophy has become itself a very specialized discipline, which has given up
the search for such a whole. Second, due to the cult of the irrelevant in one's
own discipline, partly driven by an obsession with originality, sometimes even
at the expense of truth, partly by the necessity to react to the research of colleagues in one's narrow field, the time necessary for trying to locate one's own
research in an overarching picture of knowledge has shrunk. The turn against
"essentialism" has deprived many intellectuals of the capacity to distinguish
between essential and inessential knowledge, even if it is obvious that the
narrower and narrower focus of overspecialization cannot help discovering
the connections between the field one is studying and other fields. Although
the borders drawn between the various academic departments tend to ignore
them, such connections do exist in reality. To give an example, economy is
embedded in ecology. The refusal of many economists to reflect on this fact
and to try to arrive at an appropriate system of pricing for environmental
resources that goes beyond what the market dictates is one of the causes of
many—perhaps most—current ecological disasters since the market does
not mirror preferences of future generations. This is accelerated by the high
degree of mathematical sophistication in the calculation of short-term profits.
The mathematician with no interest in the ontological nature of mathematical
objects, the psychologist without any concept of the soul or any understanding of the irreducibility of the mental to the physical, the jurist without a concept of material justice, and the sociologist who cannot grasp that there are
ideal values that are not the same thing as social values can all do highly useful
and appreciated work in their fields. But there is something very important
missing in their intellectual outlook.

But the third and most worrisome aspect of the modern system of education is the undermining of the belief that education ultimately has a moral aim. This is a break from millennial tradition, and it is worth pondering what its causes are. It does not come as a surprise that the theory of education presented in Plato's *Republic* has its apex in the vision of the Form of the Good or that the *Politics* of Aristotle offers in its last book a theory of the education of the citizens of the ideal state.[10] But not many are aware that the education theories of early modernity also strongly focus on moral education, which is not only theoretical but includes character formation. The founder of modern English empiricism, John Locke, writes in *Some Thoughts Concerning Education* (1693): "I place virtue as the first and most necessary of those endowments that belong to a man or a gentleman, as absolutely requisite to make him valued and beloved by others, acceptable or tolerable to himself."[11] "All other considerations and accomplishments should give way, and be postponed, to this."[12] For learning without wisdom and virtue makes only "the more foolish, or worse men."[13] Wisdom in Locke means what we today would call prudence, and, together with breeding and learning, it is added to virtue as a further, but subordinated, goal of education.[14] At the same time, Locke does not believe that traditional mores are the criterion of virtue, which has to be based on reason. "The far greater part of mankind received even those opinions and ceremonies they would die for, rather from the fashions of their countries, and the constant practice of those about them, than from any conviction of their reasons."[15] Kant's pedagogical ideas, published in 1803 by his pupil Friedrich Theodor Rink based on the master's lectures, are similar to Locke's, even if he rejects the ultimate reduction of morality to the prudential hedonistic calculus that Locke proposes in the *Essay Concerning Human Understanding* (II 28). Also, for Kant, moral training is the peak of education and is built on discipline (which tames the animal drives), culture (which brings out abilities), and discretion, (which corresponds to what Locke calls "wisdom"). "It is not enough that a man shall be fitted for any end, but his disposition must be so trained that he shall choose none but good ends—good ends being those which are necessarily approved by everyone, and which may at the same time be the aim of everyone."[16] Children must be taught to respect what is right among humans—"that apple of God's eye upon earth."[17] It is crucial that a child not be beaten into obedience but "learn to act according to 'maxims,' the reasonableness of which he is able to see for himself."[18] Even religious education must render it clear that morality founds theology, not the other way around. "The religion which is founded merely on theology can never contain anything of morality. Hence, we derive no other feelings from it but fear on the one hand, and hope of reward on the other, and this produces merely a superstitious cult. Morality, then, must come first and theology follow; and that is religion."[19]

What are the reasons for the evaporation of moral education, at least in the higher grades of education? For while primary education, even in Western democracies, still inculcates basic secondary virtues, such as obedience (if only in order to get the class more disciplined), at least in tertiary, if not already in secondary education, ethical skepticism is rampant—among teachers, and thus, even if with a certain delay, also among pupils. Partly, people point to the difficulty of solving moral dilemmas (as if such difficulties would spill over to nondilemmatic cases), partly they condemn judgmentalism that does not consider extenuating circumstances (as if this condemnation did not presuppose moral principles itself). If the values communicated in early childhood do not pass the assault of skepticism, to which adolescents, for good reasons, subject many of their moral beliefs and fall prey to skepticism, it is unlikely that they will survive into adulthood. The power of habit may carry them on for a while, but when there is a painful conflict between duty and inclination and one is convinced that our knowledge of duties is sketchy and problematic at best, it is more than natural to follow the inclination whose evidence is palpable.

As far as I can see, the following factors are important in the decline of moral education. First, even if Kant is doubtless right that it is religion that has to be based on ethics, not the other way around (for we know a priori that God is good, and not simply by defining "good" as that which is willed by God), historically most moral systems, at least in the Abrahamic religions, are connected to a specific religious tradition within which they are taught. Partly, the faith in these traditions has diminished. Even where this is not the case, the modern Western state, for good reasons, has become religiously neutral. The horror of the intra-Christian religious wars of Europe in the sixteenth and seventeenth centuries had to come to an end. (It has not come to an end for several other religions.) But this means that the state cannot explicitly support a value system if the latter's validity is perceived to depend on a specific religion. True enough, early modern natural theology, natural law, and rational ethics tried to find an ethics based on pure reason. But even if their achievements are much better than they are purported to be, their social success has been limited. To be more precise, their ideas inspired the elites of the eighteenth and the nineteenth centuries (the fathers of the American Constitution, among others), but they never took hold of the majority of the populace. With the decline of European and American hegemony, non-European religions have come to the forefront of the global discourse, and despite remarkable success in finding common moral ground (for example, in the Universal Declaration of Human Rights), humanity is still far from having found a moral consensus on issues that are both substantial and concrete. (It is much easier to agree on formal and procedural principles and on generalities like "unjust wars are not allowed," as long as one does not have to spell out the criteria for just wars.) The commitment to one's own religious tradition, which had concrete answers but excluded large parts of humanity, seems now parochial to many. Yet, the generalities of the overlapping consensus of all cultures do not seem to provide a moral motivation strong enough to impose, for example, the limitations on one's desires that are demanded by the impending ecological catastrophe.

Second, the epistemic system that for the educated public has widely inherited the religions' authoritative claim to have privileged access to truth, namely the natural sciences, does not have answers to moral questions. For the natural sciences describe causal connections within the natural world; such knowledge is necessary, but never sufficient, to answer normative questions. And the scientifically cogent account of the evolutionary genesis of humankind can be, and often is, interpreted as supporting a view that the existence of humans is contingent and that moral norms, a byproduct of this contingent organism, inevitably share its contingency.

Third, the social sciences enjoy the greatest social prestige in economics, partly because it has undergone a high degree of mathematization and partly because it is linked to the desire for welfare, which is general among humans but clearly has replaced in modernity all otherworldly goals. The anthropology that most economists defend, however, is not simply that of the homo economicus understood as rationally and efficiently using scarce resources but that of the homo economicus as driven exclusively or at least mainly by selfish motives. Economic rationality in the first sense is compatible with morals (and is probably even necessary if one wants to achieve a greater moral good) but in the second sense undermines a fuller understanding of humans as moral agents.

But do not at least the humanities contribute to the formation of moral values? Alas, this is even less the case. For the humanities, in the modern sense, a creation of the nineteenth century, are as value-free as the social sciences. True enough, they try to reconstruct the values permeating the past of one's own as well as of other cultures, but, qua humanities, they do not have the capacity to tell us which of the many different value systems, which are often incompatible with each other, are the right ones. On the contrary, the encounter with the plurality of value systems often strengthens the feeling that there is no such thing as objective morality. In short, the academic disciplines that dominate the contemporary system of higher education hardly contribute to offering moral clarity.

CHALLENGES AND OPPORTUNITIES: ETHICS ARE NOT THE SAME AS MORALS

Even if the two terms sometimes are used interchangeably, I will use *ethics* to refer to the intellectual discipline that deals with morals. Clearly, one can be a moral person without any ethical competence—people rooted in noble traditions and animated by a subtle moral conscience may achieve a very high moral level without being able to investigate specifically ethical questions. Is it also possible to be ethically competent without being a moral person? I am afraid that there is not only a logical possibility but that the phenomenon is quite frequent. People investigating metaethical questions—questions concerning, for example, the epistemological status of moral judgments and the ontological nature of values—need mainly conceptual clarity and logical acumen; they may never get to addressing concrete moral issues. But even those who work in normative ethics and in applied ethics—that is, those who try to determine the general principle of moral action and those who apply it to determinate areas, such as business or war—may prove unable to behave as they claim one ought to behave. Indeed, weakness of the will is compatible with intelligence. Or, even worse, they may use their analytical abilities to rationalize their amoral preferences. "The tools of good justification are the tools of good rationalizing and self-deception as well."[20] Needless to say, the incapacity of intellectuals to act according to their own moral principles does not show the falsity of their principles. But it undermines their public recognition, for moral principles are necessarily considered not easy to follow if those who uphold them in theory are unable to do so in practice. And it certainly diminishes the respect for such ethicists as persons (again, not necessarily as ethicists).[21] What we most cherish is the combination of moral and ethical competencies—we admire the person who both shows virtuous behavior and is able to justify her choices with sound arguments.

As the title of the chapter suggests, I am interested here in the teaching of ethics, not moral behavior. But such teaching will be far more successful if the students already know and esteem moral behavior, for then their desire to find its justification is rooted in a strong motive. Teaching ethics to an amoral person is not impossible, but it is analogous to teaching musicology to a deaf one. Deaf people can grasp the concept of sounds and the nature of the relations between them, but they lack the experiential content that makes such knowledge fascinating. This analogy implies that successfully teaching ethics presupposes, besides certain genetic predispositions, a prereflexive moral education that, in most cases, has to occur within the family. Where it has failed to occur, it is naïve to believe that educational ethics can step in and replace it. It will fail, too—not because it does not have good arguments but because such arguments are not able to resonate experientially and transform behavior. Ethical education will be most successful where students with a good moral education desire more intellectual clarity and have the cognitive capacities to achieve it (which, again, is not granted to every moral person). In this process, not all prereflexive moral beliefs will receive confirmation; some will be challenged, some even refuted. But it will be an enrichment of one's moral consciousness, and not its corrosion, only if there is a prereflexive foundation for reflection. Traditional religions that later in life offer space for philosophical-theological reflection on the moral assumptions inculcated into the children's minds—a space that allows for the further development of theoretical and practical tenets—often achieve a remarkable balance between moral stability and adaptation to changing environments.

Even if moral education is not the topic of this chapter, two points concerning it must be mentioned. First, education in general both produces and presupposes knowledge. Certainly, in an ideal situation, the knowledge presupposed and the knowledge produced are distributed among two different subjects, the educator and the student, respectively. But the process had to start somewhere. This means that the first educator could not yet build on the advantages of the education he is imparting for the first time. This is true not only of the first education but also of any pedagogic innovation. If it is novel and important, then the innovator must recognize that she herself lacked a crucial benefit, and this might shed doubts concerning the quality of her discovery. Kant, after writing, "For insight depends on education, and education in its turn depends on insight," points to the necessity of a slow evolution of pedagogy over the course of the generations.[22] This, one could say, is a problem common to the development of all disciplines, and the obvious progress of humankind shows that it is indeed solvable. But it seems to me that in the case of moral education, there is a specific difficulty involved, which is due to the fact that this type of education is not simply theoretical but demands behavior corresponding to the norms taught. Locke, Rousseau, and Kant all agree that few things are more important in moral education than the personal model.[23] One must teach by example more than by precepts. They do not deny my argument that an ethical theory is not confuted by behavior contradicting it. If they did, Rousseau could hardly take his own pedagogical work seriously, given that he delivered his four children to orphanages at a time when the mortality rate there was especially high. But they rightly believe that on a prereflective level, lessons contradicted by the teacher's own behavior will not prove fruitful. This, however, has the consequence that new moral insights are difficult to communicate because individuals who have just gained them often have not yet learned to live by them. Thus, their teaching lacks credibility. The new ecological ethics is a good example—it is often taught and discussed at international conferences whose settings are in strident contrast to the demand for more frugality which the new ethics entails.

The second point regarding moral education is that one of the central demands of ethics is autonomy, which the teaching of ethics as a rational discipline indeed supports. But the moral education that all ethical education, as we saw, presupposes cannot yet be based on autonomy alone. True, the fostering of the conscience of the child is an early equivalent of the rational discourse characteristic of ethics. However, this is already a relatively late step in education that has to be preceded by earlier ones. Thanks to Jean Piaget's genetic psychology and developmental psychology in general, we have today a much better grasp of the steps according to which the thought of children develops than the classical authors of pedagogy had. This is also true for the specific field of moral thought—from Jean Piaget's *The Moral Judgment of the Child*[24] to Lawrence Kohlberg's theory of the three levels (preconventional, conventional, and postconventional) and six stages of moral development (which I have to ignore here).[25] On a less sophisticated level, humanity has always known that younger children cannot be brought to reason by appealing to their reason, for what is to be brought about cannot yet be presupposed. That is why, as already mentioned, Kant introduces moral training only as a fourth step of education after discipline, culture, and discretion. Discipline, according to him, consists in constraining our animal nature in order to prevent damage to the specific human nature, while culture develops technical and discretion social abilities.[26] It is worth mentioning that an author rooted in a very different tradition, namely psychoanalysis, makes a similar point. Bruno Bettelheim insists that "a more refined morality must have as its base a once rigid belief in right and wrong" and that focused learning in school can hardly start to occur if the child has not yet subjected the pleasure principle to the reality principle and formed the content of a superego by internalizing parental authority. "For education to proceed children must have learned to fear something before they come to school."[27]

The education of ethics, based on reason, can thus only succeed if the psychodynamic structures are in place that motivate the learning of complex issues, if there is both a moral sensibility and an intellectual capacity to form abstract concepts and check inferences, and if earlier stages of moral development have already occurred. But after puberty, ethics classes should be introduced in all high schools. For neither should ethical education be limited to religion classes (for when students lose religious beliefs, the moral ones will vanish hand in hand with them), nor should ethics take place only in the form of civic education, which often enough instrumentalizes ethics for the purposes of the state and gives it a nationalist slant. What should be taught in such classes? If we want to find an answer to this question, we must keep in mind the intellectual reasons that have corroded the preeminent place of ethics in the system of traditional education that was laid out earlier.

First, the rejection of a religious foundation of ethics was mainly motivated by the need of the modern state to guarantee stability to the political system without having to enforce a homogeneous religion. In a world in which the number not only of inner-Christian denominations but also of very different religions present in the most advanced states has proliferated, there is no way to find a binding ground common to all citizens within a specific religious tradition. Religious pluralism is a fact, and among the widespread worldviews there is also an irreligious atheism. We can only, and must, help the students "to face, in as rational a way as possible, the bewildering choices of values, principles, ideologies, ways of life, etc. with which they are confronted."[28] The experience of an aporia while confronting a moral dilemma, as in several early Platonic dialogues, can be a useful starting point to motivate people to rise from concrete moral norms to the general principle that underlies them. This means that, instead of teaching certain sets of values and norms as being the valid ones because they happen to belong to our own tradition or are in our own national or class interest and then devising psychological and pedagogical techniques to spread them more efficiently, we must allow a "bracketing" of our factual mores and teach a commitment to formal philosophical methods that allow us to evaluate according to a rational, ideal standard the socially recognized values and norms. Such a standard, to be accepted by everybody, can only be the principle of universalizability—which, however, is only a necessary and not a sufficient principle of ethics. Something is obligatory, permitted, or forbidden for a person only if—ceteris paribus—it is obligatory, permitted, or forbidden for all persons. Certainly, the ceteris paribus-clause opens up many questions, not all of which are easy to handle (the main being whether rights to positive benefits do not unfairly create duties for those who have to deliver them). But it certainly shifts the burden of proof to those who claim that the clause does not hold in a particular case. The principle of universalizability must, however, be accompanied by a set of values that are ultimately grounded in the recognition of reason, which in turn presupposes life, property, and social recognition in order to operate in finite and embodies minds. Some extensions of the principle of universalizability do not come without an intellectual effort—the idea of intergenerational justice is rooted in principle, but because future generations are not yet there, it is easy to overlook this idea.

The appeal to a formal principle and certain basic values that flow from the concept of embodied mind transcends values that have only particular resonance due to historic contingencies. This is good because ethics should not help to perpetuate social mores, such as sexism or racism, which are incompatible with the principle of universalizability. But it is, at the same time, of utmost importance that the commitment to the formal principle be articulated into a concrete set of norms, some of which (not all) have to be the basis of the legal system.[29] Such norms are presupposed by any pluralist society that does not want to fall apart; for even if in a pluralist society specific norms like "Rest faithful to the religious community in which you were brought up" are no longer valid, new ones are added that might be even more difficult to internalize, such as "Respect people from other religious background and build up a common trust that is no longer rooted in common religious practices."[30] Such respect is not easy to live by and is certainly not the same as the attempt to impose on everybody a secular outlook.

The transition from the factual mores to the ideal standard must not end in moral skepticism or in an attitude that claims only one's rights without recognizing corresponding duties. It can free from duties that have been unfairly imposed. But on the whole, we should trust the moral seriousness of those who have subjected factual mores to the scrutiny of reason only if a moral consciousness ensues that demands more from oneself. Otherwise, chaos will spread, and the need to keep a society going may easily lead to a new imposition of dogmatic values, which will remain dogmatic, that is, not based on reason, even if their content changes. R. M. Hare writes: "But moral philosophers spread at least as much muddle as clarity, and it is touch and go whether the educational revolution will get into the hands of people who have this clarity or not. If not, the revolution could easily make matters worse. All that would happen would be that a different descriptive definition would be used to programme the machinery of the 'good man' factory."[31]

Second, the replacement of traditional religious ethics by an ethics based on reason needn't, and shouldn't, involve an antireligious turn. Certainly, philosophers committed to reason must reject religious voluntarism, which reduces the good to God's will without asking whether this will is just—with arguments that ultimately go back to Plato's dialogue *Euthyphro*. But most naïve religious people are not inclined toward voluntarism either—they do not think that God could or would have ordered whatever he wanted. This conviction is a powerful starting point to persuade people of the possibility of a theory of the good that is not derivative of religious beliefs: the concept of God presupposes the concept of good and thus cannot ground it—or must be identical with it. But this does not mean that the rational autonomy of ethics renders the concept of God superfluous. There are two reasons why the addition of religious beliefs to moral ones is possible and even desirable. On the one hand, the advantage of a religious position is the ontological interpretation of the Idea of the Good. For an irreligious view, the moral norms are an Ought whose implementation in the world is ultimately haphazard, while the religious person has a deep trust that the Good will prevail because it constitutes the ultimate essence of reality. In a position like that of Kant, God, whose core is the moral law, has to be understood as the principle permeating the world and directing it to an approximation to the moral end. (Nothing, by the way, excludes that this process proceeds according to general laws.) But religion does not only add a metaphysical dimension to ethics. Almost all religions are connected with some historical event that is considered constitutive of their own tradition and celebrated as such. The feeling of sharing a common history is a crucial factor in the forging of a sense of community that goes beyond the abstract recognition of the same values. We would achieve enormous progress in the moral and spiritual unification of humankind if the various religions did not only succeed in elaborating a concrete moral consensus but could also agree on a common narrative according to which the various religions are all parts of a common divine plan.

Third, since concrete moral norms are often the conclusion of a mixed syllogism, that is, of a syllogism consisting of an evaluative and a descriptive premise, an ethically mature person does not need only a formal moral principle and insight into values; she must be able to access relevant empirical knowledge. While it is utterly hopeless to appropriate all the knowledge of one's time, it is possible and even necessary to develop a sense of what is essential. The ecological crisis of our time, for example, suggests that a crucial part of a responsible education must be the communication of basic ecological insights—human activities must be placed within the natural environment. The social sciences and the humanities that lack this awareness will hardly help us to face this crisis. *Ecology* literally means "doctrine of the house"—it is a holistic discipline focusing on the framework within which life unfolds. But what we need beyond ecology as a subdiscipline of biology is a strengthening of our sense of how the various claims of validity that make us human fit together and form an intellectual home. For traditional philosophy, this was a crucial task, but late modernity has dramatically neglected it. Only if we succeed in addressing it again will we be able to overcome the aforementioned impediments to moral thought that the development of the academic disciplines has built up.

Let me briefly sketch what I mean and what, in my eyes, should be taught to as many adolescents as possible, ideally by involving them in a Socratic manner and directing them through intelligent questions to find the right answers themselves.[32] While it is both scientifically absurd and ecologically irresponsible to deny the place of humans within the evolution of life forms by variation and natural selection, naturalism is by far not the only possible ontology that does justice to the fact of evolution. And the problem of naturalism is that it does not do justice to other facts that are no less relevant. Moral principles lose their binding force if they are conceived as being the result of a contingent evolution; there is no way to *justify* their validity by merely *explaining*, or better, claiming to explain their genesis within evolution. There is no way from the Is to the Ought—and this does not entail that there is no knowledge of the Ought. If there is such knowledge, as every moral person has to assume, the evolution of life has rather to be interpreted as a slow process toward the emergence of mind and cooperative social behavior.[33] It is no less absurd to hold that the appearance of the mind—still abstracting from the moral values toward which it is oriented—can be understood on the basis of the laws of physics and chemistry alone. For the mental is not identical with the physical, even if it may supervene on it. But if it supervenes on it as a mere epiphenomenon, it has no causal power. And if it has no causal power, its appearance cannot be explained by the mechanism of natural selection. In short, matter, mind, and ideal norms seem to be three irreducible strata of reality, and the recognition of their difference and their connections should be at the core of a holistic education. A nonmaterialistic ontology must be accompanied by a nonempiricist epistemology that allows for cognitive access to ideal objects. A complex concept of God as the principle of these connections and their intelligibility will then appear not simply as an heirloom from irrational traditions but also be of deep philosophical significance.

Concerning the changes of values in human history, relativism is not the only, and not even the most plausible, response. It is not plausible because relativism is itself historically situated and thus, according to its own lights, must be relativized to a certain epoch. It is not the only one because the history of our moral consciousness can be interpreted, in analogy to the history of scientific thought, as a slow process of approximation to the demands of a universalistic moral ideal in which the rise of economic rationality plays an important but limited place. After systematic ethics, a philosophy of the history of ethics also has to be offered as soon the awareness of the historical evolution of ethical systems emerges in the students.[34] And part of the moral evolution of humankind is the recognition that we share a common responsibility to educate all human beings, not only in order to help them maintain themselves as part of the global society but also to comprehend the complex nature of our world and to attain a greater depth by grasping moral values irreducible to self-interest as well as their ultimate source.

NOTES

1. I take the term from Gehlen, Arnold, *Der Mensch: Seine Natur und seine Stellung in der Welt* (Berlin: Junker und Dünnhaupt, 1940). For an English translation, see Gehlen, *Man: His Nature and Place in the World*, trans. C. McMillan and K. Pillemer (New York: Columbia University Press, 1987).
2. Kant, Immanuel, *On Education (Ueber Pädagogik)*, trans. Annette Churton (Boston: D.C. Heath, 1900), 6. (I give also the page of the original edition of 1803 [A] in order to facilitate checking the German original: A 8). Niklas Luhmann differentiates by writing that humans are born, but persons are due to socialization and education. See Luhmann, *Das Erziehungssystem der Gesellschaft* (Frankfurt: Suhrkamp, 2002), 38.
3. The Protestant contribution to literacy and education (and thus also to liberal democracy in general) can be shown also in the former European colonies; see Woodberry, Robert, "The Missionary Roots of Liberal Democracy," *American Political Science Review* 106, no. 2 (2012): 244–274.
4. Gellner, E., *Nations and Nationalism* (Oxford: Basil Blackwell, 1983), 31.
5. That schools subject children to general norms that are valid independently of the affective bonds in the family and thus prepare them for the public spirit they need as citizens has been forcefully argued by Durkheim, Emile, *L'éducation morale* [*Moral Education*], trans. Everett K. Wilson and Herman Schnurer (New York: Free Press of Glencoe, 1961).
6. On these reasons, see chapter 1.
7. See the classical essay by Becker, Gary D., "An Economic Analysis of Fertility," in *Demographic and Economic Change in Developed Countries* (Princeton, NJ: Princeton University Press, 1960), 209–240.

8.   Malthus, *An Essay on the Principles of Population* (Harmondsworth: Penguin, 1986), 101.
9.   See the overview by Max Roser at: https://ourworldindata.org/fertility-rate. To give one concrete example: a paper studying Nigeria suggests that one additional year of female education reduces early fertility by 0.26 births. See Osili, Una Okonkwo, and Bridget Terry Long, "Does Female Schooling Reduce Fertility? Evidence from Nigeria," in *Journal of Development Economics* 87, no. 1 (2008): 57–75.
10. In Aristotle's *Nicomachean Ethics* too reflections on education can be found in the last book, book 8 (1179b3 ff.).
11. *The Works of John Locke*, vol. IX (London: Thomas Tegg, 1823), 128 (=$135).
12. *The Works of John Locke*, 58 (=$70).
13. *The Works of John Locke*, 142 (=$147).
14. *The Works of John Locke*, 128 (=$134).
15. *The Works of John Locke*, 141 (=$146).
16. Kant, *On Education*, 20 (A 23).
17. Kant, *On Education*, 104 (A 123).
18. Kant, *On Education*, 83 (A 98).
19. Kant, *On Education*, 112 (A 133 f.).
20. Puka, Bill, "Inclusive Moral Education: A Critique and Integration of Competing Approaches," in *Moral Education and Pluralism*, ed. Mal Leicester, Celia Modgil, and Sohan Modgil (London: Falmer Press, 2000), 131–148, 135.
21. See a good overview of the problem in Ammann, Christoph, Barbara Bleisch, and Anna Goppel, eds., *Müssen Ethiker moralisch sein?: Essays über Philosophie und Lebensführung* (Frankfurt: Campus Verlag, 2011).
22. Kant, *On Education*, 11 (A 14).
23. *The Works of John Locke*, 29 (=§ 37), 50 (=§ 67), 70 (=§ 82), 87 (=§ 94); Rousseau, Jean-Jacques, *Emile or On Education*, introduction, translation, and notes by Allan Bloom (New York: Basic Books 1979), 42, 52, 100, 104, 119, 131, 141, 182, 232, 251, 310, 321,334, 378, 388, 390, 397. Some of the passages are not limited to moral education;Kant, *On Education*, 94 (A 112).
24. Piaget, Jean, *The Moral Judgment of the Child* (London: Kegan Paul, Trench, Trubner, 1932).
25. Kohlberg, Lawrence, *Essays on Moral Development*, 2 vols. (New York: Harper & Row, 1981 and 1984). As a psychologist, Kohlberg presupposes the truth of an ethical theory strongly influenced by Socrates/Plato and Kant without really arguing for it. Among the various critics of Kohlberg, I want to point out Gertrud Nunner-Winkler, "Zum Verständnis von Moral—Entwicklungen in der Kindheit," in *Detlef Horster and Jürgen Oelkers*, ed. Pädagogik und Ethik, 173–192 (Wiesbaden: VS Verlag, 2005). Nunner-Winkler tries to mediate between Kohlberg and Elliot Turiel, *The Development of Social Knowledge: Morality and Convention* (Cambridge: Cambridge University Press, 1983), who ascribes moral knowledge already to young children. According to Nunner-Winkler, this is true, but moral motivation, studied by Kohlberg, is built up much later than moral knowledge.
26. Kant, *On Education*, 18 (A 22).
27. Bettelheim, Bruno, "Moral Education," in James M. Gustafson, Richard S. Peters, Lawrence Kihlberg, Bruno Bettelheim, and Kenneth Keniston, *Moral Education. Five Lectures* (Cambridge, MA: Harvard University Press, 1970), 84–107, 89.
28. Hare, R. M., "Value Education in a Pluralist Society: A Philosophical Glance at the Humanities Curriculum Project" (1976), reprinted in Hare, R. M., *Essays on Religion and Education* (Oxford: Clarendon Press, 1992), 137–153.
29. See my attempt in Hösle, V., *Morals and Politics* (Notre Dame, IN: University of Notre Dame Press, 2004).

30. Compare Crittenden, Brian, "Moral Education in a Pluralist Liberal Democracy," in *Education in Morality*, ed. J. Mark Halstead and Terence H. McLaughlin (London: Routledge, 1999), 47–61, 56ff.

31. "Platonism in Moral Education: Two Varieties," in Hare, *Essays on Religion and Education*, 178–190, 184.

32. A highly impressive example of the philosophical acumen and fantasy that a child can develop already at the ages of eleven and twelve are the letters by Nora K. in: Nora K. and V. Hösle, *The Dead Philosophers' Café* (Notre Dame, IN: University of Notre Dame Press, 2000). The fact that the German original was translated into fifteen languages, among which seven from Asia, shows that many children from all over the world could connect with Nora's imaginative creation of conversations between great philosophers of the past.

33. We owe a powerful philosophical analysis in this direction to Nagel, Thomas, *Mind and Cosmos* (Oxford: Oxford University Press, 2012).

34. See my essay "Can a Plausible Story Be Told of the History of Ethics? An Alternative to MacIntyre's *After Virtue*," in *Dimensions of Goodness*, ed. V. Hösle (Newcastle upon Tyne: Cambridge Scholars Publishing, 2013), 113–148.

10

EDUCATION FOR A PURPOSEFUL LIFE

WILLIAM DAMON AND ANNE COLBY

Purpose has long been identified in philosophy and theology as an essential component of a well-directed life. In recent years, support for this longstanding theoretical intuition has come from studies in psychological science and medicine that have documented important life benefits associated with purpose. Such benefits may include energy and motivation, resilience under pressure, a positive personal identity, emotional stability, academic and vocational achievement, faith and trust in the affirmative value of life, and a sense of direction that can withstand episodic periods of uncertainty and confusion.[1] Recent writing in medicine, especially in gerontology, has suggested that purpose may contribute to energy and health throughout the lifespan.[2] In response, nonprofit organizations worldwide are dedicating themselves to the task of helping people find and sustain purpose in their lives.[3]

The benefits of purpose can extend beyond individuals to the broader world. Purposeful people have the capacity to contribute greatly to their societies. The features of purpose that spur motivation, achievement, commitment, and direction in individuals have the potential to drive social change in ways that broadly improve the human condition. Many moral markers of human history have been created by people committed to prosocial purposes.

For education, the essential task is to provide young people with the tools they need to build lives of purpose. Some of these tools are informational and cognitive, some are social, and others are capacities related to character. The challenge for education is that there is no textbook or curriculum program for teaching purpose to schoolchildren—nor, given the nature of purpose, could any particular book, program, or other standardized approach be effective across a broad spectrum of the world's children, for the development of purpose is an individual achievement that occurs in particular ways for each person. Yet, psychological study has provided us with pedagogical principles that can be applied creatively in a wide variety of school settings to help students to become purposeful, each in their individual ways.[4] In this essay, we provide a scientific foundation for such guidelines and present a set of principles for a universal pedagogy of purpose.

AN OPERATIONAL DEFINITION OF PURPOSE FOR EDUCATIONAL PRACTICE

It is elementary that any field of practice requires clear, unambiguous definitions. Among other things, this means that every key term must have its own meaning. No word should be used to signify different things, as it is used across various contexts, and no concept of interest requires more than one term to denote it. In medicine, for example, when a doctor makes a diagnosis, it is essential that the diagnostic term that the doctor uses is understood in exactly the same way by everyone treating the patient.

The same principle applies to educational practice, and in the area of purpose, we must make a special effort to ensure that this is carried out. *Purpose* is a term that is widely used in the vernacular, and the vernacular uses of the term do not have sufficient clarity or rigor for either scientific research or educational practice. Most critically, many vernacular uses of the term do not capture the features of purpose that provide the individual and societal benefits that are special to this particular capacity.

In ordinary language, the term *purpose* is commonly conflated with the following related but conceptually distinct terms: *goal, passion, meaning, vision, mandate, dream, wish,* and *desire.* We have noticed this conflation not only among laypersons but also among professionals attempting to do scientific and educational work in this area. Such lack of conceptual rigor would be a serious impediment to progress in both science and education if not corrected.

For this reason, our team synthesized a definition from philosophical writings when we first started to investigate purpose, and we have seen some early signs of an emerging coalescence around this definition in recent scientific and educational treatments.[5] We composed this definition to (1) draw on the way purpose has been discussed in philosophy over the centuries and (2) to capture the features that give purpose its special psychological province. Our operational definition is as follows:

Purpose is an active commitment to accomplish aims that are both meaningful to the self and of consequence to the world beyond the self.

This definition includes three elements necessary to capture the distinct qualities of purpose as a unique psychological capacity. First, purpose is a *commitment*. It is not a fleeting aim or one-time effort—however noble that effort may be. If someone jumps into a river to save a drowning victim of a plane crash, this is a commendable act, but it would be an exaggeration (and thus a misnomer) to call this a purpose in life (assuming, of course, that the person does not regularly patrol rivers looking out for plane-crash victims). Rather, this is a one-time heroic response to a chance event. It may be, of course, that this person has a commitment to, say, "help people in trouble," of which this response is one of many instantiations. If so, it is this more general aim (helping people in trouble) that defines the person's purpose rather than the particular goal of saving drowning plane victims that arose in that one moment. Purpose implies a commitment over time. This does not mean that it must last forever: people take on new purposes and let others go over the course of their lives. But if a person does not stick with a goal in more than a momentary, ephemeral way, that goal does not serve as a purpose for that person.

The second essential point in our definition is that purpose must be "meaningful to the self." A person needs to "own it": to believe in it and to pursue it voluntarily. A command that feels unwelcome or externally driven will not be a purpose unless the person comes to see the value in it herself. It may be important to obey an external command, but the obedience will not be purposeful if the enterprise is not meaningful to the person. A child who does not find schoolwork meaningful will not approach homework assignments with purpose. The child still may learn something from doing it, but this will not be a purposeful activity until the child sees meaning in it.

The third essential point is that purposeful aims are "of consequence to the world beyond the self." Purpose is meaningful to the self (see point two above), but it also includes an intent to accomplish something for the world beyond the self. This additional beyond-the-self component has been frequently noted in philosophical and theological treatments of purpose. As Rick Warren said in the opening line of his popular 2002 theological book *The Purpose-Driven Life*: "It's not about you."[6] This "beyond-the-self" component of purpose generally signifies a prosocial intent. There are also purposeful intents that can be beyond-the-self without being *intentionally* prosocial. We often have heard about examples of artists and scientists whose purpose is directed toward their domain (art or science), and thus is beyond-the-self, but who construe their work as contributing to their fields—to the art or science itself—rather than being directed explicitly toward the benefit of other people. Their work may eventually contribute to human welfare, but this is not why they are doing it. Still, their work is purposeful because it aims to contribute to a domain of activity beyond the self—in such cases, the domains of art or science.

As we have defined it, the concept of purpose is distinct from other concepts that, although related, are in some ways distinct from it. For example, it is common for purpose to be conflated with meaning, as in the statement, "I hope to live a life of meaning and purpose." In our definition of purpose, the terms *meaning* and *purpose* are not the same because purpose has a beyond-the-self component that meaning lacks. This is *not* to deny the value of meaningful activities: people, for example, may find meaningful activities, such as going to movies or listening to music, uplifting as well as pleasurable. But such activities are distinct from purposeful engagements that attempt to leave a mark on the wider world beyond the self.

Similarly, each of the other associated concepts we have mentioned—*goals, passions, visions, dreams, mandates, wishes, desires*—have value in themselves, but they are not the same as purpose. (If they were, we would not need the term *purpose.*) A purpose is indeed a goal, but it is one particular kind of goal: short-term and self-oriented goals do not represent purpose. A purpose often ignites passion but not always. At times, people pursue purposes in subdued, patient, reflective, or sometimes even grim ways. Purpose is more than a dream because it includes action. Purpose is not a mandate because it is voluntary.

Purpose is a unique psychological capacity with its own particular qualities. It is these qualities that give purpose its special power to benefit purposeful individuals and their societies. For example, the enduring aspect of purpose implies the commitment that is required to accomplish consequential tasks. The meaningful aspect of purpose implies that purpose is a voluntary commitment, which creates the conditions for the energy and motivation that purpose fosters. The beyond-the-self component preempts the hazards of self-absorption and facilitates resilience and resolution under pressure. In these and other ways, defining purpose in a rigorous way captures the unique qualities that explain how purpose contributes both to social improvement and personal well-being. It also helps us understand how purpose develops through the lifespan—a question that we now turn to.

HOW PURPOSE DEVELOPS IN YOUTH

For most young people, purpose is a fairly late-developing capacity. Studies of purpose have found that only about one in five adolescents between the ages of twelve and twenty-two have a fully developed sense of purpose. It is rare for children younger than twelve to exhibit purpose, and the prevalence of purpose does not increase much between midadolescence and early adulthood.[7] In middle-aged and older adults, the prevalence of purpose has been reported as slightly less than one out of three. Younger adults tend to fall somewhere between these two groups.[8] This is an unusual phenomenon in child development: most psychological capacities grow rapidly during the childhood and adolescent years. Many young people do not find sustaining purposes until the end of their twenties, and, as we discuss in the following two sections, many never become purposeful, even as they reach middle and late adulthood.

There is a common pattern among young people who find purpose. The initial step is the child's discovery of personal interests and talents that the child finds especially compelling. The psychologist Peter Benson called such personal interests and talents "sparks" and claimed convincingly that every child has his or her own particular sparks.[9] Those who eventually turn their interests and talents into purposes experience two revelations as they learn more about the world: (1) something in the world needs to be improved, corrected, or added to; (2) I have the desire and ability to make a contribution to this. The task of doing this may be daunting, as it is for young people who dedicate themselves to heroic challenges such as curing cancer or alleviating poverty. Or it may be quite ordinary, as in those who dedicate themselves to conventional vocations, raising a family, or any number of other purposes that contribute to the healthy functioning of human society. Purposes need not be heroic or extraordinary to provide psychological and social benefits.

The adults in a young person's life play an important role in the search for purpose. Many purposeful young people have connected with role models who demonstrated lives of purpose and mentors who helped them along the way. In addition, young people who have found purpose often say that their families have supported their choices eventually. This does not always happen immediately. Often, families resist an unconventional choice that their child might make—to become, say, an artist, a chef, an athlete, a risk-taking entrepreneur. Such resistance, if not too overwhelming, actually may test and strengthen the child's resolve in the cases where that resolve is well-considered.

Finally, adults—especially schoolteachers—can play a role in young people's development of purpose by helping them learn the skills and knowledge they need to pursue their purposes effectively. In order to play this role successfully, teachers must show students how academic learning can enable purposeful pursuits. We return to this essential teaching challenge later in this chapter when we present the educational principles behind purpose learning.

Purposeful adolescents, young adults, and later-life adults from the United States exhibit a wide range of purposes that inspire their efforts and direct their daily and future choices. These include building and supporting a family, pursuing a vocation, serving God or another faith-related cause, implementing artistic aims, doing charitable work in one's community, contributing to the broader civic society, preserving the planet and its resources, and contributing to the welfare of pets and other animals.

PURPOSE IN MIDDLE AND LATE ADULTHOOD

In this paper, we have focused so far on young people—children, adolescents, and young adults. These developmental phases mark ages of special opportunity and relevance for formal education. But it is important to consider the development of purpose in the later phases of life as well in order to provide needed context for designing educational efforts at any phase. Developmental scientists who focus on the ways that particular phenomena play out across the whole of life have stressed that middle and even late adulthood provide ample prospects for positive developmental change.[10]

In our contemporary world, understanding the potential for purpose in later adulthood is more important than ever due to worldwide demographic shifts toward an aging population due to lower birth rates and greater longevity. This demographic shift offers opportunities and challenges. As the share of populations over age sixty-five grows, so does the capacity of many older people to engage more actively and meaningfully with life. On average, older people are healthier, more likely to live independently, and less likely to be disabled than ever before.[11] This recent "longevity bonus"— accompanied by a greater likelihood of a high quality of life and increased active engagement in the postretirement years—allows for an age of opportunity in which life goals, trajectory, and meaning may be reimagined, reinvigorated, and realized.

This image of older adults as purpose-driven contributors to the world beyond the self flies in the face of widespread stereotypes of older people as withdrawn from key life roles, burdens on younger adults, or focused solely on enjoying hard-earned leisure time. Yet, a study that we conducted of U.S. adults aged fifty to ninety-two revealed substantial numbers of fully purposeful individuals.[12] Overall, the prevalence of purpose in this nationally representative sample of 1,198 U.S. women and men was 31 percent, with those over sixty-five showing a rate of 33 percent. As in studies of younger people, we found that purpose was associated with higher scores on measures of many other aspects of positive adaptation and development.

The study also revealed that purpose in this age group does not meaningfully vary as a function of health status or demographic characteristics such as socioeconomic status. This means that purpose is widely accessible to people of all backgrounds, all ages across the spectrum of later life, the full range of socioeconomic statuses, both men and women, and that being in poor health need not prevent purposeful pursuits.

The search for purpose should never cease. As people age, they take on new aspirations and commitments: this is one of the hallmarks of healthy aging. In so doing, they draw on capacities they developed earlier in life. In this way, the accomplishments of the early years can set the stage for an entire life of meaning, fulfillment, and contribution to the common good. It is encouraging that the prevalence of full purpose is higher in adulthood, even late adulthood, than in young people; but, even so, too many adults miss the life satisfaction and opportunity to contribute provided by a purposeful approach to life. This reality is the basis for our sense of urgency in calling for greater attention to educating for purpose for the sake of both individual and collective well-being.

EDUCATION FOR PURPOSE IN PRIMARY AND SECONDARY SCHOOLS

Recent developmental science research on purpose has increased our understanding of how purpose develops across the lifespan. These studies show that the potential for purpose learning never ceases during one's lifetime. It is also clear that purpose is a deep psychological capacity that requires years to fully mature, and it draws on an intricate mix of cognitive skills, character dispositions, emotional regulation, social supports, and life experiences. For this reason, it is essential to initiate young people's quest for purpose during the school years.

Educational programs have risen to this challenge, introducing curricula and other classroom experiences designed to foster purposeful academic work among students and encourage students' interests in purposes beyond the classroom. One excellent source of current educational efforts directed at students' purpose learning is Heather Malin's *Teaching for Purpose*.[13] In her book, Malin articulates the implications of basic research for educational programs and reviews several multischool programs with names such as Project Wayfinder and the Open Institute. She also describes "purpose toolkits," designed by Claremont Graduate University and other research centers, that are being adopted by elementary and secondary school programs around the world. In general, these programs and toolkits implement—each in its own way—the following principles:

- Teachers help identify each individual student's talents and interests.
- Curricula present the "why" of academic subjects: why this material is important to learn, why it was created, why it is useful and enlightening, and so on.
- Teachers introduce human exemplars of purpose across the domains of knowledge (math, science, history, the arts) that students are expected to learn.
- Pedagogical strategies offer students multiple options for learning and encourage their choices.
- Educators engage students in purpose-oriented pursuits, such as long-term projects with real-world implications

Teachers also can provide examples of purpose in the ways they comport themselves in the classroom. One golden (but too often neglected) opportunity to do this is to tell students why they chose teaching as a profession, what they find fulfilling about teaching, and what they hope to accomplish with their students. The point is not to persuade their students to become teachers (students must make their own occupational choices) but rather to demonstrate what it looks like for admired adults to pursue an occupation with purpose.

Along the same lines, teachers can interject into the curriculum stories about the life choices of those who created the knowledge students are learning in school. When, for example, young people hear about the dedication, persistence, and creativity of the scientists who unravel the secrets of the universe, not only does this bring scientific knowledge to life, but it also provides young people with models of purposeful work. This is so for every field of knowledge that is taught in the classroom. It applies with special force to the field of history, which offers teachers countless opportunities to inspire students with cases of purposeful men and women who have contributed to the best traditions of civilizations.

Elementary and secondary schools around the world share the universal mission of preparing students for the fundamental opportunities and challenges of life, including productive vocations, constructive citizenship, and the literacies and numeracies that enable adaptability and continued learning across the lifespan. In contrast, university systems from country to country differ in their stated missions. And in any case, higher education does not reach all young people. Nevertheless, recent trends in university education in the United States and elsewhere have shone a spotlight on purpose learning in this context as well. We now turn to a discussion of teaching for purpose at the university level.

UNIVERSITY EDUCATION TOWARD PURPOSE

To gain a better understanding of factors that contribute to university students' purpose development, we are currently engaged in a study of purpose in a diverse group of colleges and universities in the United States. This research is still in an early stage, but some preliminary insights are beginning to emerge. First, an overview of the participating institutions reveals attention to purpose development in a number of programs. In addition to curricular offerings and particular kinds of in-class experiences, programs that are likely to address purpose development include those that engage students with their local communities and other forms of civic participation, programs that help students think about their choices of university major and vocational field, those that address purpose as a dimension of students' psychological flourishing or well-being, and those that take advantage of on-campus residence hall experiences to foster psychological growth.

In addition to collecting detailed information about the study's participating institutions, we have also surveyed samples of students at each. The study design also includes a second wave of survey data and interviews with a subset of respondents. Those follow-up data are being collected now, and findings based on the full study will be available in 2023. Since the longitudinal follow-up is not yet complete, our analyses to date cannot support causal conclusions. They can, however, suggest some preliminary conclusions, such as associations of certain undergraduate experiences with purpose development. Based on the first wave of student surveys, we have learned that purpose is more prevalent in some disciplinary majors than others. Perhaps not surprisingly, students majoring in professional/vocational fields that are prosocial in nature, such as healthcare professions, education, and social services, are more likely than average to be purposeful. We also saw higher levels of purpose attainment in students who participate in civic engagement activities, those who talk one-on-one with faculty or other advisors about their goals and plans for the future or the alignment of their own strengths with "what the world needs," and those with classroom experiences that included creative problem-solving and taking the perspectives of others different from themselves, as well as those who felt that their university experience has increased their capacity to "solve complex, real-world problems" and "understand problems facing my community."

These initial insights from our study of university students' purpose development call attention to differences between undergraduate education in the United States and other countries. Most first-year university students in the United States have not yet identified their major fields of study nor their choice of career. They are required to take courses from a broad array of disciplines, both to support general learning and development and to aid exploration of choices prior to committing to a major. In most U.S. universities, student life on campus, extra-curricular activities, psychological support systems, and institutional culture are highly salient in the student experience. And general intellectual outcomes, such as creativity, problem-solving, and critical thinking, are emphasized along with content knowledge. In contrast, undergraduate education outside the United States generally involves choosing a disciplinary focus prior to enrollment, and most universities are nonresidential, unlikely to be strongly campus-focused, and less likely to provide opportunities for students to talk with faculty individually outside of class.

Primarily due to changing workforce needs in a transforming, knowledge-based global economy in which innovation and adaptation are central, some universities in Asia and Europe are increasing their focus on educational outcomes like intellectual curiosity, creativity, complex problem-solving, and the like. In some parts of the world, notably Asia and some European countries (for example, the Netherlands), American-style liberal arts education is gaining traction. Paradoxically, these trends are inverted in U.S. higher education, where concern about the cost of education and graduates' earning potential is driving a decline in humanities and other arts and sciences majors in favor of a narrower focus on preparation for a particular career.

Because intellectual, vocational, and personal exploration; the development of new interests and commitments; preparation for active democratic citizenship; and increases in reflectiveness and awareness of one's place in the larger society are strong foundations for the development of purpose, some of these international comparisons and trends may be cause for concern. The move outside the United States toward greater emphasis on exploration, creativity, and the like may be a good sign for young people's purpose development but not if its importance is framed entirely in terms of individual and national economic competitiveness. Likewise, the move within the United States toward a more narrowly vocational approach to university education could carry risks for purpose, active citizenship, and concern for the common good. But approached with an emphasis on purpose development—a concern for students' capacities for long-term active commitment to endeavors that are meaningful to them and valuable beyond individual advancement—preparation for particular fields of work can support rather than detract from students' larger flourishing. In our view, this argues for explicit attention to the importance of purpose development in university students and assessment of current risks and opportunities in relation to that educational goal. Prevalence data from adolescent and adult samples show that we cannot take purpose development for granted; we must support it with programs intentionally designed to encourage it.

PURPOSE AND MORALITY

In closing, it is important to acknowledge that, despite its personal and social value, purpose can sometimes be misguided. Certain fanatics could meet the basic criteria of purpose (active commitments to goals that are personally meaningful and intended to promote causes beyond the self) and yet show woefully bad judgment about those causes. Even some who try to address worthy goals may use means that are morally questionable and inconsistent with the ends they claim to seek. Their passion can lead to cutting ethical corners to achieve their goals, a compromise that seldom ends well.

This raises the question of how we are to decide whether a particular goal or a means to achieve that goal is morally sound and justifiable. Distinguishing between noble and ignoble purposes or strategies, good or evil pursuits, true or false moral values cannot be accomplished by empirical research. These are *prescriptive* or *normative* questions. They must be addressed by careful thinking at the intersection of multiple disciplines, especially philosophy, theology, and psychology.

Educators must confront prescriptive questions—questions about what it means to be morally mature. Educators charged with guiding young people cannot sidestep questions of what kinds of behaviors and pursuits, including purposes or means to those purposes, are on morally sound footing and ought to be supported or nurtured. Recognizing and confronting the potential for morally misguided purposes means that educating for purpose must go hand-in-hand with educating toward moral and character growth; addressing developmental goals such as humility, wisdom, regard for truth; and enduring faith in basic human values that go beyond self-interest.[14]

We have written about how educators can bring the full range of their resources to bear on helping students develop lived moral maturity.[15] At the university level, for example, this work shows that courses in moral philosophy are far from sufficient for fostering virtue and lived moral understanding. Instead, ethical issues need to be woven into authentic problem-solving throughout the educational experience so that students will develop a habitual morality that can infuse their purposeful commitments as well as the other realms of their personal, public, and professional lives.[16]

Professional education also must demonstrate an awareness of the limitations, and even dangers, of purpose unaccompanied by strong moral character. All professions, including business, law, and medicine, have provided examples of purpose gone awry and the need to educate for professional responsibility and ethics. As they must for other critical developmental outcomes, educators must pay attention to character growth from the very outset of moral learning in primary school through the end of formal education in the university. Purpose is an important element of human flourishing, but it does not stand alone. We urge educators to embed their efforts to foster purpose in a thoroughgoing program of character development across the entire span of human development.

NOTES

1. See, for example: Weinstein, Netta, Richard M. Ryan, and Edward L. Deci, "Motivation, Meaning, and Wellness: A Self-Determination Perspective on the Creation and Internalization of Personal Meanings and Life Goals," in *The Human Quest for Meaning*, ed. Paul T. P. Wong, 81–107 (New York, Routledge, 2012), https://doi.org/10.4324/9780203146286; Ryff, Carol D., Barry T. Radler, and Elliot M. Friedman, "Persistent Psychological Well-Being Predicts Improved Self-Rated Health over 9–10 Years: Longitudinal Evidence from MIDUS," *Health Psychology Open* (July–December 2015): 1–11, https://doi.org/10.1177/2055102915601582hpo .sagepub.com; Bronk, Kendall Cotton, Patrick L. Hill, Daniel K. Lapsley, Tasneem L. Talib, and Holmes Finch, "Purpose, Hope, and Life Satisfaction in Three Age Groups," *Journal of Positive Psychology* 4, no. 6 (2009): 500–510, https://doi.org/10.1080/17439760903271439.

2. See, for example, Gawande, Atul, *Being Mortal: Medicine and What Matters in the End* (New York: Henry Holt, 2014).

3. See https://encore.org/ for a comprehensive treatment of such efforts.

4. Damon, W., *The Path to Purpose: How Young People Find their Calling in Life* (New York: Free Press, 2008).

5. Damon, William, Jenni Menon, and Kendall Cotton Bronk, "The Development of Purpose During Adolescence," *Journal of Applied Developmental Science* 7, no. 3 (2003): 119–128, https://doi.org/10.1207/S1532480XADS0703_2.

6. Warren, Rick, *The Purpose Driven Life* (Grand Rapids, MI: Zondervan, 2002).

7. Bronk, Kendall Cotton, *Purpose in Life: A Critical Component of Optimal Youth Development* (New York: Springer, 2013), https://doi.org/10.1007/978-94-007-7491-9.

8. Bundick, Matthew J., Kathleen Remington, Emily Morton, and Anne Colby, "The Contours of Purpose Beyond the Self in Midlife and Later Life," *Applied Developmental Science* 25, no. 1 (2021): 62–82, https://doi.org/10.1080/10888691.2018.1531718.

9. Benson, Peter, *Sparks: How Parents Can Help Ignite the Hidden Strengths of Teenagers* (San Francisco: Jossey-Bass, 2008).

10. Lerner, Richard M., Willis F. Overton, Michael E. Lamb, and Alexandra M. Freund, eds., *Handbook of Life-Span Development* (Hoboken, NJ: John Wiley, 2010).

11. The Federal Interagency Forum on Aging-Related Statistics, *Older Americans: Key Indicators of Well-Being* (Washington, DC: U.S. Government Printing Office, 2016), https://agingstats.gov /docs/LatestReport/Older-Americans-2016-Key-Indicators-of-WellBeing.pdf.

12. Bundick, Matthew J., Kathleen Remington, Emily Morton, and Anne Colby, "The Contours of Purpose Beyond the Self in Midlife and Later Life," *Applied Developmental Science* 1, no. 21 (2019): https://doi.org/10.1080/10888691.2018.1531718.

13. Malin, Heather, *Teaching for Purpose: Preparing Students for Lives of Meaning* (Cambridge, MA: Harvard Education Press, 2018).

14. Damon, William, and Anne Colby, *The Power of Ideals: The Real Story of Moral Choice* (Oxford: Oxford University Press, 2015).

15. Damon, William, "The Bridge to Character: To Help Students Become Ethical, Responsible Citizens, Schools Need to Cultivate Students' Natural Moral Sense," *Educational Leadership* 67, no. 5 (2010): 36–41; Damon, William, and Anne Colby, *The Power of Ideals: The Real Story of Moral Choice* (New York: Oxford University Press, 2015).

16. Colby, Anne, and William M. Sullivan, "Strengthening the Foundations of Students' Excellence, Integrity, and Social Contribution," *Liberal Education* 95, 1 (2009): 22–29.

11

EDUCATING FOR DEMOCRACY IN CONTENTIOUS TIMES

JOHN ROGERS

In all nations, hardly excepting the most rude and barbarous,[1] the future sovereign receives some training which is supposed to fit him for the exercise of the powers and duties of his anticipated station.

—HORACE MANN, 1848[2]

During his tenure as the secretary of the Massachusetts State Board of Education from 1837 to 1852, Horace Mann became a leading voice trumpeting the importance of public education for democracy. He argued that in a commonwealth where sovereignty will be enacted collectively, civic education—"instruction respecting the nature and functions of the government"— must be provided in "common schools" open to all.[3] Such schools not only would present civic knowledge, but they would also afford opportunities for social interaction and shared deliberation through which all "parties can become intelligible to each other."[4]

But even as Mann envisioned public schools as sites for preparing citizens to participate in political life, he worried that fractious partisanship might undermine the democratic project of common schooling. "If the tempest of political strife were to be let loose upon our Common Schools, they would be overwhelmed with sudden ruin. Let it be once understood, that the schoolroom is a legitimate theatre for party politics, and with what violence will hostile partisans struggle to gain possession of the stage, and to play their parts upon it!"[5]

Today, we see Horace Mann's worries manifest in many public schools across the United States and around the globe. Indeed, many public schools face not only unruly and contentious politics from the broader community but also the bitter seeds of intolerance as well (see chapter 6). These dynamics pose considerable challenges to educators committed to educating the future sovereigns. Consider, for example, the case of Linda James, a high school principal in North Carolina.[6] Ms. James believes that the greatest challenge she now faces stems from contentious national politics that stirs up "turmoil" in her school. Students have shouted down one another over important yet polarizing policy debates such as gun control. Parents have complained about what they perceive to be the liberal bias of websites recommended by their children's English teacher for research projects—at least until Ms. James showed them that these sites are on a list of reliable information sources "vetted" by North Carolina's Department of Public Instruction.

Linda James recounts sitting in her office during a class period in 2018 and hearing a loud, repetitive *thump thump thump* coming from the stairwell, causing her to run out to check on the commotion. Once there, she discovered a group of white male students clapping and shouting "Trump, Trump, Trump" as they descended the stairs. Before she could get to the boys, an African American student with an anti-Trump message handwritten on his T-shirt stepped into the hallway to challenge them. This counterprotest "ignited the boys again to pick up their cadence and their volume" until Ms. James and her fellow administrators, alongside the school resource officer, were able to establish order and begin applying consequences for the pandemonium and disruption of class time.

When students at Linda James's school reprise strains of our national political rhetoric, they often communicate racially hostile messages to their classmates. Some "students feel emboldened to say . . . 'Go back to Venezuela.' 'Go back to Colombia. You don't belong here.' " Such statements carry a particularly menacing force for Latino youth who have witnessed friends and neighbors deported in the last couple years. Noting that immigrant "parents don't like to come to school, they don't like to sign things," Ms. James describes the local Latino community as "very much on edge."

Against this backdrop of stress, division, and marginalization, Linda James sees little choice but to "deflect" attention away from politics. Her school has received recognition in the past for ensuring that 100 percent of eligible students are registered to vote. But now, she agonizes that greater political engagement is "when things fall apart." She is reluctant even to include "words like civics and democracy" in the school's mission statement. "I don't think our community would tolerate" that, Ms. James explains, as they "are a very diverse community and we have extremes on both ends." In this political moment, Ms. James does *not* believe it is her job to get students "to understand the other's viewpoints." She concludes: "I don't think anybody's been very good at doing that."

In many parts of the world today, educators like Linda James find themselves caught between a desire for their students to learn about and practice democracy and a commitment to maintaining a safe and caring learning environment in the midst of political contentiousness and racial intolerance. The "tempest of political strife" in broader society creates extraordinary challenges for principals who want to open up opportunities for young people to engage in free and open dialogue as a way to develop their civic capacities. Public schools are charged with bringing together young people from diverse backgrounds to learn from and with one another. This project requires that students engage each other with a certain degree of regard and respect. These conditions are particularly important for civic education, in which students learn to deliberate, inquire into social issues, and collaborate on shared projects. Such practices presume extensive social interaction, engagement, and voice. But as educators create more opportunities for students to share their beliefs, they potentially invite belligerent speech and intolerant ideas into classroom discourse. Such voices may threaten feelings of community and safety and undercut not just civic education but all learning.

This is not a new dilemma.[7] But it is one that is acutely felt in a time of rising intolerance and conflictual politics in society writ large. In the United States, Donald Trump's 2016 election was propelled by and has, in turn, propelled a political culture characterized by resentment of perceived elites and fear of groups considered outsiders who are perceived to threaten security as well as cultural and economic stability. The sensibility of this political culture is antiestablishment and hence disposed toward challenging social norms and conventions of correct or appropriate behavior. Political discourse has tended to be heated, combative, and coarse.[8]

Of course, the problems I describe are not confined to the United States. Many nominally democratic countries around the globe are experiencing rising illiberalism and populist nationalism— Brazil, India, Philippines, Hungary, Turkey, and more. There is no clear or easy way to cut this list short. The political scientists Roberto Foa and Yascha Mounk also see signs

of a "democratic disconnect" across wealthy democracies. Younger generations, they point out, have become increasingly likely in recent years to
view democratic governance as unwieldy and express support for authoritarian ideals.[9] Wherever we undertake citizenship education, we must thus
consider what it means to educate for democracy when democracy itself is
under threat.

As an initial response to this question, I briefly recount how the American
philosopher John Dewey addressed this issue amidst rising fascism in Europe
and reactionary politics in the United States in the late 1930s. Dewey doesn't
so much resolve the problem as he reminds us of its importance and helps us
think about democracy and citizenship education as something broader than
providing information on the workings of government. It is, he suggests, about
fostering particular habits and ways of being with one another.

I then consider whether the concept of civility offers a useful tool for framing the role of schools amid democratic threats. I examine the ways that civility
has been used to frame a particular approach to enhancing respect or at least
restraining ill-will in the context of diverse and disagreeable communities. I
consider here the ways that the rhetoric of civility has sometimes been used for
antidemocratic purposes—to impose silence and limit dissent. And I explore
some recent work that draws a distinction between top-down and bottom-up
civility. This analysis of civility sets up the main section of the chapter in which
I seek to illuminate the contours of the issue by examining three cases of high
school principals in the United States grappling with this dilemma. All of the
principals desire to take up Horace Mann's challenge of preparing "the future
sovereign[s]" so that they will be informed and engaged and have the capacity
to communicate productively with fellow community members—even those
with whom they disagree.

While the principals all take up the challenge of advancing democracy
amidst contention and intolerance, they offer very different strategies. Their
distinct approaches reflect both the particular political dynamics of their surrounding community and the distinctive ways that they frame their role in
promoting civility. None of the principals completely resolve the tensions tied
to promoting democracy in a climate of intolerance. Their cases illuminate
the possibilities and dilemmas associated with different strategic choices. In
closing, I offer a few lessons about creating democracy inside and outside of
schools in ways that might move us beyond our very contentious and consequential moment.

DEWEY, DEMOCRACY, AND EDUCATION

John Dewey wrote about democracy and education throughout his career (most famously in his 1916 book of that title), but he returns to this theme with fresh eyes in the late 1930s against the backdrop of rising fascism in Europe and right-wing backlash in the United States.[10] The "present state of the world," he reasoned in 1939, proves that democracy is in no sense inevitable. "For a long period we acted as if our democracy were something that perpetuated itself automatically; as if our ancestors had succeeded in setting up a machine that solved the problem of perpetual motion in politics."[11] What is now needed, Dewey argued, is a thoroughgoing consideration of what democracy means and how it can be cultivated in the face of growing intolerance. Dewey offered an expansive view of democracy and democratic education. Democracy, he postulated in 1937, "is much broader than a special political form, a method of conducting government, of making laws and carrying on governmental administration by means of popular suffrage and elected officers." It is "a way of life," in which all people participate in the "formation of the values that regulate the living of men together."[12] Everyone, Dewey contended, should have a voice in shaping the institutions that influence them. The flow of ideas in the course of deliberation promotes the full development of individuals and is the best assurance that institutional and societal decisions are informed and reflect a broad cross-section of interests.

Dewey introduced three reasons why the growth of fascism and racial and religious bigotry represent "treason to the democratic way of life." First, intolerance separates people into "antagonistic sects and factions" and thereby creates barriers to full and free communication. Second, the "totalitarian state" controls and distorts information, creating a vicious cycle in which "mutual suspicion . . . fear, and hatred" lead to more of the same. Third, the ideology of Nazism is fundamentally hostile to a belief in the capacity of all people for self-governance. This last point is grounded in a claim about universal intelligence as well as a moral vision for education and society. "The democratic faith in human equality," Dewey suggested, "is belief that every human being, independent of the quantity or range of his personal endowment, has the right to equal opportunity with every other person for development of whatever gifts he has."[13]

Dewey did not present any easy or simple strategies for confronting the threat of fascism and intolerance. The "depth of the present crisis" called for more "inventive effort and creative activity."[14] He contended that, whether we are talking about students and teachers in schools or citizens in the broader society, "the best way to produce initiative and constructive power is to exercise it, [since] power as well as interest, comes by use and practice."[15] Dewey thus envisioned confronting fascism and intolerance with more inquiry and dialogue. In schools, this meant supporting students to examine and talk about vital social issues, exercise voice and participate in decision making, and engage diverse classmates in mutual consultation about matters of shared concern. Democratic ends, he suggested, require democratic means.

CIVILITY

Dewey's framing poses a challenge for educators today: creating spaces for dialogue, decision making, and social interaction may be necessary to foster democracy as a way of life, but such opportunities may also embolden angry and hateful voices in the schoolhouse. How then should educators conceive of their role in developing democratic citizens in the face of heightened contentiousness and intolerance?

The concept of civility provides one way of talking about how diverse and sometimes disagreeable people relate to one another. It addresses rules, norms, or standards for living together and frequently establishes boundaries for what is acceptable or unacceptable. Sharika Thiranagama and colleagues speak of "civility as a range of practices and norms aimed at promoting restraint and respect in the face of difference."[16] These practices take on meaning within particular contexts. Benson notes that the norms governing civil communication "are always situational and contestable."[17]

Civility seems like a particularly useful concept to think about the dilemmas of democratic education because it is often referenced in discussions about deliberation within the public sphere. Robert Boyd notes that "civility is the disposition that makes political life possible because it allows those with different and conflicting views of the good to live peacefully side-by-side."[18] Some theorists, like John Rawls, associate a broad set of values—reasonableness, a willingness to listen to rival viewpoints, and so on— with the ideal of civility as a framework for public reasoning.[19] Teresa Bejan counters that this expansive set of principles stretches beyond widely accepted views of civility. She believes that it is more appropriate to focus on "mere civility," which she describes as a "minimal conformity to norms of respectful behavior and decorum expected of all members of a tolerant society as such."[20]

Whether we conceive of it in a broad or narrow sense, it is important to acknowledge that, in the words of Thirangama and colleagues, "civility has an uneasy history."[21] The concept often has been deployed—consciously and unconsciously—by people in privileged positions who wish to maintain their power and status. It sometimes has been used as a "silencing mechanism" or as a "means of social control."[22] Iris Marion Young notes that civility codes around ideals such as "articulateness" or "orderliness" mark off patterns of expression associated with particular social groups as appropriate or inappropriate.[23] Linda Zerrilli marshals historical evidence of the ways that norms of civility have been used to deride and dismiss the behavior of various subaltern groups who sought "inclusion in the public realm."[24] Her argument highlights the important role that "incivility" has played in the efforts of groups lacking formal political power to effect radical political change.[25]

Advocates of democratic education are not immune to such problematic invocations of civility and incivility. Consider, for example, the epigraph that begins this chapter. Horace Mann's appeal for public schools to educate for democracy emerges alongside his claim that certain nations are "most rude and barbarous." Those who talk about fostering inclusive participation in public life while simultaneously marking off specific political cultures as less virtuous are likely to impose ideals of civility that exclude or diminish.

Etienne Balibar not only recognizes these problems with top-down civility, but he also presents bottom-up civility as an emancipatory alternative.[26] Bottom-up civility emerges through the actions of individuals and groups who, because of their lack of power and status, often are the targets of incivility. In the words of Thirangama and colleagues, these efforts aim "to clear space for the recognition and dignity of others" and place limits on behavior that humiliates and enacts symbolic violence.[27]

Balibar's discussion of bottom-up civility is evocative rather than prescriptive. It is not entirely clear what this looks like in practice. For example, can bottom-up civility only be enacted by the most marginalized people in society? If so, what would that mean for their allies? Or for disenfranchised groups that have slightly more power or status than the most marginalized? Notwithstanding this ambiguity, bottom-up civility advances a notion that bears some similarity to Dewey's vision of everyday people participating in the "formation of the values that regulate the living of men together."[28]

THREE PRINCIPALS GRAPPLING WITH DEMOCRATIC EDUCATION, INTOLERANCE, AND CIVILITY

I turn now to three cases of high school principals in the United States who adopt different strategies for developing democratic citizens amid a climate of intolerance. They conceive of civility in slightly different ways and seek to advance it through different means. These principals, like Linda James whom I introduced earlier, are participants in a national study I began soon after the U.S. presidential election of 2016 to understand how the hostile rhetoric in the broader political climate is shaping experiences in America's public schools.[29]

It is important to note that these three cases do not represent the entire universe of principal responses. Many principals across the United States, heeding the demands of accountability systems that focus attention on standardized tests, do not place a strong emphasis on educating for democracy. Some principals, facing multiple claims on their time and/or political pressures from the surrounding community, have not been particularly attentive to contentious or even degrading student speech. And, given patterns of residential sorting, not all schools serve political communities where heightened conflict and intolerance are common. The three cases I present are selected from the subset of all principals working in diverse communities who embrace a strong commitment to developing the democratic capacities and commitments of their students *and* ensuring a supportive school climate that protects vulnerable minorities.

WE ARE SWITZERLAND

Michelle Kenup is a principal of a racially diverse high school in a politically conservative community in the southeastern United States.[30] One of her primary goals is "to prepare our students to become participatory and effective community members." She aims to build the communication skills of her students so that they can "discuss and talk through issues" and "interact with one another . . . [without] getting angry." But Ms. Kenup finds this clear sense of purpose challenged by contentious political rhetoric in the national political environment and in the surrounding community. "Politics and the news sometimes make it difficult in school because we are kind of a microcosm of society." She notes with concern: "When it starts boiling over outside, sometimes it will carry over here." The hottest topics invariably are bound up in broader issues of race and immigration.

Michelle Kenup adopts several strategies for addressing the conflict and intolerance in her school community. First, she acts proactively, communicating her commitment to what Teresa Bejan refers to as "mere civility." Ms. Kenup tells her students: "There's ways to hear one another or listen or be respectful to one another if not agree without it turning into hatred and vitriol and violence." Second, she moves quickly to address violations of these norms and tries to use dialogue to reinforce her message. "I tend to be a head on . . . that tends to shut it down much quicker than. . . . the back door." For example, when a white student told a Latino classmate that "he needed to go back to Mexico," Ms. Kenup initiated discipline proceedings and told the offending student: "We don't make comments like that." She also facilitated a discussion between the victimizer and the victim of this verbal assault and reported the affair to the white student's father. Ms. Kenup notes that "unfortunately, when I called his dad, the response I got was along those same political lines."

Because she has had only limited success with these first two strategies, Michelle Kenup also has established further restraints on what topics students can discuss in class. After another incident in which a white student referenced a recent immigration enforcement action as a way to accentuate the fear of immigrant classmates, Ms. Kenup informed students that they should not introduce politically charged ideas during class. She told them: "This is a safe place. We . . . are Switzerland. We are neutral ground because we have to be. We've got too many people coming in with too many backstories, too much history. And if we don't remain neutral and this is [not] a safe place for everybody, then it just becomes a nightmare for everybody."

By establishing clear rules of behavior, following up on transgressions, and articulating the dangers of violent rhetoric, Michelle Kenup limits the degree and scope of hostility at her school. While her efforts may have prevented more "nightmares," she does not seem to have been able to ensure a safe space for immigrant students who surely must feel the ongoing effects of past verbal assaults. Ms. Kenup's efforts to impose neutrality through prohibition on certain domains of inquiry likely make classrooms discussions less relevant and engaging. When I asked her whether it is possible both to limit harmful conflict and encourage civic development, Ms. Kenup replied: "It is a very, very delicate line. It's a very, very delicate balancing act. . . . And I'm not going to win right now."

WE'VE STOPPED AVOIDING

Cathy Burton leads a racially diverse school located in a politically contested area in the western United States.[31] Her school straddles the line between suburban and rural communities, and it enrolls both the children of farm owners (who are primarily white) and of farm laborers (who are overwhelmingly Latino, including many immigrant families). Ms. Burton aims to develop students who are civic-minded and understand their role in a democracy or republic. She is concerned about the ways that societal "rhetoric is diminishing in its civil-ness," and she wants her students to counter this trend. Ms. Burton envisions her school fostering the ability of students to understand the viewpoint of those with rival views so that they may "disagree in a way that is constructive and useful." She hopes that graduates from her school will vote, follow the laws, and speak publicly in a "responsible and civil way."

In the last three years, Cathy Burton has grown increasingly worried about the effects of national political rhetoric on her students. She describes "an ugliness about the politics that is popping up through the kids." Students see and hear politicians engaging in actions that are forbidden at school—saying outrageous and hateful things or bullying people online. Now when Ms. Burton's students violate these norms, it is harder for her to effect change. "In the past, when this occurred, there would be a certain acknowledgement and, perhaps, shame, I could elicit through discussion—an ability to see that hate speech is wrong. That is less and less true now. It takes a lot of time to walk kids through that, now, and many times, they are supported by racist, bigoted, ill-informed parents who think their child was merely stating his or opinion, and that it's perfectly fine for them to have done so."

The contentious political climate is particularly hard on Cathy Burton's students who are undocumented or who have family members who are undocumented. These students are "just flat out afraid." Ms. Burton characterizes the stress and anxiety of such students as "huge at my school, absolutely huge. . . . I can't stress that enough." Students are reluctant to access medical or educational support services out of concern that such actions will draw the attention of immigration enforcement officials.[32] Ms. Burton adds that "there is fear around that is palpable" associated with being reported for deportation.

Cathy Burton notes that her school also enrolls a substantial number of white students who are strong supporters of President Trump and advocate vigorous immigration enforcement. Some of these students freely express their views. But other Trump partisans, perhaps recognizing that they do not constitute a majority at the school, "shut down." Misconstruing or purpose-fully distorting language from teachers about why it is important to establish a supportive classroom climate for vulnerable classmates, a few white students have told Ms. Burton: "I don't feel comfortable in my class, because *it's not a safe place* for me to espouse the view that I think all illegal immigrants should be sent back."

At times, tensions between groups of students have erupted into open con-flict. "We had quite a [challenging] day, the day after [the] election," Cathy Burton recounts. "We were in the news in the area because we had a standoff between our Mexican [American kids] and our white kids. One of our kids had brought a giant Trump sign and stood on a cafeteria table and held it out like a 'ha ha.' And then one of the students grabbed it and ripped it, and the next thing you know they were at each other's throats." Amid the melee, a white stu-dent in the back of the crowd shouted: "Send them back, send them back,"—a chant heard at many of Donald Trump's campaign rallies.

While such incidents have been difficult for Cathy Burton, they have not undermined her commitment to fostering civility. She and her staff have resolved to figure out the best way to support difficult political conversations in classrooms. "We've been struggling with it. So I wouldn't say we have the answers pulled together yet. But we've stopped avoiding the conversation in classes, which is one way to handle it. We decided *not* to do that." Ms. Burton and her teachers have been working on developing facilitation skills in which students "are allowed to speak even if you disagree . . . but you have to do it civilly." She wants classrooms to be places where "hard topics are not avoided," all "viewpoints are honored, and there is a civil tone." Ms. Burton doesn't care what viewpoints are advanced as long as students are "able to articulate that viewpoint in a way that is intelligent and doesn't demean anyone."

Cathy Burton believes her teachers are "getting better and better at moder-ating those discussions." She offers the example of a classroom she observed in the last school year. "One of the Anglo country kids [said] 'Well, I just think all the Mexicans aren't helping our country. I just don't think it was a very good idea to let them all in to begin with.' The teacher did a great job in that par-ticular case of saying, 'I understand that that's how you feel, but I want you to look around this room and note that there are people here that could be upset by the way that you said that. Can you think of another way to have articulated that viewpoint?' The kid did. He was able to do that. He said, 'Okay, I guess what I'm really saying is that if you're here, you're here, but illegal immigrants shouldn't be allowed in.' The teacher said, 'Thank you,' and they were able to kind of move on. You could kind of feel the hackles going up, and then kind of going back down on kids. I think she did a stellar job."

By refusing to avoid difficult conversations, Cathy Burton and her staff embrace the challenge of fostering civil exchange in a community riven by division and intolerance. The educators try to influence *how* students speak rather than shape *what* they say or believe. They restrain tone rather than substance. This means that educators do not challenge intolerant views as long as they are advanced without overt aggression. It is possible that lowering the temperature of classroom discourse may serve as a bridge to new forms of social interaction among students that will lead to new understanding and greater tolerance. But, that hopeful outcome is in no sense inevitable. While such a strategy may lower "the hackles" associated with intense conflict, it also allows intolerant views to be normalized within classroom spaces—spaces where those views likely accentuate feelings of acute vulnerability for immigrant youth. Cathy Burton worries that her undocumented students "feel anxious as they walk onto this campus, and in classrooms." She adds: "They . . . feel a little bit like they walk on eggshells all the time."

WE DO A LOT

Anthony Montesa leads a racially diverse school in an upper-middle-class northeastern suburb that is roughly evenly split between the two political parties.[33] He wants his students to be deeply engaged in their learning so that they "fulfill their potential" and are prepared "for the world that they are going to enter." This necessitates creating an inclusive and participatory culture in the school. "You fully engage them by having a community, fostering a community, where they can participate." Engagement, Mr. Montesa reasons, is critical for learning generally as well as for civic preparation. "As an American public school," he asserts, "we believe . . . it's [a] primary responsibility to prepare them for democratic citizenship."

In the last few years, there have been a few cases when contentious political rhetoric from afar has made its way into Anthony Montesa's school. He and his staff have taken steps "to build a safe community for students that will not become fragmented due to political and societal factors." They "teach tolerance and respect for different viewpoints" and "hold students accountable when necessary." Mr. Montesa notes that they do not "tolerate bullying and harassment for any reason, specifically for someone's political views or personal or ethnic or racial background." But disciplinary efforts are few, as the school treats incidence of hate speech or intolerance as "teachable moments" in which educators "sit down with the students, talk to the students, and just say, 'Hey, look. If you have something to say, here's how you go about doing it. Here's the right way to do it.'" Mr. Montesa adds that, when needed, he employs the same strategy with his staff who speak in rude or inappropriate ways, "because sometimes it happens with teachers."

This approach reflects Anthony Montesa's commitment to promoting "a democratic culture in the building." When he first came to his school a few years ago, teachers were not "talking to each other," and students were not either. Mr. Montesa was raised with the belief that "when things are bothering you, you talk. . . . It's more productive than not dealing with things." He views dialogue as a way to encourage perspective-taking and joint work as a way to foster compromise. As a consequence, he organizes his school in ways that encourage dialogue and collaboration across adults and young people alike.

Anthony Montesa and his staff open up space inside and outside of classrooms for students to talk and work with one another on issues of shared concern. "We do a lot. . . . We have the students collaborating an awful lot in the classroom, just so that they have opportunities to work with different students and get to know different students." Perhaps even more important than these classroom opportunities are the wide array of programs and extracurricular activities that invite students to exercise voice and contribute to a more inclusive and equitable school environment. "We have student mentoring programs to try to build a friendlier, more connected community. . . . We have a district equity team, and we have an equity team in every building, and we promote the notion of an equitable environment, where every student feels comfortable, connected, and supported. And [we encourage] students to participate—having student committees, empowering the student council, using student surveys. Even if we are making some decisions that maybe they don't agree with, at least they feel they are being heard." Many of these activities focus on promoting greater understanding of issues of diversity. Students play leadership roles, organizing events, participating in small group discussions with teachers, and teaching other students. Participating in these activities provides young people opportunities to learn through practice how to work with others across lines of difference.

At times, students have organized civic activities outside the formal structure of existing school organizations. For example, after the horrific school shooting in Parkland, Florida, students at Anthony Montesa's school organized seven hundred of their classmates to join a national protest day. Mr. Montesa told the students that even though members of the staff might not agree with their platform, "their opinions are valid, and as young people, their opinions do matter." He viewed this incident as a chance to help students understand the "right way" to dissent in a democracy. He sat down with them and discussed "parameters" for how to manage the protest in ways that differed from "Antifa protestors [who] just cause damage and try to be the loudest and most violent."

While Anthony Montesa's general approach is to open up opportunities for civic or political engagement, there are a small number of exceptions—when the rights of vulnerable minorities are at stake. One such example is how educators address the concerns of undocumented students. "If that issue comes up in class, you have to be careful about it. . . . You might be the most anti-illegal immigration pro-border wall type person. But you got a kid sitting in front of you that's undocumented, and they're worried about their family getting deported in the middle of the night. You know, that kind of like takes the politics out of it because you got to think about that kid." Mr. Montesa takes a similar position in relation to transgender students at his school. For example, no matter how many students object to new rules regarding bathroom access, Mr. Montesa will defend the policy if he believes it is necessary to protect transgender students' rights. Mr. Montesa tells his students that some issues don't allow for majoritarian politics. "We can't just have a vote and" strip away fundamental rights.

By creating multiple spaces and abundant opportunities for students to participate in dialogue and collaborate with one another, Anthony Montesa and his staff contribute to a democratic culture at their school. Mr. Montesa aims to foster deep engagement of students—because such engagement supports learning generally and civic development. Hence, education for democracy lies at the core of the school's work. Dialogue also becomes a way to address incidents of intolerance. Mr. Montesa reasons that providing students with a greater sense of agency and responsibility for school culture creates a self-correcting dynamic that fosters greater understanding among students. Yet, it is important to note that Mr. Montesa's school community does not face the same level of vitriol and intolerance as is experienced in the communities where Michelle Kenup or Cathy Burton work. It is very much an open question as to whether Mr. Montesa's efforts to build a democratic culture could take hold in similar ways in those settings.

While Anthony Montesa allows for freer and more open exchange than Ms. Kenup and Ms. Burton, he too marks off limits for acceptable student behavior and hence for the practice of democracy. These boundaries arise as Mr.

Montesa establishes parameters for student dissent. His dismissal of agonistic politics (as exemplified by Antifa protestors) circumscribes the meanings of democracy available to his students. Reasonable people disagree about the value of confrontational protest. Shouldn't such questions be open to democratic debate? It is also worth noting that Mr. Montesa takes certain issues out of politics by recasting them as questions of rights. This shift from a political to a legal framework raises difficult issues of who is empowered to interpret the law. Is it Mr. Montesa alone?

FINAL THOUGHTS

The three cases suggest that there is no single approach to school leadership that eliminates the tensions associated with advancing democratic education in contentious times. Efforts to impose, build, or support civility may not ensure robust democratic development or the protection of vulnerable minorities, let alone both. But such endeavors may help educators open space for meaningful and respectful interactions across differences (by lowering the temperature) or prevent the worst (by halting or limiting assaults).

Two tentative lessons emerge from this understanding for the work of democratic educators in contentious times. First, educators should view civility not as a goal but as (at best) a provisional tool for promoting democracy amidst hostility and intolerance. The democratic purposes of schooling should be the focus—not civility per se. It is important that educators reflect continuously on the ways that their enactments of civility promote *and/or* restrict dialogue and inquiry. Second, educators should invite members of the school community to join them in reflecting on how best to advance democracy. They should talk about the dilemmas associated with encouraging participation and voice when such efforts may invite vitriol and intolerance. And they should discuss their strategies for negotiating these dilemmas. Such space for reflection and dialogue (a) serves as a check on the problematic manifestations of civility, (b) builds deliberative habits and skills, and (c) frames the problem as one that the entire school community needs to work on together. This sort of deliberation may prompt further inquiry into the historical and contemporary forces that arouse rancor and ill-will in society. Ideally, it would illuminate the ways that powerful interests at times foster discord for purposes of control, and it would sensitize participants to the pain and hurt of others.

It is worth noting one other lesson. The task of enhancing democracy in challenging times cannot solely be the responsibility of our schools. Anthony Montesa was able to build a democratic culture in his school in part because the broader political climate surrounding his school was not defined by querulousness and hate. Schools are only somewhat autonomous from broader societal dynamics. If we want schools to support the democratic development of young people, we must initiate change both inside and outside of schools.

Our challenge now is strikingly similar to that which John Dewey articulated in 1938. "We now have to re-create by deliberate endeavor" the culture and practice of democracy "as a way of life." Creative democracy remains "the task before us."

NOTES

1. Later in this chapter, I will address the notable tension between Horace Mann's description of "most rude and barbarous" nations—a reference likely drawn from David Hume's essay, "Of National Characters"—and his call for public schools to educate for an inclusive democracy.

2. Mann, *Twelfth Annual Report of the Board of Education, Together with the Twelfth Annual Report of the Secretary of the Board* (Boston: Commonwealth of Massachusetts, Board of Education, 1849), 77.

3. Mann, Horace, *Twelfth Annual Report* 84. Mann speaks of universal public education in which people across lines of class attend school together. Yet, he remained largely silent about the racial segregation of public schools. See: P, "Horace Mann and Colored Schools," *Liberator*, December 24, 1847. It should be noted that Mann was not oblivious to issues of race and discrimination. He advocated for the abolition of the slave trade while secretary of the Massachusetts State Board of Education and later, while a member of the U.S. Congress, spoke out against slavery more generally. See, for example, Horace Mann's February 23, 1849 speech, "Slavery and the Slave Trade" in Horace Mann, *Slavery: Letters and Speeches* (Boston: BB Mussey, 1853).

4. Mann, *Twlelfth Annual Report*, 86.

5. Mann, *Twlelfth Annual Report*, 86.

6. I interviewed "Linda James" (a pseudonym) via Zoom in August 2018. I use a pseudonym to protect her identity; I similarly use pseudonyms for the other three principals described later in this chapter.

7. McAvoy, Paula, and Diana Hess, "Classroom Deliberation in an Era of Political Polarization," *Curriculum Inquiry* 43, no. 1 (2013): 14–47.

8. Dionne Jr., E. J., Norman J. Ornstein, and Thomas E. Mann, *One Nation After Trump: A Guide for the Perplexed, the Disillusioned, the Desperate, and the Not-Yet Deported* (New York: St. Martin's Press, 2017).

9. Foa, Roberto Stefan, and Yascha Mounk, "The Danger of Deconsolidation: The Democratic Disconnect," *Journal of Democracy* 27, no. 3 (2016): 5–17. Foa, Roberto Stefan, and Yascha Mounk, "The Signs of Deconsolidation," *Journal of Democracy* 28, no. 1 (2017): 5–15.

10. Dewey, John, "Democracy and Education," in *The Middle Works of John Dewey 9, 1899–1924: 1916*, ed. Jo Ann Boydston (Carbondale: Southern Illinois University Press, 2008).

11. Dewey, John, "Creative Democracy: The Task Before Us," in *John Dewey. The Later Works, 1925–1953. 14: 1939–1941*, ed. Jo Ann Boydston (Carbondale: Southern Illinois University Press. 1988), 225.

12. Dewey, John, "Democracy and Educational Administration," in *John Dewey. The Later Works, 1925–1953. 11: 1935–1937*, ed. Jo Ann Boydston (Carbondale: Southern Illinois University Press. 1987), 217.

13. Dewey, "Creative Democracy," 227–228.

14. Dewey, "Creative Democracy," 225.

15. Dewey, "Democracy and Educational Administration," 224.

16. Thiranagama, Sharika, Tobias Kelly, and Carlos Forment, "Introduction: Whose Civility?" *Anthropological Theory* 18, nos. 2–3 (2018): 256.

17. Benson, Thomas, "The Rhetoric of Civility: Power, Authenticity, and Democracy," *Journal of Contemporary Rhetoric* 1, no. 1 (2011): 22.

18. Boyd, Richard, "The Value of Civility?" *Urban Studies* 43, nos. 5–6 (2006): 865.

19. Rawls, John, *Political Liberalism* (New York: Columbia University Press, 2005).

20. Bejan, Teresa, *Mere Civility* (Cambridge: Harvard University Press, 2017), 7.

21. Thiranagama, Kelly, and Forment, "Whose Civility?" 154.

22. Jamieson, Kathleen Hall, Allyson Volinsky, Ilana Weitz, and Kate Kenski, "The Political Uses and Abuses of Civility and Incivility," in *The Oxford Handbook of Political Communication*, ed. Kate Kenski and Kathleen Hall Jamieson (New York: Oxford University Press, 2017), 7.

23. Young, Iris Marion, *Inclusion and Democracy* (New York: Oxford University Press, 2002), 53.

24. Zerilli, Linda, "Against Civility: A Feminist Perspective," in *Civility, Legality, and Justice in America*, ed. Austin Sarat (New York: Cambridge University Press, 2014), 108.

25. See also Jamieson et al., "The Political Uses."

26. Balibar, Étienne, *Politics and the Other Scene* (New York: Verso Trade, 2012).

27. Thiranagama, Kelly, and Forment, "Whose Civility?" 170.

28. Dewey, "Democracy and Educational Administration," 217.

29. For an overview of this study, see Rogers, John, M. Ishimoto, A. Kwako, A. Berryman, and C. Diera, *School and Society in the Age of Trump* (Los Angeles: UCLA's Institute for Democracy, Education, and Access, 2019).

30. This case is drawn from interviews I conducted with her (a pseudonym) via Zoom in August 2018 and August 2019.

31. This case is drawn from interviews I conducted with her (a pseudonym) via Zoom in August 2018 and August 2019.

32. There is no evidence that students who accessed such services at the time of this interview increased the likelihood that they or they families would be identified for deportation proceedings. Nonetheless, the students' response speaks to the broader climate of fear.

33. This case is drawn from interviews I conducted with him (a pseudonym) via Zoom in August 2018 and August 2019.

III

EDUCATING FOR A
SUSTAINABLE FUTURE

12

CLIMATE CHANGE EDUCATION FOR ALL

Bending the Curve Education Project

VEERABHADRAN RAMANATHAN, FONNA FORMAN, MARCELO
SUÁREZ-OROZCO, ALAN ROPER, SCOTT FRIESE, KAREN
FLAMMER, HAHRIE HAN, ADAM MILLARD-BALL, PAULA EZCURRA,
AND ASTRID HSU

It is not the strongest of the species that survive, nor the most intelligent, but the one most responsive to change.

—CHARLES DARWIN

Solutions to the climate problem require a multidimensional approach to bending the curve of global warming. Such an approach was articulated in 2015 in a report titled *Bending the Curve: Ten Scalable Solutions* published by the University of California (UC).[1] The report is a collaboration among fifty researchers from the natural, technological, and social sciences, as well as the humanities. The report calls for solutions that integrate science, technology, societal transformation, governance, market instruments, and ecosystem management perspectives. In this chapter, we describe an education effort that is designed after this multifaceted and integrated approach to climate solutions.

EDUCATION AND CLIMATE CHANGE

All societies endeavor to transfer skills, competencies, virtues, and values to the next generation. The work of educating children and youth is culturally constituted, highly varied across societies, and ever-evolving.[2] Schools should reflect—and reflect upon—the cultural, environmental, and socioeconomic realities of the communities of which they form an essential part. The curiosity and joy of learning at a young age open the door to the gold standard of any education system: the molding of life-long learners who have the tools and savoir-faire to continue learning long after formal schooling stops.

Schools the world over must be at the forefront of preparing the next generation to engage and flourish in problematic times and in catastrophic contexts. A growing global challenge is unchecked climate change and its effects—known and yet to be discovered—on nature, health, economy, and society. Today, the impacts of climate disruption are intensifying across the globe, inequality is deepening, and migration is accelerating.[3] The COVID-19 pandemic was a canary in the coalmine, illustrating our profound global interdependence and exposing the disproportionate vulnerabilities of poor and marginalized people everywhere. This crisis has also exposed the susceptibility of reliable science information to political manipulation, the fragility of public commitment to collective goods, and the role that education must play in cultivating informed publics across the world committed to tackling climate change as a global public priority.

This chapter presents an overview of a host of climate change educational programs and tools designed to engage all kinds of learners in different contexts. Each program is mindful of age differences and various social considerations in making climate change teaching and learning developmentally appropriate and culturally consonant. The quest for a sustainable planet and sustainable humanity must include climate literacy for all, including pre-K–12 children and youth, college students, and adults all the way to senior citizens. This chapter outlines such a cradle-to-grave education project called Bending the Curve.[4] Our basic claim is that climate change education, carefully conceived and well-executed has inherent value and, furthermore, leads to measurable desirable outcomes. A 2020 study found that climate change education programs have the potential to change individual behaviors and attitudes, resulting in reductions in carbon emissions of similar magnitude to other large-scale mitigation strategies.[5] The goal of this project is to educate and empower millions of climate champions across the world who will help solve the problem before it is too late.

THE CLIMATE CRISIS

Unsustainable consumption of fossil fuels and other natural resources and the waste produced by this continually growing consumption pathway is a fundamental cause for polluting the air, water, and land. This pollution of the planetary climate and ecosystem has unleashed two catastrophic forces: climate disruption and species extinction, both of which pose existential threats to all of humanity and the ecosystems. With unchecked climate change and air pollution, the very fabric of life on Earth is at grave risk.[6]

We human beings are creating a new and dangerous phase of Earth's history that has been termed the Anthropocene. The term refers to the immense effects of human activity on all aspects of the Earth's physical systems and on life on the planet. With accelerating climate change, we put ourselves at risk of massive crop failures, new and reemerging infectious diseases, including COVID-19, heat extremes, droughts, megastorms, floods, and sharply rising sea levels. The economic activities that contribute to global warming are also wreaking other profound damages, including air and water pollution, deforestation, and massive land degradation, causing a rate of species extinction unprecedented for the past sixty-five million years and a dire threat to human health through increases in heart disease, stroke, pulmonary disease, mental health, infections, and cancer. Climate change threatens to exacerbate the unprecedented current flow of forcibly displaced migrants and add to human misery by stoking violence and conflict. The poorest of the planet, who are still relying on nineteenth-century technologies to meet basic needs such as cooking and heating, are bearing a heavy brunt of the damages caused by the economic activities of the rich.[7]

There is a shrinking window of time to implement climate solutions and avoid further catastrophic impacts. Climate change is a major problem that today's youth and generations unborn will have to confront and manage, as they will not have the luxury of ignoring the science and delay actions any further. The impacts of climate change are both inter- and intragenerational and have deep ethical implications with respect to how we care about each other and about how we care about creation. Society needs to embrace Pope Francis's call for an integral education (see foreword) for an integral ecology, which recognizes the intrinsic link between environmental justice and social justice. We must hear both the "cry of the earth and the cry of the poor" in Pope Francis's moving words.

ROLE OF EDUCATION

A twenty-first-century education for climate change and environmental and human sustainability must be rooted in the best natural science, social science, humanities thinking, and pedagogical practice. Furthermore, it must be:

1. Relevant to local concerns while embedded in a larger global ethic of solidarity, equity, and care

2. Developmentally and age-appropriate (how a five-year-old thinks about air pollution and how a ten-year-old thinks about climate change will differ by socio-emotional and cognitive readiness to internalize and process and make meaning of facts, concepts, and ideas).

3. Culturally appropriate as to the knowledge, values, sensibilities, and practices required to participate effectively within multiple, nested ecologies, environments, and communities (local, national, and transnational) while understanding, valuing, and respecting cultural differences.

4. Rooted in the realities of historical and systemic environmental injustices that must be understood and addressed to make progress toward equity.

5. Focused on teacher and student inquiry, agency, leadership, and civic activism.

Climate change education, from pre-kindergarten, primary school through adulthood, must play a central role in the societal transformation that is necessary to address the current crisis.

It is imperative that we nurture a generation of climate-literate and empowered young people. Further, interdisciplinary climate education must also be woven into the fabric of undergraduate education to ensure that the world's future decision makers are equipped with the knowledge to design and implement solutions to the crisis we have left them. And lastly, education via trusted community leaders can help today's generation of adults better understand the crisis before us and to make better decisions.

We live in an integral ecology; we inhabit a common home, and we share the planet like one family. We need the relevant stakeholders to do their part: teachers will need climate scientists as partners. In turn, scientists will need faith leaders to take part in the transformational moves required to communicate fact-and-science curated messages to mobilize public opinion. Scientists will need community leaders to help them carry the message of climate change science, impacts, and solutions to the public. Policy makers will need to translate the best science and best education to articulate smart new policy frameworks for teachers to best engage students. We all need enlightened business leaders to lead a revolution on sustainable business practices and products for a sustainable world.

SIX CLUSTERS, TEN SOLUTIONS

Scientists and technological innovators have identified key solutions to the climate change crisis, and the implementation of many of them is already underway. A collection of these solutions was produced in 2015 in *Bending the Curve: Ten Scalable Solutions*, a landmark report by the University of California.[8]

We outline ten scalable solutions that have made California a global leader in climate solutions over the last decades. These solutions are organized into six clusters: science, societal transformation, governance, markets and regulation, technology, and natural and managed ecosystems. The ten solutions represent an integrated approach to climate change across a wide range of expertise and sectors. They are described as *scalable* because they can be implemented in local or regional "living laboratories" and then adapted to the changing needs or demands of a variety of contexts and scaled up to national and global levels.

SOCIETAL TRANSFORMATION

For the poorest three billion of Earth's population, 2°C (3.6°F) of global warming, expected before 2050, would pose catastrophic existential threats—in effect raising an unprecedented intragenerational equity issue, which will become worse as it lingers for centuries affecting generations unborn.[9]

In the first quarter of the twenty-first century, the world witnessed the largest number of forcibly displaced human beings in history. While precise numbers are both elusive and changing, 2019 United Nations High Commissioner for Refugees data report that more than seventy million people—the equivalent of every man, woman, and child in Lagos, São Paulo, Seoul, London, Lima, New York, and Guadalajara—are escaping home into the unknown.[10] While migration is a shared condition of humanity, it is increasingly catastrophic: "The majority of new displacements in 2016 took place in environments characterized by a high exposure to natural and human-made hazards, high levels of socioeconomic vulnerability, and low coping capacity of both institutions and infrastructure."[11]

The science cluster identifies what our targets should be; it prescribes which climate pollutants we should target and defines the pathways and timelines for society to remain under 2°C of warming. The remaining clusters explore the diverse levers we need to pull to achieve these targets.

Innovations in policy and governance, business practices, and technologies are necessary for these solutions to take effect. But developing the broad societal will and motivation to take advantage of the levers will require the work of education. Implementing solutions to climate change demands that we foster a broad social understanding of the challenge and a global culture of climate action. Bending the curve requires societal transformation—a radical shift in attitudes and behaviors. We must learn to think about and behave differently in our own lives, in our interactions with each other, and in our interactions with nature. We need a bold, humanistic vision of education, as articulated by Stefania Giannini in this volume, "based on human rights, social justice, dignity, cultural and social diversity, and intellectual solidarity. This vision reaffirms a set of universal ethical principles and the need to strengthen moral values in education and society. It starts with people of all ages and the analysis of development contexts. It is inclusive and equitable, and informed by interdisciplinary research across the sciences, arts, and humanities. Finally, it is participatory and international in scope" (chapter 20). In Pope Francis's words, societal transformation requires shifting "hearts, heads, and hands" (foreword).

Education must serve to develop climate communication strategies that invest people personally in the challenge and helps everyone think about their individual and collective lives differently. Effective climate communication is not simply a matter of transmitting scientific knowledge. Having better science information, while important, does not seem to be the main reason why people accept that climate change is happening or change their behaviors accordingly. People change their attitudes and behaviors when the social becomes personal and familial: they come to care about climate change as relevant to the "me" and the "us." Climate communication should help us understand the impacts that climate change will have on things that are up-close and matter to us: our personal well-being and the well-being of our families and communities; the beloved creek where we first discovered shells and conches, the mysterious forest where we first encountered wild-life; the ageless glaciers where we learned the many shades, shapes, and colors of ice all now threatened by climate change. Climate communication is most successful in creating social motivation for change when it is tailored to audiences and their unique contexts, needs, and aspirations.[12]

We also need to harness the power of social movements early to cultivate the collective will needed to make the change we see as essential. Social movements are unlike other forms of social change in that they are designed to bring individual and collective motivation to make change into alignment with the authority to do so. Sometimes the people who have the authority to make change are also motivated. Sometimes they are not. When they are not, those who have the motivation must learn to transform the resources they have into the power they need to make the change they want. That is what social movements do. They work, thus, by teaching people to realize their own role as agents of change—what can I do, as one person, to put my hands on the levers of change? By developing people's capacities and teaching them to work with others, social movements transform people to transform the world.[13]

The foundation of societal transformation is education at every age, from pre-kindergarten through college, from early adulthood and beyond. Like climate communication more broadly, climate education should not be understood as a passive activity of absorbing science information, but it must seek to connect the learner to the challenge.

Climate education is most effective when it employs integral, inquiry-based, community-rooted strategies that invest young and adult learners in climate action. It should endeavor to help all learners understand what's at stake for them personally. But at the same time, it should cultivate empathy for one's fellows born and unborn and for vulnerable populations who are disproportionately impacted by climate disruption. Climate education must instill a sense of agency and generational purpose—the best antidotes to learned helplessness and anomic withdrawal.[14] The Bending the Curve project does all of this, targeting three distinct audiences: higher-education students and professionals; pre-kindergarten to high school and teachers; and adults of all ages, with or without a college education.

Bending the Curve is a set of educational tools and protocols that present climate disruption as a complex but solvable challenge requiring solutions that integrate science, technology, governance, finance, ecosystem management, ethics, and societal transformation. Students of Bending the Curve: Climate Change Solutions (BtC_CCS) courses become active learners and are challenged to apply their knowledge to community-based experiential learning laboratories and online dashboards.

BENDING THE CURVE EDUCATION FOR ALL COLLEGE STUDENTS AND PROFESSIONALS

The education protocol consists of four components, outlined below.

BENDING THE CURVE: CLIMATE CHANGE SOLUTIONS HYBRID COURSE

The BtC_CCS hybrid course[15] was produced with the specific goal of educating students at the university level in academic contexts. The course is designed as a hybrid course, combining the best elements of a traditional in-person class with those of online learning environments and flipped classrooms. Students watch video lectures at home and attend in-person classes that are devoted to discussions and group capstone project work facilitated by an instructor.

The course was launched in the winter of 2018 and includes over twenty recorded lectures presented by twenty-three expert faculty from across the UC system and beyond, covering multidimensional aspects of the climate problem.[16] By focusing on scalable solutions for carbon neutrality and climate stability, BtC_CCS challenges students to take matters into their own hands and identify solutions at different scales.

The BtC_CCS hybrid course introduces students to the social and natural history of climate change and the impact that climate change has on the world from various dimensions: scientific, technological, economic, and social justice perspectives. Students then learn about various solutions for carbon neutrality and climate stability and the essential interrelationships between various solutions. They examine current living laboratories of climate solutions and critique them from a multitude of perspectives. Students are encouraged to personalize the challenge to create a vision for leadership and action within their own various communities. They come to an understanding through doing that personal values and a commitment to climate change mitigation can guide personal decisions and actions. Lastly, students experiment with diverse solutions and scenarios to reduce the carbon footprint of society. Together, these are the learning outcomes of the course.

The course culminates in a capstone project through which interdisciplinary student teams apply new knowledge. The capstone project assignment consists of designing an integral set of solutions on a particular challenge—for example, wildfires in California or climate vulnerability among island inhabitants in the Pacific. Students research the challenge and come to understand that no one discipline or approach alone can "solve" the problem. They are encouraged to identify a set of solutions drawn from across the six clusters of the Bending the Curve report. Another variation of the capstone project assignment is that student teams investigate living laboratories—case studies of particularly successful integral climate action. Through their research, they come to understand why solutions require integral cooperation and action across knowledges and sectors. At the end of the course, instructors can select the most successful group capstone projects for open-access publication through the California Digital Library. Opportunities for undergraduate students to publish their work are rare, and several student group projects have been published already and are now publicly accessible.[17]

Through the 2019–2020 academic year, the hybrid course has been offered on a total of eleven campuses, including seven UC campuses (some multiple times), two additional California campuses outside of the UC system, and universities in Taiwan and Sweden.

BENDING THE CURVE: CLIMATE CHANGE SOLUTIONS ONLINE COURSE

Additionally, BtC_CCS has launched an online version,[18] which provides an opportunity for individuals to take the course without having to be physically present in a classroom. The course was designed and ready to launch before COVID-19 hit, and it became an unexpected asset for several University of California campuses that found themselves quite suddenly in need of high-quality remote learning tools. The online version of the course uses the hybrid course as its base and optimizes the design for a fully digital learning environment, emphasizing student engagement and interactivity. Lecture videos remain the foundation of the course's content, and students are required to work together to prepare for and actively participate in live sessions hosted via video conference. Students in the online course are also expected to complete a final capstone project, imagining solutions to the climate change problem in ways that demonstrate their abilities to synthesize key issues across a diverse range of disciplines and creatively apply what they have learned.

THE BENDING THE CURVE: CLIMATE CHANGE SOLUTIONS DIGITAL TEXTBOOK

The BtC_CCS digital textbook[19] was designed to accompany the course and is focused on solutions.[20] The nineteen chapters convey that the deep emission cuts that are required to bend the curve are well within our technical capabilities. This book demonstrates, however, that deploying technological solutions demands a broad understanding of the multidimensional aspects of the climate change problem. It shows how we can quicken the pace of technological innovation and create the social, political, and economic impetus to implement solutions that are already available. It also explains how we can do so in a way that helps, not harms, the most disadvantaged people in society. The book's central theme is this: climate change is not a question of political beliefs but a dominant scientific and societal issue. Without fast actions to bend the curve, it can quickly morph into an issue of enormous human tragedy.

The book itself is an open educational resource published by the Regents of the University of California that is intended for multiple audiences. It can be used as a companion text with all versions of the BtC_CCS course, including the hybrid and fully online courses and the massive open online courses (MOOC) series (described below). It can also be used in nonacademic contexts by civic, religious, and community organizations in a variety of contexts. A companion guide helps all audiences guide conversations related to the themes found in the textbook.[21] Both the digital textbook and the companion guide are available worldwide as a free PDF download through a Creative Commons license via the California Digital Library.

The book consists of three parts. The first part sets the stage for the entire book by introducing concepts and solutions. The second part consists of chapters organized into six solution clusters that capture the multidimensional aspects of climate solutions. The third part focuses on special topics that are vital for developing mitigation solutions but do not properly fit into the six-clusters structure.

While the book is designed to accompany the BtC_CCS courses, it is also written for anyone who cares about the future of the planet and human well-being. The chapters are designed to help individuals, community groups, businesses, religious leaders, mayors, heads of state—in short, everyone—to bend the emissions curve. The chapters are written for a generalist audience—nonexpert readers at the level of a second-year undergraduate student—with little assumed in the way of prior knowledge.

AUDIENCE OF LEARNERS PURSUING CLIMATE KNOWLEDGE: THE BTC_CCS EDUCATIONAL PROTOCOL

The Audience of Learners Pursuing Climate Knowledge: The BtC_CCS educational protocol also targets professionals, concerned stakeholders, and lifelong learners from all over the world through a series of four MOOCs.

Available on UC San Diego Online beginning the first half of 2020, the MOOC program of the BtC_CCS initiative consists of four self-paced courses available for learners around the world to enroll in anytime, from anywhere.[22] The same content covered in the BtC_CCS online course is distributed across the first three MOOC courses so that each stand-alone course can be completed in approximately thirty hours. These MOOC courses provide access to video lectures, homework exercises, the digital textbook, and community discussion forums that allow learners to engage with each other. In the fourth and final capstone course, learners use their acquired knowledge from the first three courses to create and share an action plan for climate change solutions in their local community. Learners can enroll in each course for free or pay a fee to access the assessments and earn a statement of accomplishment issued by UC San Diego.

KINDERGARTEN TO HIGH SCHOOL TEACHERS

We propose an educational narrative building on the idea of a sustainable planet. Our starting point is the child's innate moral sensibilities and the natural and emerging scientific curiosities of youth. It should build on their solidarity, providing a sense of connection to peers in one's local environment and community as well as with youth from around the world. The sustainable planet serves to expand the sense of "me" into "us" and the "us-vs-them" into the "us-with-them" group. It endeavors to provide a compelling moral imperative that can set youth on an active search for Bending the Curve solutions to interrupt and reverse harmful disruptions in their environment. Above all, the purpose is to expand the opportunities for every student to learn about climate change and to act on what she is learning effectively and for the common good.

The UC and California State University (CSU) systems are presently partnering with key stakeholders to advance environmental and climate change literacy for pre-kindergarten to grade 12. Together, the UC-CSU system encompasses thirty-three campuses and over 760,000 students and trains 56 percent of the pre-kindergarten to grade 12 teachers in California.

In September 2019, the leadership of the UC and CSU systems signed a declaration of climate emergency sponsored by the United Nations. Following this declaration, the Environmental and Climate Change Literacy Project and Summit (ECCLPS), a collaborative effort helping to prepare current and future teachers to respond to climate change issues, held the *Environmental and Climate Change Literacy Summit* in December 2019.[23] The purpose of the ECCLPS is to inform and encourage the advancement of pre-kindergarten–12 environmental and climate change literacy through the preparation, development, and support of future and current teachers in California. By ensuring that California educators have the knowledge, skills, support, and opportunities they need to address climate issues, the initiative aims to help more than five hundred thousand high school students each year to become literate in environmental and climate change issues and solutions.

The ECCLPS summit seeded a collaborative effort to prepare current and future teachers to respond to the need for climate change education. UC and CSU educators, California government representatives, and other global decision makers, representatives from the public K–12 school system, representatives of the indigenous communities, and others contributed to a report that provides a road map for ECCLPS's goals, objectives, and recommendations.[24] Educating the next generation on climate change impacts and solutions requires preparing teachers for the task.

ECCLPS focuses on how to best prepare teachers for facilitating climate dialogue with their students before teaching, while teaching, and for teaching different age groups. Three respective working groups focused their work on: (1) preservice, which addresses the preparation of future teachers; (2) in-service, which addresses the continued support and learning of current teachers; and (3) curriculum, which addresses the course of study for all students.

ECCLPS endeavors to integrate environmental and climate change literacy across all subjects.[25]

Both the BtC_CCS MOOC and ECCLPS are complemented by UC-CSU's NXTerra initiative, which is a resource for college teachers from across all disciplines and anyone seeking to enhance their teaching and learning about the climate crisis, critical sustainability, and climate justice studies both inside and outside the classroom. NXTerra's online platform centralizes resources including course syllabi, assignments, bibliographies, films, videos, podcasts, and sustainability news at UC and CSU campuses.[26]

CLIMATE LITERACY FOR LIFELONG LEARNERS

The BtC_CCS initiative is a strong starting point in climate education since it assembles the collective wisdom of experts from many disciplines. But formal education alone, whether in the classroom or online, cannot solve the climate crisis. Climate education needs to reach the general public beyond those for whom these materials are accessible in academic contexts.

To do this, scientists and educators must form alliances with faith leaders, tribal leaders, policy makers, and like-minded influencers to articulate and disseminate climate action messages in contexts that are personal and relevant to multiple communities. One approach is to produce an inclusive and locally relevant education program aimed at engaging the general public, including, very importantly, those who are dismissive of climate change science.

Similar to existing BtC_CCS materials, this education program, Climate Literacy for Grown-Ups, would form an alliance between four crucial sectors—academics, faith leaders, the private sector, and policy makers—to develop a locally relevant education program for faith leaders on how climate change poses risks to communities around the United States and opportunities for developing and implementing solutions. These materials would serve as tools for faith leaders to take and adapt as appropriate for their communities.

At present, a key obstacle that scientists and educators face when reaching out beyond academia is the politicization of the topic of climate change. There is a pressing need to depoliticize the subject and educate the public not only on the moral obligations we all have to the environment and to each other but to the real risks we are all facing. Though this effort is applicable globally, the present focus is on communities in the United States.

Climate Education for Grown-Ups is the culmination of brainstorming with leading theologians, religious leaders, climate and social scientists, and communicators. It also addresses an urgent issue that has long been identified by religious groups, including the Pontifical Academy of Sciences and Pope Francis, who together have advanced numerous solutions and calls to action regarding our collective responsibility to protect human health and wellness—"a moral obligation to safeguard the earth for future generations."[27]

CALIFORNIA AND BEYOND

Although the educational protocol presented here is developed primarily by experts in California, it is by no means applicable only to California or even the United States. Certain components of the educational protocol, for example, "Higher Education," have already transcended state lines and international borders. BtC_CCS was designed with flexibility and scalability in mind as a crosscampus initiative for students at different campuses within the UC system. BtC_CCS is customizable to its audience in terms of age, culture, and region. Campus coordinators design their own approach and assemble their own subset of the available materials. They are provided with teaching guides that include detailed instructions on how to facilitate group discussions and suggestions for examinations and capstone project assignments, but they are free to be as creative as they wish with their applications of the course.

The course has been piloted successfully at universities in Sweden and Taiwan, and a pilot will soon be conducted at a university in North Carolina. The digital textbook is freely available worldwide through a Creative Commons license via the California Digital Library. With the further launch of the MOOC, this protocol will be available to a global audience.

Through the components of the protocol, current and future generations will be better prepared not only to confront climate change and its technical challenges but also to become stewards of society, standing up for sustainable development.

A massive societal transformation in how we view our relationships with one another and with our planet must occur in tandem for true change to take place. This is why climate change education needs to be incorporated into schools, universities, and beyond traditional learning centers to engage professionals and the general public.

In September 2019, in the largest ever youth-led demonstrations in history, young people took to the streets by the millions to articulate in hundreds of different languages and in cities big and small, on every continent on Earth, a powerful message: we must act on climate change now. Young people are struggling to make sense of the planet's finality. While all children come to contemplate the mortality of their parents and loved ones and, eventually their own, the mortality of the planet is not easily grasped. In their collective cry, they are articulating the existential terror of planetary death.

Climate change has ignited the dynamic movement for youth agency and action in service of the common good. Climate change education for all should be a part of the solution for moving forward.

It is by nurturing socio-emotional learning, the values and virtues of engaged citizenship, and by imparting the basic skills to prepare youth for a changing world that schools and colleges become meaningful vehicles for collective empowerment and positive social action. Schools and colleges must endeavor to instill in youth humane sensibilities, empathy and compassion, communication and collaboration skills, higher-order cognitive skills for critical thinking, and the metacognitive abilities to become lifelong learners, civic agents, and environmental literacy champions.

ACKNOWLEDGMENTS

We are deeply grateful to the fifty authors of the Bending the Curve report,[28] the twenty-five lecturers of the education protocol,[29] the eighteen authors of *Bending the Curve* textbook, and all participants of ECCLPS.[30] Creation of the education protocol indeed took a village.

NOTES

1. Ramanathan, Veerabhadran, Juliann E. Allison, Maximilian Auffhammer, David Auston, Anthony D. Barnosky, Lifang Chiang, William D. Collins et al., Executive summary of the report, *Bending the Curve: 10 Scalable Solutions for Carbon Neutrality and Climate Stability* (Oakland: University of California, 2015), http://uc-carbonneutralitysummit2015.ucsd.edu /_files/Bending-the-Curve.pdf.

2. Suárez-Orozco, Marcelo M., ed., *Learning in the Global Era: International Perspectives on Globalization and Education* (Berkeley: University of California Press; New York: Ross Institute, 2007).

3. Fonna, Forman, and Veerabhadran Ramanathan, "Climate Change, Mass Migration and Sustainability: A Probabilistic Case for Urgent Action," *Humanitarianism and Mass Migration*, ed. Marcelo Suarez-Orozco, 43–59 (Oakland: University of California Press, 2018).

4. See Bending the Curve: Climate Change Solutions (website), University of California, San Diego: https://bendingthecurve.ucsd.edu/.

5. Cordero, Eugene C., Diana Centeno, and Anne Marie Todd, "The Role of Climate Change Education on Individual Lifetime Carbon Emissions," ed. Francesco S. R. Pausata, *Plos One* 15, no. 2 (February 4, 2020): e0206266, https://doi.org/10.1371/journal.pone.0206266.

6. Ramanathan, Veerabhadran et al., Executive summary of *Bending the Curve*.

7. Ramanathan, Veerabhadran, "Bending the Curve: Ten Scalable Solutions."

8. UC Carbon Neutrality (website): http://uc-carbonneutralitysummit2015.ucsd.edu/_files /Bending-the-Curve.pdf;Ramanathan, Veerabhadran et al., Executive summary of *Bending the Curve*.

9. Ramanathan, Veerabhadran, "Bending the Curve: Ten Scalable Solutions."

10. Forman, Fonna, and Veerabhadran Ramanathan, "Unchecked Climate Change and Mass Migration: A Probabilistic Case for Urgent Action," in *Humanitarianism and Mass Migration*, ed. Marcelo M. Suárez-Orosco, 43–59 (Oakland: University of California Press, 2019).

11. Suárez-Orozco, Marcelo M., ed., *Humanitarianism and Mass Migration: Confronting the World Crisis* (Oakland: University of California Press, 2019); https://www.internal-displacement .org/global-report/grid2017/pdfs/2017-GRID-part-1.pdf, 9.

12. Forman, Fonna, "Rethinking Climate Justice: Practical Ethics in Urgent Times," in *Health of People, Health of Planet: Problems and Solutions*, ed. Wael Al-Delaimy, Veerabhadran Ramanathan, and Marcelo Sánchez Sorondo, 239–250 (New York: Springer, 2020).

13. Han, Hahrie, *How Organizations Develop Activists: Civic Associations and Leadership in the 21st Century* (Oxford: Oxford University Press, 2014).

14. Schreiner, Camilla, Ellen K. Henriksen, and Pål J. Kirkeby Hansen, "Climate Education: Empowering Today's Youth to Meet Tomorrow's Challenges," *Studies in Science Education* 41, no. 1 (January 2005): 3–49, https://doi.org/10.1080/03057260508560213; Wibeck, Victoria, "Enhancing Learning, Communication and Public Engagement about Climate Change— Some Lessons from Recent Literature," *Environmental Education Research* 20, no. 3 (May 4, 2014): 387–411, https://doi.org/10.1080/13504622.2013.812720.

15. Bending the Curve (website): https://bendingthecurve.ucsd.edu/.

16. "Bending the Curve: Climate Change Solutions," University of California, December 12, 2018, https://bendingthecurve.ucsd.edu/wp-content/uploads/sites/355/2019/04/1-V1.0-OVERVIEW -BtC-Booklet-V1.0-12-20-17-spread.pdf.

17. "Bending the Curve: Climate Change Solutions Student Projects," eScholarship (University of California), accessed March 27, 2020, https://escholarship.org/uc/bending_the_curve_student _projects.

18. "Course Description Bending/Curve: Climate Change, SIO 109R" (website), University of California, accessed March 28, 2020, https://crossenrollcourses.universityofcalifornia.edu /view/80596?title=SIO+109R+Bending%2FCurve%3A+Climate+Change (site no longer available).

19. Ramanathan, Veerabhadran, Roger Aines, Max Auffhammer, Matt Barth, Jonathan Cole, Fonna Forman, Hahrie Han et al., *Bending the Curve: Climate Change Solutions* (self-pub., eScholarship, 2021), https://escholarship.org/uc/item/6kr8p5rq.

20. Veerabhadran Ramanathan et al., *Bending the Curve: Climate Change Solutions* (eScholarship, University of California, 2019).

21. Ramanathan, Veerabhadran, Roger Aines, Max Auffhammer, Matt Barth, Jonathan Cole, Fonna Forman, Hahrie Han et al., "Learning Companion" to *Bending the Curve: Climate Change Solutions* (self-pub., eScholarship, 2021), https://escholarship.org/uc/item/2b80d2k2.

22. "Bending the Curve: Climate Change Solutions, Course 1," UC San Diego Online (website), accessed April 14, 2020, https://online.ucsd.edu/courses/EXT+BTC-1/.

23. "Environmental and Climate Change Literacy Summit," ECCLPS (website), accessed April 14, 2020, https://sites.google.com/tenstrands.org/ecclps/home?authuser=0.

24. "Achieving Climate Stability and Environment Sustainability: PK–12 Education as Part of the Solution for Bending the Curve," ECCLPS (website), accessed March 27, 2020, https:// sites.google.com/tenstrands.org/ecclps/report; Veerabhadran Ramanathan et al., *Achieving Climate Stability and Environment Sustainability: PK–12 Education as Part of the Solution for Bending the Curve*, ed. Leigh Leveen (Los Angeles: University of California, Los Angeles, 2019), https://sites.google.com/tenstrands.org/ecclps/report.

25. Veerabhadran Ramanathan et al., *Achieving Climate Stability and Environment Sustainability*.

26. UC-CSU NXTerra: transformative education for climate action (website), UC-CSU NXTerra, accessed March 25, 2020, https://www.nxterra.orfaleacenter.ucsb.edu/.

27. Sorondo, Monsignor Marcelo Sánchez, Howard Frumkin, and Veerabhadran Ramanathan, "Health, Faith, and Science on a Warming Planet," *JAMA* 319, no. 16 (April 24, 2018): 1651, https://doi.org/10.1001/jama.2018.2779.

28. Bending the Curve (website): https://bendingthecurve.ucsd.edu/.

29. UC Carbon Neutrality (website): http://uc-carbonneutralitysummit2015.ucsd.edu/_files/Bending -the-Curve.pdf

30. ECCLPS, University of California, and the California State University, "Environmental and Climate Change Projects," https://sites.google.com/tenstrands.org/ecclps/home.

13

FROM KNOWLEDGE TO BEHAVIOR CHANGE

Signs, Patterns, Influences in Education for Sustainable Development

RADHIKA IYENGAR, TARA STAFFORD OCANSEY, AND HAEIN SHIN

In September 2015, leaders from around the world adopted the sweeping set of Sustainable Development Goals (SDGs), which go far beyond the "unfinished business" of the Millennium Development Goals to address seventeen urgent and interlinked challenges relating to sustainable development.[1] The UN has defined *sustainable development* in many ways, but perhaps the most common and agreed-upon definition defines it as "the ability to meet the needs of the present without jeopardizing the ability of future generations to meet their own needs."[2] Taking this generational view, it may seem, at first glance, that some of the seventeen SDGs are at odds with one another. How can we reduce poverty (SDG 1) and promote economic growth (SDG 8) while also reducing wasteful consumption (SDG 12) and making drastic cuts in carbon emissions needed to combat climate change (SDG 13) that will ensure a sustainable future for all? More broadly, the prioritization of specific goals depends on the country's stage of development and its own local environmental, economic, and social concerns. Recently, the world has come face-to-face with the need for sustainable development more than ever, with the COVID-19 pandemic exposing the real dangers of continued environmental degradation and biodiversity loss, and with grassroots mobilization against various rising forms of supremacist nationalism in places like the United States (white supremacy) and India (Hindu supremacy). One hundred ninety-three member states have taken on the challenge of meeting the SDGs by 2030 to address these intersecting challenges of environmental degradation, climate change, poverty, inequality, and more.

India has been one of the countries at the forefront of global efforts to combat climate change and environmental degradation, establishing itself as one of the leaders in investment in renewable energy sources in 2018,[3] and taking steps to ban single-use plastics by 2022.[4] While India is taking bold steps at a policy level to curb emissions and minimize waste generation, implementation has been slower. Many citizens in India are unaware of the causes of the environmental degradation they witness in their communities, unaware of the actions they can take or advocate for to address these environmental challenges, and/or they are constrained by cultural norms that make it difficult for them to gain awareness or change their behavior. For example, for the festival of Lohri, celebrated in the northern Indian states, bonfires are created in many houses that use coal or wood; similarly, for the festival of Diwali, firecrackers are a part of the celebration but cause pollution on a massive scale. In an environmental survey of five thousand individuals in major cities in India, 90 percent of the people interviewed across highly polluted cities had heard of air pollution but lacked awareness about the causes and effects.[5]

Changing individual behaviors rooted in long-held cultural norms is a daunting task. However, with the global impact of social media and access to information, young people arguably have more access to find more in common with each other across cultures than previous generations. With 42 percent of the world's population under the age of twenty-five,[6] it is these young people who will inherit these shared global challenges. Young people, therefore, must be equipped with the knowledge, skills, and lifestyle choice alternatives to make the massive shifts in ways of living, consuming, doing business, and advocating that must be made to overcome threats of climate change and pollution for a sustainable future for all. As Jeffrey Sachs—one of the world's foremost thinkers on sustainable development—has stated, "Education is the most vital input for every dimension of sustainable development."[7]

This chapter first explains the contextual setting of where this study takes place, followed by a theoretical framework that underpins the approach towards sustainable development. The paper continues with a literature review of the different components of education and sustainable development used in the framework. The methodology section focuses on operationalizing the framework and details the data collection activities. The results section presents the main themes that emerge from the data analysis. The discussion and the recommendations sections elaborate on the current trends in education for sustainable development (ESD), the research and practice gaps that remain, and recommendations for the practice of ESD.

SETTING

In a slum community, at a stone's throw to the closed, ill-famed Union Carbide factory, is a nonprofit officially established in 1998 to rehabilitate the victims of the Bhopal gas tragedy of 1984.[8] The mission of Mahashakti Seva Kendra (MSK) is twofold: (1) promoting the message of "no chemicals" to protect the environment and (2) training women in vocational skills to earn a living by producing eco-friendly, reusable bags using block printing and natural dyes. The organization has trained more than twenty thousand women in eco-friendly printing skills and, at present, has a dedicated women employee group of forty young and middle-aged women, many of who have limited formal education. The setting of this study lends itself to using the ESD framework due to its intersectoral approach, addressing gender inequality, livelihoods, and environmental and climate issues. A setup for technical and vocational education and training (TVET) was ideal for this study, as it includes many dimensions needed for sustainable development. The TVET Center provides the skills to make eco-friendly reusable bags, provides an economic means to come out of poverty, ensures that it is all-inclusive and is based in the community and has an education component, and provides consultations with doctors on healthy living. All these factors were included in the ESD intervention as context through this research.

RESEARCH QUESTIONS

The research questions informing the design of the initial sessions included the following. First, what is the general level of awareness among the participants of the environmental and sustainability issues in India? Second, what communication techniques or delivery mechanisms resonate the most with learners to influence their behaviors?

The study was designed to understand two issues. First, how should science-based content on environmental and sustainability issues be customized to the cultural and social settings of the location so that the content resonates with participants? Second, how should environmental and sustainability messages be communicated effectively to promote environment-friendly behavior? The extent to which localization of the science-driven environment content requires consideration of gender dynamics and cultural norms was identified as an area for further exploration. This paper presents the initial findings from these workshop-style sessions and discusses the implications of these findings to design programs intended to build awareness of challenges to environmental sustainability further and offer approaches to behavior change that are realistic within the cultural contexts where the work is being done.

THEORETICAL FRAMEWORK

Even after the UN Decade of Education for Sustainable Development from 2005–2014, the concept of ESD, for many in the education sphere, still lacks a clear definition or differentiation from related concepts such as environmental education (EE). EE first emerged in the late 1960s, when William Stapp, who has been called the father of EE, defined its scope as "aimed at producing a citizenry that is knowledgeable concerning the biophysical environment and its associated problems, aware of how to help solve these problems, and motivated to work toward their solution."[9] Many teachers still associate ESD as more aligned to this definition of EE and lack the competence to approach ESD through the intersecting pillars of sustainable development—originally conceived of as environment, economy, and society.[10] The fourth pillar of culture has more recently emerged, with advocates arguing that efforts to spur behavior shifts will only take root when designed with local cultures in mind.[11] Hofman argues that ESD must equip learners with "action competence."[12] Rather than ESD trying to impose behavior change on learners separated from democratic and ethical considerations, ESD must help learners identify challenges to sustainable development in their local environments, to see how different courses of action lead to different outcomes, and to have the capacity to thoughtfully decide their sustainable courses of action accordingly.

Similarly, Scott and Gough describe ESD as education in citizenship, offering learners "a responsive social learning process which is a preparation for informed, open-minded, social engagement with the main existential issues of the day."[13] Addressing the urgent global need to spread awareness of growing threats to a sustainable future and offering practical approaches for how people can take action to minimize wasteful consumption and hold their governments accountable must be approached through these four pillars in order to tap into the personal priorities and cultural norms of individuals and communities.

The four pillars can help ensure the seemingly paradoxical SDGs achieve their mission by offering a vital lens through which culturally appropriate and equitable strategies can be developed.

The theoretical framework we use to discuss the study led by MSK is grounded in this definition of ESD that aims to understand the challenges to sustainability through the lenses of the four pillars—economic, environmental, social, and cultural. This framework develops action competence among learners to identify social problems and develop and implement contextually appropriate solutions to these problems that are in harmony with intersecting SDGs. The SDGs most relevant to issues of environment, education, gender, and biodiversity are most pertinent here. Our theoretical framework further assumes that youth and young adults, as a large population who will be the future prime influencers and leaders over economic and social issues, are the audience likely to execute on the central tenets of ESD if they are woven into education curriculum and capacity development opportunities that they have access to. As Sachs notes, education at the tertiary level, including TVET, is necessary to foster "a generation of skilled young people trained in public policy and sustainable development."[14] By integrating concepts of ESD into areas of learning that are perceived to have a more direct impact on learners' abilities to improve their quality of life (such as becoming aware of water and air pollution and their implications on health), the solutions developed through these programs will have an increased likelihood of leading to behavior change in the students than will other approaches—such as stand-alone ESD curricula or other ESD educational activities that do not include the fourth pillar of culture.

Changing behaviors of adults to be more proenvironment requires a mindset shift. Therefore, the study uses existing eco-psychology literature to address four key steps as described in Steg and Vlek.[15] First, the identification of which behaviors should be changed to improve environmental quality requires selecting the behavior, assessing the feasibility of changing the behavior, and conducting measurement of baseline levels and identification of target groups. Second, the authors suggest assessing which factors promote or inhibit proenvironment behavior. These could be economic, moral and normative, contextual, and habitual factors. Third, interventions designed to address the key factors identified in step two must be selected to promote proenvironment behavior, such as informational strategies (information, persuasion, social support), or structural strategies, such as legal regulation and availability of products and services. Fourth, evaluate the effectiveness of the interventions. How did interventions contribute to changes in behavioral determinants, behaviors, environmental quality, or individuals' quality of life? This broad framework was combined with other elements that came forward using the existing literature. The interventions target women and young adults since they are the main levers for eco-friendly behavior changes, using participatory approaches resulting in eco-solutions that emerge through consensus. Government regulations, such as the single-use plastic ban that were already in place, were discussed to raise awareness of examples of lifestyle changes that could be practiced. The study incorporates the cultural pillar of sustainable development by weaving in religious concepts and local contextual factors to relate knowledge about the science of climate change to the participants' lives and beliefs. Since the study is conducted in a nonformal vocational setting, it uses the green-TVET literature to link eco-activism to their vocation. The study attempts to expand EE beyond the schools into the public domain to motivate behavior change from the communities. Finally, under the broad umbrella of climate change, the plastic issue was identified as an area that could resonate with individuals, as it demanded specific behavior change along with other factors. The plastic issue is a prominent issue that is present in everyone's homes and communities. It did not require individuals to be at a certain education level to understand the problem and take action.

RELEVANT LITERATURE

At its core, the notion of sustainability enabled by environment depends on the actions and behaviors that directly address environmental issues at the individual, household, community, and societal levels. The actual trajectory that follows awareness and knowledge gain about what needs to be done to improve environmental conditions with daily actions and behavior is a complicated one. The discourse surrounding this topic points to the complex puzzle pieces of knowledge, education, awareness, culture, psychology, and a fundamental paradigm shift that must precede meaningful change.

GAPS IN GLOBAL EDUCATION FOR SUSTAINABLE DEVELOPMENT

The considerations in the literature rest on the general assumption that education plays a critical role in societal transformation; thus, the growing conversations on the role of education in sustainable development suggest an interest in the "interrelatedness of education and societal transformation in the face of sustainability challenges."[16] Literature written in 1994 already forewarns the gaps that may be overlooked in education for sustainable development vis-à-vis environmental education as a result of the imprecision in its definition, composition, conceptualization, and understanding to elicit inquiry, debate, and perspectives that are not through prescriptive thinking. Selby maps the rise of the concept of *education for sustainable development*, which leads to the birth of the term *sustainable development*.[17] The concept and term sprung into popularity in the 1980s with World Conservation Strategy.[18] With the Brundtland Commission report, environmental protection became an integral part of sustainable development.[19] According to Selby, it was during this time that *sustainable development* became a formal term in the developing world, opening up space to address the increasing and intersecting global environmental and social crises.[20] The environment was then understood as a key aspect of development. This global approach to sustainable development provides a sound theoretical framework to understand the concept in consideration of various elements, including the environment. However, multiple authors over the course of the past two decades point to major gaps stemming from the loose and varied definitions surrounding what constitutes an education for sustainable development.[21] This rift is deepened by the assumption that education leads to sustainable development and, further, that education automatically translates to action and behavior change. ESD requires concerted efforts and a strong infusion of sustainability and notions of citizenship in education. Therefore, the type of education that citizens receive is vital to establish any links between education and sustainable development.

The loose definition of ESD not only captures the wide-ranging issues of sustainable development, but it also creates a space vague and diffuse enough for both "the environment lobby of the metaphorical North . . . and the development lobby of the metaphorical South" to imbue it with their own meaning.[22] As we reviewed, the sustainable development framework already embraces multiple layers of contradiction, including its belief that ESD embodies the misalignment and disengagement between the skills-training orientation of ESD versus the wide-ranging and key components of the human-nature relationship. ESD does not create links between the multiple layers and intersecting challenges of sustainable development, nor does it step beyond teaching simple environmental facts and knowledge, which has been echoed in ESD literature since the 1990s. Jickling states that ESD does not amply explore the topics in philosophical and critical ways.[23] For example, Jickling outlines that one would assume an "educated person" to have

> some understanding of the relationships between these bits of informa-
> tion which enable a person to make some sense of the world; the educated
> person should have some understanding about why a relationship exists.
> We might also wonder if the ability to think critically is a necessary crite-
> rion for the educated person. Again, we would expect to find considerable
> agreement; we would be reluctant to say that a person was educated if we
> judged that he or she could not think for him or herself.[24]

These types of considerations are missing in the ESD approach; ESD approaches tend to teach environmental knowledge and related information, but they do not adequately include philosophy, justice, and equity considerations or les-sons on the application and execution of ideas raised about the environment. Two decades after the emergence of views such as Jickling's, the main critique of ESD rests on the flawed assumption that there is an inherent correlation between quality education (SDG 4) and environmental awareness and behav-ior change. ESD as a field needs to find its place in the curricula at various levels. Further, even though the value of indigenous and local knowledge is acknowledged publicly, as released in the October 2018 report by the UN Inter-governmental Panel on Climate Change (IPCC), the adoption of such practices is yet to be seen—the majority of Western education models focus on eco-nomic growth and social equity over environmental concerns. Komatsu and Rappleye reiterate two issues raised in the 1990s and in the 2000s: (1) the dis-connect in approach to ESD results from the conflicting foundation of inter-national development agenda that remains Global North–centric and (2) the assumption that education alone leads to awareness and behavior change.[25]

FACTORS TO CONSIDER IN GLOBAL EDUCATION FOR SUSTAINABLE DEVELOPMENT

As if to respond to the concerns raised in ESD literature, the field of psychol-ogy has examined this link between knowledge and behavior change. Envi-ronmental psychologists found that "higher cognitive skills and knowledge do not necessarily prompt people into action,"[26] and other factors, such as culture, including the concept of self (for example, whether one considers themselves independent or interdependent), are more likely to mobilize people for proenvironmental actions.[27] Polasky and colleagues highlight the importance of economics to define sustainable development.[28] Poverty on one side and excessive consumption and wastage on the other side also define the parameters of sustainable development. This section defines some factors that were prominent in discussions with the participants.

PSYCHOLOGY AND BEHAVIOR

There are major consequences of climate change. Many individuals have the knowledge about the consequences, but not all are making their actions proenvironment. Research suggests that there are many factors that influence proenvironment behavior, such as childhood experiences, education, personality, social norms, and other personal and social traits.[29] Others may use a more moralistic or value-based approach that encourages people to opt for proenvironment choices.[30] Prior research suggested that people acted in a proenvironment manner if the action seemed to benefit them personally. However, not all proenvironmental actions are for self-interest.[31] Economics of proenvironmental choices also plays an important role in individual decisions.[32] Individuals tend to weigh the costs and benefits of their consumption habits and may opt for the cheaper options. The cost of being environment-friendly could come from time consumed in separating wet waste from dry waste at homes, being a more discerning shopper, or using public or other alternative transport. Or it could come in the form of a monetary cost difference between choosing an electric car versus a conventional car or other such eco-friendly, typically more expensive, product alternatives. On the side of value-based motivations for action, developing a sense of attachment with one's home and local area promotes more proactive behavior to protect the environment.[33] The study showed that if one feels connected with their local area and community, the individual is more likely to engage in environmental issues that impact the community and be a part of political or environmental activism. One study examined the psychological barriers to environmental protection, offering its participants the choice between eco-friendly products (proenvironment) and cheaper products (self-interest). The study found that individuals' construction of self affects their preferences when faced with the decision between proenvironmental and self-interested goals. The construction of self referred to whether individuals were more interdependent or independent. Individuals with more interdependent orientations favored proenvironmental choices and were willing to pay more for eco-friendly options than were individuals with independent orientations. This can be partly explained by the fact that interdependent people exhibited better self-control and restraint over self-interested desires than did independent people.[34]

From another perspective, a study examining the psychological factors that may influence proenvironmental engagement and willingness to engage in proenvironmental behavior hypothesized that worldview and level of skepticism about climate change could affect these attitudes. A survey of 297 American adults supported these hypotheses: the study found that when people believe the world is stable—versus malleable—they are less concerned about helping the environment. These study results show that a person's perception of the world affects their level of skepticism about climate change. Skepticism about climate change naturally influences a person's willingness and intentions in engaging in proenvironmental/climate mitigation behaviors and actions.[35]

CULTURE

Beyond the psychology of behavior, the environmental issues affecting all corners of the earth require a lens to consider the uniqueness and differences exhibited in various parts of the world. Adger and colleagues propose that climate change threatens not only the environment but also the "cultural dimensions of lives and livelihoods that include the material and lived aspects of culture, identity, community cohesion and sense of place."[36] The study finds there are "important cultural dimensions to how societies respond and adapt to climate-related risks."[37] This point is further supported by the fact that climate change stems from people's unsustainable production and consumption of goods, lifestyle choices, and social organization structures, which increase greenhouse gas emissions. Swidler and Hays define culture as the "symbols that express meaning, including beliefs, rituals, art and stories that create collective outlooks and behaviors, and from which strategies to respond to problems are devised and implemented."[38]

Simultaneously, culture relates to a physical space and the communities rooted in that space. Physical environmental impacts, such as drought, vibrancy of marine life, ice coverage, retreating snow cover, and ecosystem disturbance, all correlate to cultural impacts. The results can range from changing patterns in herding, housing, migration, pastoral communities' movement and livelihood, loss of traditional knowledge in housing and fishing/hunting specific species, loss of iconic and culturally significant habitats, and even land loss of island states.[39] Such correlation calls for attention to culture, individuals, and communities if adaptation and mitigation responses are to be effective.

GREEN TVET

In 2001, UNESCO's recommendation for TVET included three goals that paved the way forward for sustainable development. These goals are: (1) TVET should contribute toward the democratization of social, cultural, and economic development; (2) TVET should promote scientific and technological aspects in work while taking into consideration social, political, and environmental implications; and (3) TVET should empower people to contribute to environmentally sound, sustainable development through the work.[40] The 2002 World Summit on Sustainable Development also emphasized the need to build the capacity of individuals through training, providing technical know-how, and strengthening national institutions in economically viable, socially acceptable, and environmentally sound ways. In October 2004, UNESCO experts discussed the way forward on greening TVETs, under the title of "Learning for Work, Citizenship and Responsibility."[41] To operationalize this agenda, sustainable development had to be defined in the context of TVETs. Sustainable development was globally accepted, but it was not a fixed concept, as it had to be a "culturally-directed search for a dynamic balance in the relationships between social, economic and natural systems, a balance that seeks to promote equity between the present and the future, and equity between countries, races, social classes and genders."[42] The UNESCO-UNEVOC online conference further operationalized the greening of TVETs by defining "Green Jobs" as helping to reduce consumption of energy and raw materials, limit greenhouse gas emissions, minimize waste and pollution, and protect and restore the ecosystems.[43] The report also discussed the "green competencies" required for a "green economy."[44] An example from India included Toyota incorporating a three-year training program that included environmental topics as a part of the knowledge and skills relevant for car manufacturing. Another example is the Cane and Bamboo Technology Centre (CBTC) in Guwahati, India, which focuses on the economic and social development in the northeast region of India. The training aims at developing curricula on bamboo-based skills for young people in the informal sector. The creation of green industries and jobs will mean the skilling of individuals in green jobs.[45]

GENDER AND SUSTAINABILITY

The participants in this study were purposively chosen to be all women. Women in the south will be more impacted by climate change as compared to men in those countries and men in the north.[46] The irony is that while this is true, women are not a part of decision-making processes relating to climate in many developing countries.[47] Eastin notes that gender disparities in developing countries are aggravated due to climate change.[48] The author explains that with rising climate change effects, men out-migrate from their villages, leaving behind women with scarce water and food resources, which also undermines the health status of women. However, Salehi and colleagues argue that women are the ones who primarily manage household chores, have the decision power to make their household practices more environment-friendly, and are more engaged in climate change.[49] While the link between gender and the environment is not a widely discussed topic, especially in EE, growing discussions and contemporary policy briefs discuss the critical role of women in addressing the protection of the environment for sustainable development.

There are three reasons why women are central to the climate debate: (1) the percentage of women in the most marginalized groups are the highest; (2) they have a higher mortality rate during natural calamities; and (3) women are more environmentally conscious.[50] While both men and women must play crucial roles in protecting the environment, globally, women predominantly provide livelihoods for families, engage in agricultural labor, and manage household use of natural resources and consumption of services and goods. However, gender power relations discount women's roles as agents of change. This calls for a deeper gender analysis related to the roles men and women play in the environment in the areas of (1) use of natural resources such as water, forests, land, and so on; (2) consumption of services and goods such as transport and food; and (3) experiences of environmental degradation, such as pollution, chemicals, and loss of biodiversity.[51]

PLASTIC POLLUTION MENACE

In India, plastic debris is disturbing the ecological system at a great pace. While India consumes only a fraction of plastic per capita as compared to the United States (India consumes 24 pounds per capita; the United States 240 pounds per capita), its poor waste management has resulted in the accumulation of plastic waste, contaminating the beaches of Mumbai.[52] Jayasiri, Purushothaman, and Vennila found the mean abundance of plastics to be 7.49 grams (0.17–56.27 grams) and 68.83 items (12–960 items) per square meter.[53] The study results show that plastic litter predominates in Mumbai beaches. A similar study by Sruthy and Ramasamy found microplastics present in the sediments of Vembanad Lake, a Ramsar site in India. The study proves that microplastics are emerging as one of the major pollutants in the state of Kerala in India. The lake is a major source of fish and clams for the local residents, and thus their health is at stake with the occurrence of microplastic in the waters.[54] Karthik and colleagues studied twenty-five beaches on the southeast coast of India. The study recorded the highest abundance of microplastic on beaches adjacent to the river mouth. Microplastics were found in 10.1 percent of seventy-nine fish representing five species.[55]

During World Environment Day on June 5, 2018, environment minister Harsh Vardhan announced that India will, by 2022, "eliminate all single-use plastics from our beautiful country."[56] Twenty-five of the twenty-nine states have already announced a plastic ban. While the ban is great news for environmentalists, execution has varied from state to state, with many states continuing to use plastic despite the ban. Prime Minister Narendra Modi has called plastic a "menace to humanity,"[57] and many citizen-led movements have come forward to clean beaches under India's Swachh Bharat Abhiyan (Clean India Movement).[58] The Urban Development Ministry of the state of Madhya Pradesh is taking stronger and promising steps to focus on waste pollution. The Municipal Corporation of Bhopal is making great strides in waste management, especially in urban slum dwellings. Each morning, vehicles that are mandated to pick up waste are sent out to various parts of the city to collect it from households. Up until this effort started, many community dustbins overflowed with unsorted garbage. Now, community bins have been removed, and direct garbage collection at individual households has started. In discussions with the ministry, plastic waste reduction remains a daunting challenge. They are eager to work with partners to find innovative ways to educate and change the uses and practices around plastics for local residents. Because of the missing pieces in education and understanding, many community members are still not actively reducing plastics use or properly sorting waste, which has led to contamination of the Clean India program. This community, like many others across India, demonstrates why there is a huge need for fundamental knowledge—that is, the science behind the negative impacts of plastics, the benefits of waste collection, why efforts such as sorting trash and recycling are needed, and how these particular small and local actions can have important impacts on system-level processes.

METHODOLOGY

STUDY DESIGN AND SAMPLE SIZE

Positioned within the Earth Institute, Columbia University, where climate scientists focus on climate change research and studies, the Center for Sustainable Development (CSD) developed an approach to bring climate and environmental science contents to the social science and education arena. An initial needs assessment was conducted at MSK's center in Bhopal by CSD researchers. This formed the basis for content adaptation by the CSD with help from MSK's leadership. This exercise helped to put in place sessions on climate risk mitigation.[59] Lamont-Doherty Earth Observatory, Columbia University (Lamont), provided the climate and environmental science content for these discussions. The science content was then contextualized by MSK staff.

The participatory action research (PAR) method was used to collect data. PAR can be viewed as a way of "bringing participation into action research."[60] There is another view that PAR was coined by Hall to describe "an integrated activity that combines social investigation, educational work, and action."[61] PAR arises from two research approaches: action research and participatory research. Participatory research (PR) is a process that combines research, education, and action. Action research (AR) originated from "Lewin's concern to find methods that dealt with critical social problems such as poverty, fascism, anti-Semitism, and minority issues" rather than using the traditional positivist science. The first applications of PAR were in the fields of adult education, international development, and the social sciences. Since PAR, by definition, is inclusive, it is a great method of qualitative inquiry to use in a multicultural context.[62] Common to both AR and PR is the use of knowledge to bring about developmental change. Developmental change in action research attempts to provide access to social services for all. For this study, the developmental change is bringing about proenvironment thinking and action. Keeping PAR as an approach to collect data, four interactive sessions were planned, each lasting two hours. The researcher ensured that these participant reflection sessions on climate were made interactive by asking frequent questions and giving space for participants to frequently engage in discussions and activities throughout the sessions.

This study uses the discussions generated as the data collected. The discussion format was a useful data collection method since the idea was for participants to listen to one another and get ideas on how to be eco-friendly. It was very true to the idea of PAR and activity-based learning rather than conducting interviews or focus group–style discussions. It was also helpful for the participants to engage in sharing some of the practices that women follow at home and how they could improve their household and individual practices. The data for this study is the raw footage filmed during the full length of each session. The footage was first transcribed verbatim. A start list of code was prepared based on the hypothesis, problem area, and literature review.[63] The transcript was analyzed, and frequencies were created every time there was an occurrence of the code in the transcript.

THE PARTICIPANTS

Dwarka Nagar Ward of Bhopal city is a resettlement colony that hosts lower-income families. The study participants were based here. Dwarka Nagar Ward is also where MSK's center is located. The majority of the families were daily wage earners, and some were service-class families. The age group of the women was from twenty-two to about sixty years, with the average age being thirty-five. The majority of the women were married and lived with their husbands and children. The majority of the women were primary school graduates; only five completed high school, and two completed a college degree. Many women joined MSK because their families did not allow them to work anywhere else. Since this NGO only works with women, they could get their families' permission. In other cases, the women wanted to learn a skill, such as stitching, block-printing, or zari-zardosi, which MSK was offering for free using a government-funded grant.

PLANNING THE INTERVENTION

Climate scientists from Lamont provided the resources to develop the content. The topics for the first section included plastic waste, plastic in the city and oceans, consumption of plastic by animals and humans, Bisphel A (BPA) and its harmful effects, and ways of plastic waste reduction through refuse, reuse, recycle. The next session was on climate change and its harmful effects—greenhouse gases, changing seasonal patterns, harmful health effects, human impact index, population density, changes in the polar regions, natural disasters, earthquakes, floods, tsunamis, droughts, and global warming trends.

CONTEXTUAL ADAPTATION OF THE SCIENCE-HEAVY CONTENT

Since this content is science-heavy, it was necessary to contextualize the content based on India examples. The curated, nonadapted content was presented to the NGO staff, who helped provide examples that connected to the lives of the participants. The adaptation was as follows.

First, the environmental issues had to be connected to what they observed or felt in their daily lives. Therefore, the sessions were adapted to start with a series of questions encouraging participants to reflect on their observations of various changes in their local climate.

Second, when discussing floods, local and recent examples of floods were presented—for example, the Kerala floods of 2017 and the Uttarakhand Floods of 2013. Similarly, earthquake examples were limited to the region, which included the Nepal earthquake of 2015. These incidences were included since participants would be familiar with them either through the news or other means.

Third, the cultural context was kept in mind. In India, Earth is often referred to as "Mother Nature." Therefore, this term was often used to build a connection between culture and nature.

Fourth, since religion is an important factor in India, examples were consciously interwoven to keep religion integral to the content. For example, the flood discussion was based in Kedarnath, a Hindu pilgrimage spot that many families visit. The religious side was carefully approached since the topic of religion in India is very sensitive. For example, during a particular Hindu festival, the mud idols are put in water, which causes a lot of water pollution. Pictures of the waste in the water had to be discussed in a sensitive manner.

There were other general considerations taken into account. First, a lot of pictures from Bhopal city were included for various sections of the sessions. For example, the Bhopal lake was shown with a lot of plastic waste. Second, images were more effective than words on the slides since not all participants could read. Even if they could read, their comprehension of more technical words and scientific facts was low. Therefore, slides had to be verbally explained in the local language (Hindi) rather than directly read from the slides. Third, the presentation and discussion were on scientific facts, which led to action items toward the end of the session. The researcher did not lead this action agenda; it was open-ended, and participants discussed the steps they could or could not take.

The researcher led the discussions with questions that affected the daily lives of the participants. The participants presented examples that showed anecdotal evidence of the negative impacts of the polluted environment and changes in climate on their daily lives. Scientific facts were explained using graphs, and all of the photos shown were from India. Activities included taking stock of the types of plastic found near the NGO's office. Participants were also asked how they used plastic in their lives. Another activity was thinking about what goes inside their dustbins at home.

FINDINGS

Common themes that emerged from analyzing the raw footage are as follows.

CULTURAL CONTEXT IS IMPORTANT FOR ENVIRONMENTAL SCIENCES MESSAGING

As a subset of culture, religion is a critical component, and participants could relate to this topic. Discussions on the arrival of doomsday highlighted the human impact on climate. Therefore, environmental science facts connected to religious practices were very effective. For example, landslides due to deforestation and unplanned urbanization were discussed in relation to the Kedarnath floods. Kedarnath is a famous Hindu pilgrimage site, as previously mentioned. Since the participants or their relatives visited this site at least once in their lifetimes, and it is a revered site, the natural disaster affected the participants deeply. Therefore, when this incident was connected to deforestation and unplanned urbanization, it resonated with them. Similarly, it provided a recent, more contextual example of the frequent occurrence of floods that everyone could connect with. Another example was of Hindu idols being submerged in the Bhopal lake during a festival. The participants could relate to the water pollution caused by the festival with the help of photos of the pollution in the drinking source for the city.

HIGH AWARENESS ABOUT ENVIRONMENTAL ISSUES BUT LACK OF RELATION TO THEIR OWN LIVES

The general knowledge and awareness about plastic pollution were very high. Scientific facts helped participants to understand some concepts such as "plastic does not ever go away." Diagrammatic depiction of waste from plastic entering the sewage and joining the city lakes and ultimately larger water bodies helped participants further understand the life cycle of plastic. The participants were aware of the problem of cows swallowing plastic bags with food and human fecal matter containing plastic materials. The participants brought up different types of cancer associated with plastic. The general awareness about plastic causing harmful effects to human beings was present to start, but the action to stop [using plastic] was not a common consensus. There was also great awareness about plastic polluting the oceans, even though the Madhya Pradesh state is a landlocked area. The session was helpful to put some scientific facts on the table, which validated the participants' general awareness and concern about plastic. The session integrated the types of diseases related to BPA. Since the majority of the participants were not literate, all the information was presented via visual media. The majority of the participants owned a TV at home, but they complained they did not have time to watch TV regularly. Only one participant possessed a smartphone.

The knowledge about environmental hazards has not resulted in pollution mitigation. The plastic menace was so common that it had become a part of everyone's lives. It almost seemed like plastic in the community was invisible to everyone. In the activity of thinking about the plastic that goes into their home dustbins, it took some time to recollect the plastic items. The same was true for plastic waste that participants saw in their neighborhoods. The plastic waste was so ingrained into the lifestyles and local environment of the participants that it was not viewed as a menace anymore. An additional conversation was required to view it as a problem, look at examples, and then discuss plastic pollution among participants.

HEALTH AILMENTS AND ECONOMIC DISTRESS IN RELATION TO ENVIRONMENTAL POLLUTION

BPA in plastic was discussed in relation to people's health. This was a successful exercise, as the participants listed the diseases more frequent now as opposed to those from the recent past. Cancer, infertility, and miscarriages were some of the common health ailments that participants saw becoming more frequent in their environments. Therefore, linking these ailments to BPA and discussing steps that various countries have taken to ban plastic containing BPA was helpful in relating back to the health issues that have become very common.

Discussion on the economics of opting for more eco-friendly options had varied responses. Carrying a cloth bag to get groceries was considered to be an activity done by their mothers or aunts. Although, some women said this is a good idea and needs to be done more now. Others said that plastic is very convenient for daily use. The vendors could give free plastic bags very easily. Therefore, since there was no added economic loss associated with using a plastic bag, the practice of using an alternate solution was not given much thought. In addition, plastic bags were helpful to carry pickles and rotis for lunches, and the participants did not see any need for replacement. Plastic containers and one-time-use plastic items, such as straws and chocolate wrappers, had no replacement option in their neighborhood while also being very inexpensive.

INDIVIDUAL VERSUS GOVERNMENT REFLECTION TOWARD SHARED RESPONSIBILITY

Activities and discussions were framed in a manner to encourage everyone to self-reflect on their own responsibilities. This was purposely done to avoid passing the buck to the government to take on all the responsibility toward a cleaner and greener environment. Regarding the responsibility of minimizing plastic use and managing plastic waste, the participants were divided in their responses. Some said the government is cutting down trees for making roads, and the responsibility for climate risk is on them. In a similar vein, participants said that individuals could not bring lasting change and therefore do not hold themselves accountable. Others suggested they cannot wait for the government and need to do their own part. These small initiatives could be reusing plastic bottles as pots for plants in the house and adopting the strategy of reusing and recycling plastic. At the end of the session, the group did not finalize any collective decisions on actions that could be taken to become proenvironment.

RELEVANCE AND CONNECTIONS WITH SCIENTIFIC FACTS ABOUT THE ENVIRONMENT

Presentations were framed to answer the questions that came up during the needs assessment. These questions included the following:

Why have the summer months become so intense?

Why has the number of winter months reduced?

Why are seasons shifting?

Why are floods and droughts becoming so common?

The participants were keen to know the reasons for these changes. Therefore, the scientific facts were collated to specifically address them in a pictorial manner. The messaging of climate risk imparted that disasters increase in intensity every year. Thus, it was easier to imagine more heatwaves coming to an already hot summer season. The messages around climate were linked to a Hindu concept of doomsday or *prahlay.*

It was helpful to show a pictorial representation of time-series data that showed the heat extremes from 1980–2005. The heat episodes in these pictures were colored red, and the episodes increased as the years progressed. The pictures required minimal explanation to show the heat has increased every year. The climate risk was much greater for cities with an urban population, and since Bhopal is a city, everyone could connect to this issue. Graphs on the human impact show how humans have affected or altered ecosystems, such as tropical forests or deserts.[64] The larger, overall human influences on the earth, such as settlements, access or roads, landscape transformation (deforestation), and infrastructure (paving), were also color-coded; this made it easier for participants to identify them. The colors were easy guides to understand how human activity alters nature in the most harmful ways.

Every activity also required participants to be aware of the location of these regions on the map. Western eco-friendly concepts of conserving electricity and using water consciously did not apply since clean water is a scarce commodity in the city. In this part of the world, electricity and water cannot be wasted, as they have high economic costs associated with them. The participants are careful about using electricity due to its cost. Composting was also difficult since it added a chore to an already busy life. Most women already separated dry and wet waste as mandated by the municipal corporation of the city. Planting trees as a way of conserving the environment was not a solution to be environmentally conscious since space is a constraint in a resettlement colony like Dwarka Nagar.

Other aspects that did not resonate much with participants included photos and data of ocean animals consuming plastic since oceans are not close to Bhopal city. Similarly, photos of glaciers melting were a difficult concept for participants; understanding the photos' significance would require prior knowledge of the arctic pole, glaciers, and the map of the world. Therefore, all activities had to be geared toward India or the South Asian continent.

DISCUSSION

In the article *Pursuit of Common Good*, Dasgupta and Ramanathan state that all of humanity needs to check our actions and reduce carbon emissions. However, "this requires large investment and huge commitment from communities, charities, national governments and international bodies."[65] This thought needs to percolate at all levels, including at nonprofits and in the communities. The participant data gathered from the workshops with MSK was helpful to understand the links between the environment and other SDGs, such as achieving gender equality (SDG 5) and quality education (SDG 4) even outside of the formal schooling context. Oftentimes, it is the women who manage their homes and make many of the decisions about what food is purchased, how home goods are transported to the home, and how waste is disposed of. With greater awareness of the causes and potential solutions to sustainability issues, women could not only become more sustainability-oriented in how they conduct their home management activities, demonstrating how a gendered approach can drive environmental sustainability, but women could also position themselves in leadership roles on a major global issue, thereby demonstrating how prioritizing environmental sustainability issues can help elevate efforts toward gender equity. Yet, this gender and environment link is often neglected globally in discussions and implementation at policy and local levels. Sustainability-oriented strategies could lead to a greater impact if women become leaders in all sectors of society, especially in decision-making roles for agriculture, education, management over natural resources, and production and consumption of services and goods.

The workshops also confirmed the study's theory that the pillar of culture is integral to sustainable development. Discussion of scientific facts will help build general awareness for the workshop participants, but they have to be contextualized through the lens of culture in order for them to have the power to influence behavior. The methodology for teaching ESD has important ramifications for learner outcomes. Through ESD that prioritizes place and cultural context, there is higher probability participants will go on to make connections to their lived experiences and invest their knowledge in behavioral change than they would through being taught in workshop formats only presenting science-driven facts without a cultural context. Also, in this part of South Asia, parallels drawn between science and religion could help encourage citizens to reflect on environmental practices.

The workshops and women's perspectives captured through the data demonstrated that education on environmental issues should be embedded under the sustainable development agenda. Focusing on the environment alone will not solve the development-related challenges. Since environmental challenges are multidimensional, they will require a more complex and holistic approach from individual, communal, regional, and global levels. ESD provides a framework to link the environment to other issues of sustainable development.

Knowledge about environmental challenges will likely be translated into action if ESD is not a stand-alone topic. The environment needs to be discussed along with development and other sectors, including health and livelihood. The links between economic wellbeing and the environment need to be fleshed out. Making connections about how certain environmental factors can lead to health or economic ailments will ensure that discussion of environmental factors is considered as a core component of quality education. Highlighting the relationships among various topics and the health of the environment is not only an intellectual exercise but will also bring environmental issues to life for immediate and real consideration. Without this awareness felt firsthand, any consequential action to conserve and protect the environment will be impossible.

As the setting for this study was the site of the gas tragedy in 1984, it is likely that individuals living in this area are more aware of human-made environmental damages than individuals living in other cities of India. Yet, we found that making lifestyle changes is hard even for the most affected. Perhaps because they are most affected and marginalized by intersecting challenges of poverty, misogyny, and environmental degradation, making lifestyle changes is all the more challenging. It becomes difficult to take time out to, for example, keep the wet and dry waste separate or to compost organic matter. The daily economic activity of the participants does not always give them the perceived liberty to be eco-conscious. This situation is aggravated with environmental messages getting lost through poor contextualization, integration, and delivery in the school system. Communities and municipal wards do not discuss environmental issues as they relate to human health and well-being. This is despite the fact that it is a common sight to see open sewage and still water potholes, and, as a result, every monsoon season is also accompanied by dengue infestations.

There was a general awareness about environmental health ailments but no consensus around what individuals should do. For example, not using a plastic bag may seem too trivial a task to make an impact on the environment; small lifestyle changes seem too simple or do not come with a conviction. Wide-scale community mobilization efforts on behavior changes focusing on sustainability and its four pillars are needed. These efforts will help individuals see that, while their individual action may feel small, it is significant when taken together with others in their communities. Since the intervention, the TVET center has become a "plastic-free center." Some ladies have reduced plastic in their homes as a result of the ongoing discussions among their peers in their workplace. This brings hope for the current study context, where the communities are tightly woven. If the environmental psychology reviewed in this paper can offer hints to concrete strategies for building environmental consciousness and lead to meaningful behavioral change to protect the environment in various parts of the world, then leveraging the interconnectedness of people in tight-knit community contexts can offer higher chances of adopting behavior changes that positively affect not only the individuals but also the community as a whole.

RECOMMENDATIONS

INTEGRATION OF ESD INTO VARIOUS NONFORMAL AND ADULT EDUCATION AND PROFESSIONAL DEVELOPMENT PROGRAMS

As Ramanathan and colleagues argue, ESD should not be limited to schools (see chapter 12). ESD is more likely to be integrated into formal schooling contexts, while the rest of the community (including nonformal education systems, adults, village and community elders, government institutions, and others) is neglected. However, ESD must also be delivered to community leaders, women leaders, housewives, working professionals, government leaders, religious leaders, and all sectors of society in ways that fit in with their existing activities and responsibilities. Therefore, nonformal education and TVET spaces, as well as community organizations, professional development programs, and others, need to be considered as well. Adult education forms a large population that could benefit from ESD but has been neglected so far.

CONTEXTUALIZE ESD CONTENT AND MESSAGES TO LOCAL CULTURE, CHALLENGES, AND PRIORITIES

We concur with Ramanathan and colleagues (chapter 12) that much more work needs to be done on communication strategies for sustainability issues. This chapter highlights some communication strategies that have resonated with participants in the MSK study. These strategies cannot be generalized to a large population. However, they present a hint of what has potential in India to build environmental consciousness and work toward behavior change for environmental protection, and suggest a framework for working with communities facing similar challenges, opportunities, and constraints. More research is needed to understand the psychological and cultural aspects that make messaging around sustainability more effective and to understand the localized links between various sustainability issues and how contextualized messaging and knowledge can build a sense of urgency among those who have the power to positively impact the sustainability of their communities. Considering how environmental issues intersect with other SDGs that may feel more immediate in the lives of various populations could be one starting point, considering health impacts, livelihood opportunities, gender equality, and others.

Further, integration of ESD in various learning spaces, including in both formal and nonformal education, needs to be action-oriented to bring about behavioral changes in lifestyles and empowerment to advocate for systemic solutions. It was encouraging to find that some individuals did not wait for the government to take ownership of all the environmental damages; they believed in their own agency to make a change. ESD that focuses on individual solutions that can be implemented in the short term, as well as skills for advocating for systemic change over the longer term, must be prioritized across education spaces.

CONDUCT FURTHER RESEARCH ON WHAT ESD MESSAGES TRANSLATE TO BEHAVIOR CHANGE

This chapter has shown there is reasonable awareness about pollution, deforestation, and unplanned urban development, but this paper does not track participants' behavior changes. More research is needed on how messaging, communication, and capacity-building can lead to observed behavior change and how such behavioral change may lead to improvements in environmental sustainability.

NOTES

1. For a full description of the Millennium Development Goals, their progress, and existing gaps, visit: http://www.un.org/millenniumgoals/pdf/MDG_Gap_2015_E_web.pdf.

2. World Commission on Environment and Development, *Our Common Future* (Oxford: Oxford University Press, 1987), 1.

3. Sushma, U. N., "India's Investments in Renewable Energy Are Growing Faster than Even China's," *Quartz India*, July 10, 2018, https://qz.com/india/1323902/indias-investments-in-renewable-energy-are-growing-faster-than-even-chinas/.

4. Parvaiz, A., "Why India Passed One of the World's Toughest Anti-Plastic Laws," *Huffington Post*, July 3, 2018, https://www.huffpost.com/entry/single-use-plastic-ban-india_n_5b3a09b6e4b0f3c221a28a07.

5. Perappadan, B. S., "90% Citizens Aware of Air Pollution but Lack Awareness of Causes and Impact," *The Hindu*. November 17, 2018, https://www.thehindu.com/news/cities/Delhi/90-citizens-aware-of-air-pollution-but-lack-awareness-of-causes-and-impact/article25528325.ece.

6. Khokhar, Tariq, "Chart: How Is the World's Youth Population Changing?" World Bank Blogs, April 17, 2017, https://blogs.worldbank.org/opendata/chart-how-worlds-youth-population-changing.

7. UNESCO, "Education for People and Planet: Creating Sustainable Futures for All," in *Global Education Monitoring Report* (Paris: UNESCO, 2016), ii.

8. The Union Carbide factory leaked a methyl isocyanate, a poisonous gas that killed two thousand people instantaneously and injured more than 300,000 people with up to 20,000 people dying in the aftermath. The Bhopal disaster is also referred to as the Hiroshima of the chemical industry. Dhara, V. R., and R. Dhara. "The Union Carbide Disaster in Bhopal: A Review of Health Effects" *Archives of Environmental Health* 57, no. 5 (2002): 391–404.

9. Stapp, William, "The Concept of Environmental Education," *American Biology Teacher* 32, no. 1 (Jan 1970): 15.

10. Hofman, Maria, "What Is an Education for Sustainable Development Supposed to Achieve—A Question of What, How, and Why," *Journal of Education for Sustainable Development* 9, no. 2 (2015): 213–228, https://doi.org/10.1177/0973408215588255.

11. United Cities and Local Governments, "Culture: Fourth Pillar of Sustainable Development (2010)," accessed March 24, 2021, http://www.agenda21culture.net/sites/default/files/files/documents/en/zz_culture4pillarsd_eng.pdf.

12. Hofman, "What is Education for Sustainable Development," 15.

13. Scott, William, and Stephen Gough, "Sustainability, Learning and Capability: Exploring Questions of Balance," *Sustainability* 2 (2010): 3743.

14. Sachs, Jeffrey, *The Age of Sustainable Development* (New York: Columbia University Press, 2015), 255.

15. Steg, Linda L., and Charles Vlek, "Encouraging Pro-Environmental Behavior: An Integrative Review and Research Agenda," *Journal of Environmental Psychology* 29 (2006): 309–317.

16. Van Poeck, Katrien, Ariane König, and Arjen E. J. Wals, "Environmental and Sustainability Education in the Benelux Region," *Environmental Education Research* 24, no. 9 (2018): 1229–1233, DOI: 10.1080/13504622.2018.1471668.

17. Selby, David, "The Firm and Shaky Ground of Education for Sustainable Development," *Journal of Geography in Higher Education* 30, no. 2 (2006): 351–365.

18. Presented jointly by International Union for the Conservation of Nature (IUCN), United Nations Environment Programme (UNEP) and World Wildlife Fund (WWF) in the 1980s. The World Conservation Strategy provided an intellectual framework and practical guidance for conservation actions necessary calling for global collaboration and coordinated efforts (IUCN, The World Conservation Strategy. Living Resource Conservation for Sustainable Development, 1980, https://portals.iucn.org/library/efiles/documents/wcs-004.pdf).

19. Global agenda for change drafted by the World Commission on Environment and Development in response to General Assembly of the United Nations' proposal to push forward long-term environmental strategies for achieving sustainable development (UN, 1987, Report of the World Commission on Environment and Development: Our Common Future, https://sustainabledevelopment.un.org/content/documents/5987our-common-future.pdf). As part of the United Nations Conference on Environment and Development, the Rio Declaration reinstituted the principle that human environment is core to sustainable development (UN, 1992, Rio Declaration on Environment and Development: The United Nations Conference on Environment and Development, https://www.iau-hesd.net/sites/default/files/documents/rio_e.pdf)

20. Selby, "Firm and Shaky Ground."

21. Jickling, B., "Why I Don't Want My Children to Be Educated for Sustainable Development: Sustainable Belief," *Trumpeter 1994*; Selby, "Firm and Shaky Ground"; Hofman, "What Is an Education for Sustainable Development Supposed to Achieve?"

22. Selby, "Firm and Shaky Ground," 353.

23. Jickling, B., "Why I Don't Want My Children to Be Educated for Sustainable Development: Sustainable Belief," *Trumpeter 1994*.

24. Jickling, "Why I Don't Want," 233

25. Komatsu, I. S. H., and J. Rappleye, Facing the Climate Change Catastrophe: Education as Solution or Cause," Network for International Policies and Cooperation in Education and Training, October 12, 2018, https://www.norrag.org/facing-the-climate-change-catastrophe-education-as-solution-or-cause-by-iveta-silova-hikaru-komatsu-and-jeremy-rappleye/.

26. Komatsu and Rappleye, "Facing the Climate Change Catastrophe, para. 10.

27. Adger, W. N., J. Barnett, K. Brown, N. Marshall, and K. O'Brien, "Cultural Dimensions of Climate Change Impacts and Adaptation," *Nature Climate Change* 3, (2003):112–117; Y. Chuang, X. Xie, and C. Liu, "Interdependent Orientations Increase Pro-Environmental Preferences when Facing Self-Interest Conflicts: The Mediating Role of Self-Control," *Journal of Environmental Psychology* 46 (2016): 96–105.

28. Polasky, S., C. L. Kling, S. A. Levin, S. R. Carpenter, G. C. Daily, P. R. Ehrlich, G. M. Heal, and J. Lubchenco, "Role of Economics in Analyzing the Environment and Sustainable Development," *Proceedings of the National Academy of Sciences* 116, no. 12 (March 2019): 5233–5238, DOI:10.1073/pnas.1901616116.

29. Chuang and Liu, "Interdependent Orientations Increase," 96–105.

30. Steg and Vlek, "Encouraging Pro-Environmental Behavior," 309–317.

31. Chuang and Liu, "Interdependent Orientations Increase," 96–105.

32. Steg and Vlek, "Encouraging Pro-Environmental Behavior," 309–317.

33. Anton, C. E., and C. Lawrence, "Home Is Where the Heart Is: The Effect of Place of Residence on Place Attachment and Community Participation," *Journal of Environmental Psychology* 40, (2014): 451–461.

34. Chuang and Liu, "Interdependent Orientations Increase," 96–105.

35. Solima, Monica, and Anne E. Wilson, "Seeing Change and Being Change in the World: The Relationship Between Lay Theories About the World and Environmental Intentions," *Journal of Environmental Psychology* 50 (2017): 104–111.

36. Adger et al.," Cultural Dimensions of Climate Change," 112.

37. Adger et al.," Cultural Dimensions of Climate Change," 112.

38. Swidler, A., "Culture in Action: Symbols and Strategies," *American Social Review* 51, (1986): 273–286; Hays, S. "Structure and Agency and the Sticky Problem of Culture," *Social Theory* 12, (1994): 57–72.

39. Adger et al., "Cultural Dimensions of Climate Change," 112–117.

40. UNESCO-UNEVOC, *Orienting Technical and Vocational Education and Training for Sustainable Development*, discussion paper series 1 (Bonn, Germany: UNESCO-UNEVOC International Center for Technical and Vocational Education and Training, 2006), https://files.eric.ed.gov/fulltext/ED495381.pdf.

41. UNESCO-UNEVOC, *Orienting Technical and Vocational Education*, 1.

42. UNESCO-UNEVOC, *Orienting Technical and Vocational Education*, 5.

43. UNESCO-UNEVOC, *Greening TVET for Sustainable Development* (Bonn, Germany: UNESCO-UNEVOC International Center for Technical and Vocational Education and Training, 2012), https://unevoc.unesco.org/fileadmin/user_upload/docs/e-Forum_Synthesis_report_Greening_TVET.pdf. (2012): 10.

44. UNESCO-UNEVOC, *Greening TVET*, 13.

45. UNESCO-UNEVOC, *Greening TVET*, 15.

46. Arora-Jonsson, Seema, "Virtue and Vulnerability: Discourses on Women, Gender and Climate Change," *Global Environmental Change* 21 (2011): 744–751.

47. Arora-Jonsson, "Virtue & Vulnerability" 744–751; Eastin, J., "Climate Change and Gender Equality in Developing States," *World Development* 107 (2018): 289–305.

48. Eastin, "Climate Change and Gender Equality," 289–305.

49. Salehi, S., Z. P. Nejad, H. Mahmoudi, and A. Knierim, "Gender, Responsible Citizenship and Global Climate Change," *Women's Studies International Forum* 50, (2015): 30–36.

50. Arora-Jonsson, "Virtue & Vulnerability," 744–751.

51. Swedish International Development Cooperation Agency (SIDA), Gender and the Environment, gender toolbox brief, March 2016.

52. Parvaiz, "Why India Passed"; Jayasiri, H. B., C. S. Purushothaman, and A. Vennila, "Quantitative Analysis of Plastic Debris on Recreational Beaches in Mumbai, India," *Marine Pollution Bulletin* 77 (2013): 107–112.

53. Javasiri, Purushothaman, and Vennila, "Quantitative Analysis," 107–112.

54. Sruthy, S., and E. V. Ramasamy, "Microplastic Pollution in Vembanad Lake, Kerala, India: The First Report of Microplastics in Lake and Estuarine Sediments in India," *Environmental Pollution* 222 (2017): 315–322.

55. Karthik, R., R. S. Robin, R. Purvaja, D. Ganguly, I. Anandavelu, R. Raghuraman, G. Hariharan, A. Ramakrishna, and R. Ramesh, "Microplastics Along the Beaches of Southeast Coast of India," *Science of the Total Environment* 645 (2018): 1388–1399.

56. Vardhan, H., "Text of Union Environment Minister's Speech at the World Environment Day 2018 Celebrations," Press Information Bureau, Government of India, June 5, 2018, https://pib.gov.in/newsite/PrintRelease.aspx?relid=179791.

57. Parvaiz, "Why India Passed."

58. See Swachh Bharat Abhiyan website: http://swachhbharatmission.gov.in.

59. Please see videos of the two recent sessions on environmental changes below. https://www.youtube.com/watch?v=JV_KYhmCk9Q&t=16s; https://www.youtube.com/watch?v=OSURDyPRI-E.

60. Khanlou, N., and E. Peter, "Participatory Action Research: Considerations for Ethical Review," *Social Science & Medicine* 60 (2005): 2333–2340.

61. Hall, Budd, "Participatory Research, Popular Knowledge, and Power: A Personal Reflection," *Convergence* 14 (1981): 6–19E; White Glen, Monika Suchowierska, and Margaret Campbell, "Developing and Systematically Implementing Participatory Action Research," *Archives Physical Medicine and Rehabilitation* 85, no. 2 (2004).

62. Khanlou and Peter, "Participatory Action Research," 2333–2340.

63. Miles, Matthew B., and Michael Huberman, *Qualitative Data Analysis: An Expanded Sourcebook*, 2nd ed. (London: Sage, 1994).

64. Center for International Earth Science Information Network, "Global Human Footprint Index," ArcGIS, last updated May 2, 2018, https://www.arcgis.com/home/item.html?id=65518e782be04e7db31de65d53d591a9.

65. Dasgupta, Partha, and Veerabhadran Ramanathan, "Pursuit of the Common Good," *Environment and Development, Policy Forum, Science* 345, no. 6203 (2014): 1457.

IV

THE FOUNDATIONS OF
EDUCATION

14

EARLY CHILDHOOD EDUCATION IN REGGIO EMILIA AND IN THE WORLD

CARLA RINALDI

INTRODUCTION

Quality early childhood education offers children favorable conditions to flourish. Despite serious situations of educational poverty at the international level, the figures show a progressive increase in attendance in early childhood education services. Schools, along with cultural and education agencies, represent the backbone of this change, but they are not always able to offer quality education. The pedagogical experience known as the Reggio Emilia approach—developed in the early childhood education centers of Reggio Emilia—is proposed in this chapter as evidence of quality preschool education. It is based on the idea of the child as a citizen from birth. It is also based on children's rights, education as a common good, and school as a generative place for the whole community—principles that can contribute to developing a quality education worldwide.

EDUCATION AND SCHOOL—AN EVOLVING RELATIONSHIP

Human civilizations have always had education at heart. *Education* is essentially the ability to transmit knowledge, values, skills, competencies, and sensitivity from one generation to the next. Initially, this mostly took place within a local culture. In modern times, and still in the era of the global economy, every nation—each with its own methods, systems, values, and perspectives—considers school one of its main stakeholders, as it is the place of formal education. In order to talk about education, I deem it necessary to also talk about school, and this will be my starting point.

Since the nineteenth century, education has been a concern of countries. Once a country has been established, it must build its own national identity by teaching the common language, reading and writing skills, and all the competencies that enable people to work and have an economic return. The institutionalization of education has contributed in the past and continues to contribute to building the child's sense of belonging to a cultural community and the adult's sense of belonging to a working community. That is not all. School is also a key element, as evidence of policies concerning not only children (any individual from zero to eighteen years, as defined by the UN convention) but also women and work.

The relationships and interactions between early childhood and civil and economic society are clear once we reflect on some data. For instance, according to the 2019 OECD report, *Education at a Glance*, the increase in attendance in early childhood educational services in European countries is closely related to the increase in the female labor force.[1] But the intertwining of education, educational places, and labor and social policies has a further aftereffect: education and services are interpreted as a consequence of labor or social policies with reference to women's claims for emancipation, work, and the need for social equity. Although linked to social dynamics and needs, this vision prevents us from understanding and developing early childhood education and preschools first as a primary right of the child, as a citizen from birth, no matter the place. The vision also ignores the right of societies to have a place—the school—that educates children, young people, parents, and other adults to citizenship by listening to them and giving value to their contributions. Listening and valuing the contributions of all of education's stake holders enables schools, and therefore societies, to become places of innovation, participation, and democracy. Moreover, it enables the transformation of contents and modes characterizing the relationship between adults and children, the relationship between teaching and learning, and, more generally, the presence of children and young people in our society.

The educational experience known as the Reggio Emilia approach and the dialogue that this experience has been able to create with a small part of the world taught me to consider preschools as sites of a new cultural and civil awareness about childhood in the contemporary era.

The Reggio Emilia approach is an educational philosophy born in Reggio Emilia, a midsize city in northern Italy. Immediately after the Second World War, a small hamlet on the outskirts of the city decided to rebuild its community, destroyed by bombs, putting the children at the center. Together, the citizens built a preschool for everyone—a beautiful, new, and different school. In doing so, they not only built a physical school, but they also gave life to an idea of education, participation, community, and democracy.

Thanks in particular to the women's organizations in the city, a grass-roots movement surfaced and pushed the city administration to open the first municipal preschool in 1963. Many others followed up to the current network of educational services, which includes forty-one infant-toddler centers and sixty-four preschools.[2]

The definition of Reggio Emilia's pedagogical and educational identity was entrusted to Loris Malaguzzi, *pedagogista* and philosopher, who managed it until his death in 1994.

There are several protagonists in this collective story—the city administration; Loris Malaguzzi; and the many different people, especially women, teachers, *atelieristas*, cooks, mothers, and citizens, who contributed to the development of the education system of infant-toddler centers and preschools in the city of Reggio Emilia.

Today, the philosophy of the Reggio Emilia approach is based on the image of the child as a holder of rights from birth; a child competent to learn and relate to others from birth; a child provided with an extraordinary learning potential metaphorically described with the expression of "a hundred languages"—that is, the hundreds, thousands of ways of expressing themselves, thinking, understanding, and learning, as described by Malaguzzi in the following poem.

NO WAY. THE HUNDRED IS THERE

The child
is made of one hundred.
The child has
a hundred languages
a hundred hands
a hundred thoughts
a hundred ways of thinking
of playing, of speaking.[3]

THE DEMAND FOR QUALITY SCHOOLS

The data on access to early childhood education systems vary from country to country and, although full recognition of the right to preschool education is still a long way off, there is an increase in attendance.[4] Global reports show how preschool attendance positively contributes to children's socio-emotional, cognitive, linguistic, and physical development. Some of these reports agree, however, that data on the increase of early childhood education services are not per se a guarantee of the quality of education.[5] Early childhood schooling is increasing worldwide, but we have to ask: What is quality in education?

After almost fifty years of work and research in the educational context of Reggio Emilia in dialogue with the world, I am convinced that quality is not an entity in itself but a process. Many interconnected components contribute to this process, and children, young people, families, teachers, and, in a broader sense, the community are part of it.

The school, as a place designed for formal education, is therefore not only important but decisive in promoting the very concept of quality education—although quality educational places are not only limited to schools but also include multiple cultural and education agencies. Reggio Emilia is a school that, by pursuing families' and the community's participation, puts children and their relationships at the center.

THE PEDAGOGY OF LISTENING

For quality education, putting children and their relationships at the center implies, first of all, listening. The pedagogy of listening, which I presented for the first time in *Making Learning Visible*, is not just about school.[6] It has to do with our humanity—all the more so in a time of pandemics and major climate change. It concerns us as human beings not "in front of" but within the universe. Before our birth, we live for nine months inside a body that we listen to and that listens to us. So, surrounded by dialogue, listening becomes an innate, natural attitude.

The term *listening* can have various meanings.

Listening as a metaphor for openness, listening and being listened to, with all senses: sight, touch, smell, taste, orientation, not only with hearing.

Listening to the hundreds, thousands of languages and codes used by life to express itself and communicate.

Listening to the connections that hold us together as living beings; beings intimately convinced to belong to a plural dimension.

Listening that requires its own time; a time made of pauses, of silence; an inner time, and therefore listening to ourselves as regeneration, as taking care of new questions about us and the others.

Listening as interest, as curiosity, as emotion.

Listening as openness to others; welcoming differences, the value of others' points of view. Listening as an active verb, which interprets, welcomes, and gives value and meaning.

Listening that doesn't produce answers but builds questions. Listening that is generated by doubts, awareness of one's limits and by the suspension of judgment and prejudice.

Listening that calls for willingness to change, that gives value to the unknown, to the not yet known, and to emptiness as an opportunity.

Listening that gives meaning and legitimacy to the person listened to.

Therefore, listening where you learn to listen and narrate, to compare interpretations, and where the sensitivity to listening is the possibility to give shape to and communicate among different representations of the world.

The pedagogy of listening is one of the metaphors used to identify the educational philosophy of Reggio Emilia. In this context, therefore, the verb *listening* acquires a value that is not only epistemological but also ethical and political. As a matter of fact, in the educational experience of Reggio Emilia, the construction—or socio-construction—of knowledge needs listening: a theory, a hypothesis, a reflection should be able to be seen, observed, and studied but also shared with others to enrich them further with new cues and through new experiments. The outcome may provide answers but certainly other questions, other challenges.

From the very moment of birth, children are curious explorers of the world and seek communication with the people around them. Children immediately show that they can listen and want to be listened to, in turn. Listening also manifests as availability to others, trusting them, granting them time, welcoming their differences. Listening is, therefore, a verb of reciprocity and of openness to others. It is a transformative verb.

When a school is open to listening to the child, to a subjectivity that asks to be respected and put at the center of the educational project so as to affect and modify the relationship between teaching and learning and the very concept of education as a learner's right, it is then that a school can offer contexts and tools with which children can enrich their knowledge about the world, life, and the meanings of things.

Children are, in a metaphorical sense, the greatest "listeners" of the reality surrounding them; of life, in its different forms and colors; of the others, both adults and peers. What we should try to do is set up contexts and places where children can experience and construct all the hundreds, thousands of ways of walking, talking, discovering, dreaming, and loving and the hundreds, thousands of languages they can use to express themselves, learn, and narrate their feelings, discoveries, emotions, and knowledge. And as they narrate using words, bodies, hands, drawings, and the many other media they have available—including now digital media—children learn. They learn about themselves and the world.

The pedagogy of listening is this attention, this choice not to turn off the desire, joy, and wonder of communication, not to turn techniques into an end but into a means to foster children's "natural" attitude to experience life and themselves as curious researchers.

In this dimension of reciprocity, adults review their role as coconstructors of knowledge and culture together with children and must be capable of sustaining discussions and exchanges with and among children. This means that adults should be able to accept their partiality, vulnerability, the possibility of making mistakes, and their curiosity. The teaching-learning relationship is also reversed by shifting the focus to the child's learning and to the child as a member of a group. Even if teachers learn, they learn from children's learning; they learn to teach.

This dimension of reciprocity, which also concerns the relationship between children and parents, children and family members, parents and teachers, and so on, is what makes a powerful and competent teacher possible—one capable of keeping abreast with a powerful and competent child. We will be able to empower teachers if we can empower children. We will empower teaching if we empower learning. In this way, school can become a research and learning place for everyone: children, parents, and teachers—researchers and apprentices at the same time, like in a Renaissance workshop.

School, therefore, is a context where values and culture are not merely transmitted but created. It is a context where children and adults feel motivated, at ease, respected, appreciated, and welcomed. And it is a place where the child not only learns to learn but also becomes aware of the group as a learning and teaching "place" where meeting, listening, sharing, and differences are invaluable resources for constructing knowledge and essential ingredients of living together as a community.

THE CHILD AS CITIZEN, HOLDER OF RIGHTS, COMPETENT

The child is a holder of rights and a citizen from birth. Children are citizens of the present, not just the promise of the future. And the child is competent from birth. The definitions developed in the 1970s have been further elaborated over time, becoming and symbolizing a paradigm shift, which still remains partly the horizon to refer to. The child as citizen from birth—therefore, not only a private subject, "son, daughter of . . . ," but a citizen—represents a burst upon the scene of a new subject with individual, legal, civil, and social rights. However, this is a very recent issue or achievement. It was only in the 1990s that the international Conventions on the Rights of the Child recognized the separation of children's legal subjectivity from their parents'. From this perspective, the pedagogy of Reggio Emilia looked at childhood with an awareness that had not yet been expressed in international law, and this awareness is reconfirmed in the daily educational practice in Reggio Emilia, in Italy, and in the world.

The right of the child as a citizen is highlighted and reaffirmed in one of the last documents drafted by Loris Malaguzzi, *A Charter of Rights*, which outlines the "central triad" of the subjects in education: children, parents, and teachers.[7] The child as citizen asks for a new concept of citizenship in terms of belonging to a community. For example, when we think about public spaces and community services, we should make way for this new citizen and all the worlds carried within by children. A culture and pedagogy for the city and with the city that allows itself to be transformed in a permanent process of change and innovation and that questions places and contexts through a childhood culture developed "with" children.

By affirming the right to be recognized as citizens of the present, we affirm and confirm children's strength, their extraordinary potential, and their right to expand and express such a potential. Thus, the child is not only recognized as a citizen from birth but also as a competent person. The child is competent in learning, asking questions, seeking answers, and generating a culture of their own. Children are "constructors of their own experience and thus active participants in the organization of their identities, abilities, and autonomy, through relationships and interaction with their peers, with adults, with ideas, with objects, and with the real and imaginary events of intercommunicating worlds."[8]

Indeed, each child is credited with "an extraordinary wealth of inborn abilities and potential, strength and creativity. Irreversible suffering and impoverishment of the child is caused when this fact is not acknowledged."[9] The child is the essence of the human being; the young child, with their outstanding skills in terms of research and connections, is the genetics, the DNA, and the immense potential of the human race.

The child is the human able to question themselves and others, to be surprised and ask why, to change patterns and expectations, and, hence, to innovate. The human being, as a child, is the researcher par excellence. Their nature is characterized by their incredible abilities. "The child is made of one hundred," says the poem-manifesto by Loris Malaguzzi. Education has to give voice to these hundred languages and not play the role of those who steal ninety-nine of them. Quality education says: with the child—no way, the hundred is there.

The hundred languages of the child also represent children's ability to welcome differences. The child is the first "foreigner" in our midst. A foreigner because they are a stranger to rules and conventions—an "inconvenient child," as Loris Malaguzzi used to call them. A foreigner who reveals the other embedded in us: we see ourselves through the gaze of the other, and by educating ourselves, we educate each other to a new reality.

THE CENTRAL ROLE OF CHILDREN AND THEIR RELATIONSHIPS

The child as "listener"—pursuing the meaning of things and of the world and seeking the encounter and dialogue with the other—leads us to one of the key concepts in education: the child, a relational subject as a whole. I am convinced that, if there is a focus in education, this shall be the "right of children to realize and expand their potential, placing great value on their ability to socialize, receiving their affection and trust, and satisfying their needs and desires to learn"[10] thanks to the alliance with the world of adults, ready to frame learning as a process that also involves the entire family's participation. The process of educating each other together, with the "mediation of the world," as

Paulo Freire said,[11] is guided by teachers and educators, and it considers parents as public subjects, a common good, who participate in this community as political subjects.

Participation is, in this light, an educational strategy where parents, children, and teachers are all active constructors of knowledge. Participation, therefore, is understood not as "taking part in" but rather as "being part of." Participation is the essence, the substance of a common identity, of an "us" that comes to life thanks to our participation and active presence. Thus, "what" and "how"—for example, education and participation—become the form and substance of a single construction process.

Schools and cultural and educational places certainly play a fundamental role in this rich process of constructing knowledge and learning, but I would also like to point out that educational places are closely linked to the societies they are located in. In this respect, participation may not be restricted to the family circle but opened up to the community, inviting them to participation as a democratic practice so as to build an open school and a place of democratic action together.

A school based on participation that stands at the center of a community as a point of reference, as a statement about the importance of education, is a school that generates change. Change in terms of research and evolution, where each of the parties involved is invited to coevolve. In this sense, not only can the school become an "educating community," but everyone involved in the educational process comes to create an enlarged "educating community" characterized by an atmosphere of coexistence, civic consciousness, and activism—where processes and projects to improve the collective life take place.

Participation, understood and lived like that, can further enrich its original meaning. It is a participation in an educational and learning process in which all—children, teachers, parents—are in a dimension of welcome, dialogue, and exchange while playing their own roles. Without this exchange, there is no knowledge, not even of ourselves. There is a relational reciprocity between teachers and children, children and families, and families and teachers. And in this dimension, participation generates listening, attention, care of the other, and therefore responsibility, which results in the sense of belonging to a community. Rights generate rights; care generates care.

Care, taking care in a mutual way, is the dimension of education. This dimension can only come into existence in an attitude of listening and respect, being aware that people are unique and relationships are important. But care is also the dimension of coexistence and community. A community that knows how to value education, from early childhood education, puts the school at the center of its life and pays attention and listens to it. This community gives the school a key position in its life, thoughts, and projects: education as a common good, school as the regenerative place of an entire community. A community that makes such a choice will have a return in terms of trust and attention because it is taking care of its future, of its young generations, who will give back the care they received.

RIGHTS, POVERTY, AND EDUCATIONAL CRISIS

Today, prompted by Pope Francis's wisdom in giving life to the Global Compact on Education, we are wondering how we can address the most urgent questions that call for education. We are accompanied by an insatiable desire to search, that "nostalgia for the future" mentioned by Loris Malaguzzi when he invited us to have courage of the future, to seek new paradigms, to welcome the unexpected and the unknown. It is a recommendation, too, not to be overwhelmed by indifference and resignation. It is a substantial confidence in the human community capable of walking toward its own horizon, and this is also the key to a common commitment.

The right of children, young people, women, and men to quality education and to a better life, wherever they live, and considering education as an emergency that helps in dealing with other emergencies—this is the horizon we have to set.

We are faced with a betrayed childhood and humanity, locked in refugee camps. In many parts of the world, there are a childhood and a humanity disappointed in their most essential needs. Great is the grief when we think of the many children, both in megacities and in small towns and suburbs, who do not have the possibility to grow up in schools and contexts that are educational. Experiences of educational poverty occur not only at school and not only in situations of economic poverty. The impoverishment, in fact, is also of meanings and relations in the safe houses of the so-called developed countries.

The issue is not only economic, political, and ecological. The issue includes all three aspects, but the crisis is even deeper (chapter 20). This is an educational crisis, that is, a crisis of the confidence in succeeding through educational actions, which are effective and mutual relations to search and build together the meaning of life, of our being in the world, of our being the world, of our being here together.

The proposal for quality education can be, if not an answer, a way to confront this moral duty to tackle educational poverty. First of all, because childhood is recognized as the right to have rights. Rights of their own, a culture of their own, which raises the child from a person in need to a subject of rights. Children as holders and constructors of their own cultures; competent children, and citizens from birth. This allows us to frame childhood not only as an age but also as a quality of life of the human being throughout life.

Secondly, because children are in a relationship of reciprocity with the world around them. Worlds upon worlds are added to children, teachers, parents: the neighborhood, the community, the city. Circular ripples that expand, from the child to infinity, in an alliance with adults that is a search for knowledge and shared paths to reach it rather than being a mere transmission.

What results from this educational experience is an ethics of coexistence, achieved by planting seeds so as to generate processes, small plants that will grow. We need to trust our participation in a culture of rights and responsibility anywhere in the world. Rights are never given, never acquired, but rights are generative: rights generate rights.

In a context of globalization, advocating for a right throughout the world means affirming it and giving it the chance to be advocated everywhere. Rights should not only be understood as the self-affirmation of a right per se, but they encompass other meanings aimed at transforming the coexistence: choice, responsibility, sharing. Therefore, they refer to "duty" meant as the complementary face of the right. "The fact that the rights of children are recognized as the rights of other children is the sign of a more accomplished humanity," says Loris Malaguzzi.[12] This is a call for everyone to great responsibilities and the possibility of opening up horizons and better futures, which we have to try to build together. That "most accomplished humanity," which is an ethics of coexistence, which is respect, tolerance, care, dialogue, participation, reciprocity, and solidarity among all stakeholders, each with their own culture.

The city of Reggio Emilia, on the occasion of the thirtieth anniversary of the UN Convention on the Rights of the Child, felt the urgency to celebrate with commitment and solemnity by means of an open-air exhibition called Flags4Rights. One hundred artworks, designed by children and young people from all over the world, were installed as flags in the streets of the city center. These are not works "on" rights, but "due to" rights, which have been denied, experienced, lost, dreamed of. A repertoire of naïve or conscious drawings, paintings, or graphic marks, in which an experience, a feeling, an aspiration can be perceived. Listening, therefore, means understanding that each of these one hundred drawings, turned into flags, shall be interpreted as narratives of a unique and unrepeatable human being, a unique and unrepeatable child, on this and on the other side of the Earth.

It is therefore necessary to promote a real revolution that involves government, public, and religious institutions; education agencies, foundations, and social organizations; communities, educators, and families committed to creating quality education. This is possible by building a system of schools and places of nonformal, quality education, which are defined as such because they are welcoming and they value differences without indifference. Accordingly, these places are based on listening, interdependence, integration, and trust in the child and in the human being. They involve families and the community, children's culture and competencies in the perspective of an educating community. A broad educational alliance, in Pope Francis's words. A beautiful school, because it is participatory, because it is loved; a place to educate and be educated as people and as a community—hence, an inclusive school.

That is why it is important to invest in but also to believe in childhood. One must believe in childhood not only as a phase of life but as a way of thinking about life throughout life. Childhood is the most extraordinary phase of a human being's life in all societies. And children just ask to be listened to, as do so many young people today collectively. Think of the worldwide climate movement kicked off by a sixteen-year-old girl.

If listening, in its deepest sense, is changing, accepting that the encounter with the other changes both, then listening means recognizing the central role of children—listening to their hundred, thousand languages.

According to an African proverb, "it takes a whole village to raise a child," but we need children to improve a community, whether local or global, and to build that village to which Pope Francis calls us as an educating and open community.

NOTES

1. OECD, *Education at a Glance* (Paris: OECD Publishing, 2019), 163.
2. Istituzione Preschools and Infant Toddler Centres of the Municipality of Reggio Emilia, https://www.comune.re.it/retecivica/urp/pes.nsf/web/Sclprmrscndrd?opendocument.
3. The Reggio Children Foundation has granted Columbia University Press permission to print this poem, which continues:

   A hundred always a hundred
   ways of listening
   of marvelling, of loving

a hundred joys
for singing and understanding
a hundred worlds
to discover
a hundred worlds
to invent
a hundred worlds
to dream.
The child has
a hundred languages
(and a hundred hundred hundred more)
but they steal ninety-nine.
The school and the culture
separate the head from the body.
They tell the child:
to think without hands
to do without head
to listen and not to speak
to understand without joy
to love and to marvel
only at Easter and at Christmas.
They tell the child:
to discover the world already there
and of the hundred
they steal ninety-nine.
They tell the child:
that work and play
reality and fantasy
science and imagination
sky and earth
reason and dream
are things
that do not belong together.
And thus, they tell the child
that the hundred is not there.
The child says:
No way. The hundred is there.

4. Edwards, C., L. Gandini, and G. Forman, *The Hundred Languages of Children* (Santa Barbara, CA: Praeger, 2012), 3.

5. According to 2018 UNESCO data, the world average rate of preschool attendance is around 51 percent but with a very wide range among countries—for instance, in Saudi Arabia preschool attendance is 21 percent, while in Sweden is 96 percent. World Bank, Open data (https://data .worldbank.org/); The school attendance of children is an increasing phenomenon. Especially in OECD countries, from 2005 to 2017, the enrollment of children aged three to five years increased from 76 percent to 86 percent. OECD, *Education at a Glance*, 165.

6. UNICEF, *A World Ready to Learn: Prioritizing Quality Early Childhood Education* (New York: UNICEF, 2019), 68.

7. Giudici, C., M. Krechevsky, and C. Rinaldi, *Making Learning Visible* (Reggio Emilia: Reggio Children, 2009), 78–89.

8. Loris Malaguzzi, *A Charter of Rights* (Reggio Emilia: © Preschools and Infant Toddler Centres—Istituzione of the Municipality of Reggio Emilia; from the "The Hundred Languages of Children" exhibition catalogue, published by Reggio Children), 2.

9. Loris Malaguzzi, *A Charter of Rights*, 2.

10. Loris Malaguzzi, *A Charter of Rights*, 4.

11. Freire, Paulo, *Pedagogy of the Oppressed: 50th Anniversary Edition* (London, Bloomsbury Academic, 2018).

12. Loris Malaguzzi, *A Charter of Rights*, 2.

13. Loris Malaguzzi, *A Charter of Rights*, 2.

15

ADDRESSING OUR GLOBAL
DEVELOPMENTAL EMERGENCY

Early Intervention and the Think Equal Early Years Program

LESLEE UDWIN

We are currently in the midst of a development emergency with a proliferation of violence, which is worsening. What violence is not fueled by prejudice and inequality can be symptomatic of other determinants of mental and emotional ill health: stress, anxiety, greed, adverse childhood experiences, abuse, and anger among them. These can give rise to social, public, and mental health epidemics of devastating proportions, claiming and ruining lives. The economic and health burdens of these problems are global and catastrophic in magnitude.

CHALLENGES

The global challenges we are facing are multiple and include:

- $14.1 trillion was the full economic impact of violence globally in 2018, equivalent to 11.2 percent of global GDP.[1]
- More than 300 million people are now living with depression, an increase of more than 18 percent between 2005 and 2015, with eight hundred thousand resultant deaths each year.[2]
- At least two hundred million women and girls aged fifteen to forty-nine have undergone female genital mutilation.[3]
- $4.9 billion is the cost of domestic violence against women in the United States annually.[4]

- An estimated 40.3 million people were in modern slavery in 2016, more than any other given time in human history.[5]
- An estimated 150 million girls and 73 million boys under eighteen have experienced forced sexual intercourse or other forms of sexual violence.[6]
- In the last forty-five years, suicide rates have increased by 60 percent worldwide, with suicide now the second leading cause of death among fifteen- to twenty-nine-year-olds.[7]

The more violence we witness, the more inured and desensitized we become to it; the more it proliferates, the greater the sense of hopelessness about being able to stem its escalating tide. It is the most vicious of cycles.

SOLUTIONS

A clear solution to this global epidemic is achievable, easily implementable, replicable, inexpensive, and scalable. The key question, however, is what *type* of education?

Inequality can only be effectively addressed if the focus is placed on breaking the cycle of negative stereotypes and prejudicial judgments by committing to educating children with moral, social, ethical, and emotional values and competencies, and teaching them to "think equal"—in short, by changing a dominant mindset. As Nelson Mandela said, "No one is born hating another person because of the colour of his skin, or his background, or his religion. People must learn to hate, and if they can learn to hate, they can be taught to love."[8] With these words, Mandela defined what he meant by "education" being "the most powerful weapon which you can use to change the world."[9] He did not mean mere access to education nor the type of learning that is generally referred to by the word *education*. The education system as we know it is a broken model—outmoded and long overdue for reform. It was originally designed during the Industrial Revolution with the purpose of filling factories.[10] Structured on that nineteenth-century model, the modern education system neglects social and emotional learning (SEL) as a critical aspect of what education must mediate. Think Equal believes this has been an obstacle to progress in gender equality, global peace, mental and public health, and sustainable development. The lexicon surrounding this missing third dimension in education is not yet cohesive or consistent, nor is the list of its component objectives. To some degree, this is bound to hinder progress and may perhaps mean that many will unfortunately be mired in theory, talk, academic frameworks, and definition for some time to come. The OECD has dubbed its list of skills "21st-century skills,"[11] begging the question as to why these were not needed in any other century. Furthermore, despite the promise in that title of a new century's outlook on what is needed for a new global world, the skills listed are still, for the most part, closely linked to job-seeking and succeeding in a global economy (e.g., problem solving, critical thinking, written and oral communication, self-direction, collaboration, etc.). "Soft skills," a phrase that was rather unsurprisingly coined by the U.S. military in the early 1970s,[12] ignores the fact that neuropathways created in empathetic response, for instance, cannot be "less hard" in their physical manifestation than those created in habits of aggression.

Other nomenclature includes: "noncognitive skills" and "life skills" or "socio-emotional competencies" (which at least do describe more closely what we are, or should be, dealing with). Whatever we call this list of outcomes, it should amount to those values, competencies, behaviors, and attitudes required to live a life that is dignified and respectful of the dignity of others, of the earth, and all of its species. Many lists attempt to agglomerate these foundational capacities and fall far short of this overriding objective, typically looking no further than the route to the labor market or the accumulation of wealth and ignoring critical and urgent objectives, such as gender equality, self-esteem, inclusion, and empathy. More than a unified theoretical framework or commonly understood lexicon, what is needed is action and tangible tools—and urgently so.

WHY EARLY CHILDHOOD?

If we are to teach real peace in the world . . . we shall have to begin with the children

—MAHATMA GANDHI[13]

There is an indisputable scientific rationale for starting with very young children.[14] Neuroscience evidences a unique and optimal brain sensitivity in the early years when habitual ways of responding and modes of control are learned and fixed by neural connections and pathways in the developing architecture of the brain.[15] The human brain undergoes extremely rapid growth during childhood, with development in all domains being finely integrated across neural circuitry. This is a developmental trajectory during which attitudes and behaviors can be optimally formed, encouraged, improved, and modified.

While there are undoubtedly some further opportunities (notably in adolescence and possibly beyond) for neuroplasticity of the brain,[16] there is a wealth of evidence that suggests that an early focus on personal, social, and emotional learning provides the critical foundation and preparation for children to succeed and prosper as youths and in adulthood.[17] These studies posit that high-quality early childhood education programs will produce better, more rooted and assured life outcomes, and greater health, economic, and social (and even academic) outcomes for children, families, and nations.

Much data support this claim. A twenty-year longitudinal study for the Robert Wood Johnson Foundation offers research-based evidence that early years' social competence is a consistent and significant indicator of both positive and negative future outcomes across all major domains: education, employment, criminal justice, substance abuse, and mental health in adulthood. Jones and colleagues evidenced a connection between socio-emotional learning (SEL) in the early years and positive outcomes in adulthood. For every point higher in social competence, children are two times as likely to attain a college degree and 46 percent more likely to have a full-time job by the age of twenty-five.[18]

Other research suggests that many outcomes (both positive and negative) in overall health and well-being are rooted in the window of opportunity presented by early childhood, with 90 percent of brain density developing before the age of six.[19]

Nobel laureate in economics, James Heckman, states, "Those seeking to reduce deficits and strengthen the economy should make significant investments in early childhood education."[20] He suggests that providing quality SEL in one's early years is an effective fiscal and economic policy, likely to bring a substantial injection into economic development, major productivity gains, and greater savings in healthcare, incarceration of prison populations, and so on.[21]

National budgets and the economic and social development of adopting countries would be positively impacted by the education policy change envisioned by the Think Equal program. By way of example, the average cost of incarceration in the United States is estimated at just over $36,000 per year.[22] The Think Equal program costs just $2 per child per year and $6 per child for the entire three-year program. Eighteen thousand children can be taught Think Equal for a year at the same cost of incarcerating a single violent offender in the United States for a year.

Rigorous economic analyses have modeled both the cost of inaction and also returns on investment when it comes to early intervention programs. Heckman documents that for every dollar spent on early childhood education, particularly for the neediest children, the return is $7 in improved academics and productivity and lower social costs like prison and welfare. He also notes that this is a greater return on investment than annual returns of the stock market since World War II.[23] Research from Columbia University suggests an $11 return from each $1 invested in SEL.[24]

A health perspective additionally yields that damage done in the early years (including damage through toxic stress) has long-lasting and potentially irreversible consequences: "Stressors in early childhood can disrupt neurologic, metabolic, and immunologic systems, leading to poorer developmental outcomes."[25] Psychological stress can lead to chronic diseases, such as diabetes, depression, eating disorders, chronic pain, and symptoms of mental disorders.[26] It can also lead to an increased risk of cardiovascular disease, with a risk that is as attributable as that of other major cardiovascular risk factors.[27] Tawakol and colleagues further state that "psychosocial stress is . . . an important precipitant of morbidity."[28] The cumulative and lifelong impact of early experiences on a child's development is far-reaching and profound.

For those who might adhere to a view of the education system where "education" leads to a job and in which academic achievement and testing matter most, there is even strong evidence that exposure to SEL in the early years leads to increased academic achievement and higher report card grades in domains of learning in addition to health and social-emotional development.[29] In a meta-analysis of 213 school-based SEL programs involving 270,034 students from kindergarten to high school from studies produced between 1970 and 2007, students demonstrated improved social and emotional skills, attitudes, behavior, and significantly higher academic performance. The study reflected an 11-percentile-point gain in achievement for the students involved in SEL programs when compared to the control group.[30]

We have a duty of care to children in the early, vulnerable years, and they have the fundamental right to a foundation for positive outcomes in life on an even playing field. Children have the right to *not* grow up and rape or bully because they have been handed down prejudices. They have the right to *not* grow up to become depressed, stressed, or suicidal because they have not been equipped with the tools, competencies, and skills that they require to fulfill their potential and succeed in life. Think Equal provides the opportunity to ensure children grow up with positive life outcomes.

THINK EQUAL: A PRESCRIPTION AND
TOOLBOX APPROACH

The Think Equal program was designed as a response to this development emergency. It is both a movement and a practical, action-oriented early years' intervention program that envisions a safe, peaceful, sustainable, and equal world. Its focus is policy and systems change in education and, alongside advocacy, it insists upon tangible and measurable action with urgent and immediate effect. Thus far, it has reached approximately 134,000 children in sixteen countries across six continents. Its goal for the next three years is to reach 1.1 million children.

Think Equal's programmatic work has been designed directly and tangibly to address ten of the seventeen UN Sustainable Development Goals: goal 3 (good health and well-being); goal 4 (quality education); goal 5 (gender equality); goal 8 (decent work and economic growth); goal 10 (reduced inequalities); goal 13 (climate action); goal 14 (life below water); goal 15 (life on land); goal 16 (peace and justice); and goal 17 (partnerships for the goals).[31]

The Think Equal initiative is committed to a transformational agenda with a simple, clear, replicable, scalable model and strategy for investing in people in synergy with the former UN secretary-general's synthesis report *The Road to Dignity by 2030: Ending Poverty, Transforming All Lives, and Protecting the Planet*.[32]

The Think Equal program has been designed with the input of global thought leaders in the fields of psychology, neuroscience, human rights, gender, and education who are experts in social and emotional health and intelligence. The program committee of experts and patrons includes Sir Ken Robinson, Professor Richard Davidson (Center for Healthy Minds), Dr. Urvashi Sahni (Brookings and Ashoka Fellow), Vicky Colbert (Fundación Escuela Nueva, Colombia), Barbara Isaacs (Montessori Institute), Dr. Marc Brackett and Dr. Robin Stern (Yale Center for Emotional Intelligence), among others. The Think Equal team collaborates with national ministries of education and curriculum development to translate and contextualize the program to each adopting country's cultural context while maintaining the overall integrity of nurturing inclusion, diversity, and global citizenship.

Think Equal experientially mediates a prescribed set of twenty-five values and SEL competencies. These are specifically: empathy, emotional literacy, emotional self-regulation, critical thinking, self-esteem, problem-solving, gender equality, inclusion, peaceful conflict resolution, kindness, self-confidence, mindfulness, goal-setting, resilience, communication skills, collaboration, relationship-building skills, global citizenship, perspective-taking, environmental awareness and sensitization, standing up for others, creativity, self-awareness, moral and ethical values, and celebration of diversity. Doses are meted out a prescribed number of times per week (three), over three thirty-week levels or years (corresponding to ages three to six), in a prescribed order, and with a concretely delineated methodology of mediating them. Resources are given for free to new teachers who require only the skill of being able to read the simple and clear lesson plan instructions in order to carry them out. The focus is on the children getting what they require to form habitual ways of responding born of a physical brain architecture with neuropathways for sympathetic, pro-social, and emotionally and socially intelligent attitudes and behaviors.

At a global level, the Think Equal initiative works in partnership with education ministers and their departments, the United Nations and its agencies, civil society organizations, and independent experts in achieving its goals of a safe, free, and equal world in which all human beings, animals, and the planet itself are respected. Since the inception of Think Equal, the program team has worked closely with the United Nations Office of the High Commissioner for Human Rights (OHCHR) and with regional offices of the United Nations Children's Fund (UNICEF) and the United Nations Educational, Scientific and Cultural Organization (UNESCO) in a number of countries. Think Equal has a partnership approach and has collaborated with Pope Francis's Scholas Occurrentes Foundation, Montessori Group (UK), the Yale Center for Emotional Intelligence, Charter for Compassion, the Center for Healthy Minds at the University of Wisconsin-Madison, the Center for Contemplative Science and Compassion-Based Ethics at Emory University, among others.

Since systemic transformation and large-scale adoption are inextricably linked, Think Equal has a global, all-schools, every-child approach, with extremely inexpensive resources and a minimal training requirement to support it. Typically, the program begins with a small pilot program comprising approximately twenty sites. In the second year, a broader program is rolled out (e.g., to a whole district, town, or region), scaling up ever wider until the implementation of the program becomes national policy. The goal is to reach government-led rollouts in adopting countries within three to five years.

Think Equal has thus been designed specifically to cater to a landscape where there is not yet consistency of practice, nor a sufficiently trained workforce, nor reliable expertise in how to mediate the competencies and skills of what is, after all, a "new subject." The materials and lessons present a comprehensive, easy-to-implement, consistent, and holistic road map of what to teach and how to teach it.

Teachers can be trained over two days because the materials contain step-by-step instructions, which effectively means they train as they teach. All teachers need is to receive the introductory training in the purpose and methodology of the program, be given the set of materials with which to teach the new subject, and be able to read the instructions.

Narrative is a key vehicle in the Think Equal program and an ideal one through which to share personal and experiential social and emotional learning. Narrative has, for years, been held as a crucial element in the instruction of young children, with theories and anecdotes supporting the power of narrative dating back centuries.[33] Story and character engage the heart and encourage the experience of empathy and development of the skill to see things from the perspectives of others. Narrative describes the basic conflicts of human life and helps the children devise ways to resolve them in a safe environment. Additionally, narrative introduces new concepts to children in a comfortable space, allowing them to live new ideas through the perspective of story characters.[34] Think Equal proposes that through the use of hopeful narratives, which focus on a regulated, respectful, inclusive, and positive self, the development of social and emotional skills and competencies, and a knowledge of and respect for equality, that the individual stories of children will change. These children will, in turn, begin to affect the stories of others in their world, ultimately leading to a positive and concrete change in the collective narrative of society.

Recently, early childhood development (ECD) has surfaced as worthy of prominent focus within domestic and international policy agendas. In 2018 in Buenos Aires, a declaration prioritizing ECD and supporting a whole-child approach to education and health was signed by the G20. Unfortunately, in 2019 at the G20 Summit in Japan, momentum by global leaders was lost again. Despite or because of this setback, it is critical that decision and policy makers in the field build upon the consensus surrounding the importance of quality ECD in impacting well-being, prosperity, and sustainable development. Pressure must be kept up on global leaders to keep their 2018 promises to prioritize ECD for all children regardless of race, culture, or socioeconomic status to build on the action plan on the 2030 Agenda for Sustainable Development Goals.

In conclusion, policy makers and leaders must commit now, in no uncertain terms, to a shared future that rises above hatred and divisions of race, gender, and economic injustice. The moral compass must be reset, and mindsets governed by greed, self-interest, and selfishness must be recalibrated. Adoption of high-quality SEL programs will not only revolutionize global education but will also create a generational systemic change in how people think, interact, and solve the world's increasingly complex problems. Violence, discrimination, climate change, inequality, and other issues require a new generation of thinkers who have the skills, competencies, creativity, will, and integrity to solve them. Think Equal began piloting in January 2017 and hopes to see this emergent new generation of leaders in just fifteen years.

Policy makers and educators must at last commit to their duty of care in providing every child with the inalienable right to be provided a solid foundation for later life. They must work actively and practically to fulfill this duty of care. A new humanism is nothing short of an urgent necessity, and it will only be achievable through educating children's hearts and not just their heads, starting as soon as possible in a child's earliest years.

NOTES

1. Institute for Economics and Peace, "Global Peace Index 2019: Measuring Peace in a Complex World," Vision of Humanity, accessed January 15, 2020, http://visionofhumanity.org/reports.

2. "Depression, Let's Talk: Says WHO, as Depression Tops List of Causes of Ill Health," World Health Organization (WHO), March 30, 2017, https://www.who.int/news/item/30-03-2017 --depression-let-s-talk-says-who-as-depression-tops-list-of-causes-of-ill-health; "Depression," World Health Organization, September 13, 2021, https://www.who.int/news-room/fact-sheets /detail/depression.

3. "What Is Female Genital Mutilation: 7 Questions Answered," United Nations Children's Fund (UNICEF), March 4, 2019, https://www.unicef.org/stories/what-you-need-know-about -female-genital-mutilation.

4. Peterson, Cora, Megan C. Kearns, Wendy LiKamWa McIntosh, Lianne Fuino Estefan, Christina Nicolaidis, Kathryn E. McCollister, Amy Gordon, and Curtis Florence. "Lifetime Economic Burden of Intimate Partner Violence Among US Adults," *American Journal of Preventive Medicine* 55, no. 4 (2018): 433–444.

5. "Global Estimates of Modern Slavery: Forced Labor and Forced Marriage," International Labor Organization, accessed January 29, 2020, https://www.ilo.org/wcmsp5/groups/public /---dgreports/---dcomm/documents/publication/wcms_575479.pdf.

6. "Global and Regional Estimates of Violence Against Women: Prevalence and Health Effects of Intimate Partner Violence and Non-Partner Sexual Violence," World Health Organization, October 20, 2013, https://www.who.int/reproductivehealth/publications/violence/9789241564625 /en/?.

7. World Health Organization, "Depression."

8. Nelson Mandela, *Long Walk to Freedom: The Autobiography of Nelson Mandela* (London: Little Brown, 1994), 749.

9. Nelson Mandela, "Lighting Your Way to a Better Future," Nelson Mandela Foundation, July 16, 2003, http://www.mandela.gov.za/mandela_speeches/2003/030716_mindset.htm.

10. Robinson, Ken, and Lou Aronica, *Creative Schools: The Grassroots Revolution That's Transforming Education* (New York: Penguin, 2016), xiv-xv.

11. "The Future of Education and Skills: The Future We Want," Organization for Economic Co-Operation and Development (OECD), accessed January 29, 2020, https://www.oecd.org/education/2030-project/teaching-and-learning/learning/learning-compass-2030/OECD_Learning_Compass_2030_Concept_Note_Series.pdf.

12. Whitmore, Paul, and John Fry, *Soft Skills: Definition, Behavioral Model Analysis, Training Procedures* (Washington, DC: ERIC Clearinghouse, 1974).

13. Bylund, Lynnea, "Gandhi Spoke at Montessori London 1931," Gandhi Worldwide Education Institute, November 10, 2011, https://www.gandhiforchildren.org/gandhi-spoke-montessori-london/.

14. Barnett, Steven, Clive Belfield, Jeanne Montie, Milagros Nores, Lawrence Schweinhart, and Zongping Xiang, "Lifetime Effects: The High/Scope Perry Preschool Study Through Age 40," High/Scope Educational Research Foundation, accessed January 15, 2020, http://nieer.org/wp-content/uploads/2014/09/specialsummary_rev2011_02_2.pdf; Heckman, James, "Schools, Skills and Synapses," *Economy Inquiry* 46, no. 3 (June 2008); Heckman, James, and Ganesh Karapakula, "The Perry Preschoolers at Late Midlife: A Study in Design-Specific Inference, Centre for the Economics of Human Development" (National Bureau of Economic Research working paper 25888, May 2019), https://www.nber.org/papers/w25888; chapters 3 and 14 in this book.

15. Barnett et al., "Lifetime Effects"; Heckman, "Schools, Skills and Synapses"; Heckman and Karapakula, "The Perry Preschoolers."

16. Fuhrmann, Delia, Lisa Knoll, and Sarah-Jayne Blakemore, "Adolescence as a Sensitive Period of Brain Development," *Trends in Cognitive Sciences* 19, no. 10 (October 2015): 558; Koll, Lisa, Delia Fuhrmann, Ashok Sakhardande, Fabian Stamp, Maarten Speekenbrink, and Sarah-Jayne Blakemore, "A Window of Opportunity for Cognitive Training in Adolescence," *Psychological Science* 27, no. 12 (December 2016): 1620–1631; Valkanova, Vyara, Rocio Eguia Rodriguez, and Klaus Ebmeier, "Mind Over Matter—What Do We Know About Neuroplasticity in Adults?" *International Psychogeriatrics* 26, no. 6 (Jun 2014): 891–909; chapter 3.

17. For example, Barnett et al., "Lifetime Effects"; Brackett, Marc, and Susan Rivers, "Emotions in Education: Transforming Students' Lives with Social and Emotional Learning," in *International Handbook of Emotions in Education*, ed. Reinhard Pekrun and Lisa Linnenbrink-Garcia (New York: Routledge, 2014); Durlak, Joseph, Allison Dymnicki, Molly Pachan, John Payton, Kriston Schellinger, Rebecca Taylor, and Roger Weissberg, *The Positive Impact of Social and Emotional Learning for Kindergarten to Eighth Grade Students: Findings from Three Scientific Reviews* (Chicago: Collaborative for Academic, Social, and Emotional Learning, 2008), http://www.mentalhealthpromotion.net/resources/packardes.pdf; Flook, Lisa, Simon Goldberg, Laura Pinger, and Richard Davidson, "Promoting Prosocial Behavior and Self-Regulatory Skills in Preschool Children Through a Mindfulness-Based Kindness Curriculum," *Developmental Psychology* 51, no. 1 (Jan 2015): 44–51; Heckman, "Schools, Skills and Synapses"; Heckman and Karapakula, "The Perry Preschoolers"; Jones, Damon, Mark Greenberg, and Max Crowley, "Early Social-Emotional Functioning and Public Health: The Relationship Between Kindergarten Social Competence and Future Wellness," *American Journal of Public Health* 105, no. 11 (Oct 2015): 2283–2290.

18. Jones et al., "Early Social-Emotional Functioning and Public Health," 2283–2290.

19. Brown, Timothy, and Terry Jernigan, "Brain Development During the Preschool Years," *Neuropsychology Review* 22, no. 4 (Dec 2012): 313–333.

20. Heckman, "Schools, Skills and Synapses."

21. See also chapter 2.

22. Prisons Bureau, "Annual Determination of Average Cost of Incarceration," *Federal Register*, April 30, 2018, https://www.federalregister.gov/documents/2018/04/30/2018-09062/annual -determination-of-average-cost-of-incarceration.

23. Heckman, "Schools, Skills and Synapses."

24. Belfield, Clive, Brooks Bowden, Alli Klapp, Henry Levin, Robert Shand, and Sabine Zander, "The Economic Value of Social and Emotional Learning," *Journal of Benefit-Cost Analysis* 6, no. 3 (December 2015): 508–544.

25. Robinson, Lara, Rebecca Bitsko, Ross Thompson, Paul Dworkin, Mary Ann McCabe, Georgina Peacock, and Phoebe Thorpe, "CDC Grand Rounds: Addressing Health Disparities in Early Childhood," *Morbidity and Mortality Weekly Report* 66, no. 29 (July 2017): 770.

26. Dimsdale, Joel, "Psychological Stress and Cardiovascular Disease," *Journal of the American College of Cardiology* 51, no. 13 (April 2009): 1237–1246.

27. Tawakol, Ahmed, Amorina Ishai, Richard AP Takx, et al., "Relation Between Resting z Activity and Cardiovascular Events: A Longitudinal and Cohort Study," *Lancet* 389, no. 10071 (Feb 2017): 834.

28. Tawakol et al., "Relation Between Resting Amygdalar Activity," 834.

29. Flook, Lisa et al., "Promoting Prosocial Behavior," 44–51.

30. Durlak, Joseph, Allison Dymnicki, Kriston Schellinger, Rebecca Taylor, and Roger Weissberg, "The Impact of Enhancing Students' Social and Emotional Learning: A Meta-Analysis of School-Based Universal Interventions," *Child Development* 82, no. 1 (2011): 405–432.

31. "Transforming Our World: The 2030 Agenda for Sustainable Development," United Nations General Assembly, October 21, 2015, https://www.un.org/ga/search/view_doc.asp?symbol=A /RES/70/1&Lang=E.

32. United Nations, *The Road to Dignity by 2030: Ending Poverty, Transforming All Lives and Protecting the Planet* (New York: United Nations General Assembly, 2014), https://www.un.org /disabilities/documents/reports/SG_Synthesis_Report_Road_to_Dignity_by_2030.pdf.

33. Baldock, Peter, *The Place of Narrative in Early Years Curriculum: How the Tale Unfolds* (London: Routledge, 2006).

34. Cotti, Painy, and Michael Schiro, "Connecting Teacher Beliefs to the Use of Children's Literature in the Teaching of Mathematics," *Journal of Mathematics Teacher Education* 7, no. 1 (December 2004): 329.

16

THE FUTURE OF LITERACY IN A DIGITAL CULTURE

Promise and Perils

MARYANNE WOLF

Where is the wisdom we have lost in knowledge?
Where is the knowledge we have lost in information?

—T. S. ELIOT, "CHORUSES FROM 'THE ROCK'"[1]

The great nineteenth-century French novelist, Gustave Flaubert, gave humanity one of its most beautiful descriptions of language: "Human speech is like a cracked kettle on which we beat crude rhythms for bears to dance to, all the while we long to make music that will melt the stars."[2] For many years, I have conducted research on the processes used by the human brain to read, comprehend, and reflect on such a sentence. They include the use of many of our most sophisticated, intellectual achievements: background knowledge and analogical thought; inference and deduction; perspective-taking and empathy; critical analysis; and the still mysteriously generative *drive* within all forms of language that Flaubert captures here and which helps us to create insights and wisdom of our own.[3] Each of these special faculties contributes to what I have called the deep reading processes.[4] And, each of them is under one form of threat or another, as we move ever more imperceptibly into digital-based modes of reading. Understanding both the threat and the promise of digital reading for ourselves and for the next generation is the underlying theoretical goal of this paper. There is another goal that is more long-term in nature: using this knowledge to address the ramifications of the two pandemics of our time, the COVID-19 virus and structural racism and the concomitant inequities in health and education exposed and intensified around the world.

BACKGROUND

We exist today in what Harvard scholar Robert Darnton calls a historical "hinge moment"—between print and digital culture—without sufficient
understanding of either the advantages or disadvantages of both. If T. S. Eliot
were to live in this moment in time, he might reorder the above two lines of
his poem to underscore our society's growing inability to discriminate knowledge from information, much less appreciate the ineffable role of wisdom in
its discernment. Indeed, our world is awash in instantaneously provided information that often contradicts rather than illumines. Our society is replete with
multiple sources of knowledge, and its usefulness is sometimes diminished or
even falsely negated by profit-driven interests. As a society and as individuals,
we are increasingly unable to discern the truth in either information or knowledge, and many are too distracted by the glut of information to consider the
potential loss this represents.

In this chapter, I suggest that how we approach contradicting sources of
information and opposing bases of knowledge can have a profound impact on
the intellectual development of our next generation and our future as a species.
More specifically, I will argue that digital and print mediums for reading both
embody different, sometimes contradicting, cognitive characteristics and also
represent opposing forces within our culture. For, while the digital medium
holds great promise for the dissemination of knowledge around the world and
thus greater opportunities for health, education, and equity, it can pose significant threats to the critical analysis of that same knowledge with unexamined
consequences for a democratic society. By contrast, although the print medium
poses significant and sometimes insurmountable challenges in reaching children in parts of the world with few schools, teachers, and resources, it advantages the allocation of time to critical analysis and empathy in the readers who
are to become the world's future leaders.

To approach these contradictions, I turn to the work of three philosophers
in three historical epochs who sought to reconcile what occurs in the presence of opposing "truths" or forces. Described by philosopher Ernst Cassirer as
the "first modern thinker," the fifteenth-century philosopher Nicholas of Cusa
(who predated Copernicus in his conceptualization of the earth as a sphere
that revolved around the sun) wrote compellingly about how to approach the
convergence of opposing ways of thinking.[5] Influenced by Thomas Aquinas
and Plato, Nicholas of Cusa argued that when one is confronted by a "coincidence of opposites"—that is, when two "truths" appear to contradict each

other—our intellect should be informed by both the available conceptual knowledge and a more transcendent form of intellectually informed intuition.[6] His concept of learned ignorance, while directed largely to the human limits of ever understanding G-d, has relevance to today's coincidence of opposites in a digital culture. Specifically, such a stance is informed by knowledge (learned) about each truth but acknowledges the limits of our understanding (ignorance) and the need for a lens that is a transcendent, active searching for wisdom.

Many later historical characterizations of conceptual disequilibrium were influenced by Nicholas of Cusa. For example, Hegel famously portrayed human history as the product of tensions between opposing movements of thoughts (i.e., thesis and antithesis) whose synthesis propelled us forward (see chapter 8). In more recent times, the German-Italian Jesuit philosopher, Romano Guardini, provided our last century with a new approach in which two opposing bodies of thought are not to be synthesized as Hegel wrote but rather held together within a tension that itself moves us forward.[7] The unfinished thesis of Pope Francis, then Jorge Mario Bergoglio, has recently been brought to life in an intellectual biography. The title of his unfinished thesis, "Polar Opposition as Structure of Daily Thought and Christian Proclamation," reflects a view by Pope Francis that we are confronted daily by polar opposites in our world. Influenced by Guardini, Pope Francis's approach eschews the Hegelian concept of synthesis and rather invokes the concept of a transcendent plane from which we can construct a new view through "reconciliation thinking."[8]

Perhaps nowhere is this perspective more visible than in the encyclical Laudato Si, where Pope Francis examines the effects of the opposing forces of a technocratic, profit-directed society and the ethics of an ecological perspective on the future of our earth. Within this encyclical, Pope Francis describes how scientific knowledge about climate change lies in direct opposition to political, economically based forces that deny that knowledge to preserve corporate gain.[9] As Los Angeles Bishop Robert Barron wrote, Pope Francis used the work of Guardini to urge that we use both our best knowledge and "reconciliation thinking" to preserve and sustain care for "our only world."[10] Within this view, Pope Francis has used the term *tensionate* to describe the importance of using reconciling thought to preserve the productive tension that is emitted when "opposing elements pull in opposite directions."[11]

I wish to employ a similarly reconciling approach to understanding the opposing elements involved in the role of different mediums (print and digital) in the development of full literacy around our world. Toward those ends, this chapter will be divided disproportionately into three sections: (1) an intentionally cursory view of the promise of digital mediums for literacy learning; (2) a description of the cognitive and affective threats posed by digital mediums and the advantages for print mediums; and (3) a proposal for a new framework for future literacy based on the tensions between print and digital mediums. Within the second section, I will address how these tensions have been exacerbated by the twin pandemics of our time.

THE PROMISE OF DIGITAL MEDIUMS

The extraordinary dissemination of knowledge made possible by the spread of digital devices is at the heart of the indisputable promise that technology holds for the citizens of our world. This is especially the case for those who have never had access to literacy or to schools that provide anything beyond the most primitive forms of literacy education.

My colleagues and I in the global literacy initiative, Curious Learning, have been actively pursuing the potential of digital culture to give access to people long disenfranchised from the rest of the world due to the lack of schools and education available to them. Toward those ends, we have developed apps and digital games that have helped the spread of literacy across multiple villages and remote regions in Africa and India, where literacy was nonexistent. In recent years, under the leadership of Stephanie Gottwald and Tinsley Galyean, my colleagues have developed a foundational reading-skills app, Feed the Monster, that helps nonliterate children and youth learn the most basic elements and precursors of literacy. This open-source app is readily available and has been translated into more than forty-seven languages and downloaded in over 120 countries. This game-like, basic app can help jumpstart many young would-be readers, with some beginning evidence that children acquire about two months of growth for every twenty-two hours spent using the app.

There are by now various forms of evidence demonstrating the capacity of such early apps to lay the groundwork for later literacy. For example, we brought digital tablets to children in two remote regions of Ethiopia. After one year, the great majority of the children had learned the rudiments of print, impressive vocabulary knowledge, and some basic precursors to literacy. A few years later, our group returned to see the progress of the children. One of the original two villages had disappeared in a drought, thus preventing any follow-up on the progress of the children. In the second village, our field representatives were able to test one-third of the original children; the other children were either in the fields or had moved to other hill villages. Results, albeit limited to only a small sample, indicated that most of those tested had learned to read at a basic level through their continued use of the digital tablets. This includes the wonderful child whom we called the Lion Prince and who was a case study in an earlier paper. (Note: He was the first child to turn on the tablet and, in his excitement, shouted, "I turned mine on! I'm the Lion!") Although disappointed that we could not follow more of the children, my colleagues and I were deeply gratified that a small group of children had learned to read at a very basic level in both English and Oromo through digital mediums.[12]

To summarize, the extensive work done by many global literacy initiatives, including my own group's, demonstrates the powerful impact that digital reading can have to help ameliorate the devastating effects of nonliteracy, with all the concomitant consequences for equity, health, and economic stability.

THE PERILS OF DIGITAL MEDIUMS

Wendell Berry, an American novelist, poet, essayist, environmental activist, cultural critic, and farmer, argues that "we have accumulated a massive collection of 'information' to which we may have 'access.' But this information, by being accessible, does not become knowledge."[13]

Despite a continued belief in the transformational roles that digital mediums can play in disseminating knowledge and promoting global literacy, Berry's concerns, as articulated in his essay collection *Our Only World*, are close to my own.[14] I have come to worry about the tension between the benefits of greater access to knowledge afforded by digital technologies and the threat to deeper forms of literacy that these technologies represent. These concerns, which stem from my work as a cognitive neuroscientist on the reading brain, are based on both biological and cultural factors.

The biological concerns stem from the premise that learning to read isn't natural, despite what most of us mistakenly assume. Rather, the fact that reading is a cultural invention means that the brain has to build a new circuit or system for connecting networks that already exist, particularly for language, conceptual knowledge, and vision, to accommodate this new skill.[15] The invention of literacy requires the brain of every new reader to build a new circuit that is and remains plastic across the reader's development.

Over time, this coupling of nature and nurture propels the growth and repurposing of neuronal networks for visual, language-based, cognitive, and affective processes. The circuit of any reader is as basic or as complex as the reader's education and experiences, moving from the simplest of circuits in the young to the most elaborated of circuits in the older, expert reader. The *reading brain* is one of the most important, epigenetic-based changes in modern history and is the scaffolding for developing many of our species' most complex intellectual skills, referred to earlier as the "deep reading processes" of expert readers.

Furthermore, this deep reading circuit has importance for the rest of human development. The consistent strengthening of the connections among our analogical, inferential, empathic, and background knowledge processes generalizes well beyond reading. When we learn to connect these processes over and over in our reading, it becomes easier to apply them to our own lives, teasing apart our motives and intentions, and understanding with ever greater perspicacity and, perhaps, wisdom, why others think and feel the way they do.

That said, there is both an Achilles-like strength in a plastic reading circuit and an Achilles-like heel. First, the plasticity of the circuit makes it able to adapt to the cultural requirements of different writing systems, instructional emphases, life experiences, and mediums. Secondly, the Achilles heel in having a plastic circuit means that adapting to the characteristics (affordances) of different mediums does not ensure that the development of deep reading processes will occur; or, that if learned on one medium, will be maintained across other mediums. This depends on the affordances of each medium and which medium dominates reading over time.

In other words, the specific reading circuit will develop and/or atrophy according to the emphases of the medium(s) used. If the dominant medium advantages processes that are fast, multitask-oriented, and well-suited for large volumes of information, as is the digital medium, less attention and time will be allocated to slower, time-demanding cognitive and reflective functions that comprise deep reading processes. Even if the latter processes previously shaped the expert reading brain through the medium of print, a plastic reading circuit will change as a result of the processes emphasized or de-emphasized in the medium used most. The biological-cultural principle is this: use or lose it. An expert reading circuit is not a given; rather, it is built and rebuilt by emphases in its environment and by the reader's intention and purposes for reading.

Within this context, there are multiple questions that we must ask about factors whose cascading effects have far-reaching implications. They begin with the quality of our attention. Will attention change as we read on mediums that advantage immediacy, dart-quick task switching, and continuous monitoring of distraction, as opposed to the more deliberative focusing of our attention? The reality is that each of us is bombarded with more stimuli than ever before, particularly visual. We don't look away. Indeed, homo sapiens survived in part because of a biological mechanism, the novelty bias reflex, which forces us to attend to any new stimulus, whether the tracks of a predator or the "breaking-news" crawl on television.[16] The combination of stimulus bombardment and this evolutionary reflex affect attention and memory, especially for children, whose inhibitory systems are least developed. The oft-discussed "continuous partial attention" of the young child stems, in part, from their inability to inhibit the steady stream of stimuli they receive.[17] When constantly distracted, they can never fully concentrate their attention. When never able to fully focus their attention, the child (and adult, for that matter) are less able to consolidate information in memory.

There are all too many statistics behind these worries.[18] The crux of many facts is this: children are being given digital devices from the minute they can sit in a high chair without regard to the qualitative and quantitative changes in children's attention, their increasing needs for continuous sensory stimulation, and the decreasing ability by our older youth to fully comprehend what they read.

I do not worry that any of these children will fail to develop the important cognitive and perceptual skills honed by digital devices and necessary for the twenty-first century. I am buoyed by that. But I worry that along the way to becoming technically competent, they will never know the joy that quickens at the first page of every new book or the quiet grief felt when a favorite hero or heroine dies in a place they never knew existed. I worry that many of our youth will never have the time to meet all the complicated friends and fiends to be met in books and learn their complex thoughts, when their days at school are filled with tests and exercises on digital screens, and their hours at home are consumed with addictive video games and one-dimensional characters who fight and quest for things of little value. In short, I worry a great deal for the many children today who will never discover the power of print—books— to lift them out of their lives to discover whole new places, historical epochs, other cultures, and the feelings and thoughts of others they would never otherwise experience.

The problems, however, only begin there. There are now increasing pressures on parents to allow their older children longer time online instead of outside or at least out of their chairs. Current research on older youth and young adults in Europe, the United States, and Israel demonstrates the close connections among digital medium use, attentional problems, and obesity,[19] and between distracted reading styles and decreased comprehension.[20] Research by Jean Twenge and her colleagues on young people's reading habits over the last fifty years is summarized in their subtitle: "The Rise of Digital Media, the Decline of TV, and the (Near) Demise of Print."[21] Perhaps the most depressing statistic that these researchers cite is the decline of daily reading of some form of print—whether magazine, book, and so on—from 60 percent in the late 1970s to 16 percent today.[22] The authors used the notion of "displacement theory" to contextualize their results, where 82 percent of young people use social media today, more than likely *displacing* time they formerly might have given to reading.

The more unexpected and most worrisome changes appear in the comprehension capacities of college-aged students when reading on print or digital-based mediums. The largest meta-analysis ever conducted on this topic was recently reported by European researchers in the E-READ Consortium with over 170,000 subjects in fifty-eight studies conducted between 2000 and 2017.[23] Results indicated that young people were significantly better in comprehension skills when reading the same text in print rather than on digital screens. The researchers found that print enabled higher comprehension across genres, and the gap became more marked when a student was being timed. Perhaps most surprisingly, the superior performance when reading of print *increased* over the most recent years. In other words, the readers most likely to be digital natives were actually comprehending text better when reading it in print rather than on screens. This research portrays a generation that has grown up with digital reading and yet appears to be less likely or potentially less able to use more sophisticated cognitive processes to the fullest when reading on screens.

A related body of research in Israel by Ackerman and colleagues compared the reading skills among young adults on print and digital mediums and demonstrated the same trends with an important caveat: when asked which medium produced their best performance, Israeli students "perceived" that they were better on digital. They had no knowledge that they read with less understanding and attention to detail when reading on screens. They falsely associated faster speed with understanding.[24] A similar study in Israel by developmental neuroscientist Tami Katzir with much younger readers again showed similar, worrisome effects on comprehension (see chapter 17). The fundamental illusion by many of our young people is that speed increases their understanding rather than subtracts from the time the brain could allocate to the more demanding, deep reading processes that require *more time, not less.*

Adults fare little better, even with our more developed inhibitory systems. Increasing evidence from eye-movement research in Germany and the United States indicates that all of us tend to skim, word-spot, and divide our attention frequently when using digital screen devices. "To skim to inform" is the new mode for reading.[25] If more and more readers allocate less and less time to the more sophisticated processes like critical analysis, inference, and the more time-consuming contemplative functions, our society will change inexorably. For, in our sometimes obsessive desire to respond to the glut of information that daily bombards each of us, we are altering *how we read* (skimming and word-spotting our way through the text), which alters *what we read* (shorter, less dense material; more familiar, less challenging silos of information that demand less cognition and perspective-taking of alternative viewpoints), which eventually alters *what is written* (the pressure on publishers to adapt to the hows and whats of the present reader), which ultimately changes *why we read*. What goes missing in this set of changes are the deep reading processes that until now were integrated into the expert reading brain circuit. These processes, the basis for eliciting the furthest reaches of human thought and empathy, can no longer be taken for granted—either in the next generation or in ourselves.

This is the digital chain hypothesis of reading that affects how we think, act, and even, I worry, vote for our leaders and how we respond to crises like global climate change and the horrors of the current dual pandemics. When we retreat from the intrinsic complexity of human life on earth—whether through gruel-thin Twitter messages or superficial triaging the daily digital overflow of information—often as not, we turn to what conforms to the narrowing confines of what we already know. We seek silos of information that require little questioning, little movement outside the boundaries of our past thought with all its earlier assumptions, and sometimes never-examined prejudices. We do not know that unless we attend to what we are choosing—in how, what, and why we read—we may lose, literally, more than we think.

Never have the concerns about digital immersion been more evident to educators and parents than in the time of COVID-19, when many children are tethered to their screens and digital devices because they cannot be in school. There are multiple, deeply troubling realities occurring simultaneously. First, there is the reality of a large regression in academic learning for most children when their academic learning takes place only in digital forms. Second, there is even greater regression among our less privileged families, especially the 20 percent of children living in poverty in the United States who do not have sufficient access to digital platforms. Problems range from actually possessing a device, to bandwidth issues in the household, to enough time on the device because of the needs of the rest of the family, to insufficient understanding of digital platforms. The multidimensional impacts of both these co-occurring realities on the acquisition of full literacy and the psychological and physical development in our young must be the first priority among educators and policy makers alike.

There is a third reality that is an offshoot. One of the sequelae of COVID-19 is that many parents are faced with unparalleled pressure to allow excessive amounts of screen time to children and adolescents, which they use largely for social media and games. There is little question that the quality of attention and motivation by these youth are increasingly shaped by digital media and its affordances. Understanding both the potential of digital culture for positive learning experiences and for negative influences on cognitive, linguistic, and affective processes is paramount during this defining moment for our species.

From my perspective as a guardian of deep literacy, my greatest concern for young and old alike is the insidious loss of deep reading processes when we read—the basis for much of our culture's best thought and feeling. This is not a phenomenon limited to our young. We need only observe changes in ourselves, particularly the quality of our ability to immerse ourselves in reading, to recognize differences in the *cognitive patience* we expend when we read now. Like a phantom limb, we might remember who we were as readers before digital reading dominated our lives, but we cannot summon that ineffable joy we once felt in being transported somewhere outside the self to that interior space that once was home to our best thought. Just as Flaubert and Charles Taylor described for spoken language and Proust ascribed to reading, the great invitation within written language is to aspire to go beyond whatever is written to discover the furthest reaches of our thinking.[26]

A PROPOSAL

To ensure the preservation of these intellectual and affective processes that are advantaged by print reading and the addition of those new processes advantaged by digital mediums, we need to insert a pause in our transition to a fully digital culture, particularly after the onset of the COVID-19 pandemic, so as to examine both the better-known promise and the less understood threats. This examination, I have come to believe, is best served from the vantage point of what Pope Francis and Guardini describe as "reconciliation thinking."[27] Within this mode of thought, we step outside of both opposing forces and find what is positive in their *tensionate*—that is, the tension between them.

Toward those ends, in my most recent research, I have been working upon the concept of a biliterate reading brain, one that will develop over time and ultimately allow the child to grow into a reader capable of deep reading across every medium. It begins at the beginning: on a beloved parent's lap—reading books, reading to their children daily, if possible, from infancy through early childhood. I wish to emphasize the role that books play in the complex development of children, particularly children growing up in a digital culture. My concerns involve what young children might miss if digital devices and social media increasingly replace the multiple intellectual, social-emotional, and ethical roles that books can play in a life. As Israeli scholar Tami Katzir has beautifully written in her chapter for this volume (chapter 17), the importance of empathy and perspective-taking in the development of the moral imagination of our young cannot be exaggerated either for the child or for the health of our society.

My proposal, therefore, is to ensure that those skills begin and are consistently developed through the medium of print books for the first ten years of childhood. Not unlike Vygotsky's parallel developmental pathways for language and thought, I envision parallel paths of development for print-based literacy and for digital skills.[28] For example, I conceptualize the initial development period from infancy to five years of age as largely separated into two domains, with print dominating all forms of reading by parents and caretakers to the child and digital devices invisible until around two years, when they appear in the nursery like any other toy. That is, digital devices would be available occasionally but never dominating the child's day nor ever either used by the parent as a reward or withheld as a punishment. At five years, the parallel paths for print and digital mediums would be more clearly demarcated—with print and hard copy books used largely for teaching children to read. Digital mediums would be the platform of choice for developing those critical inferential, spatial, and conceptual skills needed by every twenty-first-century child and provided by programming and coding activities. They would also be used both where appropriate to supplement curricula and also for children with reading challenges as a vehicle for giving multiple exposures to the decoding processes that must become automatic.

During the child's early literacy period, from five to ten years, books would become a foundation for introduction to the deep reading processes. The world of books—from *Charlotte's Web* to *Harry Potter* to *Jane Eyre*—represents the single most important source of our next generation's ability to take on the perspectives and realities of others and make ever more sophisticated inferences and insights over a lifetime. Books provide their readers not only with geometrically growing repositories of knowledge but also with incalculable capacities at the root of human progress: the ability to understand the multiple perspectives of others; to go beyond the constraints of former beliefs to propel discovery and novel thought; and to wrestle with the meaning of their lives, as eloquently described by Katzir (chapter 17).

The rich, internal background knowledge we receive through books is as essential to the deep reading circuit as salt was to King Lear's pork and as little understood by us as him. We make sense of our world by making references to things we know. Our greatest leaps of imagination and discovery occur when making an analogy between what we know and what we hope to know. I fear that the formation of background knowledge in our youth and their ability to make these analogies is imperceptibly threatened by the great changes in both what they read and how they read. Without the diverse forms of knowledge conveyed by books, they will not know what they do not know. In short, I am concerned that the diminishing quantity and content of our youth's reading provides insufficient background knowledge for the formation of the deep reading brain circuit of expert readers.

Just as Vygotsky had processes underlying thought and language more intertwined over development,[29] I conceptualize the major intersections between the two mediums occurring after deep reading processes are firmly grounded in the fluent comprehending reader. For some children, this may occur around fourth grade; for others, much later. Individual variation will play an important role when teachers begin the careful introduction of deep reading skills on the digital medium. In addition, there will be no simple recipes here for individual children, particularly neurodiverse learners like children with dyslexia, who are sometimes indeed better served by complementing their early acquisition of reading with practice on digital mediums.

Understanding the purpose of whatever the child (or adult) reads is essential for understanding what medium is better for any particular text. There is an important set of lessons to be taught and learned about the advantages and disadvantages of print and digital for different kinds of reading materials. In addition, there is already a pressing need for teaching all our children digital wisdom—to prepare them with skills of discernment concerning the power of advertising, the cruelty of bullying, and the insidious nature of false information, falsely raised hopes and fears, and other tools of demagoguery in all its forms.[30] Within such a context, it is the powerful foundation of deep reading processes like critical analysis and empathy that can serve as an antidote to the negative effects of digital culture. Most importantly, in a biliterate read-ing brain, such processes prepare our youth to think for themselves on any medium, wisely and well.

———— ⊕⊕⊕ ————

We are so distracted by and engulfed by the technologies we've created and by the constant barrage of so-called information, that more than ever to immerse yourself in an involving book seems socially useful. . . . The place of stillness that you have to go to write, but also to read seriously, is the point where you can actually make responsible decisions, where you can actually engage productively with an otherwise scary and unmanageable world.

—JONATHAN FRANZEN[31]

It is incumbent upon us, as stewards of the next generation, to understand both the promise and perils of the digital culture for the intellectual, social-emotional, and ethical development of the young, especially after wit-nessing the still emerging detritus of our twin pandemics. In previous writing, I sought to elaborate on the power of digital devices to help the spread of literacy to children whose environments cannot help them sufficiently learn to become fully literate. In this chapter, I emphasize the potential threats that digital culture can have for the development of deep reading processes, par-ticularly critical analysis, empathy, and the contemplative function. I believe that the digital chain, which leads from the proliferation of information to the eye-byte servings consumed daily by many of us, will need more than simple vigilance by our shared culture, lest the quality of our attention and memory, the perception of beauty and recognition of truth, and the complex decision-making capacities based on all of these atrophy along the way.

Marilynne Robinson says that the "greatest tests ever made of human wis-dom and decency will come to our generation or the next."[32] Understanding the potential promise and potential loss that digital culture represents for our species is one of those tests. I have used the concept of "reconciliation think-ing" from Romano Guardini and Pope Francis as a possible way to preserve the tension between print and digital mediums (tensionate) and the good in both while knowing and avoiding the pitfalls and losses. To achieve such a goal will take no small amount of intelligence, a good deal of common sense, and our collective moral conscience if we are to protect and propel the human wisdom and decency that is our greatest legacy.

NOTES

1.   Eliot, Thomas Stearns, "Choruses from 'the Rock,' " in *The Complete Poems and Plays of T. S. Eliot* (1934).

2.   Flaubert, Gustave, *Madame Bovary*, trans. W. Blaydes (New York: P. F. Collier, 1902), 234.

3.   Taylor, Charles, *The Language Animal* (Cambridge, MA: Belknap, a division of Harvard University Press, 2016).

4.   Wolf, Maryanne, *Reader, Come Home: The Reading Brain in a Digital World* (New York: Harper, 2018).

5.   See descriptions in Dunne, John S., *The House of Wisdom: A Pilgrimage* (New York: Harper & Row, 1985); Dunne, John S., *A Vision Quest* (Notre Dame, IN: University of Notre Dame Press, 2006).

6.   Nicholas of Cusa, *Complete Philosophical and Theological Treatises of Nicholas of Cusa*, trans. J. Hopkins (Minneapolis: Banning, 2001).

7.   See Unger, Roberto Mangabeira, *The Religion of the Future* (Cambridge, MA: Harvard University Press, 2014).

8.   Borghesi, Massimo, *The Mind of Pope Francis: Jorge Mario Bergoglio's Intellectual Journey* (Milan: Liturgical Press, 2018).

9.   Francis (Pope), *Laudato Si: On Care for Our Common Home* (Vatican: Libereria Editrice Vaticana, 2015).

10.   Berry, Wendell, *Our Only World: Ten Essays* (Berkeley, CA: Catapult, 2015).

11.   Francis (pope), *Laudato Si.*

12.   Wolf, Maryanne, Stephanie Gottwald, Tinsley Galyean, and Robin Morris, "Global Literacy and Socially Excluded Peoples," in *Proceedings from the Socially Excluded Peoples Meeting, Pontifical Academy of Social Sciences* (2014).

13.   Berry, *Our Only World: Ten Essays*, 11.

14.   Berry, *Our Only World: Ten Essays.*

15.   Wolf, Maryanne, *Proust and the Squid: The Story and Science of the Reading Brain* (New York: HarperCollins, 2007); Wolf, Maryanne, *Tales of Literacy for the 21st Century* (Oxford: Oxford University Press, 2016); Wolf, *Reader, Come Home.*

16.   Levitin, Daniel J., *The Organized Mind: Thinking Straight in the Age of Information Overload* (New York: Dutton, 2014); Wolf, *Tales of Literacy.*

17.   Stone, Linda, "Beyond Simple Multi-Tasking: Continuous Partial Attention," Linda Stone (website), November 30, 2009, https://lindastone.net/2009/11/30.

18.   Wolf, *Tales of Literacy*; Wolf, *Reader, Come Home.*

19.   Steiner-Adair, Catherine, and Teresa H. Barker, *The Big Disconnect: Protecting Childhood and Family Relationships in the Digital Age* (New York: HarperCollins, 2013).

20.   Delgado, Pablo, Cristina Vargas, Rakefet Ackerman, and Ladislao Salmerón, "Don't Throw Away Your Printed Books: A Meta-Analysis on the Effects of Reading Media on Reading Comprehension," *Educational Research Review* 25 (2018): 23–38; Mangen, Anne, and Adriaan Van der Weel, "The Evolution of Reading in the Age of Digitisation: An Integrative Framework for Reading Research," *Literacy* 50, no. 3 (2016): 116–124; Barzillai, Mirit, Jennifer M. Thomson, and Anne Mangen, "The Influence of e-books on Language and Literacy Development," in *Education and New Technologies: Perils and Promises for Learners*, ed. Kieron Sheehy and Andrew Holliman (New York: Routledge, 2017).

21.   Twenge, Jean M., Gabrielle N. Martin, and Brian H. Spitzberg, "Trends in US Adolescents' Media Use, 1976–2016: The Rise of Digital Media, the Decline of TV, and the (Near) Demise of Print," *Psychology of Popular Media Culture* 8, no. 4 (2019): 329–345.

22. Twenge, Martin, and Spitzberg, "Trends in US Adolescents' Media Use," 338.
23. Delgado et al., "Don't Throw Away Your Printed Books," 23–38.
24. Ackerman, Rakefet, and Tirza Lauterman, "Taking Reading Comprehension Exams on Screen or on Paper? A Metacognitive Analysis of Learning Texts Under Time Pressure," *Computers in Human Behavior* 28, no. 5 (2012): 1816–1828.
25. Baron, Naomi S., *How We Read Now: Strategic Choices for Print, Screen, and Audio* (Oxford: Oxford University Press, 2021); Liu, Ziming, "Digital Reading," *Chinese Journal of Library and Information Science,* English ed. (2012): 85.
26. Flaubert, *Madame Bovary*; Taylor, *The Language Animal*; Wolf, *Proust and the Squid.*
27. Francis (pope), *Laudato Si.*
28. Vygotsky, Lev S., *Thought and Language* (Cambridge, MA: MIT press, 2012).
29. Vygotskij, *Thought and Language*
30. Barzillai, Thomson, and Mangen, "The Influence of e-books"; Barzillai, Mirit, Jenny Thomson, Sascha Schroeder, and Paul van den Broek, eds. *Learning to Read in a Digital World*, vol. 17 (Amsterdam: John Benjamins Publishing Company, 2018); Coiro, Julie, "Online Reading Comprehension: Challenges and Opportunities," *Texto Livre: Linguagem e Tecnologia* 7, no. 2 (2014): 30–43; Wolf, Maryanne and Mirit Barzillai, "The Importance of Deep Reading," *Educational Leadership* 66, nos. 32–35 (2009).
31. Grossman, Lev, "Jonathan Franzen: Great American Novelist," *Time* 176 (2010).
32. Robinson, Marilynne, *The Givenness of Things: Essays* (New York: Farrar, Straus and Giroux, 2015), 96.

17

THE FEELING OF READING IN A CHANGING WORLD

From Neurons to Narratives

TAMI KATZIR

What is the nature of childhood today? According to a new OECD report, on many levels, great improvement is evident in important measures: safety, health, and support for mental health and well-being. At the same time, children in the twenty-first century are reporting increased levels of anxiety and depression, among other things, as a result of heightened pressure to excel in educational environments. New technologies allow children to stay connected, but, at the same time, the sense of loneliness among human beings is growing. Children today are reported to spend less time on old-fashioned activities, such as running around and socializing, and more time on computer screens.[1] Childhood is a critical neurological developmental period. It is a period when important foundational cognitive and affective skills and neuronal connections are formed.[2] Stable and positive relationships with parents, teachers, and peers are crucial for improving children's wellbeing and social and emotional thriving.[3] Supportive parents and teachers can provide children with skills and knowledge on how to deal with adversities in life.[4]

In this chapter, I will argue that meaningful reading programs in school can stimulate academic achievement and a sense of community, purpose, and meaningful tools for dealing with the challenges of growing up in the twenty-first century. In fact, well-designed, evidence-based reading instruction can prepare children in the three important subcategories of defined twenty-first-century skills: literacy, learning, and life skills.

Reading books is a door to the world of imagination, other realms, and endless possibilities of identifying with literary characters, working through challenges in one's personal life, and developing dreams of a wonderful future.[5] Educators have the ability to grant students the gift of reading—not reading as a homework assignment but rather reading that has a magical effect and generates strong feelings, sometimes even stronger than those facilitated in everyday life. Developing the identity of a reading self in young people—a person who takes time to learn about the environment, world, and one's self—will equip them with a strong foundation for building a caring society.[6]

In this chapter, I will first address what reading looks like in a changing world. I will then review the literature linking cognition and emotion in reading in a mind, brain, and education framework. I will claim that an important component linking cognition and emotion in reading is listening (chapter 14). Listening can be widely defined and can propel cognitive and affective understanding of texts and human beings. I will then describe a national reading program we developed in Israel, called Island of Understanding, and the impact it has not only on reading but also on the feelings of children, teachers, and the community.

THE GLOBAL STATE OF READING AMONG CHILDREN AND ADOLESCENTS

The topic of reading comprehension has become a focus of particular attention in the OECD and in other international organizations. International surveys support a strong link between cognition and emotion in reading habits and performance.

Children and young people who enjoy reading and read daily are five times more likely to read above the level expected for their age compared to their peers who don't enjoy reading. Overall, according to the National Literacy Trust, children's and young people's reading engagement, their enjoyment of reading, and reading frequency, especially of novels, have declined steadily over the past five years.[7] The challenges we face as educators and researchers are to understand the circuits that support reading in the brain and then translate them into meaningful, engaging instruction in schools and communities.

THE FEELING OF READING IN
THE BRAIN: INSIGHTS FROM MIND, BRAIN,
AND EDUCATION

Recent converging research from behavior and brain science points to the importance of linking cognition and emotion in educational theory and practice. To quote Douglas Newton, "In today's world, there is often so much emphasis placed on the intellect that the interaction between feeling and thinking is rarely identified. Nonetheless, emotions have a powerful effect on how we perceive the world and learn new knowledge."[8]

In the field of reading, there are two rich yet often disconnected bodies of research and practice on the linguistic and affective components linked to comprehension.[9] New multicomponential models suggest that beyond language, memory, and visual systems, a wide set of emotions also play a role in the critical reading performance of children.[10] Each reader comes to a text with different experiences, social-emotional skills, and certain attitudes toward a particular story and text.[11] Readers might be interested in the topic of the text or bored by it, motivated to read and learn new information or merely to pass a test, anxious that the task requires reading out loud or dealing with a painful subject from the past.[12] Readers may even have a mental model of themselves as readers, one that affects their interaction with the text.

Recent research suggests that both positive and negative feelings are related to different levels of reading in children of all ages.[13] Interestingly, rate of performance rather than accuracy is linked to reading self-concept and reading anxiety. In today's school culture, speed is an appreciated ability. Our studies suggest that children fear being the last one to hand in a worksheet or assignment. One of the lessons learned recently from distance learning is that individual-paced learning diminishes stress related to timed tasks in school. In addition to slow readers, young girls display higher levels of reading anxiety and lower confidence than boys.[14] A study examining galvanic skin response patterns during reading reported more arousal in poor versus strong readers.[15] In addition, poor readers across all grades exhibit low reading self-concept.[16]

New findings from brain imaging studies support the critical role of emotions in reading. The amygdala and temporal pole are considered important for social scripts, emotions, and judgments.[17] Children's processing of stories eliciting affective and cognitive empathy is associated with more medial and bilateral orbitofrontal cortex activation.[18] In addition, there are different patterns of brain activities when children listen to their mothers read stories versus hearing them from a recording.[19]

Reading is both a personal and communal act. Reading is influenced by interactions at home, in school, and in wider cultural settings. Studies indicate that home literacy is correlated with word reading and reading comprehension of children.[20] Children who come from homes with many books are significantly better readers than children with fewer books at home. In a recent study, poor readers, as compared to good readers, reported being more controlling and negative about shared reading time.[21] Children born to mothers addicted to drugs show delays in reading and math ten years after birth.[22] Moreover, children from a low socio-economic background have significantly lower achievements on general vocabulary, reading comprehension, and knowledge of emotion words compared to children raised in wealthier environments.[23]

The importance of high-quality relationships at home and of meaningful interactions around books is receiving initial support in neuroscience research. Innovative brain imaging studies indicate that when reading is shared, especially with a mother, the pattern of activation is different than when children view videos of the same stories.[24] Greater frontal lobe activation was found in children when they were engaged in a picture book reading task with their mothers as opposed to passive viewing of a videotape in which the story was read to them. These findings support the hypothesis raised by Lipina (chapter 3) that the most important pathways in which child poverty would modulate the cognitive and emotional neural and self-regulatory development during the first two decades of life would be the quality of parenting environments and stress regulation.

Emotions are important not just within the reader and within the family but also between the child and her teacher.[25] In our lab, we found that the quality of the relationship between a teacher and a struggling child she tutors predicts how much the child will improve in reading over the course of a year.[26] This is a self-fulfilling prophecy that the teacher sets for the child.

Despite the growing evidence from affective neuroscience and behavior research, most reading programs tend to focus on technical skills associated with reading, with less of an emphasis on enhancing interest, excitement, and dealing with anxiety and boredom that may arise in students.[27]

LINKING COGNITION AND EMOTION IN READING THROUGH VALUE

One way to entice children to engage in reading is to let them read about topics they encounter every day in their development, moral dilemmas, and core values they form in these critical years. Teaching through exposure to dilemmas lets children concurrently develop the three important skills of literacy, learning, and life. Damon and Colby (chapter 10) make a very important call for an education for purpose. They claim that one aspect of purpose is purpose to self. That is, children need to be taught meaningful, relevant topics for themselves in school. Another important aspect is purpose beyond self—purpose to society. Literacy skills are important for both.

Morais argues that the more literate individuals are, the better they participate in exercising control over the affairs of their community and can contribute to true democratic governing.[28] This idea is particularly challenging in light of the fact that, as Morais reminds us, illiteracy rates remain quite high worldwide (see introduction).

The traditional approach is that values are taught in the homeroom or in social studies rather than in language lessons, but in the multidimensional approach, learning from role models and reading about dilemmas are considered the most comprehensive ways of learning about values while observing and listening to others and to oneself.[29] This is especially relevant in light of the digital revolution.

THE VALUE OF LISTENING IN AN ERA OF DIGITAL LITERACY

Contemporary literacy encompasses interactions with the written word on screens, oral language, and processing images via videos, podcasts, and other digital communication formats.[30]

Digital media have, in fact, revived the importance of listening and oral literacy.[31] In the twenty-first century, listening can play an essential role in supporting learners with diverse needs, abilities, and styles. Tools such as digital text, text-to-speech, and audiobooks offer powerful alternatives to traditional classroom materials that rely almost exclusively on printed text. In Chapter 14, Carlina Rinaldi presents the beautiful idea of a pedagogy of listening. In her work, she suggests that listening is an active verb. Listening to children allows them not only to be heard but also to shape their thoughts externally.

However, at present, listening does not always involve an active interlocutor. That is, one can listen to a digital device by pressing a button. As such, listening does not necessarily entail nor promote dialogue nor empathy. As this is the new reality, we need to make a point of emphasizing the development of active empathic listening to others, to the environment, to one's self, rather than only the technical taking in of surface facts involved in person-computer interactions. Shared reading, as stemming in origin from religious contexts and in the educational context, can serve to advance these skills.

In order for children in the twenty-first century to not only listen to technology but truly engage in transformational listening, let us revisit the ideas of German philosopher Martin Buber. Martin Buber's famous text, *Me and You*, presents a philosophy of personal dialogue in that it describes how personal dialogue can define the nature of reality.[32] Buber's major theme is that human existence may be defined by how we engage in dialogue with each other, with the world, and with God.

According to Buber, human beings may adopt two attitudes toward the world: *I-Thou* or *I-It*. In the I-Thou relationship, human beings are aware of each other as having a unity of being. In the I-Thou relationship, human beings engage in a dialogue involving each other's whole being. In the I-It relationship, which is becoming much more prevalent in children's reality, where the *It* can represent a screen of a YouTube video, human beings perceive each other as consisting of specific, isolated qualities and view themselves as part of a world that consists of things. This may be because we relate to the other instrumentally, as the means to attain some desired end, and not as a human being with their own desires and being. The relationship that education systems should focus on enhancing in children, and for which reading can serve as a vehicle, is the I-Thou relationship of empathic listening and reciprocity.

According to the International Listening Association, listening is a critical language skill necessary for competent communication in its many manifestations (e.g., reading, speaking).[33] Listening can also be defined as an ethical endeavor, a pure nonegocentric form, a way of knowing and valuing the other person.

Finally, listening can be defined as part of an experiential and social interaction, as a communal activity. This perspective incorporates theories and principles from storytelling, narrative theory, therapeutic listening, experience, and phenomenology.

These aspects of listening are typically not part of the language arts and reading curriculum. When reading, a child can be taught to listen to herself, listen to the environment, and listen afterward to the community that reads a similar or different text. Active emphatic listening will allow the child to come out of the reading experience changed and enriched.

The need to develop emphatic listening through reading builds on the understanding that cognition and emotion are strongly linked in every human action on the brain and behavior levels.

In a large national-based study, we developed a universal reading program that builds on cutting-edge research in cognitive and affective neuroscience and behavior. We also consulted with value researchers, literature scholars, teachers, and students. Our goal was to create an encompassing experience for elementary school children, one in which reading will take them on an adventure that will teach them about themselves, their environment, and how to listen to each other.

FINDINGS FROM THE ISLAND OF UNDERSTANDING

We constructed a background story about students who find themselves on an island where they must survive on their own. On the island, the students encounter social dilemmas that involve both physical and emotional predicaments. The dilemmas were chosen to map Schwartz's value system.[34] In order to learn life lessons about friendship, survival, listening, and self-identity, the students read journals and letters as well as historical and current texts. In the program, the students are also exposed to role models from whom they can learn about coping with stressful situations, overcoming difficulties, and acquiring values that can be applied to their personal lives.

Thus, in this program, reading is performed for the purpose of survival—physical, emotional, and social. After reading, students are required to carry out different assignments aimed at developing a rich vocabulary, reading flow, and skills of oral and written expression. The approach underlying the program is that reading is an essential source of learning both about the world and about oneself. In this program, reading entails not just passive reading of texts but listening to ideas and discussing them orally with each other, all with the purpose of surviving together on an island.

In addition, the program focuses on the topic of active listening. The children learn that we often "hear" others but do not necessarily listen to them attentively. In the program, after the topic of listening has been grasped, students learn about active listening to the text. They learn that reading requires active listening to the text without jumping to conclusions, while attending to the perspectives of the author or of various characters in the story and developing the ability to formulate the text's words reflectively after listening. The message for students is that the purpose of reading is not to answer questions on a test but rather to understand the author, his or her aim, the information conveyed, what meaning this information has for them as readers, what emotions the text arouses in them, what thoughts, to what prior knowledge the content is related. The assumption is that promoting listening on all levels will facilitate verbal and nonverbal communication among the students and will even change their patterns of active reading. The program teaches, both directly and indirectly, foundational literacy skills such as strategies for reading comprehension before, during, and after reading a text.

Over the past two years, we ran the program with nearly 2,500 students and 120 teachers.[35] In a randomized controlled study, we found that the children who participated in the program reported more excitement, interest, and confidence in reading after their experience "on the island" compared to a control group. They also significantly outperformed children who did not participate in all reading measures. Teachers who took part in this program shared that their relationship with the children improved and that a sense of community was created through this experience. C. Suárez-Orozco (introduction) discusses the basic need of children to belong. This is especially true for immigrant and refugee populations who suffer xenophobia. One of the most important findings from our study is that children both native and immigrant reported a higher sense of belonging to their school, their peers, and, most importantly, to themselves.

SUMMARY: THE FEELING OF CONNECTED VALUE-BASED READING

In conclusion, the key to promoting literacy in twenty-first-century children should be through meaningful shared learning experiences. Literacy impacts not only individual minds but also society and humanity as a whole. In order to retain reading as a central human experience, the links between cognition, emotion, and value should be embedded in reading instruction and curriculum. Further, an important skill to add to the twenty-first-century list is empathic listening. The skills addressed in the program tie together cognition and emotion and allow for literacy learning as well as building life skills. The Island of Understanding program demonstrates that reading is first and foremost an emotional process. Reading builds on a foundation of rich vocabulary, reading flow, and cognitive and metacognitive abilities. Improving students' reading comprehension, however, must begin by encouraging them to willingly and enthusiastically engage in considerable and thorough reading and open their minds and hearts to listening. In order to expand and improve not only the state of literacy but also to develop a strong community of contentious young people who experience reading with feeling, there is a need to shift to a model of reading programs that incorporate values, relationships, and evidence-based pedagogical practices informed by multiple disciplines ranging from linguistics and literature to cognitive and affective neurosciences. In order to truly promote literacy not merely for purposes of international or local exams, we must place reading at the center of the learning process. Lessons from imaging, behavioral, and educational research indicate there is a shift from "cognitive-centric" teaching to integrated reading instruction, which impacts society by helping close important educational gaps.

NOTES

1. Burns, Tracey, and Francesca Gottschalk, eds, *Educating 21st Century Children: Emotional Well-Being in the Digital Age* (Paris: OECD Publishing, 2019).

2. Barrett, Lisa Feldman, *How Emotions Are Made: The Secret Life of the Brain* (Boston: Houghton Mifflin Harcourt, 2017).

3. Choi, Anna, *Emotional Well-Being of Children and Adolescents: Recent Trends and Relevant Factors*, no. 169 (Paris: OECD Publishing, 2018).

4. Pianta, Robert C., "School Psychology and Developmental Psychology: Moving from Programs to Processes," in *Handbook of School Psychology*, 4th ed., ed. Terry B. Gutin and Cecil R. Reynolds, 107–123 (Medford, MA: John Wiley, 2008); Hamre, Bridget K., and Robert C. Pianta, "Early Teacher–Child Relationships and the Trajectory of Children's School Outcomes Through Eighth Grade," *Child Development* 72, no. 2 (2001): 625–638; Goldman, Eliot, Joan Stamler, Kimberly Kleinman, Sarah Kerner, and Owen Lewis, "Child Mental Health: Recent Developments with Respect to Risk, Resilience, And Interventions," *Health Promotion for Children and Adolescents* (2016): 99–123.

5. Roth, Merav, *A Psychoanalytic Perspective on Reading Literature: Reading the Reader* (New York: Routledge, 2020).

6.   Katzir, Tami, and Orly Lipka, *An Island of Understanding—Teacher's Manual* (University of Haifa, Israel: 2017).

7.   National Reading Panel (U.S.), *Report of the National Reading Panel: Teaching Children to Read: An Evidence-Based Assessment of the Scientific Research Literature on Reading and Its Implications for Reading Instruction: Reports of the Subgroups* (Bethesda, MD: National Institute of Child Health and Human Development, 2000).

8.   Newton, Douglas P., *Thinking with Feeling: Fostering Productive Thought in the Classroom* (Oxfordshire, UK: Routledge, 2014).

9.   Katzir and Lipka, *An Island of Understanding.*

10. Primor, Liron, and Tami Katzir, "Linking Cognition and Emotion: Into Reading Comprehension Instruction," in *Linking Emotion, Cognition and Reading Comprehension: From Theory to Practice*, ed. Orly Lipka and Tami Katzir, 1–25 (Israel: University of Haifa, 2006); Katzir, Tami, Young-Suk G. Kim, and Shahar Dotan, "Reading Self-Concept and Reading Anxiety in Second Grade Children: The Roles of Word Reading, Emergent Literacy Skills, Working Memory and Gender," *Frontiers in Psychology* 9 (2018): 1180; Meer, Yael, Zvia Breznitz, and Tami Katzir, "Calibration of Self-Reports of Anxiety and Physiological Measures of Anxiety While Reading in Adults with and Without Reading Disability," *Dyslexia* 22, no. 3 (2016): 267–284; Katzir, Tami, Orly Lipka, Anat Prior, and Michal Shany, "From Mapping to Intervention, A Multi Componential Model for Teacher Training" (report submitted to the chief of science, Israeli Ministry of Education, 2019).

11. Conlon, Elizabeth G., Melanie J. Zimmer-Gembeck, Peter A. Creed, and Melinda Tucker, "Family History, Self-Perceptions, Attitudes and Cognitive Abilities Are Associated with Early Adolescent Reading Skills," *Journal of Research in Reading* 29, no. 1 (2006): 11–32; Katzir, Tami, Vered Markovich, Einat Tesler, and Michal Shany, "Self-Regulation and Reading Comprehension: Self-Perceptions, Self-Evaluations, and Effective Strategies for Intervention," in Executive Function in Education: From Theory to Practice, ed. L. Meltzer, 240–262 (New York: Guilford Press, 2018).

12. Cartwright, Kelly B., Timothy R. Marshall, and Erica Wray, "A Longitudinal Study of the Role of Reading Motivation in Primary Students' Reading Comprehension: Implications for a Less Simple View of Reading," *Reading Psychology* 37, no. 1 (2016): 55–91; Guthrie, John T., and Susan Lutz Klauda, "Effects of Classroom Practices on Reading Comprehension, Engagement, and Motivations for Adolescents," *Reading Research Quarterly* 49, no. 4 (2014): 387–416.

13. Kasperski, Ronen, and Tami Katzir, "Are Confidence Ratings Test- or Trait-Driven? Individual Differences Among High, Average, and Low Comprehenders in Fourth Grade," *Reading Psychology* 34, no. 1 (2013): 59–84; Kasperski, Ronen, Michal Shany, and Tami Katzir, "The Role of RAN and Reading Rate in Predicting Reading Self-Concept," *Reading and Writing* 29, no. 1 (2016): 117–136.

14. Katzir, Young-Suk, and Dotan, "Reading Self-Concept and Reading Anxiety," 1180.

15. Meer, Breznitz, and Katzir, "Calibration of Self-Reports of Anxiety," 267–284.

16. Kleider-Tesler, Einat, Anat Prior, and Tami Katzir, "The Role of Calibration of Comprehension in Adolescence: From Theory to Online Training," *Journal of Cognitive Education and Psychology* 18, no. 2 (2019): 190–211.

17. Northoff, Georg, and Felix Bermpohl, "Cortical Midline Structures and the Self," *Trends in Cognitive Sciences* 8, no. 3 (2004): 102–107.

18. Brink, Tila Tabea, Karolina Urton, Dada Held, Evgeniya Kirilina, Markus Hofmann, Gisela Klann-Delius, Arthur M. Jacobs, and Lars Kuchinke, "The Role of Orbitofrontal Cortex in Processing Empathy Stories in 4-to 8-Year-Old Children," *Frontiers in Psychology* 2 (2011): 80.

19. Hutton, John S., Kieran Phelan, Tzipi Horowitz-Kraus, Jonathan Dudley, Mekibib Altaye, Tom DeWitt, and Scott K. Holland, "Shared Reading Quality and Brain Activation During Story Listening in Preschool-Age Children," *Journal of Pediatrics* 191 (2017): 204–211.

20. Katzir, Tami, Nonie K. Lesaux, and Young-Suk Kim, "The Role of Reading Self-Concept and Home Literacy Practices in Fourth Grade Reading Comprehension," *Reading and Writing* 22, no. 3 (2009): 261–276.

21. Bluma, Segal, Michal Shany, and Tami Katzir, "A Diadic Study About Mother-Child Perspectives on Reading" (in preparation).

22. Lee, Samantha J., Lianne J. Woodward, and Jacqueline M. T. Henderson, "Educational Achievement at Age 9.5 Years of Children Born to Mothers Maintained on Methadone During Pregnancy," *PloS One* 14, no. 10 (2019): e0223685.

23. Sabag Shoshan, Tami, "The Role of Emotion Words in Reading Comprehension" (PhD diss., University of Haifa, Israel, 2021).

24. Hutton, John S., Kieran Phelan, Tzipi Horowitz-Kraus, Jonathan Dudley, Mekibib Altaye, Thomas DeWitt, and Scott K. Holland, "Story Time Turbocharger? Child Engagement During Shared Reading and Cerebellar Activation and Connectivity in Preschool-Age Children Listening to Stories," *Plos One* 12, no. 5 (2017): e0177398.

25. Bluma, Shany, and Katzir, "A Diadic Study"; Cheung, Cecilia Sin-Sze, and Eva M. Pomerantz, "Parents' Involvement in Children's Learning in the United States and China: Implications for Children's Academic and Emotional Adjustment," *Child Development* 82, no. 3 (2011): 932–950.

26. Gallili Kama, Michal Shany, and Tami Katzir, "The Self-Fulfilling Prophecy of Teachers Beliefs and Students' Achievement" (in preparation).

27. National Reading Panel (US), *Report of the National Reading Panel.*

28. Morais, José, "Literacy and Democracy," *Language, Cognition and Neuroscience* 33, no. 3 (2018): 351–372.

29. Narvaez, Darcia, Jennifer Bentley, Tracy Gleason, and Jay Samuels, "Moral Theme Comprehension in Third Graders, Fifth Graders, and College Students," *Reading Psychology: An International Quarterly* 19, no. 2 (1998): 217–241.

30. Wolf, Maryanne, *Reader, Come Home: The Reading Brain in A Digital World* (New York: Harper, 2018); see also chapter 16.

31. Meyer, Anne, David Howard Rose, and David T. Gordon, *Universal Design for Learning: Theory and Practice* (Wakefield, MA: CAST Professional Publishing, 2014).

32. Buber, Martin, *Ich und du* [Me and you] (Stuttgart: Reclam, 1923).

33. Imhof, Margarete, "How to Listen More Efficiently: Self-Monitoring Strategies in Listening," *International Journal of Listening* 15, no. 1 (2001): 2–19.

34. Schwartz, Shalom H., "Universals in the Content and Structure of Values: Theoretical Advances and Empirical Tests in 20 Countries," in *Advances in Experimental Social Psychology*, ed. Mark P. Zanna, vol. 25, 1–65 (Cambridge, MA: Academic Press, 1992.)

35. Katzir et al., "From Mapping to Intervention."

V

THE FUTURES OF EDUCATION

18

GLOBAL LEARNING ECOLOGIES

Leveraging Technologies for Equity

BRIGID BARRON

A cross the globe, digital technologies continually transform the ways people work, communicate, learn, and play. Rapid innovation has led to great enthusiasm about the potential for networked tools to provide more children with low-cost access to learning opportunities that might help minimize existing educational inequities. Ambitious initiatives to provide inexpensive computing power to those most in need have distributed networked laptops to children in remote villages and urban centers in the hope that the provision of access to content and modern tools will fuel learning. Although prior experiments have yielded important insights, they have largely failed to lead to a significant transformation of educational practice.[1] Schools vary in how well they envision the purposes of using technology, prepare their teachers, and provide the infrastructure to sustain working tools, aspects of use that correlate with affluence and serve to amplify preexisting privileges.[2]

Outside of schools, families leverage their financial resources, prior education, and connections to knowledgeable social networks as they incorporate technology into their daily routines to support children's learning and social development. Diversity in the functionality of devices, stability of internet access, and the quality of content further contribute to variability in the affordances of technology for learning at home. The 2020 global pandemic and emergency school closures have revealed the ongoing cost of these inequities, as schools across the world turn to digital technologies to continue the education of millions of children. Unequal access to the internet and devices, significant gaps in preparation to connect homes and schools to technology, and differential assistance to teachers and parents have limited our capacity to sustain learning and social well-being in a time of crisis.[3]

The uneven success of prior educational experiments shifts our attention from a sole focus on physical access to technology to concerns about *the learning opportunities* within sociotechnical systems that will allow more empowered and generative uses of technology to develop new literacies, domain knowledge, creative capacities, and critical perspectives.[4] To make progress on the important agenda of using technologies to bridge divides in learning opportunities, it is critical to build on advances in our knowledge regarding human development and learning and to acknowledge the risks and opportunities presented by a rapidly shifting digital landscape. Now, more than ever, teachers, parents, principals, industry leaders, policy makers, and the higher education community must come together to understand the importance of access and the need for intentional use. We need to collectively learn from the current moment and plan for a future where all families and educators are prepared to leverage technology to support one another in and out of school.

CONTRASTING IMAGES OF THE ROLE OF TECHNOLOGY IN HUMAN DEVELOPMENT

The need for empirical research to guide innovation in the form and content of learning opportunities for educators, parents, and children is reflected in shifting narratives about the potential harms and benefits of technology for human development. In a dramatic portrayal of the possible consequence of widening divides between more and less prepared populations, Castells envisioned a future in which people become members of two different groups—the interacting or the interacted. The interacting will have the background and resources to find, choose, develop, and critique new technologies, while the interacted will be passively subjected to its influence, possibly without their awareness.[5]

Fast forward to 2020, and the insightfulness of this prediction is clear, yet the realities are far more complicated. As devices and internet connections become more available to a greater proportion of the world, empirical studies reveal that even highly educated people are both "interacted" and "interacting." Most young people are unable to distinguish online news from advertisements or opinions.[6] Adults, too, are at a loss, as trusted sources of information disappear, and "news" includes manipulated video while partisan websites portray themselves as policy-neutral curators of information.[7] Few people are able to read and understand online privacy agreements and, even if they could, often give up personal data in exchange for free access to the digital tools they have come to depend on. Large-scale survey studies suggest that bullying, hate speech, inappropriate content, and "fear of missing out" represent some of the risks of online activity. Overuse of social networking sites is correlated with markers of emotional distress.[8] Children and adults are subject to disruption of attention as they are drawn into their personal media ecologies, leading to what psychologist Sherry Turkle calls a tendency to be "alone together."[9] From this view, characterizations of young people as "digital natives" and older folks as "digital immigrants" are called into question, as digital divides are increasingly conceptualized as multidimensional, overlapping, and intersectional.

Yet, alongside this sobering portrait, there are hopeful signs that the human capacities to reflect, critique, resist, manage, and leverage resources in the service of a creative agency for valuable purposes are alive and well. Accounts of technological experimentation and adoption provide rich examples of generating family-focused collaborative learning opportunities, supporting one's community, creating locally relevant inventions, and new forms of civic engagement.[10] Take, for example, the case of Greta Thunberg. At age fifteen, Thunberg launched what was to become a widespread global movement demanding political action on climate change policy. What started as a solo school strike in 2018 escalated into a global effort after Thunberg posted photos to her Twitter and Instagram accounts and called on youth to join her in public rallies, coordinated through youth-led Fridays for Future events.[11] In 2019, there were at least two coordinated global multicity protests involving over a million students across 150 countries. In the popular press, this collective wave of action has been called the "Greta effect." From a learning sciences perspective, it is an example of a new form of collaborative learning that reflects collective efficacy made possible by social media and increasing interconnectedness.[12]

By her own account, Thunberg first became concerned about climate change at the age of eight, introduced to the topic by her classroom teacher. She found herself unable to forget the images and went into a period of depression, refusing to talk or attend class. In May 2018, at age fifteen, she wrote an essay on the topic, winning a competition and garnering recognition for her views. This consequential feedback led to an invitation from activist Bo Thoren to attend a climate change group that offered a community of adult champions who believed that teens could make a difference and facilitated brainstorming among potential change agents. These collaborative sessions focused on generating new projects that would bring attention to the climate crisis. Thunberg was drawn to the idea of a school strike, inspired by peers in the United States who refused to go to school in response to the high school shooting in Parkland, Florida.

Her project got little attention from local peers, so she took the idea up on her own, suspending her participation in the joint meetings.[13] On August 20, 2018, armed with fact-filled fliers, a sign reading "School Strike for the Climate," and the mobile phone she used to post activity to Twitter and Instagram, Thunberg launched her effort in front of the Swedish Parliament building. Before long, adult climate activists were championing her cause through photo documentation and digital distribution of her story. Within the year, Thunberg had marshaled the support of her family and thousands of young people across the world. Like other youth activists, she has been attacked online and on television and criticized by politicians and business leaders. Rather than ignoring their harsh comments, she has revoiced them, utilizing insults and critiques to advance her arguments, profile her opponents, and model the resilience required of those who enter the fray of social media.[14]

CONNECTIONS TO THE SCIENCE OF LEARNING

Thunberg's example is extraordinary for a number of reasons.[15] Yet, it is also consistent with recent theories of learning that shift attention from learning as a cognitive phenomenon, driven by knowledge acquisition, to a highly participatory social process that takes place over time, settings, and interpersonal interactions.[16] Consequential learning is increasingly recognized as interest-driven, linked to emotions, aided by a diverse set of learning partners, and distributed across home, school, and community, including online virtual spaces. Parents, educators, community members, and peers may take on diverse sets of learning partner roles as they broker opportunities, collaborate to explore possibilities, share resources, and teach, becoming learners as expertise shifts over time.[17]

Studies that chart the evolution of interests, either prospectively or retrospectively, point to the important roles of early experiences and family-supported hobbies as well as schools in sustaining engagement in the sciences and humanities.[18] Sustained engagement may be thought of as multidimensional; ideas, types of experience, and a desire for social connection can jointly contribute to staying involved in learning activities.[19] The incorporation of identity has become increasingly important for conceptualizing cross-setting learning dynamics, making visible relationships among persons, domains, and pursuits over time, with the intertwining of learning.[20] When young people are positioned as outsiders or are negatively stereotyped, conditions for disengagement may arise. However, when young people are invited to participate, valued for their input, and recognized through recruitment to new roles, conditions for a virtuous cycle of continued engagement and development are created.

IMPLICATIONS FOR GLOBAL EDUCATION

Along with many young people who have set foot on the global stage in the service of racial justice, humanitarian initiatives, and environmental causes, Thunberg's example makes the case that although traditional literacy goals are fundamental to achieving equity of opportunity, they are not adequate.[21] In these cases, we see young people teaching as well as learning, and inspiring as well as critiquing adults who hold positions of power. A collective wave of action was made possible by access to networked systems but, most importantly, by the uniquely human resources of cooperation, empathy, sense of justice, passion, and the capacity to invent and adopt different ways of learning within a supportive community.

Beyond illustrating contemporary theories of learning, Thunberg's pathway offers a compelling case for the design of new forms of personally relevant, project-based, and distributed collaborative learning. This and other learning biographies reflect the importance of providing varied opportunities for engagement across disciplines and communities, as it is impossible to predict how early experience may be taken up later in life.[22] It is not enough to assume that because of increasing connectedness all young people will have a chance to learn. Instead, intentional efforts are needed to create youth-relevant, equity-aware, civically oriented learning opportunities.[23] Learning pathways are deeply rooted in culture, subject to privilege and marginalization, and often linked to the structural supports provided by schools, families, and communities.[24]

LEVERAGING TECHNOLOGIES FOR
EQUITABLE LEARNING BY DESIGN

Given the potential uses of technology for human agency and collaboration, it is essential that we do everything we can to ensure that all young people are positioned for its empowered use. As digital activities become a growing part of experience at increasingly younger ages, it is vital to consider not only the content young people have access to but also *how* schools, families, and communities can use technology collaboratively to support learning and development, both in and out of school. In particular, we need to develop novel pedagogical approaches that will help adults and young people curate, critique, design, create, invent, manage, and use technologies that enhance their personal lives and social worlds.[25]

In the rest of this chapter, three design directions for supporting learning will be summarized, building on theory and contemporary research in the learning sciences. These include designing family-based intergenerational learning, providing school-based catalysts for interest-driven learning through project- and problem-based learning opportunities, and connecting institutions to connect activities across schools, communities, and homes.

DESIGN FOR FAMILY-BASED
INTERGENERATIONAL LEARNING

Young children learn long before school begins through everyday activities, imaginative and constructive play, and conversations with caregivers and peers. These early years are foundational for later learning. Through routine interactions, the child comes to own not only skills but also cultural tools such as writing systems, maps, language, and numerical systems.[26] Increasingly, these symbolic cultural tools are shared through digital interactive media that can be accessed from smartphones or other mobile devices such as tablets. Global estimates suggest that one out of three children are users of the internet, and research confirms that much of this use is taking place outside of school.[27] In the United States, young children's time spent on mobile devices more than tripled between 2013 and 2017, from an average of fifteen to forty-eight minutes daily, with much of this time spent playing games or watching online videos.[28]

International studies also reflect the rapid diffusion of mobile computing and show that children in many countries spend more than an hour on average using devices to access the internet, with more time on weekends.[29]

As conversations around digital media and young children evolve from quantifying screen time to considerations of content and context, learning sciences research offers valuable perspectives for caregivers, educators, and designers.[30] Digital media resources can serve as powerful learning tools when adults and children use them as catalysts for collaborative exchanges around meaningful content.[31] Digitally anchored activities shared with parents, siblings, grandparents, and extended family can generate questions, explanations, and extended conversations that build connections to real-world experiences and support the development of language and literacy.[32] Digital tools also allow for the cocreation of artifacts that document experiences and perspectives. Research in the learning sciences emphasizes that these forms of joint media engagement can be a powerful mechanism for fostering cultural knowledge, coordinating activities between home and school, and codeveloping interests that evolve over time.

In these emergent family collaborations, children and adults have unique and complementary perspectives and forms of expertise.[33] Children and adolescents can serve in the role of information and technology brokers, helping caregivers learn and find information, explore new tools, and manage digital life.[34] Relying on young people for help is especially common in immigrant families, where parents may need help finding and translating information.[35] In other cases, parents leverage technology to help children with school. In a study of immigrant families in the United States, parents used multiple resources to assist children with homework, including YouTube and apps that translate from English to the parents' native languages, such as Spanish.[36] This body of research suggests the importance of understanding families as intergenerational learning teams with unique needs and assets that can benefit from experiences that amplify possibilities for reciprocal and bidirectional learning.[37]

There is growing evidence that caregivers want ways to leverage technology that supports children's learning, but many are uncertain about the value of digital resources and shy away from using them. In a survey of over fourteen thousand families in eleven countries, researchers found that parents' view of technology was a pivotal factor in digital exploration and developing skills.[38] Parents who adopt a restrictive style for children's technology use may shield them from the risks of online engagement but undermine their ability to learn and benefit from digital activities. When parents adopt an enabling style that includes monitoring and mediation, sharing online experiences, and supporting children's efforts when they request it, children may encounter more risks but take advantage of more online resources and activities, developing their own unique forms of digital literacy. The researchers also reported variability within and across countries; on average, the children from lower-income countries were more likely to spend time on entertainment activities, raising concerns that valuable time for learning was being lost.[39]

INSPIRATIONS FOR DESIGN

As devices and internet connections become more available, the prospects of supporting families through strong content and caregiver support are significant. Family media ecologies often reflect the transmedia connections that children explore, encountering connected content in traditional or digital books, videos, digital games, and toys. The Ready to Learn initiative leverages the potential of transmedia design to engage preschoolers in science inquiry, using PBS-created videos, interactive games, and reading materials. Classroom activities were designed to connect to children's daily lives at home, and parents reported that children had initiated conversations about content introduced at school, suggesting a potential for cross-setting learning.[40]

In other efforts, public media organizations are developing materials that support the socio-emotional well-being of families experiencing trauma while also supporting literacy development. For example, Sesame Workshop is developing early learning materials for children and caregivers affected by the Syrian conflict.[41] This model connects to families wherever they are, from classrooms and health clinics to TV and mobile devices, featuring characters who have been displaced. The stories are based on children's own experiences and model calming and connecting strategies designed with the intention that both parents and children will benefit.

Digital libraries of books accessible at school and on devices at home can provide ways for parents and children to engage with the same texts while they provide data to educators on the reading that students do outside of class.[42] Some nonprofit efforts have produced culturally relevant child-level reading materials by partnering with authors. For example, World Reader works with authors to create content in more than a hundred languages, distributing books on mobile devices, and engaging community organizations to support literacy activities with parents and children.[43] To go beyond traditional literacies, other efforts offer family creative learning workshops that combine community-building activities with computational design projects to support intergenerational media production, offering multiple entry points that connect to the skills and interests of all.[44]

CATALYZE AUTHENTIC LEARNING THROUGH PROJECT-BASED WORK IN SCHOOLS

Schools are essential sites for providing young people opportunities to go beyond basic literacy, grapple with challenging real-world problems, explore disciplinary frameworks, experiment with contemporary tools, and begin to develop identities as potential innovators and civically engaged change-makers. The calls for educational approaches that connect knowledge to applications are not new; they have roots in the theories of constructivist learning like those of John Dewey and Jean Piaget, and the progressive education movement that emphasized the importance of inquiry-oriented, interest-driven, and project-based learning for connecting knowledge with contexts of authentic application. Thirty years ago, the SCANS report suggested that in order for today's students to be prepared for tomorrow's workplace, their learning environments must allow them to explore real-life situations and consequential problems.[45] Such arguments are echoed in scholarly research, national commission reports, and policy proposals, urging instructional reforms that can help students gain vital media literacy, critical thinking skills, systems thinking, and interpersonal and self-directional skills.

A rationale for these recommendations comes in part from research demonstrating that students do not develop the ability to analyze, think critically, communicate effectively, and solve complex problems when only working on more constrained tasks. To nurture these capacities, students must have the opportunity to develop them in the context of complex, meaningful projects— ones that require sustained engagement, collaboration on research, and management of resources that can lead to an ambitious performance or product.[46] Evidence from a range of design experiments suggests that longer-term projects are particularly inspiring when they invite learners to contribute as designers, authors, and investigators; they provide access to tools, time, and learning resources; they offer connections with mentors and opportunities to share with broader communities; and they provide assessments that lead to visible improvements. Although technology can provide resources to support these activities, schools are not always prepared to use them, adding to the structural inequities that can occur as a function of family or community resources.[47] Investment in the ongoing professional development of teachers through workplace learning opportunities is needed in order to answer the increasingly urgent need for ambitious problem- and project-based approaches.

Schools can also introduce students to the cultural, social, and ethical dimensions of newer participatory online cultures. The examples of young activists shared earlier make the case that new forms of civic and social agency can benefit from the peer learning made possible by a broad range of networked tools. Beyond single cases, studies of out-of-school affinity groups have documented that when young people contribute, circulate, and curate content for their peers and communities, they develop insights into the possibilities of participatory cultures.[48] Networked technologies play important roles in these extended journeys, as they offer connections to content, ideas for projects, tools for creation, and new ways to learn through varied forms of distributed mentoring.[49] However, the capacity to find and evaluate sources of information online and determine their credibility is garnering increasing attention, and empirical work shows how education levels and experience with networked resources can contribute to these skills.[50] Formal opportunities to learn how to establish credibility are essential.

INSPIRATIONS FOR DESIGN

Students learn more when they apply classroom knowledge to real-world problems. Inquiry and design-based approaches are important ways to nurture communication, collaboration, creativity, and deep thinking. We know from prior work that teaching practices that emphasize intellectual authority, accountability to others, and responsibility for problematizing content can lead to higher levels of engagement.[51] In the area of science education, a National Research Council report highlights the potential for an interest-driven, identity-focused learning STEM ecosystem that can span school, home, and community-based science settings.[52] For example, in citizen science projects, students are given opportunities for local and distributed collaboration as they collect data within the classroom or district and share it with others working on the same problem for purposes of collective analysis.[53] In formal classroom settings, students learn to navigate websites, upload investigations, and use technologies like GPS devices, sensors, and Google Maps. For some projects, students venture outside to collect data in the field—around school, in backyards, at a local beach, and so on. As they submit their investigations online, students enter a networked community where information is shared, and participants communicate virtually across locations. Thus, students are not simply using technologies; they are learning how to use them within a structured context facilitated by their teachers, the site administration, and a curriculum in a larger educative endeavor.[54]

Experiments to advance new forms of civic education through project-based learning are underway. Some of these leverage social media to engage young people in dialogue across politically distinct geographic communities to nurture mutual understanding and civic engagement through writing, critical media analysis, relationships building, and creative production. Rather than focusing on learning the history and practice of traditional civic engagement, these classroom approaches employ dialogue that flows from local and international concerns, and research and writing are translated into podcasts, films, and photo essays.[55]

To address the increasing need for critical news analysis and authorship, out-of-school apprenticeship approaches such as "collegial pedagogy" have been designed to support young journalists in National Public Radio's Youth Radio program.[56] To prepare for original reporting work, novices are guided through a series of increasingly intensive experiences, including organized classes and peer mentoring, focused on establishing what would count as credible news. Later, they work directly with adult reporters or editors and are paid as interns to produce material. Consistent with the established practice of documentary newsrooms, both the youth and adults engage in collaborative framing of original work, although ultimately, the young journalists have the editorial power. By working closely with established journalists, beginning authors get a chance to see how seasoned writers anticipate the reactions of diverse audiences to stories they help create, making once-hidden aspects of expertise available for reflection.

CONNECT INSTITUTIONS AND DIVERSIFY LEARNING OPPORTUNITIES ACROSS SETTINGS

Lately, there has been a move away from conceptualizing learning as tied to specific places but rather as distributed and assembled across a variety of environments and long-term trajectories of participation.[57] Understanding that learning pathways may be extended over time and place requires that we understand them as subject to structural dimensions of inequality, which can limit and constrain access to the opportunities inside and outside of school. These include financial, social, institutional, and personal barriers that can alter or disrupt pathways of learning.

Such a broad view draws attention to the ways that schools may be embedded in the broader ecologies of learning and the ways in which non-school resources contribute to inequities. Studies that investigate extracurricular expenditures have highlighted the ways in which disposable income allows parents to supplement school learning with enrichment activities, materials, and a wide range of academic support outside the classroom, taking place during the school year and over the summer.[58] Such compounded privileges include books, computing tools, travel opportunities, summer camps, organizational memberships, gear and clothing for specialized hobbies, transportation and enrollment fees, tutors, test preparation classes, access to academically oriented online communities, and entry fees to such cultural institutions as museums.

Differences in access to these supports contribute to variability in academic achievement, and there is increasing evidence that lack of access is linked to missed opportunities for the development of domain-related interests and identities.[59] To counter these sources of inequity, systemic approaches to design are needed to organize more out-of-school spaces for learning and build synergy between school and out-of-school activities.[60] Questions about how we can intentionally catalyze cross-setting learning have gained currency given the rapidly changing technologies that provide novel opportunities to design hybrid forms of curriculum-based learning, which can span virtual and collocated settings. The hope is that participation in such intentionally designed activities can build cultural learning pathways over time, linking experiences in discrete learning settings to developmental trajectories of participation.

INSPIRATIONS FOR DESIGN

Experiments to create more equitable learning pathways are still in their infancy. Others are needed that will reflect the realities of diverse communities across the globe. The MacArthur Foundation has funded the Connected

Learning network, a critical champion and sponsor of both design-based and basic research.[61] To counter layered inequities, spaces are being designed for schools, after school, and online programs tailored to the interests and needs of learners. For example, the Youth Network (DYN) Digital Media Citizenship design framework has guided the development and iteration of a program that will cultivate "digital media citizenship" as youth become constructive producers of digital media, social advocates for a better future, and critical consumers of digital media.[62]

Within DYN, multiple participation structures provide focused opportunities to generate ideas and refine skills. Mentors blend aspects of formal learning in classrooms and apprenticeships using a range of demonstration and work sessions common in the visual arts.[63] Workshops offer demonstrations, suggested readings, and provide models of adult expertise and practices to which learning may aspire. Forums introduce important issues, invite reflection through production, and provide a setting to share work. The school-based media arts classes offer compelling projects and ensure that everyone has an opportunity to engage with mentors. The online space is a place for any time posting, sharing work, and exchanging commentaries. Less frequent events such as class-wide projects and contests are also available. Longer-term projects introduce mentors and provide a chance for collaborative engagement across cohorts. Contests in pods and classes generate enthusiasm for production and heighten joint attention to norms and quality contributions. Showcasing quality work occurs through online venues and behind-the-scenes interviews that offer a glimpse of the histories, people, and inspiration for creating. These opportunities for engagement increase the odds that learners will find people, projects, and tools that connect to their own interests and preferences for content and social interaction.[64]

Other experiments focus on using technology to connect independently conceived and conducted out-of-school activities. A notable example includes a city-level intervention designed to connect young people with summertime activities in Chicago.[65] Hundreds of organizations were mapped in a website to help parents and educators locate opportunities for young people.[66] This mapping work revealed a lack of youth organizations in many neighborhoods, highlighting inequities in the geography of opportunity in the United States.[67]

As social design experiments move forward, the roles and needs of distributed brokers, mentors, and caregivers have become increasingly important.[68] In community mapping projects, it is often librarians, educators in after school clubs, or other community-based organizations who support family caregivers in coordinating and connecting resources that support learners' engagement over time. Though technology can make connections across settings and support learning within them, human relationships are what is central to cultivating purpose, empathy, and inspiration (see chapter 10).

—————— ∞ ——————

Although unequal access to information technologies was documented well before the COVID-19 pandemic, dramatic school closures have brought a significant digital divide into sharp relief and exposed the ongoing cost of inequities as teachers across the world scrambled to continue the education of millions of children. Radio, television, and the internet were deployed in an attempt to connect schools and homes. Learners in rural areas, citizens from less affluent countries, families who have less wealth, and female students were the least likely to have access to any of these forms of remote learning. In the United States, what was conceptualized as the "homework gap," a recognition of schools' increasing reliance on technology as a core resource, now represents a much more serious "learning opportunity gap." In a recent analysis that accounts for both quality of a device and speed of internet access, it was estimated that more than three hundred thousand teachers and 15–16 million students lacked what they needed to participate in the distance learning advocated by experts.[69] These consequential gaps have affected students across the world and need to be understood in terms of overlapping, multidimensional inequities in access to learning opportunities.[70] At the same time, new ways to engage families and communities have emerged, opening up possibilities for future collaboration and the reimagining of home and school relationships.[71]

The COVID-19 pandemic has made it clear that technology will be a crucial tool for accessing social, educational, and health-related resources. At the same time, it is recognized that access to devices alone is insufficient. To recover fully, schools will need to support the needs of teachers, families, and students by investing in efforts that revitalize communities with extended opportunities for learning and emotional well-being.[72] As the international community explores strategies to prepare learners for an increasingly complex and interconnected world, we need design studies that follow a use-inspired genre of basic research, notably referred to as "Pasteur's quadrant"—one that can tailor approaches to specific community needs, values, and constraints.[73] Use-inspired basic research is distinguished from research driven only by practical goals or only as a quest for basic scientific understanding. There is an urgent practical need to create dynamic learning ecologies that can prepare educators, caregivers, and young people to sustain learning opportunities and relationships under conditions that disrupt schools while working collectively to harness what may be a new moment to transform possibilities for those who do not have the benefit of expansive education under normal conditions.

An equally important case can be made for research that reveals how technologies were used in innovative ways to sustain well-being and catalyze learning during a pandemic that has affected global communities. Their rapid evolution and the ways in which they were appropriated require that we capture the examples of innovation by young learners, teachers, and communities. The need to connect and adapt has led to rapid adoption of tools, new forms of collaboration to share resources, and unique learning practices. Beyond standardized tests, it is important to document the forms of civic engagement and ingenuity that have emerged. As schools across the globe reimagine education in preparation for what may be an ongoing need for remote learning, we will expect to see new approaches to home-school-community connections. This essential reimagining of education and opportunity requires the mobilization of social networks, innovative pedagogical approaches, new technical designs and approaches to research, and careful attention to who will have resources and why.

ACKNOWLEDGMENTS

This chapter originally appeared as a paper for *Education: The Global Compact*, Pontifical Academy of Social Sciences, Rome, March 6–7 2020. Preparation and delivery of this paper has been supported by the TELOS initiative at the Graduate School of Education at Stanford University.

NOTES

1. Ames, Morgan G., *The Charisma Machine: The Life, Death, and Legacy of One Laptop per Child* (Cambridge, MA: MIT Press, 2019); Wagner, Daniel A., *Learning as Development: Rethinking International Education in a Changing World* (New York: Routledge, 2017).

2. OECD, *Students, Computers and Learning: Making the Connection* (Paris: OECD Publishing, 2015).

3. UNICEF, "COVID-19: Are Children Able to Continue Learning During School Closures?" Brochure (2020): 17.

4. World Bank, *World Development Report 2018: Learning to Realize Education's Promise* (Washington, DC: World Bank, 2018).

5. Castells, Manuel, *The Information Age: Economy, Society and Culture*, vol. 1, *The Rise of the Network Society* (Oxford: Blackwell, 1996).

6. OECD, *Students, Computers and Learning.*

7. "CIGI-Ipsos Global Survey on Internet Security and Trust," Center for International Governance Inovation-Ipsos, accessed October 8, 2021, www.cigionline.org/internet-survey-2019.

8. Lin, Liu Yi, Jaime E. Sidani, Ariel Shensa, Ana Radovic, Elizabeth Miller, Jason B. Colditz, Beth L. Hoffman, Leila M. Giles, and Brian A. Primack, "Association Between Social Media Use and Depression Among US Young Adults," *Depression and Anxiety* 33, no. 4 (2016): 323–331.

9. Turkle, Sherry, *The Second Self: The Human Spirit in a Computer Culture* (New York: Simon & Schuster, 1984). Also see chapter 16.

10. Mirra, Nicole, and Antero Garcia, "Civic Participation Reimagined: Youth Interrogation and Innovation in the Multimodal Public Sphere," *Review of Research in Education* 41, no. 1 (2017): 136–158.

11. Jung, Jieun, Peter Petkanic, Dongyan Nan, and Jang Hyun Kim, "When a Girl Awakened the World: A User and Social Message Analysis of Greta Thunberg," *Sustainability* 12, no. 7 (2020): 2707.

12. Bandura, Albert, "Self-Efficacy: The Foundation of Agency," in *Control of Human Behavior, Mental Processes, and Consciousness: Essays in Honor of the 60th Birthday of August Flammer*, ed. Walter J. Perrig and Alexander Grob, 17–33 (Mahwah, NJ: Lawrence Erlbaum Associates, 2000).

13. Thunberg, Greta, *No One is Too Small to Make a Difference* (New York: Penguin, 2019).

14. O'Connor, Mary Catherine, and Sarah Michaels, "Shifting Participant Frameworks: Orchestrating Thinking Practices in Group Discussion," *Discourse, Learning, and Schooling* 63 (1996): 103.

15. After speaking at the UN, other invitations to address adult leaders quickly followed. Over the course of two years, Thunberg was invited to address the World Economic Forum, European Economic and Social Committee, film award ceremonies, the European Parliament, the Austrian World Summit, the French National Assembly, the UN General Assembly, and Facebook in Stockholm among others.

16. Brofenbrenner, Urie, and Gregory Evans, "Developmental Science in the 21st Century: Emerging Questions, Theoretical Models, Research Designs and Empirical Findings," *Social Development* 9 (2000): 115–125, DOI:10.1111/1467-9507.00114; Rogoff, Barbara, *The Cultural Nature of Human Development* (Oxford: Oxford University Press, 2003).

17. Barron, Brigid, Caitlin Kennedy Martin, Lori Takeuchi, and Rachel Fithian , "Parents as Learning Partners in the Development of Technological Fluency," *International Journal of Learning and Media* 1 (2009): 55–77.

18. Crowley, Kevin, Brigid J. Barron, Karen Knutson, and Caitlin K. Martin, "Interest and the Development of Pathways to Science," in *Interest in Mathematics and Science Learning and Related Activity*, ed. Ann Renninger, Martina Nieswandt, and Suzanne Hidi (Washington, DC: AERA, 2015); Tai, Robert H., Christine Qi Liu, Adam V. Maltese, and Xitao Fan, "Planning Early for Careers in Science," *Science* 312 (2006): 1143–1144.

19. Azevedo, Flavio, "The Tailored Practice of Hobbies and Its Implication for the Design of Interest-Driven Learning Environments," *Journal of the Learning Sciences* 22 (2013): 462–510, DOI: 10.1080/10508406.2012.730082.

20. Calabrese-Barton, Angela, Hosun Kang, Edna Tan, Tara B. O'Neill, Juanita Bautista-Guerra, and Caitlin Brecklin, "Crafting a Future in Science: Tracing Middle School Girls' Identity

Work over Time and Space," *American Educational Research Journal* 50 (2013): 37–75; Delors, Jacques, *Learning: The Treasure Within* (Paris: UNESCO, 1996); Holland, Dorothy, and Kevin Leander, "Ethnographic Studies of Positioning and Subjectivity: An Introduction," *Ethos* 32, no. 2 (2004): 127–139; Hull, Glynda A., and James G. Greeno, "Identity and Agency in Nonschool and School Worlds," in *Learning in Places: The Informal Education Reader*, ed. Zvi Bekerman, Nicholas C. Burbules, and Diana Silberman-Keller (New York: Peter Lang, 2006), 77–98; Lave, Jean, and Etienne Wenger, *Situated Learning: Legitimate Peripheral Participation. New Learning Technologies* (Cambridge: Cambridge University Press, 1991).

21. See Malala Yousafzai, human rights activist and Nobel Peace Prize recipient, and Emma González, founder of Never Again and March for Life, whose gun control advocacy efforts were launched after the Parkland school shootings in Florida.

22. Barron, Brigid, and Philip Bell, "Learning Environments In and Out of School," in *Handbook of Educational Psychology*, 3rd ed., ed. Lyn Corno and Eric M. Anderman (New York: Routledge, 2015). Consider the career pathway of another influential activist, Rachel Carson. While famous for launching the environmental movement with her 1962 book *Silent Spring*, Carson was a latecomer to science. In fact, her passion did not emerge until she was a junior in college, the result of a biology class taken to fulfill a science requirement. Both her family's nature walks and immersion in reading and writing were likely influential in her later career and groundbreaking contribution to environmental science, which took the form of beautifully written works on the role of pesticides in damaging human and ecosystem health.

23. Mirra, Nicole, and Antero Garcia, " 'I Hesitate but I Do Have Hope:' Youth Speculative Civic Literacies for Troubled Times," *Harvard Educational Review* 90, no. 2 (2020): 295–321; see introduction.

24. de Royston, Maxine McKinney, Brigid Barron, Phillip Bell, Roy Pea, Reed Stevens, and Shelley Goldman, "Learning Pathways: How Learning Is Culturally Organized," in *Handbook of the Cultural Foundations of Learning*, ed. Na'ilah Nasir, Carol Lee, and Roy Pea, 195–211 (New York: Routledge, 2020).

25. Castells, *The Information Age*; World Economic Forum, *New Vision for Education: Unlocking the Potential of Technology* (Vancouver, BC: British Columbia Teachers' Federation, 2015)

26. Vygotsky, Lev, "Interaction Between Learning and Development," in *Mind in Society: The Development of Higher Psychological Processes*, ed. Michael Cole Vera John-Steiner, Sylvia Scribner, and Ellen Souberman, 79–91 (Cambridge, MA: Harvard University Press, 1978).

27. Keeley, Brian, and Céline Little, *The State of the World's Children 2017: Children in a Digital World* (Paris: UNICEF, 2017).

28. Rideout, Victoria, and Michael B. Robb, *The Common Sense Census: Media Use by Kids Age Zero to Eight* (San Francisco: Common Sense Media, 2020).

29. Livingstone, Sonia, Daniel K. Winther, and Marium Hussein, *Global Kids Online Comparative Report: Innocenti Research Report* (Paris: UNICEF, 2019).

30. Lauricella, Alexis R., Courtney K. Blackwell, and Ellen Wartella, "The 'New' Technology Environment: The Role of Content and Context on Learning and Development from Mobile Media," in *Media Exposure During Infancy and Early Childhood*, 1–23 (New York: Springer, 2017).

31. Takeuchi, Lori, and Reed Stevens, *The New Coviewing: Designing for Learning Through Joint Media Engagement* (New York: The Joan Ganz Cooney Center at Sesame Workshop, 2011).

32. Barron, Brigid, and Amber Levinson, "Media as a Catalyst for Children's Engagement in Learning at Home and Across Settings," in *Children and Families in the Digital Age: Learning Together in a Media Saturated Culture*, ed. Elizabeth Gee, Lori Takeuchi, and Ellen Wartella, 17–36 (New York: Routledge, 2017).

33. Barron, Brigid, Caitlin Kennedy Martin, Lori Takeuchi, and Rachel Fithian, "Parents as Learning Partners in the Development of Technological Fluency," *International Journal of Learning and Media* 1, no. 2 (2009): 55–77.

34. Katz, Vikki S., *Kids in the Middle: How Children of Immigrants Negotiate Community Interactions for Their Families* (New Brunswick, NJ: Rutgers University Press, 2014).

35. Yip, Jason C., Carmen Gonzalez, and Vikki Katz, "Children of Immigrants' Experience in Online Information Brokering," *Children and Families in the Digital Age: Learning Together in a Media Saturated Culture* (2017): 137–152.

36. Levinson, Amber Maria, "Latino Immigrant Families Bridging Home and School Learning with Technology," in *Children and Families in the Digital Age: Learning Together in a Media Saturated Culture*, ed. Elisabeth Gee, Lori Takeuchi, and Ellen Wartella, 174–191 (New York: Routledge, 2017).

37. Katz, *Kids in the Middle*; Rogoff, Barbara, *The Cultural Nature of Human Development* (Oxford: Oxford University Press, 2003).

38. Livingstone, Sonia, Kjartan Ólafsson, Ellen J. Helsper, Francisco Lupiáñez-Villanueva, Giuseppe A. Veltri, and Frans Folkvord, "Maximizing Opportunities and Minimizing Risks for Children Online: The Role of Digital Skills in Emerging Strategies of Parental Mediation," *Journal of Communication* 67 (2017): 82–105.

39. Livingstone, Sonia, Kjartan Ólafsson, Ellen J. Helsper, Francisco Lupiáñez-Villanueva, Giuseppe A. Veltri, and Frans Folkvord, *Global Kids Online*.

40. Pasnik, Shelley, and Carlin Llorente, *Preschool Teachers Can Use a PBS KIDS Transmedia Curriculum Supplement to Support Young Children's Mathematics Learning: Results of a Randomized Controlled Trial. Summative Evaluation of the CPB-PBS Ready To Learn Initiative* (Waltham, MA: Education Development Center, 2013).

41. Cole, Charlotte F., June H. Lee, Abigail Bucuvalas, and Yasemin Sırali, "Seven Essential Elements for Creating Effective Children's Media to Promote Peacebuilding: Lessons from International Coproductions of Sesame Street and Other Children's Media Programs," in *Towards a More Peaceful World: The Promise of Early Child Development Programmes*, ed. James F. Leckman and Pia Britto, 55–69 (Medford, MA: New Directions for Child and Adolescent Development, 2018).

42. Levinson, "Latino Immigrant Families."

43. Heavner, Rachel, and Zev Lowe, *Reading Programs in The Digital Age: The Case for Format Neutrality* (San Francisco: World Reader Global Insights, 2017).

44. Roque, Ricarose, "Building Projects, Building Relationships: Designing for Family Learning," in *Designing Constructionist Futures: The Art, Theory, and Practice of Learning Designs*, ed. Nathan Holberg, Matthew Berland, and Yasmin Kafai (Cambridge, MA: MIT Press, 2020).

45. Secretary's Commission on Achieving Necessary Skills, *What Work Requires of Schools: A SCANS Report for America 2000* (Washington, DC: U.S. Department of Labor, 1991).

46. Levy, Frank, and Richard J. Murnane, "Education and the Changing Job Market," *Educational Leadership* 62, no. 2 (2004): 80–84; National Research Council, *Identifying and Supporting Productive STEM Programs in Out-of-School Settings* (Washington, DC: National Research Council, 2015).

47. Technology in less affluent schools often features "individualized" progression through workbook-type activities; phonics, grammar and punctuation exercises; drills on math items; and practice with multiple choice test questions. Although these approaches may support some aspects of learning, they are very different than those offered by simulations, content creation, data analysis, or writing that is part of interactive learning, where the technology is used to engage with data, explore and create, express ideas, and develop presentations of learning;

and where peer discussions and teacher-led activities are also part of instruction. See Darling-Hammond, Linda, Molly B. Zielezinski, and Shelley Goldman, *Using Technology to Support At-Risk Students' Learning* (Washington, DC: Alliance for Excellent Education, 2014).

48. Jenkins, Henry, *Confronting the Challenges of Participatory Culture: Media Education for the 21st Century* (Cambridge: MIT Press, 2009).

49. Aragon, Cecilia, and Katie Davis, *Writers in the Secret Garden: Fanfiction, Youth, and New Forms of Mentoring* (Cambridge, MA: MIT Press, 2019).

50. Hargittai, Eszter, "An Update on Survey Measures of Web-Oriented Digital Literacy," *Social Science Computer Review* 27 (2009): 130–137.

51. Engle, Randi, and Faith R. Conant, "Guiding Principles for Fostering Productive Disciplinary Engagement: Explaining an Emergent Argument in a Community of Learners Classroom," *Cognition and Instruction* 20, no. 4 (2002): 399–483.

52. National Research Council. *Identifying and Supporting Productive STEM Programs in Out-of-School Settings* (Washington, DC: National Academies Press, 2015).

53. Sharples, Mike, Eileen Scanlon, Shaaron Ainsworth, Stamatina Anastopoulou, Trevor Collins, Charles Crook, Ann Jones, Lucinda Kerawalla, Karen Littleton, Paul Mulholland, and Claire O'Malley, "Personal Inquiry: Orchestrating Science Investigations Within and Beyond the Classroom," *Journal of the Learning Sciences* 24, no. 2 (2015): 308–341.

54. Patrichi, Mugurel, "Threats to Using Mass Collaboration in Education," in *Conference Proceedings of E-learning and Software for Education (eLSE)*, no. 01 (2011): 526–533.

55. Mirra and Garcia, "I Hesitate but I Do Have Hope."

56. Soep, Lisa, and Vivian Chávez, *Drop That Knowledge: Youth Radio Stories* (Oakland, CA: University of California Press, 2010), 49.

57. Barron, Brigid, "Interest and Self-Sustained Learning as Catalysts of Development: A Learning Ecology Perspective," *Human Development* 49, no. 4 (2006): 193–224; Nasir and Pea, eds., *Handbook of the Cultural Foundations of Learning* (New York: Routledge, 2020).

58. Bennett, Pamela, Amy C. Lutz, and Lakshmi Jayaram, "Beyond the Schoolyard: The Role of Parenting Logics, Financial Resources, and Social Institutions in the Social Class Gap in Structured Activity Participation," *Sociology of Education* 85, no. 2 (2012): 131–157; Chin, Tiffani, and Meredith Phillips, "Social Reproduction and Child-Rearing Practices: Social Class, Children's Agency, and the Summer Activity Gap," *Sociology of Education* 77, no. 3 (2004): 185–210; Duncan, Greg J., and Richard J. Murnane, *Restoring Opportunity: The Crisis of Inequality and the Challenge for American Education* (Cambridge, MA: Harvard Education Press, 2014).

59. Archer, Louise, Jennifer DeWitt, Jonathan Osborne, Justin Dillon, Beatrice Willis, and Billy Wong, "Science Aspirations, Capital, and Family Habitus: How Families Shape Children's Engagement and Identification with Science," *American Educational Research Journal* 49, no. 5 (2012): 881–908; Ben-Eliyahu, Adar, Jean E. Rhodes, and Peter Scales, "The Interest-Driven Pursuits of 15 Year Olds: 'Sparks' and Their Association with Caring Relationships and Developmental Outcomes," *Applied Developmental Science* 18, no. 2 (2014): 76–89.

60. Vossoughi, Shirin, and Bronwyn Bevan, "Making and Tinkering: A Review of the Literature," *National Research Council Committee on Out of School Time STEM* (2014): 1–55; Itō, Mizuko, Kris Gutiérrez, Sonia Livingstone, Bill Penuel, Jean Rhodes, Katie Salen, Juliet Schor, Julian Sefton-Green, and S. Craig Watkins, *Connected Learning: An Agenda for Research and Design* (Irvine, CA: Digital Media and Learning Research Hub, 2013).

61. Itō, Mizuko, Kris Gutiérrez, Sonia Livingstone, Bill Penuel, Jean Rhodes, Katie Salen, Juliet Schor, Julian Sefton-Green, and S. Craig Watkins, *Hanging Out, Messing Around, Geeking Out: Living and Learning with New Media* (Cambridge, MA: MIT Press, 2009); Itō et al., *Connected Learning: An Agenda for Research and Design.*

62. Pinkard, Nichole, and Kimberly Austin, "Digital Youth Network: Creating New Media Citizens through the Affinity Learning Model," *International Journal of Learning and Media* 2, no. 4 (2010).

63. Hetland, Lois, Ellen Winner, Shirley Veenema, and Kimberly M. Sheridan, *Studio Thinking 2: The Real Benefits of Visual Arts Education* (New York: Teachers College Press, 2015).

64. Azevedo, "The Tailored Practice of Hobbies."

65. Pinkard, Nichole, "Freedom of Movement: Defining, Researching, and Designing the Components of a Healthy Learning Ecosystem," *Human Development* 62, no. 1–2 (2019): 40–65.

66. Barron et al., "Parents as Learning Partners;" Ching, Dixie, Rafi Santo, Chris Hoadley, and Kylie Peppler, "On Ramps, Lane Changes, Detours and Destinations: Building Connected Learning Pathways in Hive NYC through Brokering Future Learning Opportunities," Hive NYC, https://www.researchgate.net/publication/282365450_On-Ramps_Lane_Changes_Detours _and_Destinations_Building_Connected_Learning_Pathways_in_Hive_NYC_through _Brokering_Future_Learning_Opportunities, accessed November 5, 2021.

67. Chetty, Raj, Nathaniel Hendren, Patrick Kline, and Emmanuel Saez, "Where is the Land of Opportunity? The Geography of Intergenerational Mobility in the United States," *Quarterly Journal of Economics* 129, no. 4 (2014): 1553–1623.

68. Gutiérrez, Kris, A. Susan Jurow, and Sepehr Vakil, "Social Design-Based Experiments: A Utopian Methodology for Understanding New Possibilities for Learning," in *Handbook of the Cultural Foundations of Learning*, ed. N. Nasir, C. Lee, and R. Pea, 195–211 (New York: Routledge, 2020).

69. Chandra, Sumit, Amy Chang, Lauren Day, Amina Fazlullah, Jack Liu, Lane McBride, Thisal Mudalige, and Danny Weiss, *Closing the K–12 Digital Divide in the Age of Distance Learning* (San Francisco: Common Sense Media, 2020).

70. de Royston, Maxine McKinney, Brigid Barron, Phillip Bell, et al., "Learning Pathways."

71. "COVID-19: Are Children Able to Continue Learning During School Closures," UNICEF, August 2020, https://data.unicef.org/resources/remote-learning-reachability-factsheet/.

72. McBurnie, Chris, Taskeen Adam, and Tom Kaye, "Is There Learning Continuity During the COVID-19 Pandemic? A Synthesis of the Emerging Evidence," *Journal of Learning Development* 7, no. 3 (2020), 485–493.

73. Darling-Hammond, Linda, Abby Schachner, and Adam K. Edgerton, *Restarting and Reinventing School: Learning in the Time of COVID and Beyond* (Palo Alto, CA: Learning Policy Institute, 2020); Stokes, Donald. E., *Pasteur's Quadrant: Basic Science and Technological Innovation* (Washington, DC: Brookings Institute Press, 1997).

19

IMPROVEMENT SCIENCE

The Social Glue that Helps Helpers Help?

LOUIS M. GOMEZ, MANUELITO BIAG, AND DAVID G. IMIG

The insights and proposals in this volume will require careful coordination and long-term collaborations among different stakeholders, including the research community, policy makers, faith leaders, the philanthropic sector, and, above all, education practitioners on the frontlines. Multisector stakeholder collaboration is at once essential and hard to achieve.[1] The available science, technology, and practice to reliably achieve cooperation and coordination is, at best, weak. We argue that the developing field of educational improvement science carried out in networks, along with other efforts that bear a family resemblance, can offer essential lessons and tools for the work of improving the quality of education in disparate settings.[2]

We contend that intellectual movements like improvement science create social glue that leads to infrastructures that engender cooperation and coordination and are foundational interpersonal and interorganizational resources for the improvement of quality goals in education.[3] As we conceive it, social glue generates within a locality mutual bonds of recognition and connectedness that span the boundaries of existing communities and organizations; in doing so, diverse people feel connected and experience a common purpose. For the Global Compact proposed by Pope Francis to make progress toward success, it will rely on accelerating the development of the social glue that binds people who aspire to be helpers together in shared intention and coordinated action, along with the people they seek to serve in the compact's mission.

COVID-19 AND THE CHALLENGE OF
COLLABORATIVE ENGAGEMENTS

The COVID-19 pandemic has gripped the world with death, untold suffering, and has contributed to the further widening of preexisting divides. For example, in the United States, the pandemic has been especially detrimental to economically disadvantaged communities and people of color. Recent data from the Bureau of Labor Statistics indicate that African American and Latinx workers were more likely to be unemployed than their white counterparts despite making up the disproportionate share of essential workers who had to remain on the job (e.g., grocery clerks, custodial staff).[4]

Chaotic policy responses to COVID-19 have also exacerbated inequalities in health outcomes by race/ethnicity and socioeconomic status. Recent studies on vaccination efforts suggest that groups most vulnerable to catching and dying from the virus are not receiving the most shots.[5] Researchers find that infection and death rates among African Americans are higher than their vaccination rates and that vaccine appointments are going largely to wealthier white residents in many cities instead of those populations living in under-resourced communities experiencing high numbers of COVID-19-related cases and deaths.

Among young people of color and those living in poverty, the sudden shuttering of schools is likely to cause disproportionate learning losses—particularly those already behind in their learning. For instance, low-income, minoritized students are less likely than their wealthier counterparts to have access to reliable internet connections for remote learning or devices that they do not need to share with siblings or other family members. COVID-19 has significantly disrupted many of the traditional structures and supports students need to succeed in school, such as strong relationships with teachers, mentors, and peers; academic and enrichment services; and safe and stable home environments.

From nation-states to local communities, we find in this global crisis an important message for all of us: learn to work together or perish. We are seeing how a common enemy, in this case, a virus, can devastate us if we do not collaborate and coordinate for a common purpose. In particular, those of us who aspire to support the social, emotional, and cognitive development of children and youth should take heed. Without robust tools and procedures to organize and work together, the world's educationally underserved will surely continue to be a sad testament to wasted human promise.

OPPORTUNITIES OF THE GLOBAL COMPACT FOR EDUCATION

Pope Francis's Global Compact for Education offers us an opportunity to work in partnership to address undereducation worldwide and especially in the metaphoric Global South. Taking up this opportunity is more than a matter of aspiration. It is hard, fundamental work that requires foundational resources. It is fundamental work because it requires that we do what is, at the same time, the easiest of human endeavors—working with others. The COVID-19 near-global stay-at-home orders compelled people all over the planet to find new ways to be together while apart. Although it is easy and desired to be in the company of others, it is a different matter to create concerted arrangements of people who work together intentionally on a shared problem. In our judgment, this latter task demands powerful interpersonal tools and perspectives not in wide use today in the service of education. As such, this chapter seeks to examine the work and resources it might take to help all of us who want to work better together to be more coordinated and collaborative helpers with a shared desire for improvement.

The compact seeks to attack problems of equity, access, and quality. While we know that schooled societies offer undeniable benefits, such as longer life, societal and intergenerational wealth, and well-being, better systems to effectively educate the world's most disadvantaged people have largely eluded us. Even though governmental and nongovernmental organizations, private industry, and the general citizenry share an aspiration to formal schooling with quality for all, we have collectively failed to provide equity in opportunity, access, and quality for all—despite the billions of dollars that have already been spent in its service.

Marshaling diverse human resources to remove access and quality as barriers is the task that Pope Francis sets before us. Rallying people to work together is the perennial challenge. Those of us who seek to help—educators, designers, policy makers, social service managers, healthcare providers, and other stakeholders—could be more effective if we partnered together. We posit that developing a useful and usable practical infrastructure that enables us to work together is essential to the compact's success. The collective energy of helpers—both indigenous (or Global South) helpers as well as those from the Global North—may be the most potent wellspring for improvement that we currently have at our disposal. We are given to believe that people can accomplish more together than even the best of us can accomplish by working alone.[6]

Collectively, we can learn from each other and build our knowledge to respond to the needs of humanity. Yet, how do we intentionally build knowledge together?

According to Hecker, there are at least three primary components to the act of collective knowledge building: information sharing, information coordination, and externalization of knowledge in tools and artifacts.[7] Collective knowledge-building to solve complex problems involves these three components working together and acting synergistically. Consider Wenger's example, where one mechanic notices a bit of unexplained oil on the tarmac while another reports that a hydraulic light on the plane is engaged.[8] This example is not unlike the science teacher who greets students who she knows are without permanent physical homes. She observes how they often appear sluggish and hungry when they arrive at school. Her colleague, a math teacher, observes that these same children are more likely to be disruptive in math class. Just as the mechanics can engage together in synergistic problem solving with the right social systems in place, these teachers would be able to design more effective learning environments for all of their students.

Despite the promise of impact, when we work together at the individual level[9] and the organizational level,[10] far too often the obvious stakeholder to a problem fails to avail herself of the collective advantage—what Hobbes in his sixteenth-century text *Leviathan* and more recently others have called the "collective wisdom" or "shared expertise."[11] An infrastructure for individuals to work and learn together can be seen in contemporary examples, such as Doctors Without Borders, which provide the coordination and communications scaffolding for medical professionals to quickly form teams and collaborate on health. Likewise, large engineering consortia provide coordination and communication scaffolding to create engineering marvels, such as aircraft and massive oceangoing vessels. We are hard-pressed to find a plethora of these kinds of examples in any field, but they are especially hard to find in education.

CREATING SOCIAL GLUE

In this chapter, we explore interpersonal coordination and communications infrastructure, which, we suggest, determine why we as stakeholders to problems in education fail to work together more regularly to solve pressing problems of practice. Examples of how we might leverage collective advantage are difficult to find in multicausal problem spaces because, as Senge suggests, these problem spaces are complex, often large, and unwieldy.[12] This multicausal fog compels us, as individuals as well as in our institutional silos, to have problem-solving myopia. We are attracted to and latch on to aspects of a problem that are most comfortable for us, perhaps because of previous experiences and our developed expertise. An infrastructure that corrects our natural intellectual nearsighted-ness needs to, on the one hand, allow us to communicate the perspective we hold. On the other hand, this infrastructure should encourage problem solvers—both local and external—to communicate and organize the different perspectives and values that they hold. Most importantly, such an infrastructure should make val-ues and held doctrine visible to all stakeholders. While they may come to shared values, the first essential step is mutual recognition.

In the sense we mean it here, an interpersonal coordination and communi-cations infrastructure should have the properties of what Churchill calls social glue.[13] Social glue is a property of contexts where feelings of social connec-tion are strengthened through shared experience. The word *glue* emphasizes joining, adhering, and the fixing and cementing together of things that would otherwise be separate, such as problem solvers who have different perspec-tives on the same problem. Social glue brings people together and holds them fast in some social dynamic. Conduits, such as shared narratives of a common experience of pain or trauma[14] or ritual behaviors like those that occur among people with shared diasporic forms of participation,[15] can provide social glue to engender routines and activity structures with organized groups of people.[16] In turn, these ritualized environments can provide fertile ground for coordinated activity, learning, and innovation.[17]

It is important to note that social glue is related to but not the same as social capital.[18] Social glue inheres to both physical and technological environments, while social capital is composed of the specific set of interpersonal relation-ships that create value for individuals. Environments with social glue may help to develop capital for those who use them. It seems to us that for initiatives like the compact to be successful, they need to attend to catalyzing work environ-ments that place a premium on providing social glue and a sense of common purpose to the helpers who seek to work together.

THE HELPER'S CHALLENGE:
ENGAGING VOICE AND AGENCY

The inability to create the social glue necessary to work successfully is, perhaps, most evident when we think of stakeholder engagement. Some stakeholders suffer from losing or never attaining a sense of voice—the ability to represent a perspective effectively—as well as agency—the ability to act consequentially. Frequently, those engaged in the work lose sight of the need to attend to resident needs and aspirations.

INNOVATIONS MISSING THE MARK:
SESAME STREET AND KHAN ACADEMY

Untapped voice and agency can be observed in the things we make to help other people. Humans are inveterate inventors. Faced with a challenge, we create things to meet the demands at hand. Education and the inequities and challenges it presents are no different. Consider, for example, *Sesame Street,* one of the earliest innovations designed to bolster literacy development among disadvantaged children. Although hailed as a general success, in its early incarnations Sesame *Street* did not reach those for whom it was originally intended. While middle- and upper-middle-class families used *Sesame Street* extensively, it was underutilized by those in their target demographic, which were lower-income, inner-city children and families that did not leverage television for educational programming.[19]

Another example is Khan Academy, a well-conceived innovation that seeks to extend access to high-quality instructional materials. As an educational website with thousands of videos and other resources, Khan Academy allows anyone interested, as its tagline puts it, to "learn almost anything—for free." Khan Academy holds the promise of revolutionary power for some of the world's most disadvantaged students. Recognizing this, companies such as Comcast cable television and internet services have partnered with Khan Academy in the Comcast Internet Essentials Program to bring affordable internet service to low-income families.[20] By doing so, students can access Khan Academy's resources and other applications to help cross the digital divide.

While a study of the use of Khan Academy reports positive reception by teachers and students, it also reports significant variation across sites.[21] In addition, data suggest that a majority of teachers believed that Khan Academy would be most useful for their most advanced students and not the disadvantaged populations they were hoping to serve. For example, only 25 percent of teachers reported that Khan Academy resources would be effective with students who lag most behind their age group in mathematics. Perhaps, more often than we would naively expect, innovations like *Sesame Street* and Khan Academy, which are designed to assist those most in need, often experience underuse or potentially detrimental use.

The foregoing examples are not unique. In education, as in other fields, we find promising innovations that fail to have an impact on the important constituents for which they were designed. One challenge that leads to mismatches like these is that designers, as helpers, fail to engage the voices of and provide agency to key constituents. Voice, and making sure that it is engaged, is perhaps at the center of what it means to genuinely help. After all, helping is a dialectic. In complex social settings, such as schools, teachers cannot teach unless learners are engaged and take part in the learning. Writing about healthcare, Biggs argues that patients are experts in the consumption of care.[22] By analogy, we suggest that one can view students, particularly those who have experienced many years of schooling, as experts in the consumption of instruction. It follows then that designers, as helpers, should find ways to enlist students (or their representatives) in crafting innovative solutions to leverage platforms like *Sesame Street* or Khan Academy to the problems of teaching and learning.

To illustrate, in the process of developing *Sesame Street*, the caregivers of disadvantaged students are the sort of helpers who may have been silenced or never provided an opportunity to share their perspectives. A part of the responsibility of helpers is to engage a diverse colleagueship of voices. This is only possible if helpers have working environments within which social glue is attended. In the learning sciences, for instance, perhaps the most direct route to engage the user's voice is through user participation in acts of design and with intentionality in the use of designed artifacts. While cataloging the many forms that engaging user participation can take is beyond the scope of this chapter,[23] what is certain is that design that aims to create an equitable, problem-centered space for voice must, from the onset, have the means to enlist all interested and necessary voices to the work. Without this recognition, helpers are drawn into the trap of designing solutions primarily informed by the aspect of the problem that the most powerful members of the colleagueship perceive.

So too with agency, successful helper-colleagueships provide opportunities for active access to craft the artifacts and tools that enable their work across the partnership. When most helpers are agentive, potential helpers are effectively engaged in the consequential work of helping. For example, residents from historically marginalized communities, who may not have conventional scholarly credentials that certify the ability to engage in the work of change, can effectively engage in helper-colleagueship. Locals have legitimately acquired knowledge gained through first-hand experiences, or what Moll[24] and others have characterized as funds of knowledge.[25] We have seen examples of how deference to outside experts, who have little to no familiarity with the local context, has impeded positive transformation. By contrast, engaging the funds of knowledge of indigenous constituents can help provide social glue, offering an important interpersonal opportunity to allow the agentive potential to unfold.

ENGAGING COMMUNITY AGENCY: THE CINCINNATI CHILDREN'S HOSPITAL

An example of a positively engaging community agency can be found in the community improvement work currently underway in Cincinnati, Ohio. In a partnership between Cincinnati Children's Hospital and local community grandmothers from low-income communities near the hospital, the grandmothers are a recognized collective that has a preexisting role in the care and positive development of neighborhood children. As helpers, Cincinnati Children's Hospital staff formed a group they called the Caring Families Reading Bears, tapping into the agentive potential of grandmothers as reading teachers. Together, they have brought books into a variety of community spaces, including churches, hair salons, barbershops, and local homes.

It is important to recognize that Cincinnati Children's Hospital, as a helper, has created opportunities for voice and local contribution—specifically, for the grandmothers to emerge as a critical peer helping class. These types of community examples underscore the need to know how to create the social glue that, in this case, binds hospital professionals and grandmothers into a coordinated colleagueship. Collectives like the Caring Families Reading Bears do not happen by accident. Rather, the infrastructure afforded social arrangements that set the conditions for coordinated action among diverse partners.

In the sections that follow, we consider educational improvement science, carried out in networks, as an infrastructure that might engender social glue.[26] We turn to improvement science because it is undergirded by a perspective that offers voice and agency to those on the front lines of work (i.e., the helpers). Improvement science also consists of methods, tools, and protocols meant to guide practice step-by-step. By way of examples, we examine improvement science at play in rural schools in Chile to accelerate achievement for the poorest children. We also describe a partnership arrangement and the factors and conditions that support the arrangement, which allow universities and school districts in the United States to effectively prepare leaders that can help children from disadvantaged urban neighborhoods succeed in school.

SOCIAL INFRASTRUCTURES AND TOOLS: HELPING THE HELPERS

Typically, when we discuss infrastructure, we refer to the physical systems of a business or nation, such as its transportation, communication, sewage, water, and electric systems. Each, in its own way, provides the technical basis for a business, city, or nation to be operationally connected and whole. By contrast, social infrastructures allow people at various organizational levels to be socially connected and whole. Social infrastructures house and maintain social relationships by supporting formal and informal connections through meetings and convening structures. Social infrastructures provide a means to make explicit how values, such as mutual respect and accountability, are enacted in the social settings that are under its purview. The social infrastructure helps to keep roles, role groups, and their interaction in view.

In the Cincinnati Children's Hospital case, for instance, the social infrastructure gives prominence to governing interaction among different role groups, including physicians, social service agents, and grandmothers. In general, social infrastructure helps to put in place, and maintain, the social ground rules. When physical infrastructures are in place, people build tools that use and take advantage of them. Infrastructures and the tools that use them are cogenerative. To wit, roads as infrastructure coevolved with the vehicles, as tools, that use them. Similarly, social infrastructures coevolve with the tools that use them (e.g., meeting protocols). Schools that house professional learning communities might evolve routine ways to build agendas, manage standards, or capture instructional progress from one meeting to the next. This kind of coevolving is mutually reinforcing, where tools shape infrastructure and infrastructure shape tools. What we call social glue is the substrate that allows this expanse of collaboration and coordination to grow.

A set of methods including networked improvement science,[27] implementation science,[28] and design-based implementation research are beginning to take hold in districts and schools throughout the United States.[29] We conjecture that these methodologies and the tools that accompany them are creating a new social glue among a diverse set of school professionals. They are growing alongside some of the more established infrastructures that have been optimized over the past three decades of school reform around making visible which interventions are effective in helping students learn and which are not. Beginning in 2002, the "what works" social infrastructure was organized around tools, such as randomized field trials. By contrast, these newer approaches are organized around being able to discern the *how, where,* and *who* of innovation efficacy and utility. These newer social infrastructures are optimized to see iterative development rather than summative judgment. For purposes of illustration, we describe below how educational improvement science in the context of networks is shaping infrastructure.

SIX CORE PRINCIPLES OF IMPROVEMENT TO GUIDE SOCIAL INFRASTRUCTURE

Educational improvement science is organized around six core principles.

1. *Make the work problem-specific and user-centered.* It starts with a single question: "What specifically is the problem we are trying to solve?" It enlivens a codevelopment orientation: engage key participants early and often.

2. *Variation in performance is the core problem to address.* The critical issue is not what works but rather what works, for whom, and under what set of conditions. Aim to advance efficacy and reliability at scale.

3. *See the system that produces the current outcomes.* It is hard to improve what you do not fully understand. Go and see how local conditions shape work processes. Make your hypotheses for change public and clear.

4. *We cannot improve at scale what we cannot measure.* Embed measures of key outcomes and processes to track if the change is an improvement. We intervene in complex organizations. Anticipate and measure unintended consequences.

5. *Anchor practice improvement in disciplined inquiry.* Engage in rapid cycles of plan, do, study, act (PDSA) cycles to learn and fail fast and improve quickly. That failure may occur is not the problem; that we fail to learn from it is.

6. *Accelerate improvements through networked communities.* Embrace the wisdom of crowds. We can accomplish more together than even the best of us can accomplish alone.

FIGURE 19.1 Six core principles of improvement.

Source: Bryk, Anthony S., Louis M. Gomez, Alicia Grunow, and Paul G. LeMahieu, *Learning to Improve: How America's Schools Can Get Better at Getting Better* (Cambridge, MA: Harvard Education Press, 2015).

For us, these six principles (figure 19.1) have an air of necessity about them. There may be more principles that could be added, but we believe these six are necessary to engender the social glue for helpers to evolve an infrastructure that is both inclusive of stakeholders and helpful. Looking across these six principles, they address both voice and agency. The first principle, being problem-centered and user-focused, puts voice front and center. In an educational setting, users can include students, teachers, administrators, family members, and other youth-serving individuals. A user-centered strategy is premised on the idea that those who face problems day-to-day are the ones who best understand them and, therefore, are most likely to hold the keys to their answer. Accordingly, a user-centered approach holds promise in creating democratic and desirable solutions that work in context and endure over time.

In addition to taking the user environment earnestly, the social infrastructure must take users' funds of knowledge seriously. The voices and experiences of users should shape the center of conversations among collectives of helpers. Improvement science has evolved the use of tools, such as empathy interviews, in-context observations, and journey maps, among other ethnographic methods to keep users' voices, interests, and concerns in focus.[30] The aim of these user-centered approaches is to understand, as best as possible, a person's thoughts, emotions, and motivations and to determine how to bring the individual's voice into the design conversation.

As a companion, the second core improvement principle—attention to variation—encourages helpers to see that what appears to be reasoning about the problem for one kind of stakeholder is not the same process or approach for another. Thus, attending to variation encourages helpers to both expand their collectives to more diverse stakeholders and understand that a solution that seems to have traction in one community may need modification in another.

Like improvement science principles 1 and 2, seeing the system (principle 3) encourages helpers to look to the dynamics among users, their range of motivations and settings, to see the multicausal nature of the problems they confront. We noted above that most of us who are helpers are compelled to see a complex problem from our own perspective. This third principle encourages us to break free from this tendency. Improvement science also provides analytic tools, such as process mapping, to help us better understand a system and how its interrelated components operate to produce the results it gets.[31]

Giving voice to the whole user experience is another key aspect of improvement science as social infrastructure. We know that the work of teachers is embedded within larger complex social structures. Classrooms are situated within schools that have their own identities, cultures, and climate issues. Schools are embedded within districts focused on reform initiatives to meet accountability demands. Districts operate within communities wrestling with unique challenges—from poverty to crime to unemployment. We know that many urban systems are characterized by a high turnover of leadership and staff that can impede the ability of stakeholders to scale and sustain change efforts. As such, considering the forces within each of these domains and how they interact to influence the work that happens inside classrooms is critical for meaningful and lasting improvement to take place.

System change is often iterative and incremental in nature. The fourth and fifth improvement principles attend to this aspect of developing social infrastructure and, in so doing, they underscore opportunities for the collective to take agency. Measurement (principle 4) is the only way to know if an intended change has been achieved or that a collective of helpers is making progress toward it. This fourth principle envisions measurement residing squarely in the hands of all the helpers in a collective rather than with central authorities like school district central offices that tend to be outside the purview of front-line helpers like teachers. When measurement capacity is remote from the frontlines, measurement systems can become punitive.

When measures of accountability become outsized and detached, educators can respond in ways that are maladaptive for learning and improvement. Nichols and Berliner observe such maladaptation when teachers focus instruction on the "bubble kids"—those who are really close to a test norm—at the expense of other students (especially children at the bottom and very top of the achievement distribution).[32] We imagine these kinds of distortions of proper instructional values are less likely when measurement capacity is in the hands of frontline workers and focused on continuous improvement rather than administrative accountability.

Educational improvement science also has, in its toolkit of support for the efforts of leveraging collective agency, the PDSA cycle.[33] The PDSA is a tool that provides the scaffolding for small-scale, iterative development of changes. It is emblematic of principle 5 and an element of social infrastructure that confers agency. PDSAs enable rapid assessments and provide helpers with the flexibility to adapt efforts, responding to the improvement knowledge gained. While seemingly a simple and straightforward model, PDSAs are multifaceted and consist of interdependent steps shaped by local circumstances. PDSAs encourage helpers to think more deeply about changes they envision, and from the perspective of social infrastructure, who ought to be involved in the change effort to maximize the likelihood of the change being successful.[34] The disciplined inquiry prefigured by this fifth principle involves a kind of cascading involvement on the part of helpers. As a collective learns more about a change and that change is extended to more settings, the circle of helpers who join the work should also expand. If, for example, an innovation seems positive in one or two schools, it might then expand to five or ten schools. In that case, the team of frontline testers is also envisioned to expand.

Undoubtedly, educational improvement is a collective undertaking. The sixth principle of improvement views educators as working together in networks, which affirm the value of human work in helping all students learn across varied social, economic, political, and cultural circumstances. To accomplish this aspiration, principle 6 sees voice and agency working in tandem across distributed sites, inside one organization or in multiple organizations, operating together to discern the best way to move forward. Moreover, as part of the social infrastructure, networks encourage stakeholders to focus not only on the technical aspects of problems but also on their effects on real people.

We suspect network diversity serves to make stakeholders' concerns more transparent and evident—in essence, in full view for helpers. Networks like Un Buen Comienzo, which we describe below, are powerful precisely because of diversity, interdependence, and genuine and spontaneous cross group communication.[35] These factors may keep helpers concentrated on the real concerns of stakeholders.

UN BUEN COMIENZO

The improvement network Un Buen Comienzo (A Good Start) is a case of a third-party nongovernmental organization (NGO) called Fundación Educacional Oportunidad (FEO). FEO is a social infrastructure comprised of over a hundred disadvantaged rural and urban school organizations in the VI region of Chile working together to address a national problem of providing effective early learning educational opportunities to children. The work of Un Buen Comienzo is one of infrastructure building—more than a decade of developing improvement science expertise focused on tackling some of Chile's most vexing social problems. FEO took up the early educational opportunity problem as a disciplined quality improvement effort.[36] While the effort is in its early stages, just under three years old, the work is noteworthy as an example of an organization blending insights from scholarship, improvement science, and on-the-ground resident expertise to support children's learning. They have created a social infrastructure capable of bringing diverse people together energized by the use of quality improvement tools to address longstanding problems in early childhood education.

FEO understood from extant research that for young children to make progress (1) there should be adequate time on task; (2) children must attend school regularly; and (3) a sharp focus on early literacy must be present in teaching and learning, especially quality interactions between teachers and children. They also recognize that they needed to both to determine if these issues are at play in local Chilean communities in early childhood teaching and learning contexts and whether school locals recognize these as problems that they experienced and wished to correct.

Among the earliest efforts of FEO was to help community members identify for themselves that at least one of these problems was evident and faced in their schools. FEO helped locals see and name for themselves concerns such as chronic absenteeism, ineffective use of time, inadequate focus on literacy in their schools, and lack of quality interactions. It is noteworthy that FEO is bringing this analytic capacity to educational contexts where historically and currently, there are scarce social and fiscal resources. In the network, over 70 percent of the schools can be described as having high social vulnerability.

FEO constructed a preparation regime that taught local Chilean school leaders, teachers, and parents to use improvement science tools. For example, they jointly built a theory using a quality improvement tool—a driver diagram[37]—and helped schools engage in PDSA cycles to test whether their approaches to improvement were helping schools to make progress in absenteeism, teacher time on task, literacy, and effective interactions. Traditionally, NGOs and helpers have built programs for the people they aim to help, but FEO helpers actively engaged local actors to become active agents in their own contexts.

Early results suggest that these efforts are paying off. Un Bien Comienzo was able to make progress on the core problems that users face. The schools in the network were able to share and help one another make disciplined progress. For instance, figure 19.2 displays their instructional time results. In one academic year, 80 percent of teachers improved, and 50 percent of teachers met their instructional goals of having 80 percent of instructional-focused classroom time.

Similarly, figure 19.3 shows that upwards of 80 percent of pre-kindergarten and kindergarten students significantly showed increases in language proficiency. In all, the work of Un Buen Comienzo underscores the universality and

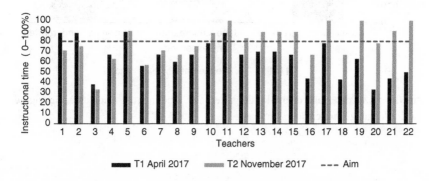

FIGURE 19.2 Percentage of time focused on instructional tasks, by teacher.

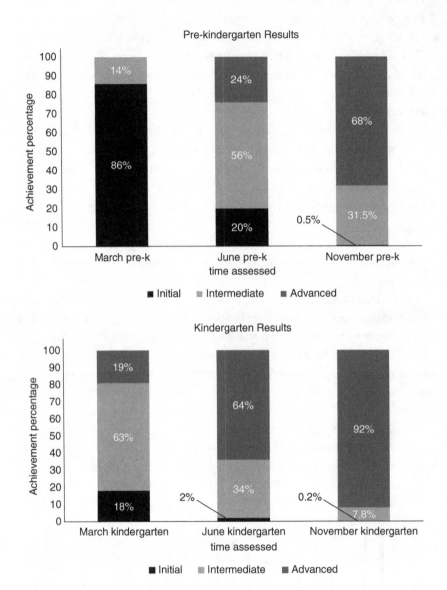

FIGURE 19.3 Percentage of pre-kindergarten and kindergarten students achieving advanced language proficiency.

power of improvement science–energized social infrastructures that coordinate the work of diverse stakeholders to spur positive change in settings with high social vulnerability.

Next, we take up a case from the United States where a disciplined and improvement-centered infrastructure is part of the force that brought together two large institutions, a public university and an urban school district, and the helpers that reside within them to better serve children in the city of Chicago.

THE CHICAGO PUBLIC SCHOOLS AND UNIVERSITY OF ILLINOIS AT CHICAGO ILEAD PARTNERSHIP

Preparing leaders with improvement know-how requires more productive partnerships between institutions of higher education (IHEs) and their local education agency (LEA) partners.[38] For these types of arrangements among diverse partners to thrive, a viable social infrastructure needs to exist. A partnership between the Chicago Public Schools (CPS) and the University of Illinois at Chicago (UIC) is noteworthy because they sustained a relationship that created a social infrastructure that prepares leaders who can effectively educate children from some of that city's most challenged neighborhoods. The CPS-UIC partnership has been in the business of creating a new social infrastructure for more than seventeen years. We focus on this collective to exemplify the profound institutional change that a collective social infrastructure can catalyze.

The CPS-UIC partnership illustrates a social infrastructure that uses improvement science-centered thinking to develop mutual dependency and interests in a diverse collective. Here, people who aim to help educate Chicago's children have effectively stretched the responsibility of school leadership preparation across two organizations. They have demonstrated that their collective wisdom can lead to a deep transformation at the core of universities and public school districts, which, in turn, can stimulate disruptive institutional change. Change of this sort involves faculty collectively and explicitly uniting theory and practice in a manner that focuses on a praxis of equity. This partnership required collective action and institutional change.[39]

The Chicago partnership is one of a family of similar efforts initiated by the Carnegie Foundation for the Advancement of Teaching called iLEAD.[40] The iLEAD network is presently made up of eleven district-university partnerships from across the United States. These partnerships were selected by the Carnegie Foundation based on their expressed commitment to improvement science, evidence of support from leadership and peers within their respective institutions, and willingness to build and sustain a collaborative community. CPS and UIC are vital members of iLEAD, even though their partnership predates the network's founding in 2017.

ILEAD'S DEVELOPMENTAL PROGRESSIONS FRAMEWORK

As a tool to support helpers to forecast and document the development of their social infrastructure, the CPS-UIC partnership is utilizing the iLEAD network's developmental progressions framework. The progressions are a working tool that members can use to enhance their communications within and among partnership groupings. These progressions identify twenty-four areas of work across the IHE, LEA, and partnership domains (table 19.1) to which district-university partnerships must attend and build the elements of infrastructure necessary to institutionalize an improvement approach in leadership development and solve local problems.

Each of the twenty-four dimensions in the developmental progressions exists on a continuum, where growth is characterized as "piloting," "emerging," "articulating," and "institutionalizing." For instance, in the area of "learning to improve," a partnership at the emerging phase would be involved in "exploring how to work together using improvement science/networked improvement communities (NICs)," while a partnership at the institutionalizing phase is "documenting and jointly reviewing evidence from a quality improvement system" and using this evidence to plan the next set of improvement cycles for the partnership.

IHEs and LEAs use the developmental progressions framework to periodically self-assess where their local efforts have resulted in substantial development and where they remain in the early stages of work. The progressions regulate the communication and actions within and across partnerships. For example, the progressions have been used as a network-wide tool to identify the development of partnership progress across key dimensions; where they seek to focus efforts and resources; and how partnerships might be grouped together to advance common aims (e.g., creating a regional hub focused on leadership development).

TABLE 19.1 Description of the domains and areas of work in the developmental progressions framework

Domain	Area of work	Working description
Partnership	Partnership relationships	Cultivation of partnership relationships built around active joint work and characterized by positive attitudes and strong bonds of trust
	Joint development of targeted problems of practice	Joint identification of one or more problems of practice that can focus EdD and/or masters students' capstones
	Formalizing partnership data agreement	Establishment of formal agreements around data collection and data sharing to support improvement efforts
	Learning to improve	Joint development of a continuous quality improvement system that capture, consolidate, and use data and evidence for ongoing improvement
	Formalizing a joint LEA-IHE "new leaders development program"	LEA cohort participation in IHE programs as central to the development of place-based and problem-focused district leadership
	A shared partnership narrative	Development of a shared narrative and set of norms
	Public communications	Communication about partnership improvement work is part of both the IHE and LEA communications program
Local education agencies	District leadership engagement	Active engagement of district leadership in improvement science (IS)/networked improvement communities (NICs) and partnership work
	Professional development of district staff	IS/NICs training for teachers and leaders is a standard part of professional development offerings
	Implementation of improvement science (IS)/ networked improvement communities (NICs)	IS/NICs are integrated into planning processes and utilized to make measurable improvements in local problems of practice
	IS and networks as district policy	IS/NICs are integral to strategy and policy conversations among district leadership

(continued)

TABLE 19.1 (*continued*)

Domain	Area of work	Working description
	Funding support	External funding stream(s) are secured and internal resources are properly allocated to support partnership work and participation
	IS/NICs expertise integrated into promotion and hiring decisions	Recognition of IS/NICs expertise in hiring, development, and promotion strategies
	Broadening stakeholder engagement	Strategies exist to actively include students, parents, and community stakeholders in improvement efforts
Institutions of higher education (IHEs)	Commitment to the idea of IS/ NICs	Active faculty engagement in IS/NICs and recognition of IS/NICs as departmental or divisional priority
	Curriculum/ program development	Integration of IS/NICs into curriculum, ranging from the adaptation of discrete courses to the development of a coherent program of study
	Faculty development and promotion	Supports exist for developing faculty improvement capability, and there is recognition of IS/NIC work in promotion and tenure policies
	Faculty engagement	Active, regular, and supported faculty engagement in IS/NICs
	IS as a signature pedagogy	Recognition of IS as a signature pedagogy
	Institutional leadership commitment	Active support from dean(s) cabinet and public recognition of IS/NICs as a distinctive contribution
	Institutional and state approvals	Resolution of possible issues around institutional and state approvals on courses, programs, and accreditation
	Scholarship of improvement: an academic community is forming	Presentation of improvement research in scholarly venues and publications
	IHE as a support hub for improvement networks	Development of IHE capacity to serve as a network hub
	A new professional education narrative	Development of an institutionally recognized and broadly owned narrative

Source: Data from Al Bertani, Louis Gomez, Michael Hanson, Randy Hitz, David Imig, and Steve Tozer. Improvement Leadership Education & Development (iLead) Nework. Palo Alto, CA: Carnegie Foundation for the Advancement of Teaching. https://www.carnegiefoundation.org/our-work/ilead/

In the language of the developmental progressions, perhaps Chicago's most significant change was in their collective narrative about *who* the work of the partnership was essentially organized to serve. They determined that the primary clientele of the partnership's work was not graduate students who were seeking a credential but Chicago Public School students who deserve committed and capable school leaders. This switch in frame for the partnership was transformative. Among other things, it meant that the school district and university now had the same client focus. This mutuality in understanding and commitment made cross institution communication vastly easier. It is a concrete example of unifying praxis.

The CPS-UIC partnership put the life outcomes of thousands of Chicago children as the focus of their work rather than follow the path of far too many leadership preparation regimes that consider the adults in front of them as the primary clientele, regardless of whether the leadership preparation program is centered in universities or local education agencies. Members of this collaborative will, of course, see the import of the adult leadership aspirant in a classroom or in a practicum, moment by moment, as the focus of the work. However, the north star of the partnership is the pre-kindergarten to high school student.

Such a north star leads to basic changes in the ways that both the school district and the university engage in the business of improvement. In the case of the university, helpers formed a new Center for Urban Education Leadership to focus efforts on funding a team of leadership coaches and researchers committed to the study of the program's impact on schools. In addition, the university replaced the master's program in educational administration with an education doctorate (EdD) program. This change meant that they could develop the school-leader-candidates during the preservice and novice years of school leadership over a minimum four-year period, and typically longer. As part of this effort to lengthen the period of training, the Chicago Public Schools created a year-long, fully paid supervised residency for every aspiring principal who was part of the partnership. To underscore the partnership's single-minded focus on placing only capable people in Chicago's most challenged schools, the partnership worked with the state legislature to redesign the principal eligibility assessment to make it more rigorous for Chicago applicants. Today, 60 percent of state license holders who are not in a full-year residency partnership with CPS, as UIC leaders are, fail the assessment.

The school district also created a partnership office charged with facilitating interaction with UIC and other partners. One might conjecture that because the university and school district shared easy lines of communication, it was more straightforward for the collective to recognize the need for a much longer training period than is typical in leadership preparation. Changes such as these are emblematic of the trust that the partners were able to accumulate through their social infrastructure. Among other dimensions represented in the developmental progressions framework, programmatic and legislative transformations like these represent institutionalization of the work in areas such as "broadening stakeholder involvement" and "funding support" (table 19.1).

As in the case of Un Buen Comienzo, the social infrastructure between UIC and CPS produced noteworthy results. Ninety-six percent of the partnership's program completers have become principals or assistant principals, positions in which they are not placed but for which they must compete, and most of them are professionals of color in a role where they are typically underrepresented. The partnership currently has over 170 people at various stages of program completion who are already leading urban schools at the school or district level, with over 110 of them having completed a doctorate. During the period of the partnership, Chicago Public Schools gained national attention as one of the fastest rising school districts in the nation in student achievement and increased high school graduation rates.[41] Of the fifty-five largest districts in Illinois, Chicago elementary students, at every grade level and in each demographic group, have the greatest achievement gains over the past fifteen years. Chicago's Black and Latinx elementary students, a population that constitutes 90 percent of the district's enrollment, now outperform their counterparts in the rest of Illinois by a substantial margin.[42]

THE WAY FORWARD: PEERAGE AMONG HELPERS

The task of being a committed helper is no small challenge. Whether the helper is a teacher, social worker, lawyer, physician, or cleric, the task is a daunting one. In today's modern world of problems, it is necessary to construct inter-dependence to be effective helpers. We visualize this interdependence, as we have characterized it over the course of this chapter, in figure 19.4.

First, at the heart of this visualization, external helpers must find and cross the values and community boundaries that separate them from local or indigenous helpers. In essence, the goal is to create a peerage with resident communities and others that share a common notion of improvement. We have argued

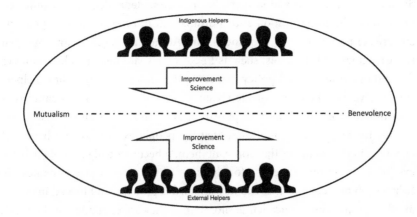

FIGURE 19.4 Social glue to promote common purpose.

that improvement science and other similar methods contain tools and engender routines that enable those outside and within the communities to understand values and approaches on both sides of the boundary.[43] In improvement, methods create social glue that allows a diverse community of peers to engage with mutualism and benevolence.

We conjecture that many efforts to help have fallen short in the past because of a failure to engender peerage. Without this peerage, efforts to help fall victim—as they have in the past—to epistemic inequality.[44] According to Zuboff, epistemic inequality arises when the ability to produce meaning is imbalanced.[45] We see imbalance when outside experts hold their tools and insights privately rather than finding ways to share expertise and coproduce improvement with those who are living and experiencing the problems day to day. The challenge is creating social glue and building peerage that span (not remove) cultural and background differences. Without this social glue, outside assistance teams will almost certainly become ineffective instruments for new institution building.

A second challenge facing aspiring helpers is that they often do not use all the professional networks potentially at their disposal to address the human problems that confront them. In schooling, for instance, the challenges that face many teachers are centered in the professional spheres of others. For the teacher, whose students cannot show up physically or intellectually because of immigration difficulties, instructional impediments can and often do stray into the purview of the law and lawyers. Each of these dependencies is connected to matters of communication and coordination. In essence, these dependencies are connected to matters of social glue. At their core, the notions of social infrastructure and the tools, such as PDSA cycles, are meant to be resources that aid practitioners and policy makers in the understanding of how helpers can achieve useful connections to create meaningful activities and patterns of coordinated work that improve opportunities for those they aim to assist.

Our fundamental assumption is that the people we aim to help have vast expertise in the problems that confront them. It becomes a big part of the helper's job to mine that expertise for the keys to progress. It also becomes the helper's job to recognize that the way forward is probably not locked in one or another professional or academic silo. Rather, they are contained in the funds of knowledge that live in communities. Modern problems are multicausal, and, often, diverse partnerships are needed to solve them.

NOTES

1. Brown, Chris, and Cindy L. Poortman, eds., *Networks for Learning: Effective Collaboration for Teacher, School and System Improvement* (New York: Routledge, 2018).
2. Bryk, Anthony S., Louis M. Gomez, Alicia Grunow, and Paul G. LeMahieu, *Learning to Improve: How America's Schools Can Get Better at Getting Better* (Cambridge, MA: Harvard Education Press, 2015).
3. Churchill, Elisabeth, "Introduction: Social Glue," in *Shared Encounters*, ed. Katharine S. Willis, George Roussos, Konstantinos Chorianopoulous, and Mirjam Struppek, 229–233 (London: Springer, 2009).
4. "The Employment Situation—February 2021," Bureau of Labor Statistics, March 5, 2021, https://www.bls.gov/news.release/pdf/empsit.pdf.
5. Ndugga, Nambi, Olivia Pham, Latoya Hill, Samantha Atiga, and Salem Mengistu, "Latest Data on COVID-19 Vaccinations Race/Ethnicity," Kaiser Family Foundation, October 6, 2021, https://www.kff.org/coronavirus-covid-19/issue-brief/latest-data-on-covid-19-vaccinations-race-ethnicity/.
6. Bryk et al., *Learning to Improve*.
7. Hecker, Achim, "Knowledge Beyond the Individual? Making Sense of a Notion of Collective Knowledge in Organization Theory," *Organization Studies* 33, no. 3 (2012): 423–445.
8. Wenger, E., *Artificial Intelligence and Tutoring Systems: Computational and Cognitive Approaches to the Communication of Knowledge* (Los Altos, CA: Morgen Kaufman, 1987).
9. Lave, Jean, and Etienne Wenger, *Situated Learning: Legitimate Peripheral Participation* (Cambridge: Cambridge University Press, 1991);Wenger, *Artificial Intelligence and Tutoring Systems*.
10. Orlikowski, Wanda J., "Knowing in Practice: Enacting a Collective Capability in Distributed Organizing," *Organization Science* 13, no. 3 (2002): 249–273, https://doi.org/10.1287/orsc.13.3.249.2776.
11. Christakis, Alexander N., and Kenneth C. Bausch, eds., *CoLaboratories of Democracy: How People Harness Their Collective Wisdom to Create the Future* (Charlotte, NC: IAP, 2006).

12. Senge, Peter M., *The Fifth Discipline: The Art and Practice of the Learning Organization* (New York: Doubleday Currency, 1990).

13. Churchill, "Introduction: Social Glue."

14. Bastian, Brock, Jolanda Jetten, and Laura J. Ferris, "Pain as Social Glue: Shared Pain Increases Cooperation," *Psychological Science* 25, no. 11 (2014): 2079–2085.

15. Whitehouse, Harvey, Jonathan A. Lanman, Greg Downey, Leah A. Fredman, William B. Swann Jr, Daniel H. Lende, Robert N. McCauley et al., "The Ties that Bind Us: Ritual, Fusion, and Identification," *Current Anthropology* 55, no. 6 (2014): 674–695.

16. Smith, Aaron C. T., and Bob Stewart. "Organizational Rituals: Features, Functions and Mechanisms," *International Journal of Management Reviews* 13, no. 2 (2011): 113–133.

17. Legare, Cristine H., and Mark Nielsen, "Imitation and Innovation: The Dual Engines of Cultural Learning," *Trends in Cognitive Sciences* 19, no. 11 (2015): 688–699; Watson-Jones, Rachel E., and Cristine H. Legare, "The Social Functions of Group Rituals," *Current Directions in Psychological Science* 25, no. 1 (2016): 42–46.

18. Coleman, J. S., *Foundations of Social Theory* (Cambridge, MA: Belknap Press of Harvard University Press, 1990).

19. Cook, T. D., H. Appleton, R. F. Conner, A. Shaffer, G. Tamkin, and S. J. Weber, "*Sesame Street*" *Revisited* (New York: Russell Sage Foundation, 1975); Cook, Thomas D., and Ross F. Conner, "*Sesame Street* Around the World: The Educational Impact," *Journal of Communication* 26, no. 2 (1976): 155–164.

20. King, Rachel, "Comcast Adds Khan Academy to Internet Education Program," ZDNet (2013). https://www.zdnet.com/article/comcast-adds-khan-academy-to-internet-education -program/

21. Murphy, Robert, Larry Gallagher, Andrew E. Krumm, Jessica Mislevy, and Amy Hafter, *Research on the Use of Khan Academy in Schools: Research Brief* (Palo Alto, CA: SRI International, 2014).

22. Biggs, Simon, "Interprofessional Collaboration: Problems and Prospects," in *Interprofessional Working for Health and Social Care*, 186–200 (Palgrave, London, 1997).

23. Gomez, Kimberly, Eleni A. Kyza, and Nicole Mancevice, "Participatory Design and the Learning Sciences," in *International Handbook of the Learning Sciences* (New York, Routledge, 2018).

24. Moll, Luis C., ed., *Vygotsky and Education: Instructional Implications and Applications of Sociohistorical Psychology* (Cambridge: Cambridge University Press, 1992).

25. Neri, Rebecca Colina, Maritza Lozano, and Louis M. Gomez, "(Re) Framing Resistance to Culturally Relevant Education as a Multilevel Learning Problem," *Review of Research in Education* 43, no. 1 (2019): 197–226.

26. Bryk, Anthony S., Louis M. Gomez, and Alicia Grunow, "Getting Ideas into Action: Building Networked Improvement Communities in Education," in *Frontiers in Sociology of Education*, 127–162 (Dordrecht: Springer, 2011).

27. Bryk et al., *Learning to Improve*.

28. Fixsen, Dean L., Sandra F. Naoom, Karen A. Blase, Robert M. Friedman, Frances Wallace, Barbara Burns, William Carter et al., *Implementation Research: A Synthesis of the Literature* (Tampa, FL: University of South Florida, Louis de la Parte Florida Mental Health Institute, 2005).

29. Fishman, Barry J., William R. Penuel, Anna-Ruth Allen, Britte Haugan Cheng, and Nora Sabelli, "Design-Based Implementation Research: An Emerging Model for Transforming the Relationship of Research and Practice," *National Society for the Study of Education* 112, no. 2 (2013): 136–156.

30. Sustar, Helena, and Tuuli Mattelmäki, "Whole in One: Designing for Empathy in Complex Systems," *Nordes* 7, no. 1 (2017).

31. Bryk et al., *Learning to Improve*; Langley, Gerald J., Ronald D. Moen, Kevin M. Nolan, Thomas W. Nolan, Clifford L. Norman, and Lloyd P. Provost, *The Improvement Guide: A Practical Approach to Enhancing Organizational Performance* (San Francisco, CA: Jossey-Bass Publishers, 2009).

32. Nichols, Sharon L., and David C. Berliner, *Collateral Damage: How High-Stakes Testing Corrupts America's Schools* (Cambridge, MA: Harvard Education Press, 2007).

33. Moen, Ronald, "Foundation and History of the PDSA Cycle" (Asian network for quality conference, Tokyo, 2009), https://www.praxisframework.org/files/pdsa-history-ron-moen.pdf.

34. Donnelly, Peter, and Paul Kirk, "Use the PDSA Model for Effective Change Management," *Education for Primary Care* 26, no. 4 (2015): 279–281.

35. Page, Scott E., *The Difference: How the Power of Diversity Creates Better Groups, Firms, Schools, and Societies* (Princeton, NJ: Princeton University Press, 2008); Pentland, Alex, *Social Physics: How Good Ideas Spread the Lessons from a New Science* (New York: Penguin, 2018).

36. Arbour, Marycatherine, M. P. Collao, and Marcela Marzolo, "Spotlight on Un Buen Comienzo Improvement Network," (Fundación Educacional Oportunidad, Washington, D.C.: Carnegie Summit on Improvement in Education, April 2019).

37. Langley et al., *The Improvement Guide*.

38. Miller, Teresa N., Mary Devin, and Robert J. Shoop, *Closing the Leadership Gap: How District and University Partnerships Shape Effective School Leaders* (Thousand Oaks, CA: Corwin Press and Sage Publications, 2007);Tozer, Steve, Paul Zavitkovsky, Sam Whalen, and Peter Martinez, "Change Agency in Our Own Backyards," in *Handbook of Urban Educational Leadership*, ed. Muhammad Khalifa, Noelle Witherspoon, Azadeh F. Osanlod, and Cossette M. Grant (Lanham, MD: Rowman & Littlefield, 2015), 480;Young, Michelle D., George J. Petersen, and Paula M. Short, "The Complexity of Substantive Reform: A Call for Interdependence Among Key Stakeholders," *Educational Administration Quarterly* 38, no. 2 (2002): 137–175.

39. Tozer, Steve, "Social Foundations of Education as an Unwelcome Counter-Narrative and as Educational Praxis," *Educational Studies* 54, no. 1 (2018): 89–98.

40. Velásquez, Camila, Manuelito Biag, Louis M. Gomez, David G. Imig, "Partnering for Leadership Development and Continuous Improvement: Carnegie's Improvement Leadership Education and Development Network" (AERA Learning and Teaching in Educational Leadership newsletter, 2019).

41. Reardon, S. F., and R. Hinze-Pifer, *Test Score Growth Among Chicago Public School Students, 2009–2014* (Redwood City, CA: Stanford Center for Education Policy Analysis, 2017).

42. Zavitkovsky, Paul, and Steve Tozer, *Upstate/Downstate* (Chicago: Center for Urban Education Leadership, University of Illinois, 2017), https://urbanedleadership.org/wp-content/uploads/2020/02/UPSTATE-DOWNSTATE-FINAL-w-Appendices-06.16.17.pdf.

43. Gomez, Louis M., Manuelito Biag, and David G. Imig, "Learning at the Boundaries: Reconsidering University-District Partnerships for Educational Leadership," in *Handbook of the Cultural Foundations of Learning*, ed. Na'ilah Suad Nasir, Carol D. Lee, Roy Pea, and Maxine McKinney de Royston (New York: Routledge, 2020).

44. Czerniewicz, L., "Inequitable Power Dynamics of Global Knowledge Production and Exchange Must Be Confronted Head On," LSE Impact Blog, April 29, 2013, http://blogs.lse.ac.uk/impactofsocialsciences/2013/04/29/redrawing-the-map-fromaccess-to-participation/#more-10331.

45. Zuboff, Shoshana, "You are Now Remotely Controlled," *New York Times*, January 24, 2020.

20

UNESCO AND THE FUTURES OF EDUCATION

STEFANIA GIANNINI

his chapter makes a case for global efforts to rethink education, learning, and knowledge so that education systems can develop the capacities that humanity needs for sustainable development. It calls for a bold, humanistic vision based on human rights, social justice, dignity, cultural and social diversity, and intellectual solidarity. This vision reaffirms a set of universal ethical principles and the need to strengthen moral values in education and society. It starts with people of all ages and the analysis of development contexts. It is inclusive and equitable, and informed by interdisciplinary research across the sciences, arts, and humanities. Finally, it is participatory and international in scope.

UNESCO's Futures of Education initiative, led by an international commission chaired by the president of Ethiopia, is employing a humanistic approach to foster a forward-looking global conversation about probable, possible, and preferred futures. Through conversing about the future beyond established social boundaries, it is hoped that education will become better able not only to respond to current development crises but also to positively transform the future of humanity. A postscript sets the commission's work in the context of the COVID-19 pandemic, which has exposed and exacerbated educational inequalities and reinforced the necessity of global solidarity and intelligent collective action: "Broad dissemination of ideas and knowledge, based on the freest exchange and discussion, is essential to creative activity, the pursuit of truth and the development of the personality."[1]

Below, I begin by introducing the development and education crisis and call for a bold, humanistic approach based to human rights, social justice, dignity, appreciation of cultural diversity, and intellectual solidarity. I then consider the possible implications of this approach and introduce UNESCO's Futures of Education initiative as a global conversation on education and humanity and "learning to become."

A MULTIDIMENSIONAL DEVELOPMENT CRISIS

The idea that the world is at a critical juncture, characterized by a deep multidimensional social, moral and environmental crisis, is increasingly accepted. Climate change has been described by the United Nations secretary-general as the "defining issue of our times."[2]

The sense of crisis is in itself not new, but todays' development challenges appear deeply entrenched and difficult to resolve. Some trends, including the disruption related to digital technologies, exhibit daunting levels of complexity and contradiction.

Economic growth and the creation of wealth have reduced global poverty rates, but vulnerability, inequality, exclusion, and violence have increased within and across societies throughout the world. The precarity of economies, the strains to peaceful coexistence, and natural ecosystems are becoming more and more apparent. Unsustainable patterns of economic production and consumption contribute to climate change, natural disasters, and environmental degradation. Moreover, while international human rights frameworks have been strengthened over the past several decades, the implementation and protection of these norms remain a challenge. Women continue to face discrimination in public life and in employment. Again, while technological development contributes to greater interconnectedness and offers new avenues for exchange, cooperation, and solidarity, there is an increase in cultural and religious intolerance, identity-based political mobilization, and conflict.

Recent assessments indicate that the scale of climate change and its implications are worse than what had been imagined even five years ago when the 2030 Agenda for Sustainable Development was adopted by the United Nations General Assembly. According to the NASA Goddard Institute for Space Studies, the past decade was the hottest on record, and every decade since the 1960s has been warmer than the decade previously. Human activities are estimated to have caused approximately 1.0°C of global warming above preindustrial levels.[3]

Persistent inequalities, social fragmentation, and political extremism con-tinue to undermine social cohesion and trust in established institutions, bring-ing many societies to the point of crisis. These pose significant new governance challenges at a time when multilateralism, international cooperation, and global solidarity are under assault.

Advances in digital communications, artificial intelligence, and biotechnology are fundamentally transforming the way we live, work, communicate, process knowledge, and learn. While these hold great promise for human welfare, they also raise serious ethical, social, and political concerns, especially as past techno-logical innovations have an uneven record of contributing to human flourishing.

Technological advances—artificial intelligence, automation, and robotics—will create new jobs, but those who lose their jobs in this transition may be the least equipped to seize the new opportunities. According to International Labour Organization projections, women, workers with a lower secondary degree educa-tion, and workers in lower-wage occupations will be most affected by automation.[4]

Another important trend is demographics. According to the United Nations Population Division, between 2010 and 2015, about thirty-six million migrants changed their country of residence. This corresponds to 0.5 percent of the global population and an average of seven million international migrants moving per year.[5] There is a rapidly aging population, especially in Asia (see chapter 6).

All of these changes in the international development context generate ten-sions for which education is expected to prepare individuals and communities.

LIMITS OF CURRENT EDUCATION SYSTEMS TO RESPOND TO CRISES AND TO IMAGINE ALTERNATIVE FUTURES

Global assessments of education, including UNESCO's independent Global Education Monitoring Report, reveal unprecedented increases in access and participation in all levels of education in recent decades.[6] The gender gap in access to education has narrowed, and increasing attention has been given to the quality and relevance of education. Although the world is not on track to achieve the goal of "inclusive and equitable quality education and promote life-long learning opportunities for all" by 2030, according to conventional mea-sures, progress is being made.[7]

Yet, despite these education success stories, the persistence and deepening of development problems lead to the question of why, as currently organized, education systems are unable to respond adequately to the scope of current challenges and to contribute more toward a more inclusive, just, and sustainable world. Indeed, it raises uncomfortable questions about education's own roles in the multidimensional social, moral, and environmental crises that education is being expected to equip learners to address. Historically, education was an instrument of colonization and indoctrination. It has fostered competition between learners and institutions, unsustainable production and consumption, and exacerbated discrimination and social inequalities. Yet, education is also a force for liberation, freedom, human rights, and the public good.

At this critical juncture, the case is clear for a concerted global effort to rethink education so that education systems develop the capacities needed to defend humanity from self-destruction and to realize its potential for human flourishing, lasting peace, and sustainable development. This will not only involve changes to governance, financing, organization, human resources, and reforms to teaching and learning, curriculum, and assessment. More fundamentally, it is necessary to rethink the purposes of education, knowledge, and learning without being constrained by past or present arrangements. The aspiration of sustainable development requires stakeholders in education and beyond to resolve common problems and tensions and to recognize new horizons for humanity and the planet.

The 2030 Agenda for Sustainable Development, adopted in 2015, integrates education and learning within Sustainable Development Goal 4 (SDG4) "to ensure inclusive and equitable quality education and promote lifelong learning opportunities for all." It also recognizes the potential of education as a force for good by including a dedicated target (SDG 4.7) to:

> Ensure all learners acquire knowledge and skills needed to promote sustainable development, including among others through education for sustainable development and sustainable lifestyles, human rights, gender equality, promotion of a culture of peace and non-violence, global citizenship, and appreciation of cultural diversity and of culture's contribution to sustainable development.[8]

SDG 4.7 is arguably the most innovative target in the new international education agenda because of its focus on the relevance of what is learned for sustainable development, including socio-cultural learning and global citizenship. Yet, at the moment, this target is sometimes perceived as an extra burden to be added onto existing systems and practices, as an addition to already overloaded curricula, without requiring fundamental changes to the way that education is conceptualized or conducted.

This chapter argues that simply adjusting the current arrangements for education and learning will not be sufficient. Such is the depth of the crisis that it requires a more fundamental rethinking of visions and purposes for education and learning and how learning should be organized and fostered. It has the intention to stimulate forward-looking public policy debate on the future of education. This chapter recalls the vision provided by the two landmark UNESCO publications: *Learning to Be: The World of Education Today and Tomorrow* (1972), the "Faure Report," and *Learning: The Treasure Within* (1996), known as the "Delors Report." It also considers how this rethinking might best be done.

Education must find ways of responding to such challenges, taking into account multiple worldviews and alternative knowledge systems. This means greater attention to learning in the arts and humanities, social and emotional learning, and new frontiers in science and technology, such as the advances in neurosciences and the developments in digital technology. Rethinking the purpose of education and the organization of learning has never been more urgent.

TOWARD A HUMANISTIC APPROACH TO DEVELOPMENT AND EDUCATION

Addressing the complex challenges above requires the adoption of humanistic values, including "respect for life and human dignity, equal rights and social justice, cultural and social diversity, and a sense of human solidarity and shared responsibility for our common future."[9] With the multifaceted crises resulting from models of development centered on economic growth in the twenty-first century, a humanistic vision of development must be guided by a central concern for sustainability understood as the responsible actions of individuals and societies toward a better future for all and the planet. A humanistic vision reaffirms a set of universal ethical principles that should be the foundation for an integrated approach to the purpose of education and the organization of learning.

The ethical and moral principles of a humanistic approach to development stand against violence, intolerance, discrimination, and exclusion. This approach emphasizes the inclusion of people who are often subject to discrimination—women and girls, Indigenous people, persons with disabilities, migrants, the elderly, and people living in countries affected by conflict.

A humanistic approach implies attention to the strengthening and development of moral values within education systems and for society. Beyond those skills directly relevant to labor markets, learners need the knowledge and values to live meaningful and purposeful lives in harmony with others and the planet. Such an approach has implications for the design of learning processes that promote the acquisition of relevant knowledge and the development of competencies in the service of our common humanity. A humanistic approach takes the debate on education beyond its utilitarian role in economic development (see chapter 7). It has a central concern for inclusiveness and for an education that does not exclude and marginalize. It serves as a guide to dealing with the transformation of the global learning landscape, one in which the role of teachers and other educators continues as central to facilitating learning for the sustainable development of all.

Education alone cannot hope to solve all development challenges, but a humanistic and holistic approach to education can and should contribute to achieving a new development model. In such a model, economic growth must be guided by environmental stewardship and by concern for peace, inclusion, and social justice. It requires an open and flexible approach to learning that is both lifelong and life-wide—an approach that provides the opportunity for all to realize their potential for a sustainable future and a life of dignity. This humanistic approach has implications for the definition of learning content and pedagogies as well as for the role of teachers and other educators. It is even more relevant given the rapid development of new technologies, in particular, digital technologies.

The quality of education is inextricably linked to its relevance as a human right and as a vehicle for inclusive, socially just, and sustainable development. Education is both a human right in itself and an indispensable means of realizing other human rights. As an empowerment right, education is the primary vehicle by which economically and socially marginalized adults and children can lift themselves out of poverty and obtain the means to participate fully in their communities. Education has a vital role in empowering women, safeguarding children from exploitative and hazardous labor and sexual exploitation, promoting human rights and democracy, protecting the environment, and controlling population growth. Increasingly, education is recognized as one of the best financial investments states can make. But the importance of education is not just practical: "a well-educated, enlightened and active mind, able to wander freely and widely, is one of the joys and rewards of human existence."[10]

EDUCATION, LEARNING, AND KNOWLEDGE
AS A COMMON GOOD

The escalating levels of social and economic complexity present a number of challenges for education policy making in today's globalized world. The intensification of economic globalization is producing patterns of low-employment growth, rising youth unemployment, and vulnerable employment. While the trends point to a growing disconnection between education and the fast-changing world of work, they also represent an opportunity to reconsider the link between education and societal development. Furthermore, the increasing mobility of learners and workers across national borders and the new patterns of knowledge and skills transfer require new ways of recognizing, validating, and assessing learning. Regarding citizenship, the challenge for national education systems is to shape identities and to promote awareness of and a sense of responsibility for others in an increasingly interconnected and interdependent world. The expansion of access to education worldwide over the past several decades is placing greater pressure on public financing. Additionally, the demand has grown in recent years for voice in public affairs and for the involvement of nonstate actors in education at both national and global levels. This diversification of partnerships is blurring the boundaries between public and private, posing problems for the democratic governance of education. In short, there is a growing need to reconcile the contributions and demands of the three regulators of social behavior: society, state, and market.

In light of this rapidly changing reality, we need to rethink the normative principles that guide educational governance—in particular, the right to education and the notion of education as a public good. Indeed, we often refer to education as a human right and as a public good in international education discourse. Yet, while these principles are relatively uncontested at the level of basic education, there is no general agreement in much of the discussion about their applicability to post-basic education and training.

To what extent does the right to education and the principle of public good also apply to nonformal and informal education, which are less institutionalized, if at all? Therefore, a concern for knowledge—understood as the information, understanding, skills, values, and attitudes acquired through learning—is central to any discussion of the purpose of education.

Knowledge is an inherent part of the common heritage of humanity. Given the need for sustainable development in an increasingly interdependent world, education and knowledge should, therefore, be considered global common goods.

Inspired by the value of solidarity grounded in our common humanity, the principle of knowledge and education as global common goods has implications for the roles and responsibilities of diverse stakeholders. This holds true for international organizations such as UNESCO, which has a global observatory and normative function qualifying it to promote and guide global public policy debate.

UNESCO's publication *Rethinking Education* (re)affirmed that knowledge is an inherent part of the common heritage of humanity. Because of the need for sustainable development in an interdependent world, we should be inspired by the value of solidarity grounded in our common humanity and recognize knowledge as a global common good. If public goods are resources managed as part of a social mandate, frequently by governments, common goods are less instrumentally configured collective resources whose production, protection, and use are properly ensured through transparent social collaboration, participation, and trusteeship.

AN INTEGRATED APPROACH TO KNOWLEDGE, LEARNING, AND EDUCATION

The humanistic approach offers an integrated approach to knowledge, learning, and education, and, indeed, to education as an integrated, lifelong learning system more than the sum of its parts.

Knowledge, broadly speaking, can be conceived as information, understanding, skills, attitudes, and values—in sum, as the ways individuals and societies apply meaning to experience. There are diverse ways of knowing and diverse forms of knowledge. As much as humans organize the world through knowledge, knowledge also organizes our being in the world and the principles that guide our reflections and actions. In the past few decades, digitalization and globalization have radically transformed the ways that data, information, and knowledge are created, processed, managed, governed, and used. Machine learning, information and communication technologies, and the proprietary commercialization of data have generated tensions on how to ensure the flourishing of scientific, cultural, and Indigenous knowledge, as well as on how to manage their equitable and democratic circulation and utilization.

Learning is understood to be the process of acquiring knowledge. It is both a process and the result of that process, a means as well as an end, an individual practice as well as a collective endeavor. Learning is a multifaceted reality defined by the context. What knowledge is acquired and why, where, when, and how it is used represent fundamental questions for the development of individuals and societies alike.

Education is understood as encompassing formal and nonformal educational and training programs as well as other less institutionalized learning processes, such as workplace-based and community-based, as well as self-directed learning—in sum, all forms of organized learning throughout the life cycle.

While the concept of learning has been core to UNESCO's work over the past seventy-five years, in recent decades, learning has gained increased global prominence in policy and public discussions about education. Alongside the input factors of teaching and curriculum, learners are increasingly recognized as active creators, designing and determining their own educational pathways, with teachers increasingly seen as guides and facilitators. While this trend may be applauded, robust definitions of education are required that encompass development that is effective as well as cognitive; processes of becoming that unfold over time; and the relational dimensions of pedagogy. Above all else, learning is a social endeavor rooted in communities and plural social worlds. It is within these settings that we should discuss what values and practical knowledge should be taught/learned. Furthermore, it is at local levels that the collective purposes of education need to be deliberated upon and acted upon.

Seen as part of the global commons, knowledge, learning, and education represent *humanity's greatest renewable resource* for responding to challenges and inventing alternatives. While education may be considered to be a "necessary utopia,"[11] it is important to recognize that the organization and pursuit of learning is a world-making fact of the here and now. It is also an area where values are lived and where being, knowing, doing, and living together are not just prepared for but are actualized.

POTENTIAL THEMATIC AREAS TO BE EXPLORED

The humanistic approach also suggests various thematic areas for further exploration, including the following.

GOVERNANCE OF KNOWLEDGE

Knowledge must be respected as a global common good. Education must recognize the plurality and fluidity of knowledge while also addressing persistent asymmetries. Research, scientific, and other processes for generating, sharing, and applying knowledge should be inclusive, democratic, transparent, and participatory.

HUMAN AND PLANETARY SUSTAINABILITY

We must take collective and collaborative responsibility for fostering sustainable life on the planet. Education has a key role to play not only in changing mindsets but also in changing existing unsustainable practices. Education must channel human capabilities in directions that improve the quality of human life while respecting supporting ecosystems.

CITIZENSHIP AND PARTICIPATION

Participation is fundamental to creating preferred futures. Education must strengthen capacities for collective action and deepen commitments to democratic values, including intellectual emancipation and human freedom. At the same time, education institutions and systems must live out and enact these commitments in their own operations and processes.

WORK AND ECONOMIC SECURITY

Meaningful employment and economic security are cornerstones of human dignity and flourishing. Education must interrupt patterns of exclusion and systems oppression. This means supporting learning across the lifespan and considering higher-order cognitive and socio-behavioral competencies as foundational within learning systems.

A GLOBAL CONVERSATION ON THE FUTURES OF EDUCATION

UNESCO was founded shortly after the Second World War as an organization that would embody a culture of peace and the "intellectual and moral solidarity" of humankind. Its vision was laid out seventy-five years ago, most famously in the UNESCO Constitution's call to construct the defenses of peace in the minds of people. UNESCO is committed to the democratic principles of dignity, equality, and mutual respect; it works to advance education and culture for purposes of justice, liberty, and peace; and it seeks to further the rule of law and human rights. International cooperation and collaboration—the spirit of mutual assistance and concern—has been the basis of UNESCO's work for three-quarters of a century. Today, more than ever, our work must be based on intellectual and moral solidarity that extends across the planet. Advancing cooperation in education, the sciences, culture, communication, and information holds strategic stakes at a time when societies across the world face the rising pressures of change and the international community faces new challenges.

The director-general of UNESCO, Audrey Azoulay, in her message on the second International Day of Education, January 24, 2020, noted that:

> Education is the cornerstone of peace. Education is an opening up to others, a path of intelligence which leads to intercultural understanding, to reconciliation, to fellowship. This is the meaning of the global citizenship education promoted by UNESCO. . . .
>
> High-level political authorities and citizens, States and associations, teachers and parents of students: everyone, in their own way, has a role to play in making the right to education a reality for all. It is our responsibility to future generations.

In a global conversation on the future of education, the following questions may serve as helpful starting points for debate:

While Delors's four pillars of learning—to know, to do, to be, and to live together—are still relevant, they are threatened by globalization and by the resurgence of identity politics. How can they be strengthened and renewed? How can education respond to the challenges of achieving economic, social, and environmental sustainability? How can a plurality of worldviews be reconciled through a humanistic approach to education? How can such a humanistic approach be realized through educational policies and practices? What are the implications of globalization for national policies and decision making in education? How should education be financed? What are the specific implications for teacher education, training, development, and support? What are the implications for education of the distinction between the concepts of the private good, the public good, and the common good?

Diverse stakeholders with their multiple perspectives should be brought together to share research findings and to articulate normative principles in the guidance of policy. UNESCO, as an intellectual agency and think tank, can provide the platform for such debate and dialogue, enhancing our understanding of new approaches to education policy and provision, with the aim of sustaining humanity and its common well-being.

What would it take to envisage the future of education in a world of increasing complexity, uncertainty, and fragility? The relationship between education and society is rapidly changing, and UNESCO is currently leading a global initiative on the futures of education that seeks to generate an agenda for debate and action on the futures of education, learning, and knowledge in a world of increasing complexity, uncertainty, and precarity. It is a global conversation that acknowledges that all voices must be heard in order to shape and transform education. This conversation begins with a humanistic and transformative vision of education and development, and it recognizes the value of foresight for envisioning a better world and, as far as necessary, rethinking and reimaging education's roles and purposes.

WAYS FORWARD

Two decades into the twenty-first century, the traditional model of economic growth is in crisis, calling into question established development and education approaches. The multiple interconnected challenges in the current historical juncture require that we urgently explore alternative development models. Development cannot be simply framed in terms of economic growth—human flourishing and the accessibility of lives of meaning and dignity must be primary concerns. Continued technological change and continued transformation of human cultures and societies seem inevitable. Furthermore, we might be shaping futures where there are fundamental transformations in human consciousness and human identities. As we come to terms with the Anthropocene as a geological era of human-caused change to the planet, and as we grapple with a more-than-human world, the key question before us is: What do we want to become?

To conclude, existing models of development and education are in crisis. This crisis is multidimensional. There are severe and continuing challenges of access to schooling, especially in low-income countries. Even when children have a school place, they are struggling to learn the basic skills, and the relevance of what is being taught is not always clear. There are also new challenges arising from digitalization and new learning spaces that also bring into question current models of schooling and education systems.

FIRST, START WITH DEVELOPMENT CONTEXTS

It is argued that an analysis of changing local, national, and international development contexts is an essential starting point for the education community. Whereas much research, reflection, and analysis have focused on trying to understand and reform education systems to improve access and quality, deep consideration of the crisis of development itself is also required. Modern education systems have been influential in shaping ideas about human progress and are, to some extent, implicated in the unsustainable development trends witnessed today. An assessment of the global development crisis adds to the imperative to rethink education and, more broadly, knowledge and learning. Making education an object of inquiry without sufficient attention to these changing contexts will result in a partial diagnosis of the challenges and partial recommendations for the future.

SECOND, A HUMANISTIC PHILOSOPHY

UNESCO has a distinctive, humanistic—and human-rights-based approach to education. Applying principles of equity and inclusion to education is a basis for socially just and sustainable societies. It means privileging historically marginalized voices, such as those of Indigenous peoples and disadvantaged groups. Education certainly has a role to play in developing technical and vocational skills. But, consistent with SDG 4.7, values are also important for future societies that will be inclusive, appreciate cultural diversity, and support a sense of truth and fullness of life. Education is and will continue to be an incubator of values and essential for sustainable development.

THIRD, A MORE INTEGRATED APPROACH TO EDUCATION AND LEARNING

If children are in school but not learning, then something is wrong. Where learners' prospects are determined narrowly by their grasp of the language of instruction, results in high-stakes examinations, distance from college or university, or their gender, then education is failing future generations. Lifelong learning provides a more comprehensive framework for thinking about the future of education, and it highlights the importance of attention to transitions between levels and the metacompetencies needed, such as "learning to learn." Furthermore, attention to the relation between education and learning, and the governance of knowledge itself, is needed.

FOURTH, AN INTERDISCIPLINARY AND INCLUSIVE APPROACH

It is often said that complex problems require complex solutions. Education studies is an interdisciplinary research field, but, nevertheless, there are risks of privileging one field over another. Learning is both individual and social. Neuroscientists, sociologists, anthropologists, artists, linguists, and historians have insights to contribute, as do the wide range of education stakeholders, including learners of all ages, across society. Beyond scientific knowledge and expertise, values and wisdom are required. As the president of Ethiopia, H. E. Sahle-Work Zewde, said at the launch of the International Commission on the Futures of Education on September 25, 2019:

> As we face the profound challenges and exciting opportunities before us, we have a deep obligation to listen to children and youth and fully involve them in decisions about the future of our shared planet. It is through knowledge and learning we reach across generations. Through knowledge and learning we reach backwards to draw on the wisdom of previous generations. Through knowledge and learning we reach forwards to inspire and find inspiration in the hopes, dreams and plans of future generations.

FINALLY, A MORE INTERNATIONALIST AND COORDINATED APPROACH

Many commentators fear that multilateralism is being undermined, and they attribute this to a combination of factors, including increased nationalism, a breakdown in social contracts, declining trust, and a collective amnesia by leaders and citizens who underestimate the horrors of war. Reflection and actions on the futures of education need to mobilize people from all countries and offer diverse perspectives in a spirit of international cooperation. In this perspective, education for national competitiveness, or even national identity, is insufficient in today's global village. Furthermore, international aid and development assistance should be informed by the aspirations of local communities, and much closer donor coordination is needed to develop shared visions of the future.

From UNESCO's perspective, new approaches to imaging the futures of education are needed. It requires interdisciplinary assessments of the development trends and challenges facing humanity as a whole. Whilst recognizing weaknesses in current models of schooling and education more broadly, rethinking education also requires reflection on the future of humanity and the planet and on the question of: What do we want to become?

This chapter has made a solid case for mobilizing the collective attention to foresight and the rethinking of development, education, and learning through vigorous and inclusive debates that seek to overcome professional, disciplinary, national, gender, linguistic, and other social boundaries in the interests of human flourishing.

What happens in the societies of the future and what happens in education are inextricably linked. Far from simply responding to social, economic, and environmental change, education is a transformative force that can shape the changes that take place in the coming years.

POSTSCRIPT: ONE YEAR INTO COVID-19 AND BEYOND

The perspectives presented in this chapter have taken on pressing urgency with the COVID-19 pandemic that has exposed the dramatic impact of inequalities on learning opportunities, the tremendous resourcefulness with which countries have reacted to provide alternative learning models, and the dedication and creativity of teachers. At the peak of the pandemic, 1.6 billion students in 190 countries were affected by school closures.[12] As this publication goes to press, half the world's students are still affected by full or partial closures. This disruption is historically unprecedented.

Despite the laudable efforts of governments to provide digital and distance learning alternatives to overcome the disruption of in-person education, the world was unprepared for such a massive and sudden shift. Some 460 million students did not have access to remote learning solutions. An additional 100 million children could fall below the minimum proficiency level in reading because of the pandemic.[13] Lost learning is being counted in months and taking a rising toll on the mental health of students. Progress made toward narrowing gender gaps in education over past decades could be reversed, with girls at increased risk of exposure to early marriage and drop out. The most vulnerable children and youth have been deprived of essential health services, nutritious meals, protection, and psycho-social support. The UN secretary-general warned of the risk of a generational catastrophe without prioritizing education in the recovery as a bulwark against inequalities, a driver of economic and social development, and the basis for nurturing responsible, democratic citizenship.

The crisis has reminded us of how crucial public education is in societies, communities, and individual lives. It offers an exceptional opportunity to transform educational practices and environments. We cannot return to the world as it was before. As such, the pandemic is not a parenthesis in education but a bridge to transform education systems, to make them more inclusive, resilient, and responsive to global societal trends and challenges, including the reality of the digital revolution. The right to education has become nearly inseparable from connectivity, making this crisis a turning point in factoring digital skills and learning into education systems and more boldly addressing the injustice of the digital divide.

In building back more equal, three core commitments must always be remembered: public education, common goods, and global solidarity. This is not the time to step back and weaken these principles but rather to affirm and reinforce them and to take innovative and resolute action now to address an education crisis that puts the future of an entire generation at stake.

NOTES

1.   UNESCO, "Declaration of Principles of International Cultural Cooperation," article 7.1, 1966.
2.   Guterres, A., "Secretary-General's Remarks on Climate Change," United Nations, September 10, 2018, https://www.un.org/sg/en/content/sg/statement/2018-09-10/secretary-generals-remarks-climate-change-delivered.

3. The Intergovernmental Panel on Climate Change (IPCC), *Global Warming of 1.5°C* (Geneva: UN/IPCC, 2018).

4. International Labour Organization, *Work for a Brighter Future—Global Commission on the Future of Work* (Geneva: ILO, 2019), https://www.ilo.org/wcmsp5/groups/public/---dgreports/---cabinet/documents/publication/wcms_662410.pdf.

5. United Nations, Department of Economic and Social Affairs, Population Division (2019), *International Migration 2019: Report* (ST/ESA/SER.A/438).

6. UNESCO, *Global Education Monitoring Report 2019 Report,* https://en.unesco.org/gem-report /taxonomy/term/210.

7. United Nations Department of Economic and Social Affairs Report Sustainable Development Goal 4: Ensure inclusive and equitable quality education and promote lifelong learning opportunities for all. https://sdgs.un.org/goals/goal4.

8. United Nations General Assembly. *Transforming our World. The 2030 Agenda for Sustainable Development* (New York: United Nations, 2015), https://sdgs.un.org/2030agenda.

9. UNESCO, Rethinking Education: Towards a Global Common Good (Paris, UNESCO: 2015).

10. Adopted by the Committee on Economic, Social and Cultural Rights at the twenty-first session, E/C.12/1999/10, December 8, 1999.

11. Delors, Jacques, In'am Al Mufti, Isao Amagi, Roberto Carneiro, Fay Chung, Bronislaw Gremek, William Gorham et al. *Learning: The Treasure Within: Report to UNESCO of the International Commission on Education for the Twenty-First Century* (Paris: UNESCO, 1996), https://unesdoc.unesco.org/ark:/48223/pf0000109590?posInSet=12&queryId=f9897ad1-e31b -4acf-a2d8-e64997ad28ab.

12. United Nations Educational, Scientific and Cultural Organization "Education in a Post-COVID World: Nine Ideas for Public Action," International Commission on the Futures of Education, https://bit.ly/3nejF11.

13. UNESCO, "Education in a Post-COVID World."

AFTERWORD

UNIVERSAL EDUCATION: AN ESSENTIAL PILLAR FOR ALL SUSTAINABLE DEVELOPMENT GOALS

JENNIFER GROSS, PETER STENGAARD, AND VANESSA
FAJANS-TURNER

Universal education is an essential pillar to achieve the Sustainable Development Goals (SDGs), without which reaching all other goals will be in jeopardy. As governments and multilateral institutions grapple with the question of how to raise the funding necessary to meet their education commitments, the philanthropic community is asking itself a similar question: how can private philanthropy catalyze and augment the global efforts necessary to mobilize larger-scale, higher-quality resources to meet the world's education needs?

The Sustainable Development Solutions Network released a 2019 report estimating that it would cost a total annual average of $258 billion USD to achieve all education-related SDG targets in the world's fifty-nine poorest countries through 2030. The funding gap that exists between the resources already available in these countries and the resources still needed to meet their education costs varies by country, but it is safe to say that, especially in the wake of COVID-19's catastrophic impacts, it is economically untenable to expect any low-income country to fill this gap on its own without jeopardizing its overall SDG progress. This means that the international community must step up to provide them with the aid they need to get the job done.

What does stepping up look like?

Since 2000, education aid has increased dramatically, but it has stagnated over the course of our most recent decade. While domestic finance is still the

Jennifer Gross and Peter Stengaard are the cofounders of the Blue Chip Foundation; Vanessa Fajans-Turner is an advisor at the Blue Chip Foundation.

dominant source for education budgets in terms of volume, education aid continues to play an important role, especially for the world's most vulnerable peoples. Unlike aid to health sectors, education aid has barely grown since 2010, and its share of overall aid spending has fallen.

When we examine the education aid that is given, it's evident that much of that aid is given bilaterally, rather than through coordinated multilateral channels, and that bilateral donors have very different priorities from each other, and often from recipient governments, for their education spending. The philanthropic sector has been a particularly bad actor in this way.

Additionally, the highest share of education aid is not directed to low-income countries. Data from this past year reveal that Armenia, an upper-middle-income country, and Georgia, a lower-middle-income country, rank as the top two recipients of global education aid.

Education aid is also highly fragmented. For seven recipient countries, all in sub-Saharan Africa, no one donor gives more than 25 percent of each country's education aid. This can quickly become a logistical nightmare for recipient countries and has implications for the efficacy of aid spending.

To address this, there has been a recent push to establish donor collectives, like Co-Impact, established by the Rockefeller and Gates Foundations, to aggregate individual donor funds and channel them toward specific issues for maximum impact. These are useful in areas where there are currently no official funds established, but their capacities are still limited by their smaller scale.

The international community must establish a global education fund that streamlines multiple donors, aligns donor strategies with recipient country demands, and targets low-income countries. The Blue Chip Foundation supports these efforts. There are already myriad conversations about such a fund, to design it to mimic the successes of the Global Fund as well as others, such as the Green Climate Fund. There is also progress on some regionally specific education funds, like the African Union's Secondary Education Fund.

There is a strong precedent for private philanthropy playing a catalytic role in calling for the establishment of such a fund, and for backing up its calls with notable seed funding. As of July 2019, private sector and nongovernment partners had contributed nearly $3 billion USD to the Global Fund. In support of Pope Francis's global compact for education, the Blue Chip Foundation is ready to utilize its platform to assist in coordinating private donors and businesses to help galvanize the philanthropic community to seed an Education Fund. We invite others to help galvanize the necessary institutional actors to move this idea forward.

CONTRIBUTORS

J. LAWRENCE ABER is Willner Family Professor of Psychology and Public Policy at the Steinhardt School of Culture, Education, and Human Development, and university professor, New York University. Aber also designs and conducts rigorous evaluations of innovative programs and policies for children, youth, and families, such as violence prevention, literacy development, welfare reform, and comprehensive services initiatives.

BRIGID BARRON is professor of education at Stanford University. She is founder of the YouthLAB at Stanford and a colead of TELOS, a Stanford initiative to investigate how technologies can provide more equitable access to learning opportunities.

MANUELITO BIAG is a senior associate of networked improvement science at the Carnegie Foundation for the Advancement of Teaching.

DAVID E. BLOOM is Clarence James Gamble Professor of Economics and Demography at the Harvard T. H. Chan School of Public Health and director of Harvard's National Institute of Aging Demography Center. Bloom is an elected fellow of the American Academy of Arts and Sciences, an elected member of the board of directors of the Population Association of America, and an Andrew Carnegie Fellow of the Carnegie Corporation of New York.

DANA BURDE

is an associate professor in the Steinhardt School of Culture, Education, and Human Development at New York University.

ANNE COLBY

is adjunct professor at Stanford University, former director of the Murray Research Center at Harvard University, and senior scholar at the Carnegie Foundation for the Advancement of Teaching. She is the author of numerous books, including *The Power of Ideals* (with William Damon) and *Educating Citizens: Preparing America's Undergraduates for Lives of Moral and Civic Responsibility*. She has received a number of awards, including the Kuhmerker Award for contributions to the field of moral psychology and the 2017 Influencer on Aging award for her studies of purpose in older adults.

MAURICE CRUL

is a Distinguished Professor of Sociology at the Free University in Amsterdam. He coordinated the TIES project (the Integration of the European Second generation) in ten countries and the ELITES project on the upcoming elite among the second generation in four countries. In 2017, Crul was awarded the prestigious ERC advanced grant for the project Becoming a Minority on the integration of people of native descent in majority-minority cities in five European countries. He is the author of numerous books, among them *Superdiversity: A New Perspective on Integration* and *The Changing Face of World Cities*.

WILLIAM DAMON

is professor of education at Stanford University and director of the Stanford Center on Adolescence. He is a leading researcher on the development of purpose in life and the author of *The Path to Purpose*. Damon's other books include *Greater Expectations* (winner of the Parent's Choice Book Award), *Some Do Care: Lives of Moral Commitment* (with Anne Colby), *Good Work* (with Howard Gardner and Mihaly Csikszentmihalyi), and *The Power of Ideals* (also with Anne Colby). Damon is a member of the National Academy of Education and a fellow of the American Academy of Arts and Sciences

SARAH DRYDEN-PETERSON

is associate professor of education at the Harvard Graduate School of Education where she leads a research program on the connections between education and community development, specifically the role that education plays in building peaceful and participatory societies. Dryden-Peterson's research has played critical roles in shaping global policy and local programs that have the potential to create quality, conflict-informed, and future-creating education for millions of children globally in settings of migration and displacement.

PAULA EZCURRA is a Climate Resilience Fellow at the Scripps Institution of Oceanography, University of California, San Diego.

VANESSA FAJANS-TURNER is an advisor at the Blue Chip Foundation.

MADDALENA FERRANNA is a research associate at the Harvard T. H. Chan School of Public Health.

KAREN FLAMMER is the director for digital learning at the University of California, San Diego.

FONNA FORMAN is associate professor of political science and founding director of the Center on Global Justice at the University of California, San Diego.

POPE FRANCIS is the head of the Catholic Church. He was elected supreme pontiff on March 13, 2013. Born Jorge Mario Bergoglio in Argentina, he is the first pope from outside Europe since Gregory III in the eighth century. His encyclicals include *Fratelli Tutti* (On fraternity and social friendship) and *Laudato Si* (On care for our common home) and his books include *Amoris Laetitia: The Joy of Love* and *The Name of God Is Mercy*.

SCOTT FRIESE is the assistant director, of instructional design in the Office of the President at the University of California.

HOWARD GARDNER is the John H. and Elizabeth A. Hobbs Research Professor of Cognition and Education at the Harvard Graduate School of Education. He is best known for his theory of multiple intelligences, a critique of the notion that there exists but a single human intelligence that can be assessed by standard psychometric instruments. Since the middle 1990s, Gardner has directed the Good Project—a group of initiatives (founded in collaboration with psychologists Mihaly Csikszentmihalyi and William Damon) that promotes excellence, engagement, and ethics in education, preparing students to become good workers and good citizens who contribute to the overall well-being of society.

STEFANIA GIANNINI is the UNESCO assistant director-general for education. Previously, as a senator of the Republic of Italy and as minister of education, universities, and research, she developed and implemented a structural reform of the Italian education system centered on social inclusion and cultural awareness. She is closely involved in an advisory capacity with the European commissioner for research and innovation.

LOUIS M. GOMEZ is professor of education at the University of California, Los Angeles, and a social scientist dedicated to educational improvement. With colleagues, he has worked to bring networked-based improvement science to the field of education. This work is aimed at helping the field take a new perspective on design, educational engineering, and development efforts that catalyze long-term, cooperative initiatives in the context of networked improvement communities.

JENNIFER GROSS is the cofounder of the Blue Chip Foundation.

HAHRIE HAN is a professor of political science and the inaugural director of the Stavros Niarchos Foundation Agora Institute at the John Hopkins Krieger School of Arts and Sciences.

VITTORIO HÖSLE is the founding director of the Notre Dame Institute for Advanced Study at the University of Notre Dame. He is also a member of the Pontifical Academy of Social Sciences.

ASTRID HSU is a research associate at the Marine Biology Research Division of the Scripps Institution of Oceanography, University of California.

DAVID G. IMIG is a senior fellow of strategic initiatives at the Carnegie Foundation for the Advancement of Teaching.

RADHIKA IYENGAR is an associate research scholar at the Center for Sustainable Development, which is part of the Earth Institute at Columbia University. She leads multicountry research projects on language literacy, promoting and implementing the Sustainable Development Goals for education and gender.

TAMI KATZIR is a professor at the Edmond J. Safra Brain Research Center for the Study of Learning Disabilities at the University of Haifa. She leads the committee on language and literacy at Israel's Ministry of Education as well as the first nationally implemented multicomponential reading comprehension intervention for elementary school children that links cognition, emotion, and technology.

FRANS LELIE is a visiting fellow of sociology at the Free University of Amsterdam.

SEBASTIÁN LIPINA is a researcher and the director of the unit on applied neurobiology at the National Council of Scientific and Technical Research (CONICET) in Argentina. He is a professor of childhood poverty and cognitive development and the codirector of the Mind, Brain and Education School at the Ettore Majorana Foundation in Italy. He is also a fellow of the Center for Neuroscience and Society at the University of Pennsylvania.

ADAM MILLARD-BALL is a visiting associate professor of urban planning at the University of California, Santa Cruz.

VEERABHADRAN RAMANATHAN is Edward A. Frieman Endowed Presidential Chair in Climate Sustainability at the Scripps Institution of Oceanography, University of California, San Diego. In 1975, he discovered the greenhouse effect of CFCs (cholorofluorocarbons), establishing that non-CO_2 gases are a major contributor to planet warming. For this work, he was awarded the Tyler Prize by Nobel Laureate Sherwood Rowland in 2009. He is the chair of Bending the Curve: Climate Change Solutions, a multifaceted education project initiated by the University of California with participation of all ten campuses of the UC system.

CARLA RINALDI is founder and president of Reggio Children Foundation and professor at the University of Modena and Reggio Emilia. She has received numerous honors, including the 2015 LEGO Prize.

JOHN ROGERS is a professor at the Graduate School of Education and Information Studies, University of California, Los Angeles. He is also the director of UCLA's Institute for Democracy, Education, and Access and faculty director of Center X, which houses UCLA's teacher education program, principal leadership program, and professional development initiatives. He has written extensively on the relationship among democracy, education, and different forms of inequality as well as on democratic participation and community organizing as strategies for advancing educational equity and civic renewal. Since 2016, his research has examined how political division and racial hostility in the age of Trump affect student well-being and civic learning.

ALAN ROPER is a senior instructional designer at the Office of the President of the University of California.

JEFFREY D. SACHS is University Professor and director of the Center for Sustainable Development at Columbia University, where he directed the Earth Institute from 2002 until 2016. He is also director of the UN Sustainable Development Solutions Network and a commissioner of the UN Broadband Commission for Development. He has been advisor to three United Nations secretaries-general and currently serves as an SDG advocate under Secretary-General Antonio Guterres. He has authored numerous bestselling books, including *A New Foreign Policy: Beyond American Exceptionalism*. Sachs was twice named as one of *Time* magazine's 100 most influential people, and he was ranked by the *Economist* among the top three most influential living economists

HAEIN SHIN is an education technical adviser at the Earth Institute at Columbia University.

MAHA SHUAYB is the director of the Center for Lebanese Studies at the Free University of Amsterdam.

TARA STAFFORD OCANSEY is a senior education technology specialist at Columbia University.

PETER STENGAARD is the cofounder of the Blue Chip Foundation.

CAROLA SUÁREZ-OROZCO is Professor-in-Residence at the Harvard Graduate School of Education and the Director of the Immigration Initiative at Harvard. She is the cofounder of Re-Imagining Migration and the author of numerous award-winning books, including *Children of Immigration; Learning a New Land: Immigrant Students in American Society;* and *Transitions: The Development of the Children of Immigrants*. She has been awarded an American Psychological Association (APA) Presidential Citation for her contributions to the understanding of cultural psychology of immigration, has served as chair of the APA Presidential Task Force on Immigration, and is a member of the National Academy of Education.

MARCELO SUÁREZ-OROZCO is chancellor of the University of Massachusetts, Boston, and a member of the executive council of the Pontifical Academy of Social Sciences in Vatican City. He has also served as the Victor S. Thomas Professor of Education at

Harvard University; as University Professor at New York University; and as the inaugural Wasserman Dean of the School of Education and Information Studies at the University of California, Los Angeles. He is the author of numerous award-winning books and edited volumes, most recently *Humanitarianism and Mass Migration: Confronting the World Crisis.*

LESLEE UDWIN is a human rights advocate and filmmaker. Her films include *East is East*, which received thirty-five prestigious awards worldwide, including a BAFTA for Best Film, and did much to promote tolerance and the celebration of diversity as between the Asian and British communities. Her documentary *India's Daughter*, which contributed to the global movement to end violence against women and girls, has been critically acclaimed around the globe and won thirty-two awards, including the Peabody Award and the Amnesty International Media Award for Best Documentary 2016. She is the cofounder and CEO of the global education initiative Think Equal.

MARYANNE WOLF directs the Center for Dyslexia, Diverse Learners, and Social Justice at the School of Education and Information Studies at the University of California, Los Angeles. A scholar and advocate for global literacy, her awards include the Einstein Prize; Researcher of the Year for Learning Disabilities; Distinguished Teacher of the Year, American Psychological Association; a Fulbright fellowship; the Christopher Columbus Award for global literacy; IDA's and Reading League's highest awards for reading brain research; and the Walter Ong Award. Author of 170 scientific publications, her books include *Proust and the Squid: The Story and Science of the Reading Brain; Tales of Literacy for 21st Century*; and *Reader, Come Home: The Reading Brain in Digital Culture.*

HIROKAZU YOSHIKAWA is University Professor and Courtney Sale Ross Professor of Globalization and Education at the Steinhardt School of Culture, Education, and Human Development at New York University. He codirects the NYU Global TIES for Children Center, which focuses on evaluations of programs and policies for children and youth in low-income and conflict-affected countries. His recent books include *Cradle to Kindergarten: A New Plan to*

Combat Inequality and *Immigrants Raising Citizens: Undocumented Parents and Their Young Children*. He leads research and evaluation for the MacArthur Foundation 100&Change partnership between the Sesame Workshop and the International Rescue Committee to provide and evaluate early childhood development (ECD) services for Syrian refugees in the Middle East. He also leads the Lego Foundation–funded partnership between Sesame, BRAC, and the IRC to provide ECD services for Rohingya refugees in Bangladesh. He is an elected fellow of the American Academy of Arts and Sciences, the American Academy of Political and Social Science, and the National Academy of Education.

STEFANO ZAMAGNI is professor of economics and former dean of the economics faculty at the University of Bologna. He is president of the Pontifical Academy of Social Sciences in Vatican City. He is a member of the editorial boards of *Sociologia*, *Migration Studies*, and *Diritti umani e diritto internazionale*; he is also the associate editor of the *International Review of Economics*. He is a fellow of the Academy of Sciences of Bologna, Modena, and Milan. He is author of numerous books and journal articles on welfare economics, theory of consumer behavior, social choice theory, economic epistemology, ethics, the history of economic thought, and civil economy.

INDEX